Commonwealth

*A Study of the Role of Government
in the American Economy:
Massachusetts, 1774–1861*

D1376839

Commonwealth

*A Study of the Role of Government
in the American Economy:
Massachusetts, 1774–1861*

Revised Edition

Oscar Handlin & Mary Flug Handlin

The Belknap Press of
Harvard University Press
Cambridge, Massachusetts
and London, England

To
Arthur Meier Schlesinger

Preface to the Revised Edition

Rarely do the authors of a scholarly monograph have the opportunity to reconsider and revise their work after the lapse of two decades. The privilege of doing so has challenged us not only to review our conclusions in the light of the scholarship of the past twenty years, but also to re-examine the procedures by which we arrived at our formulation of the problem. The results of this introspective process may be of general interest, both because of the subject itself, and for the light it casts on the function of the monograph in American historiography.

The monograph, an intensive probe into a subject narrow enough so that the evidence bearing upon it can be totally encompassed, is the neglected tool of modern historians. Conventionally this is an instrument left to doctoral candidates who have to prove themselves by demonstrating the ability to master their data. Once having earned their credentials, mature scholars, more often than not, are too weary to invest the time and effort required for a second sustained piece of research. Biographies, broad sweeping subjects, and textbooks are, understandably enough, more likely to attract the attention of a wide public; and only the exceptional historian persists in the continued use of the methods learned in graduate school.

The pity is that there are kinds of historical knowledge which only the monograph can uncover. This study is a demonstration of the value of the monographic approach. *Commonwealth* was well received by the small group of scholars to whom it was initially addressed. In addition, it had the somewhat unusual distinction of being cited in a Supreme Court decision within a few years of its publication. Nor have its main conclusions been substantially challenged. Indeed, it has been gratifying through the years to see its basic concepts gradually incorporated into the literature.

Yet we could not have learned what we did through any other method than that which we used. We could not even have known what there was to learn. However plausible our answers were by the time the manuscript went to press, we must nevertheless acknowledge that we did not even know what the right questions were when we set to work. Indeed, the most demanding aspect of our task, intellectually, was the proper definition of the subject. To the extent that we succeeded, we did so by using the methods of the monograph.

No such book, of course, can escape the influences of the time and place in which it is written. That was particularly the case with this volume, which was sponsored by a group which not only provided the funds for the research but also made a consistent effort to formulate the subject of the inquiry. Today, part of our interest in reviewing and revising this book arises from the wish to examine the extent to which externally proposed guidelines based on current assumptions affected the course of our research and the character of the conclusions we reached.

The initial impulse toward the project of which *Commonwealth* was a product stemmed from a perception of the declining state of the subject of economic history in the interwar years. The very fruitful lines of inquiry pursued at the beginning of the twentieth century in this country under the aegis of Edwin F. Gay had begun to peter out. American economic historians had usually been located academically in departments of economics, and the state of that discipline in the 1930's did not encourage historical investigation. In the 1930's, the study of economics revolved about concepts of static equilibrium and was as yet limited by its statistical techniques to current data. The historical development of the productive system therefore seemed largely of antiquarian interest to the theorists who dominated the field. The only large projects of research, like the international price history series, were fragmentary and episodic.

Concern about these trends led to a determined effort to revive research in this subject. Through the influence of Dr. Joseph

H. Willits and Dr. Anne Bezanson of the Rockefeller Foundation, a committee of inquiry explored the needs of the discipline. In accordance with its recommendations, a grant in 1940 permitted the establishment of the Committee on Research in Economic History under the sponsorship of the Social Science Research Council. The moving spirit in the Committee for many years was to be Professor Arthur H. Cole. About the same time, the Economic History Association was established. The two were parts of a concerted drive, the former to supply resources, the latter to mobilize scholarly talent.

Given the nature of the movement, it was plausible to conceive that the initial effort should be a large, cooperative endeavor such as those which had attained notable success in other fields of economics. The Committee resolved not to scatter its grants among unrelated studies, but rather to concentrate on a collaborative project, at least to begin with.

External conditions influenced the choice of a subject. In the decade or so before the Committee's establishment, the most striking impact upon the study of academic economics had come from government intervention; both the experience of the depression and the broadening scope of state action after World War I had challenged classical assumptions. The Committee therefore focused upon the role of government in the economy as the central subject of its investigations. The outbreak of the war in Europe forced it also to fix its attention on the United States.

The Committee which devised the project, the leading members of which were Professors Cole, Herbert Heaton, and E. A. J. Johnson, proposed a multipronged attack on the question of the influence of the government on the economy of the United States. One study was to deal with eighteenth-century antecedents, particularly in the decades between 1750 and 1790, while other inquiries would analyze the activities of four representatives states: Massachusetts, Pennsylvania, Georgia, and Illinois. The Committee did not impose a single, uniform hypothesis upon the scholars in charge of the several investigations, "not even," Professor Cole explained, "the commonly voiced belief" that for a long time "the country had pursued a policy of laissez faire." Nevertheless the discussions among the participants did reveal a common area of concern about precisely that issue; and the guiding question when the research began was an assessment of the extent to which laissez faire was important in the American economy before 1860. The effect of the interwar experience and of the New Deal on this formulation was perfectly obvious. The symposium which brought together the authors of the several studies at the 1943 meeting of the Economic History Association bore the general title "The Development of American Laissez Faire." [1]

We began our research late in 1941. Progress reports to the Committee in April and August 1942 and in March 1943 and 1944 recall the gradual development of our thinking about the subject. Our task, we thought, was to discover instances of intrusion by the state, in an area originally free of its intervention. Once we had done so we expected to proceed to categorize these activities within the terms already outlined in a memorandum by Professor Heaton.[2] The task, we thought, would take a year or two and would demand only a sampling of the abundant available material.

We therefore proceeded at once to an exhaustive examination of Massachusetts legislation, beginning with the years between 1826 and 1861, partly because the public documents for the period were in print and partly because initially that promised to be the era of greatest interest to us. It proved not at all difficult to find instances of state action and soon the accumulation of laws proposed, enacted, amended, and repealed mounted into the thousands. Meanwhile an examination of the expressions of opinion in the state added to the volume of the evidence.

More slowly than appears in retrospect credible, it dawned upon us that the questions posed at the start were not the appropriate ones. In April 1942 we expressed doubt about an early assumption, that "Regulation in the Public Interest" was one of the tendencies that induced the government to act, and we tried to devise a scheme that would classify the state's activities in terms of the interests they served. But we still assumed that inactivity was the norm, so that action had to be explained in terms of motives, rationale, and ideas.

A year later, the issue was clearer. Asked to summarize our probable conclusions at the 1943 meeting of the Economic History Association, we asserted that the subject was not worth talking about. "Discussion of the development of economic pol-

1. "The Development of American Laissez Faire," *The Tasks of Economic History* (December 1943), pp. 51ff; also Herbert Heaton, "Twenty-Five Years of the Economic History Association," *Jour. of Econ. Hist.*, 25 (1965), 477.

2. See below, Appendix G, no. 2.

icy in terms of laissez faire" was "hardly meaningful." The concept was no guide to action; and even as an abstract proposition it did not make itself felt until the development of economics as an academic discipline in the United States after 1880.[3] At that point we might have wound up the study. We had, to all intents and purposes, answered the question initially put to us; and while the answer was not very enlightening, it was adequate to the original purpose of the project.

That, however, left us with thousands of items of legislation; in our file boxes were expressions of human intentions which demanded an explanation. The hundreds of laws regulating the flow of water to mills, setting the time for the taking of alewives or providing for the inspection of potash were a challenge. What was their meaning? Why did men enact them? What function did they serve?

At that point our research took an entirely different character. We discarded the original questions and sought others inherent in the data. The reversal demanded several changes of strategy.

We found it necessary to push back the date at which the study began. At first, this was simply a mechanical matter. The year 1790 had little significance in the history of the state. Laws enacted in that year often repealed or amended earlier pieces of legislation, and it was necessary to go back into the preceding decade to seek out the antecedents. The search for a more proper starting point brought us into the revolutionary era.

Here, for a time, we followed a false scent. Partly, no doubt, because we were writing (1942–1945) in a period of wartime controls over our own economy, we were impressed with the importance of efforts by the state between 1774 and 1783 to fix prices, control supplies, and regulate the terms of labor. We believed, for a time, that we could find a take-off point for our inquiry in the necessities of wartime legislation imposed by the conflict with Britain.

Some of the results of our research on the subject later appeared in a separate article.[4] But as we organized this material, it became apparent that to use the war as a start was inappropriate. The actions we described were there, but they made sense as part of some larger framework. The Revolution was im-

3. Oscar Handlin, "Laissez-Faire Thought in Massachusetts, 1790–1880," *The Tasks of Economic History* (December 1943), p. 65.

4. Oscar and Mary F. Handlin, "Revolutionary Economic Policy in Massachusetts," *Wm. and Mary Quar.*, 4 (1947), 3ff.

portant not merely as a military event but also as the moment of the foundation of the state.

The data thus informed us that the more appropriate starting point was the inception of the state. The Revolution was significant not only as war, and not only in its larger context as the separation from Britain, but also because it offered people the opportunity to reconsider the nature of their government and to formulate explicitly the assumptions on which they wished state power, including that over the economy, to rest.

The analysis which grew out of this perception threw unexpected light upon a theretofore puzzling document. We had, all along, been aware of the frequent acts of incorporation enacted by the legislature. In examining the relevant documents, we uncovered a puzzling statement by James Sullivan. The Attorney General of the Commonwealth, who was intimately familiar both with the affairs of government and with banking, had delivered a strange opinion on the charter of the Massachusetts Bank in 1802.[5] The opinion did not square with the character of the corporation as we knew it. Yet we could not conceive that the Attorney General was ignorant of the law. The juxtaposition of his views with the conception of the state we had begun to perceive in the revolutionary era showed the necessity for rethinking all our assumptions. That led us first to an intensive analysis of the origins of the business corporation and then to a total restructuring of the book in a form that brought us to a fresh understanding of the role of government in the economy before 1820.[6] Ultimately, too, that perception supplied us with a foundation from which we could trace the developments of the four decades before the Civil War.

Once we had completed the argument, we could perceive a relationship between the concepts traced in *Commonwealth* and the patterns of mercantilist action elsewhere in the western world. We touched on the analogy in the concluding pages of the book. But we had not started with those views, even as hypotheses, and we did not find it helpful to use this terminology or typology in our own exposition.

The course by which we discovered the meaning of our data had little relevance to the forces conventionally presumed to operate in the American historiography of the 1940's. In that

5. See below, Appendix D.
6. Oscar and Mary F. Handlin, "Origins of the American Business Corporation," *Jour. of Econ. Hist.*, 5 (1945), 3ff.

decade, it is often asserted, interpretations based on group and sectional conflict, such as those of Charles A. Beard and Frederick J. Turner, gave ground to a consensus view of American history and American society.[7] However plausible it may seem in retrospect, that assertion was utterly alien to the actual problems of a historian working with the original materials. True, the Beardian idea in the simple form sometimes given it in the 1920's and the 1930's did not square with the facts for Massachusetts.[8] But neither did the data lead us to describe a consensus in the state. Within the scope of our monograph, the issue was irrelevant. On the one hand, we could certainly discern the interests and ideas of a self-conscious economic and social group, the Boston merchants, whose influence ran through the whole development. On the other hand, we could also see large areas of agreement which enabled this group to work with others in the society. Whether in the incidents of the 1780's when the merchants confronted the debtor farmers, or in the events of the 1840's and 1850's when a later generation of merchants confronted reform-minded artisans and intellectuals, the issues never polarized but took a complex and subtle form that involved both conflict and consensus in the Commonwealth.

Nor has it been necessary to revise these judgments after a review twenty years later. There have been changes in our emphasis. In our original analysis, for instance, the Constitution of 1780 seemed to have been the handiwork of John Adams, imposed by him upon a weary populace. Our subsequent examination of the evidence, in the process of editing the documents bearing upon the development of the Constitution, showed that the relationship was more complex than we originally thought. The Constitution was the work of John Adams. But it did not spring full-blown from his mind. In compiling it, he drew upon the experience of the previous six years, during which the people of the state had made clear their desires. The document consequently was the product of an interplay between his ideas and theirs.[9]

In retrospect, it seems to us crucial that we were able to find

7. John Higham, "The Cult of the 'American Consensus,'" *Commentary*, 27 (1959), 93–100, touched off an extensive but unenlightening controversy. See also the concluding chapter in Richard Hofstadter, *The Progressive Historian* (New York, 1968).

8. Oscar and Mary F. Handlin, "Radicals and Conservatives in Massachusetts after Independence," *New England Quarterly*, 10 (1944), 343ff.

9. *Popular Sources of Political Authority*, ed. Oscar and Mary Handlin (Cambridge, Mass., 1966), pp. 18ff.

in the documents expressions of the views of the people of the state. The preface that originally introduced this work brought into focus our concern not with the activities of an impersonal economic system nor of a remote legislature, but with the aspirations and intentions of the people of the state.

Certain gaps remain because some subjects were not central to our concern. We did not then attempt, nor have we attempted since, to measure the actual effect of legislation on economic development. The statistical tools required for such an analysis are more available now than they were a quarter-century ago. But we doubt that even now such a study could be confined to a single state; comparative data would be essential to handle all the variables. In any case, we found it necessary to retain the perspective of contemporaries in describing the effects of "what the state did" upon the conceptions of state action at the time. It would have been useful to add an analysis of whether the effects then perceived were actual or imagined. But the absence of such an analysis does not diminish the accuracy of the description of what the people of Massachusetts thought they saw during the period under examination.[10]

In general, the stylistic changes in this edition have aimed to loosen an exposition that was excessively taut for our present tastes. We have also expanded the abbreviations in the quotations, where the intent and meaning were clear. The references have been simplified to eliminate redundant citations to secondary sources and to make room for the more important books of the past two decades.

Oscar Handlin
Mary Flug Handlin

Cambridge, Massachusetts
May 15, 1968

10. Robert A. Lively, "The American System," *Business History Review*, 29 (1955), 84, underestimates the complexity of the problem of isolating the consequences of state action from other forces playing upon the economy. Recent efforts to quantify the relevant data have not yet yielded fruitful results. See Lance E. Davis and John Legler, "The Government in the American Economy, 1815–1902," *Jour. of Econ. Hist.*, 26 (1966), 514ff.

Preface to the First Edition

We seek in this study the meaning of men's efforts to bend an immediate portion of the visible universe to their wills. The sense of confidence that nature and the forms of nature were thus pliable, gaining scope after the Renaissance, pushed almost into the realm of the axiomatic the assumption that human society in all its forms was most readily amenable to human aspirations. That assumption was held with particular persistence and tenacity when it came to the system of production. The rare thinkers, who from time to time cast doubts on the basic belief in the malleability of the economy, could not disrupt the unanimity with which opinion everywhere affirmed it. Whether or not was rarely pertinent; the significant questions were rather how and toward what end.

The men of action who strove to effect or to prevent changes, to control the character of the productive system, made use of whatever tools came to hand. After the sixteenth century they could hardly pass by the instruments of coercion developed by the modern state. And the men of ideas who strove to explain, to justify, or to guide faced the compulsion of developing formalized schemes describing the relations of the polity to the economy. Behind the logic of the scholar and the acts of the venturer lay a large body of ideas, unformalized preconceptions, that embodied peoples' notions of the kind of world in which they lived and the kind of world in which they wanted to live. These conceptions under specific historic circumstances are the subject of this book.

The system of government and the system of production by their very nature as systems developed institutional character-istics, significant elements of internal development and organic growth. But our concern with the relations between the two areas, or, rather, with the evolving picture of those relations, drove us to seek a mode of analysis other than the institutional. We discovered our point of departure in the common denomina-tor of both politics and the economy — in the condition and thoughts of the human beings who were the subjects of both. Treating the sword and the plow, the scales of justice and of trade as aspects of men's needs and desires, of their struggles for betterment and advantage, we hoped to understand how men came to hold the ideas they did about the role of government in the economy.

That emphasis accounts for the historic character of this study, the analysis of a concrete situation in a special time and place. The nature of our approach has also constrained us to slight a number of interesting aspects of the whole subject. We at-tempted, for instance, to judge the efficiency of administration only when that was relevant to matters of more direct concern to us. We did not venture to assess the effects of government ac-tion upon economic trends. And generally we refrained from considering problems of the motivation of individuals. We skirted such issues unless they threw light upon our central problem, the delineation of the developing conception of the role of government in the economy of the United States before the Civil War.

In America, the peculiar complexity of federalism has often, in the last half-century, misled those who have touched on the subjects of government and business enterprise. The usual con-centration of attention upon the doings in Washington has ob-scured the most critical aspects of a period in which large sectors of the economy were organized on a local or regional basis. Too often the absence of activity by the federal government has been taken for the absence of all activity, the denial of its right to act, the denial of the right of any government to act. Yet before 1860, the affairs of the states were not only of greater public con-cern than those of the nation but they also had a more pervasive and more significant influence. While each state had its own idiosyncrasies, Massachusetts was, on the whole, representative. And it furnished a particularly useful specimen for study be-cause the tradition of literateness in politics and the loquaciousness if not the eloquence of its statesmen left abundant material to the student.

Two wars set the termini of this work. These were social cataclysms of the first order of magnitude; each opened into a period critical for the history of our problem. Out of the Revolutionary era emerged a vigorous conception of the state, but also complex circumstances that conditioned the application of that conception. Pruned away and grafted upon in the process of growth during the ensuing decades, the original body of ideas steadily if imperceptibly took on a new aspect until the Civil War put a halt to this cycle of evolution.

In the course of this study we have profited from the resources of many libraries and collections and from the kindness of many friends. A generous grant from the Committee on Research in Economic History of the Social Science Research Council made possible the whole project. The members of the committee were also liberal with their time and advice and we profited from discussion of common problems with the authors of parallel studies in other states. Yet we must acknowledge a special debt to Edward C. Kirkland and to Arthur H. Cole for sympathetic assistance through the whole course of the study; it was gratifying to be able to draw freely against an unfailing account of patience and faith, of good humor and warm friendship.

The manuscript also received the advantages of a critical reading by Samuel J. Hurwitz and of careful editing by Winifred C. Ferguson and Anne Koreny. And in all the years of its preparation Joanna Flug and David Paltiel gave patiently of their time.

Oscar Handlin
Mary Flug Handlin

Harvard University
October 15, 1945

Contents

Commonwealth

*A Study of the Role of Government
in the American Economy:
Massachusetts, 1774–1861*

Abbreviations

Acts and Resolves	See Note on the Sources
Amer. Hist. Assoc.	American Historical Association
Amer. Hist. Rev.	*American Historical Review*
Col. Soc. Mass.	Colonial Society of Massachusetts
Colls. Worc. Soc.	*Collections of Worcester Society of Antiquity*
Danvers Hist. Soc. Hist. Colls.	*Danvers Historical Society Historical Collections*
Essex Inst. Hist. Colls.	*Essex Institute Historical Collections*
HCL	Harvard College Library
House Docs.	*Massachusetts House Documents*
Hunt's Merchants' Mag.	*Hunt's Merchants' Magazine and Commercial Review*
Jour. of Econ. and Bus. Hist.	*Journal of Economic and Business History*
Jour. of Econ. Hist.	*Journal of Economic History*
MA	Massachusetts Archives
MHS	Massachusetts Historical Society
Mass. Hist. Soc. Colls.	*Massachusetts Historical Society Collections*
Mass. Hist. Soc. Proceedings	*Massachusetts Historical Society Proceedings*
NYPL	New York Public Library
North Amer. Rev.	*North American Review*
Public Docs.	See Note on the Sources
res.	Massachusetts Resolves
Senate Docs.	*Massachusetts Senate Documents*
st.	Massachusetts Statutes
Wm. and Mary Quar.	*William and Mary Quarterly*
Worc. Mag. and Hist. Jour.	*Worcester Magazine and Historical Journal*

1 | Foundations of Political Power

The dissolution of imperial authority in 1774 hurled Massachusetts society into a period of violent flux. As the government collapsed beneath the weight of popular insurrection, and as a series of de facto administrations carried on the work of ruling, complex forces struggled to determine the character of the state that would rise from the revolutionary effort.

Few had as yet caught a glimpse of the larger perspective, of the breakdown of royal power, of the disorderly interregnum, or of the new political system that would emerge in the next six years. The crisis had been so long in coming that it was difficult to realize which step was the irrevocable one. Bickering with the governor had become a political pastime. The course of trade had already been disrupted in many ways; and the closing of the Port of Boston, serious though it was, seemed another vagary of the misguided royal powers. Throughout the summer of 1774 the town meetings had seethed with bravado, courts had suspended their sessions, and committees of correspondence had already begun to put Tories and tea drinkers on their lists. But the consequences were still unclear. Even John Adams coolly considered the practicability of living "wholly without a Legislature and Courts of Justice as long as will be necessary to obtain Relief." The likelihood of a real conflict, which would shake the entire society, was still remote.[1]

1. John Adams to Palmer, Sept. 26, 1774, *Letters of Members of the Continental Congress*, ed. E. C. Burnett (Washington, D.C., 1921–1936), I, 48. For a general

The men who met in Salem against Governor Gage's orders and then withdrew to join the Provincial Congress in Concord did not turn completely against the existing order; they insisted that they were acting within legal and constitutional limits.[2] Based on representation broader than that of any General Court, the Concord meeting did not claim the powers of a central government and professed that it was merely collecting the wisdom of the province until an obstinate governor and a tyrannical Parliament would allow a return to traditional forms.[3] This was a new tactic in an old struggle. Instructed by their respective towns, the delegates to the Congress asserted their loyalty to the King, reiterated their grievances, and sought an "adequate Remedy for preventing impending Ruin, and providing for the public Safety." [4]

Nevertheless the break was open and marked a radical change, ideological as well as practical. As royal authority broke down, the voice of the governor ceased to be heard outside the narrow limits of Boston, where bayonets commanded attention. Nor did the Provincial Congress know with assurance what power it could exercise. It refused, for instance, to enact statutes since it had no mandate to do so.[5] As a result, the conviction slowly spread — to the fear of some and the exhilaration of others — that the revolutionary crisis had destroyed the social compact embodied in the Charter of 1691: with "the Dissolution of the power of Great Britain over these Colonies they have fallen into a state of Nature," announced one petition.[6]

In terms of contemporary ideas, the Provincial Congress, the only existing governing body with jurisdiction over all Massachusetts, derived its authority from, and existed at the behest of, the towns which had commissioned it through county conventions in the summer of 1774. The towns therefore were no

account of the revolutionary crisis, see Lawrence H. Gipson, *The British Empire before the American Revolution* (New York, 1965), XII, 133ff, 313ff.

2. Gage's proclamation is in *Massachusetts Spy*, Oct. 6, 1774. For the attitude of the Provincial Congress, see *Journals of Each Provincial Congress of Massachusetts in 1774 and 1775* (Boston, 1838), pp. 5ff; *Massachusetts Spy*, Oct. 13, 1774.

3. *Boston Gazette and Country Journal*, Oct. 17, 1774. See also the statements of the county convention, *Journals of Each Provincial Congress*, pp. 601ff, 609ff, 618ff, 621ff.

4. *Boston Gazette*, Oct. 17, 1774.

5. As a result, the first General Court in 1775 felt it necessary to confirm all the acts of the Provincial Congress because the state had been "deprived of the free exercise of its usual powers of government," and its business had "to be conducted by congresses." St. 1775, ch. 1.

6. Pittsfield Memorial (1776), MA, CLXXXI, 42ff.

longer local units within the state. They were sovereign entities which delegated a portion of their authority to a central body and held the same relation to the Provincial Congress as did the former colonies to the Continental Congress.[7]

After the tumultuous excitement of the first weeks of struggle many communities managed alone much of the business of ruling. Attleboro organized a judiciary of its own, complete with superior and inferior tribunals. Unincorporated places like Amherst assumed political functions without any particular mandate. Often the machinery of justice fell into the hands of committees of inspection with the occasional aid of boards of arbitrators, while the nonjudicial activities of the old courts, such as licensing and control over highways, passed directly to the selectmen. In general, these officials preserved as much order as they wished, jealously guarding their prerogatives even in matters vital to the war effort.[8]

Theory and exigency alike justified for the time being these pretensions of local sovereignty; in face of the desperate challenge of revolution, safety seemed at first to lie in the smallest unit, in the town where neighbors knew each other's strength and weakness and the trustworthy stood apart from the doubtful and vacillating. Some stray individuals placed their newfound freedom of action before every other consideration, seeking thus fulfillment of the diverse expectations that provoked rebellion. But more generally, unifying factors, as deeply rooted in the social structure as the elements of division, held Massachusetts together.

In the trading and fishing towns, commerce, the prosperity of which benefited artisan and shipowner, seaman and shopkeeper, supplied a nucleus of common concern. And many farmers too were aware of the obvious circumstance that they lived in a hinterland, the business of which was to supply the

7. For the enactment by towns of provincial acts, see, e.g., D. P. Corey, *History of Malden, Massachusetts, 1633–1785* (Malden, 1899), p. 741. For the Middlesex, Suffolk, Plymouth, Essex, Worcester County Conventions, see, e.g., *Massachusetts Spy*, Sept. 8, 15, 22, Oct. 6, 13, 1774; Timothy Pickering Papers, 1760–1800 (MSS, MHS), V, 12.

8. Thus in 1775 Worcester refused to lend its cannon to the state without security (MA, CXCV, 397, 398). See also *Boston Gazette*, Feb. 13, 27, 1775; MA, CLXXXI, 50ff; Corey, *Malden*, pp. 737, 751; J. E. A. Smith, *The History of Pittsfield (Berkshire County,) Massachusetts, from the Year 1800 to the Year 1876* (Springfield, 1876), pp. 342ff, 348ff, 375–384; H. A. Cushing, "Political Activity of Massachusetts Towns during the Revolution," *Amer. Hist. Assoc. Annual Report, 1895*, pp. 105–106; Frederick Freeman, *History of Cape Cod* (Boston, 1869), I, 430ff.

coastal towns with food and with products for export. Concrete conditions forced them to recognize what had often been preached to them, that the value of their produce depended upon the demand "which an extensive commerce, the opulence of the merchant, and the number of mechanics necessarily occasion." [9] This link, strengthened by the continuity of settlement — the progressive movement from the Braintrees and Salems to the New Braintrees and New Salems — was a cohesive element of remarkable strength and vitality.

The ideas in terms of which the people of Massachusetts fought their great war also counteracted the canker of division. Revolution was a risk all had assumed together; all would share the success or failure, the danger or satisfaction. Independence transformed revolutionary insurgency into a yearning for a place of respectability and esteem among the great nations of the world. By fostering self-sufficiency and by developing its internal economy, the new state might at once acquire the resources to stand as an equal with the old and prove the wisdom of its course. To show that a free republic could match and surpass the achievements of Europe would justify the Revolution. Victory would be the first, not the last, step of a forceful, aggressive, benevolent destiny laden with benefits for all. "The past madness of Great Britain," which had compelled Americans "to become independent," was "the greatest blessing which Providence ever bestowed upon them," the best means of rendering them happy, free, and great.[10]

The fresh start, the opportunity to shape anew institutions elsewhere beyond men's control, was impressive and exciting. "We are trying, by a thousand experiments, the ingenuity as well as virtue of our people," wrote John Adams. "Imagine four hundred thousand people without government or law, forming themselves in companies for various purposes, of justice, policy, and war! You must allow for a great deal of the ridiculous, much of the melancholy, and some of the marvellous." [11]

The new venture generated an exuberant hopefulness at every level. The same theory that justified reversion to the state of nature also anticipated a moment of emergence into a state of settled constitutionality. Even the most independent towns

9. "O.P.Q.," *Massachusetts Spy*, May 18, 1776.

10. J. Adams to Genet, May 9, 1780, John Adams, *Works*, ed. C. F. Adams (Boston, 1850–1856), VII, 16off; see below, p. 51.

11. To Biddle, Dec. 12, 1774, J. Adams, *Works*, IX, 349.

recognized with Holden that "no political community . . . can truly enjoy Liberty without civil government . . . an invaluable divine blessing." [12] While full discussion of the questions of ultimate shape and control raised deeply troubling issues long pondered in New England, it rested upon a foundation of essential agreement on principles.

In the years of controversy that preceded the rebellion much thought and argument had been devoted to the nature of political relations. Everywhere were some who enlivened the town meeting with philosophical disquisitions on the role of government and men's place in it. While only a well-scattered minority concerned themselves seriously with intricate theories, years of attendance at town meetings had attuned the majority to elementary concepts, if not to detailed systems; to the idea of a state of nature, of a social compact, and of consent by the governed.

Many elements had coalesced into a common body of ideas on the nature of the state. The federal theology of the first settlers supplied the concept of a society formed by a covenant voluntarily entered into; the Baptists and the influence of the Great Awakening destroyed the notion of a community of the elect; and from Locke and his contemporaries came the theory of natural rights. Civil government was a covenant among men to further their common interests and welfare by means of a social compact in which the participants surrendered certain privileges for the better attainment of others.[13] But as a typical Pittsfield petition of 1776 pointed out, "every man by Nature has the seeds of Tyranny deeply implanted within." A wise people would erect as a barrier against any possible aggression "a fundamental Constitution securing their sacred Rights & Immunities against all Tyrants that may spring up." The constitution was "of the Nature of a most sacred Covenant" adopted "in emerging from a State of Nature, into a State of well regulated Society" and in which the participants surrendered some natural rights "to maintain secure and defend those retained." [14]

12. S. C. Damon, *History of Holden, Massachusetts, 1667–1841* (Worcester, 1841), p. 43. See also "Statement of a Berkshire County Convention" (1778), *Province Acts, 1769–80,* in *Acts and Resolves, Public and Private, of the Province of the Massachusetts Bay* (Boston, 1869–86), p. 1031; MA, CLXXXI, 42ff; J.E.A. Smith, *The History of Pittsfield . . . 1734 to . . . 1800* (Springfield, 1869), pp. 338, 351.

13. See Stoughton Instructions (1779), MA, CLX, 266, 269–271.

14. Lexington Memorial (1778) and Pittsfield Memorial (1776), MA, CLX, 24ff, CLXXXI, 42ff; *Province Acts, 1769–80,* p. 1030; J.E.A. Smith, *Pittsfield, 1734 to 1800,* pp. 338, 351ff.

There was, as well, ultimate agreement that since "power Alwaise resides in the Body of the People," legislatures cannot "give Life to the Constitution . . . it being the foundation" upon which the legislature itself stands.[15] A constitution could be adopted only with "the approbation of the Majority of the People in this Colony." The form of that approbation was also clear; it was the combination of town meetings in deliberation that "together make an act of the Body of the People." [16]

The legitimate constitution central to these ideas did not materialize until 1780. Practical experience in the intervening years left a significant impress upon the shape of the document that finally emerged. In the interim an elaborate legal fiction filled the lack. When the mirage of reconciliation vanished in April 1775, the need for an agency fully to exercise the power to govern revived the Province Charter of 1691.[17] Because the governor and council had abdicated by leaving the state, it was reasoned, their powers devolved upon the remaining body, the House of Representatives. With the approval of the Continental Congress, a legislature was elected and it, in turn, chose an executive council in which were merged the functions of the governor.[18]

The new government had the constitutional authority and the machinery, if not always the power, to enforce decisions directly without dependence upon the option of intermediaries. But few saw there the end of the quest for an elusive legitimacy that was the product of their own elaborate rationalizing against imperial authority. The fund of revolutionary theory, universally accepted, supplied an insurmountable obstacle: here was not consent by the governed, only a relic of the tyranny Massachusetts was fighting. Even those who defended the charter reasoned only in terms of a tolerable makeshift, perforce admitting that a new constitution was ultimately desirable. Not whether there should be a new instrument but when and how to frame it was the problem.

Earnest debaters and prolific contributors to the patriotic

15. See Bellingham petition (1777), MA, CLVI, 198; *Massachusetts Spy*, Dec. 4, 1776; *Province Acts, 1769–80*, p. 1031; Smith, *Pittsfield, 1734 to 1800*, pp. 357, 361.
16. Pittsfield petition (1776), MA, CLXXXI, 42ff.
17. See Leicester Instructions quoted in Emory Washburn, "Topographical and Historical Sketches of the Town of Leicester," *Worc. Mag. and Hist. Jour.*, 2 (1826), 109.
18. See General Court Proclamation, Jan. 23, 1776, *Province Resolves, 1765–80*, in *Acts and Resolves, Public and Private, of the Province of the Massachusetts Bay* (Boston, 1869–86), pp. 947ff; *Boston Gazette*, Feb. 12, 1776; *Journals of the*

press phrased their demands in terms of broad doctrine. But constitutional questions were inextricably linked to concrete problems of immediate advantage under wartime circumstances. Discomfort under the status quo, where such discomfort existed, and faith in the prospect of improvement by change, where such faith existed, gave urgency to the general desire for a new regime.

The implications of the unfolding Revolution emerged soon enough at this practical level, as war and independence altered the circumstances of participants. The initial connotation, removal of irksome royal restraints, receded rapidly under the pressure of cataclysmic mutations in fortune.

War ruined the seaports, particularly those engaged in the fisheries and in the allied whale-oil and candle business. In addition, the outlying commercial towns languished and fell into debt as their wealthy citizens gravitated toward Boston, leaving the less fortunate to bear alone the burden of taxes still under the old valuations, particularly after the act of October 1777 changed the tax from the locale of the property to the locale of the property owner.[19] Towns like Manchester, Marblehead, Hingham, Wellfleet, and Truro and all of Martha's Vineyard and Nantucket were hard hit. Nantucket's 140 ships at the beginning of the war had fallen to ten by 1780. With Plymouth, these communities begged that they "may not be Tax't . . . for the Future by reason of the Great losses . . . met with at sea & being almost totally Deprived of the fishery since the Present war which was our principall support." [20]

In all these towns, grinding hardships were the prize of war for those whose welfare depended on their own efforts. Laborers and artisans whose wages rose more slowly than prices, seamen who did not share the prosperity of privateering shipowners, suffered badly. Disruption of the normal channels of trade, diversion of manpower from civilian pursuits, and extraordinary activity by the state as a large-scale purchaser, all contributed to a fabulous increase in the price of commodities and to an inability to procure even the essentials of life.[21] Early exhortations

---

Continental Congress, 1774–1789, ed. W. C. Ford (Washington, D.C., 1904–1934), II, 76ff, 83ff.

19. See also Salem petition (May 27, 1778), MA, CLXXXIV, 143, 144.

20. *Records of the Town of Plymouth, 1636–1783* (Plymouth, 1889–1903), III, 383; Salem petitions (Jan. 1, 1776, May 27, 1778), MA, CLXXX, 275, CLXXXIV, 141ff. See also MA, CLXXX, 33, 53, 373, CLXXXI, 32, CLXXXV, 118, CLXXXVI, 370; R. A. East, *Business Enterprise in the Revolutionary Era* (New York, 1938), p. 216.

21. For manpower see *Massachusetts Soldiers and Sailors of the Revolutionary*

by the towns, the General Court, and by Congress did not prevent persons "lost to all Virtue, and the Love of their Country"
from taking unreasonable advantage. A temporary price-fixing
act in 1777 and an embargo to conserve precious resources within the state frightened farmers and reduced to a trickle the flow
of provisions to the cities.[22]

For the artisans, for the fisherfolk, for the humbler urban elements, prices were the paramount issue. The struggle to make
narrowing resources cover necessities brought occasional raids
upon shopkeepers and middlemen. But ultimate resentment
found its mark in the agrarian communities from which supplies
failed to come. These were the immediate enemies — the selfish
farmers, the hoarders who failed to feed the people at reasonable
prices because higher profits could be got elsewhere. The hard-
hit commercial community of Salem, complaining against the
farmers, "cruel as death," pointed out, "We see the produce of
land increased not less than six-fold by means of the war, and
the land itself more than doubled in value, while the proprietors
suffer no losses, and daily exhaust our interest, for the necessaries
of life, which are purchased by us at a most exhorbitant price."[23]

On this question some traders saw eye to eye with their poorer
neighbors. For many merchants the conflict occasioned grave economic readjustments. Commerce, dislocated at the outset, never
recovered. Revolution "drained the sources of some as much as
it . . . replenished others." The coasting business was dangerous
and at times mere speculation. Unable to adapt to the new times,
the old, established merchants who had not emigrated were often
forced to lay aside trade. "Salary men," those on fixed stipends,

War (Boston, 1896–1907), I, ix, xxiv-xxxix; Council to Hancock, July 19, 1776,
MA, CXCV, 425, 426. For shortages and high prices, see Abigail to John Adams,
and John to Abigail Adams, July 7, 16, 1775, June 3, 1776, Abigail Adams, *Letters*,
ed. C. F. Adams (Boston, 1840), I, 56; John and Abigail Adams, *Familiar Letters*,
ed. C. F. Adams (Boston, 1841), pp. 76, 183; W. P. and J. P. Cutler, *Life, Journals
and Correspondence of Rev. Manasseh Cutler* (Cincinnati, 1888), I, 52; *Province
Acts, 1769–80*, p. 669; J. T. Austin, *Life of Elbridge Gerry with Contemporary
Letters* (Boston, 1828–1829), I, 219ff; *Letters*, ed. Burnett, II, 252.

22. See, e.g., MA, CLXXXI, 351, CLXXXIII, 4, 106, 125, 131, CXLII, 46; Eliot
to Belknap, June 17, 1777, *Mass. Hist. Soc. Colls.*, 6 ser., IV (1891), 124; C. R.
King, *Life and Correspondence of Rufus King* (New York, 1894–1900), I, 25. For
legislation see st. 1776–77, chs. 9, 14, 15, 46; res. 1776–77, chs. 653, 877, 928; st.
1778–79, ch. 36; st. 1780, ch. 7; Freeman, *Cape Cod*, II, 121; C. F. Swift, *History
of Old Yarmouth* (Yarmouth Port, 1884), p. 157. For repeal of the act see, e.g.,
st. 1777–78, ch. 6; res. 1777–78, chs. 117, 274; *Province Acts, 1769–80*, pp. 811, 1012.

23. See *Journals of the Continental Congress*, IX, 1071ff; MA, CLXXXIII, 93,
CLXXXIV, 39, 125, 143; E. M. Stone, *History of Beverly* (Boston, 1843), pp. 83ff.

also got by with difficulty, smarting from the rising prices which dwarfed once-comfortable incomes.[24]

By contrast, wartime developments aided those prepared to grasp opportunities as they saw them. The emigration of loyalists eliminated at one stroke a significant portion of the old merchant class, and social lines became remarkably fluid as the disruption of the state's economy further upset the equilibrium of the class structure. "The Revolution brought new strata everywhere to the surface," threw "property into channels, where before it never was, and . . . increased little streams to overflowing rivers," so that, as a disgruntled contemporary complained, "when the pot boils, the scum will arise." "Fellows who would have cleaned my shoes five years ago, have amassed fortunes," observed James Warren in 1779. Enterprising traders from the outlands, ambitious ship captains, and shrewd young sons of artisans or of farmers prospered in the wake of every disturbance. Imagination brought benefits from diverse forms of trade, legal and illegal; patriotic connections gained profitable government contracts, and resourcefulness found means of satisfying unusual demands for luxuries. The daring, who looked forward to the moment when privateers would be commissioned, were not disappointed; both state and continental governments encouraged this profitable warfare. In addition, many invested most successfully in the confiscated estates of loyalists. "Moneys in large sums, thrown into their hands by these means," enabled "them to roll the snow ball of monopoly and forestalling." [25]

But they enjoyed no easygoing prosperity. Lacking the sense of security in possessions that gave confidence to those old in riches, they fought aggressively to hold what was theirs. The sources of their gains were evanescent; peace would dam up speculation and privateering. As a growing proportion of their property became involved in government money and securities that fluctuated in value, continued safety came to rest upon the success of the Revolutionary venture and upon the character of the new society to emerge from it. Enterprises heavy with risk and under

24. Fixed incomes were particularly hit by the relatively high tax on money at interest (see "O.P.Q.," *Massachusetts Spy*, May 18, 1776). See also Ezra Ripley, *Half Century Discourse* (Concord, 1829), p. 8; John Adams to Van Der Capellen, Jan. 21, 1781, J. Adams, *Works*, VII, 357ff; Swift, *Old Yarmouth*, p. 163.

25. See Paine to Gerry, April 12, 1777, Austin, *Elbridge Gerry*, I, 221; Billerica petition, MA, CLXXXIII, 292ff; S. E. Morison, *Life and Letters of Harrison Gray Otis* (Boston, 1913), I, 21. Eliot to Belknap, *Mass. Hist. Soc. Colls.*, 6 ser., IV (1891), 103, 104; Samuel Adams, *Writings*, ed. H. A. Cushing (New York, 1904–1908), IV, 19ff; *Letters*, ed. Burnett, IV, 269.

constant threat of total loss left the newly risen anxious, tensely, irascibly concerned with their recently accumulated wealth.

An analogous line between those who fared well and those who did not ran through the agrarian community. Farmers close to market profited from ever increasing demands for their supplies of food and fuel and from steadily rising prices. The flourishing condition of household industries added to their fortunate condition. Scarcity of manufactured goods, the curtailment of competitive imports, and government encouragement brought forth a rich harvest from the husbandman's loom and last, as well as from his fields. Satellitic middlemen, provision dealers who were often army contractors, benefited as much as the farmer whose livestock they drove to metropolitan markets. Jeremiah Wadsworth undoubtedly exaggerated, but there was a large measure of truth in his complaint in 1778 that "the purchasers of Flower from the Eastward . . . have amassed much wealth by a disgraceful inland trade; and the inhabitants of the New England states in general have neglected the cultivation of wheat and turned their attention to trade." Like the aggressive on the seaboard many accumulated enough surpluses to invest in public securities, make loans, and become large-scale creditors.[26]

There were also agriculturists for whom the times bred hardship. In the Maine lumber towns, which were harassed by British raiders, war and embargoes ruined the market for masts and timber. For a time the position there was desperate. Petitions from Cumberland and Lincoln counties asked not only for relief from assessments but often for relief from starvation. The General Court sent flour to keep alive and loyal "People . . . destitute of Bread & many of them of Meat for a considerable part of the year, and [with] . . . few or no materials for cloathing." But such assistance hardly met the more fundamental difficulties.[27]

Most depressed were the areas only recently settled, where subsistence agriculture still prevailed. The prosperity of other farmers did not touch those who lived on a hand-to-mouth basis;

26. East, *Business Enterprise*, pp. 21, 54. For the connection of industry and agriculture and the effect of the war, see John Adams to Calkoen, Oct. 27, 1780, J. Adams, *Works*, VII, 310ff. See also J. F. Jameson, *The American Revolution Considered as a Social Movement* (Princeton, 1940), p. 70; W. B. Weeden, *Economic and Social History of New England* (Boston, 1891), II, 779.

27. See *Massachusetts Soldiers and Sailors*, I, xxxv; G. J. Varney, *Gazetteer of the State of Maine* (Boston, 1886), p. 462; petitions in MA, CLXXX, 13, 14, 15, 21, 39, 287, 315, 315b, CLXXXI, 14, 16, 100ff, CLXXXV, 56, 63, 65, 111.

constricted acreage or lack of access to markets deprived them of the salable surplus. Perennially short of cash, already in debt when the Revolution began, the luckless sank deeper into the hopeless bog as money flowed to the seaboard and "Did not Circulat Back into the Country Very Quick." [28]

To farmers, debt was an ever impending threat. It menaced their land, which was the source of their livelihood, the guarantee of their independence, and the mark of their status in the community. More than anyone else, the husbandmen put their security in the balance when driven to the table of the money-lender. Foreclosure meant the end of a way of life and opened the unenviable prospect of working for others. Unlike the impecunious in fishing or trading towns, these, once landless, could expect little relief, even from the end of the war.[29]

Deficiencies in judicial organization, the maze of incomprehensible forms and fees, compounded the harsh effects of the times upon debtors. To throw off the incubus was almost impossible when the expense of suits was higher than the sums involved. Two complaints were almost universal, the use of offices as political plums and exorbitantly high costs of legal proceedings.[30] The services of lawyers were essential and made expensive by laws which put a premium on delays. Official charges were also steep and by 1779 rose to eight times their usual level.[31] Furthermore, by an outmoded act, the presence of two justices and a clerk was necessary to confess judgment to avoid litigation, a procedure which "overwhelmed great multitudes in Destruc-

28. [William Manning], "Some Proposals for Making Restitution to the Original Creditors" (MS, Houghton Library, Harvard University), pp. 15, 16.

29. For the pressure of debt and taxes see, e.g., MA, CLXXX, 275, CLXXXI, 42ff; G. W. Chase, *History of Haverhill* (Haverhill, 1861), pp. 407, 414; Paine to Gerry, April 12, 1777, Austin, *Elbridge Gerry*, I, 219ff. See petitions from Worcester, Monson, Sylvester, Charlestown, Shirley, Tisbury, Hingham, Great Barrington, Hull, Conway, Buxton, Truro, Wellfleet, Marblehead, Billerica, Chelmsford, Lincoln County, MA, CLXXX, 373, CLXXXI, 14, 16, 32, CLXXXIII, 292ff, 298, CLXXXIV, 216ff, CLXXXV, 27, 34, 118, 250, 301, 414, 418ff, CLXXXVI, 26, 43, 101; Enoch Pratt, *Comprehensive History, Ecclesiastical and Civil, of Eastham, Wellfleet, and Orleans* (Yarmouth, 1844), pp. 129, 130; *Records of the Town of Braintree*, ed. S. A. Bates (Randolph, 1886), pp. 448, 463, 467, 485, 493, 512; J. H. Temple, *History of North Brookfield* (North Brookfield, 1887), pp. 237–241, 243; Damon, *Holden*, pp. 47, 74; J. G. Holland, *History of Western Massachusetts* (Springfield, 1855), II, 593.

30. For the attitude that political office should serve to relieve personal financial embarrassments, see the following letters by Timothy Pickering, 1774–86, Pickering Papers, V, 383, XXXIII, 114, 176, XXXV, 1.

31. See st. 1775–76, ch. 23; st. 1778–79, ch. 21; st. 1779–80, chs. 1, 28; Theophilus Parsons, *Memoir of Theophilus Parsons* (Boston, 1859), pp. 192, 193.

tion & affoarded Encouragement to mercenary lawyers to riot upon the spoils of the people." [32] Early petitions for reform had few results. Not until February 1779 was an act to allow justices of the peace to deal with small debts even considered. Meanwhile, judicial sticklers at the letter of the law gave suspected Tories comparative freedom and added to the grievances against the gentlemen of the bar.[33]

Facing such difficulties, debtor farmers found no solace in the effects of war or of government economic policy. Military measures involved a chain of bitter consequences. Recruitment thinned the ranks of productive manpower while the demands of the armed forces quickly outran the financial resources of Massachusetts. The new state was at first too weak to call upon either the power to collect taxes or the confidence to evoke loans. Its "single available asset: the hope of winning the war" was convertible only through the liberal issue of paper money, a cure that soon proved more hazardous than the disease. Competing against the overwhelming mass of continental, Rhode Island, Connecticut, and other currencies, Massachusetts quickly saw its bills slope into a precipitous, disastrous decline.[34]

Laws enacted at the behest of creditors, urban and rural, failed to halt the trend; even stopping state emissions in December 1776 was of no avail, for the printers of Philadelphia and Providence remained busy.[35] By 1777 many insisted that salvation would come only through a return to taxation and borrowing and through a reduction of the amount of paper in circulation. In this effort, the proponents of deflation gained the support of artisans and others interested in price-fixing with the argument, sedulously propagated, that only the radical cure of putting finance on a sound basis by stopping the emission of money and by heavy taxation would halt the debilitating rise in the price of commodities.[36] A drastic act of October 1777 deprived Massa-

32. Pittsfield Memorial (1775), MA, CLXXX, 150; Smith, *Pittsfield, 1734 to 1800*, pp. 340, 343.

33. See MA, CXLII, 173a, CLXXX, 156; Sedgwick to Sullivan, Jan. 10, 1779, Theodore Sedgwick Papers, 1768–1858 (MSS, MHS), I, 83ff; E. B. Greene, *The Revolutionary Generation* (New York, 1943), p. 86; st. 1775–76, ch. 25.

34. See R. V. Harlow, "Aspects of Revolutionary Finance," *Amer. Hist. Rev.*, 35 (1929), 48; st. 1775, ch. 2; st. 1775–76, chs. 9, 18; st. 1776–77, chs. 1, 10, 16, 26, 28; J. B. Felt, *Historical Account of Massachusetts Currency* (Boston, 1839), pp. 162–189.

35. St. 1775–76, ch. 18; st. 1776–77, chs. 37, 44; st. 1779–80, ch. 7, sec. 2; *Province Acts, 1769–80*, p. 1452.

36. See J. Adams to Palmer, Feb. 20, 1777, Lee to S. Adams and to Jefferson, Nov. 23, 1777, Oct. 5, 1778, *Letters*, ed. Burnett, II, 250ff, 268, 568, III, 438; S.

chusetts bills of their legal-tender quality and provided for their exchange into interest-bearing bonds in denominations of £10 or more.[37] Meanwhile burdensome taxes and further short-term loans hastened the drain of notes back into the hands of the government.[38]

These positive steps inflamed large numbers of debtor farmers for they thereby lost the possibility of recouping their fortunes through the effects of depreciation. The policy which forced the currency into large notes that could not be readily redeemed or used took the money out of their pockets. It was "a violation of Public faith" which deprived them "of the Free use of their Proberty." Impassioned protests berated the selfish monopolizers who "made great gains by oppression," who had engrossed the bills of credit, and in whose interests the contract writ plain on the face of the bills was now being violated. A Belchertown petition was emphatic: "whether these People are in Boston or in the country we are not able to Say, but we apprehend they have persuaded your Honours to Call in their Bills — which they have unrighteously gained, and put them upon Intrest & that is to make Money Secarce, and . . . it will greatly answer the End of the monopolizer, and what Little of our Estates will be Left at the End of the war must go to pay the principal & Intrest of said Contract." [39]

To the debtors the government seemed out of reach, out of control. The course of economic legislation confirmed earlier misgivings first aroused by the activities of self-seeking representatives. The whole administration was suspect when every member from Berkshire County in the first General Court somehow obtained a substantial civil position. "That such persons

Adams, *Writings*, IV, 19ff; J. to A. Adams, Feb. 7, 1777, J. and A. Adams, *Familiar Letters*, p. 240; *Boston Gazette*, Feb. 2, 1778. For price legislation, see A. M. Davis, "Limitation of Prices in Massachusetts, 1776–1779," *Col. Soc. Mass. Publications*, X (1905), 119–134.

37. See res. 1776–77, ch. 531; MA, CXLIV, 13, CXCV, 379, 380; *Province Acts, 1769–80*, p. 813; res. 1777–78, ch. 346; MA, CXLII, 89; *Province Acts, 1769–80*, p. 815; st. 1777–78, ch. 7.

38. For loans see st. 1776–77, chs. 4, 24, 27, 43; st. 1777–78, chs. 12, 19. For taxes see st. 1776–77, ch. 13; st. 1777–78, chs. 13, 26; st. 1778–79, chs. 12, 39; st. 1779–80, chs. 12, 30, 44, 49; st. 1780, chs. 9, 16; "Squaretoes," *Independent Chronicle*, Nov. 2, 1780; res. 1778–79, chs. 405, 406, 444; res. 1779–80, ch. 302; *Province Acts, 1769–80*, p. 668; S. Adams, *Writings*, IV, 19ff; Paine to Gerry, Apr. 12, 1777, Austin, *Elbridge Gerry*, I, 220.

39. Belchertown, Billerica Remonstrances, MA, CLXXXIII, 292ff, 307. See also *Province Acts, 1769–80*, p. 817; John Adams to Gerry, Dec. 6, 1777, J. Adams, *Works*, IX, 470ff.

should nomenate and vote for themselves" was all too reminiscent of the tactics of colonial officials. "Greediness of office" flourished in a faulty system, and, flourishing, would perpetuate an unpopular regime introduced as temporary.[40]

Moreover, political changes which reduced agrarian influence in the General Court crippled the chance of adopting an alternative policy within the existing framework. The seacoast had resented the dominance of inland towns in the legislature after an act of 1775 extended representation to any incorporated place with thirty or more voters, for Boston had only four seats and no other community had more than two. Ipswich, equal in population and wealth to as many as thirty westerns towns, had only one fifteenth the voices. In response to such complaints, a rump session of the General Court in May 1776, after the country members had left, extended the powers of large towns almost indefinitely by giving them an extra representative for every 100 voters above 120.[41] The additional influence that went to the commercial cities was hardly pleasing to farmers, who insisted that, as it was, the old system had discriminated against them. Unavailingly, they asked the repeal of the Act, because it was "calculated to raise a jealousy between the landed and mercantile interests," since "four or five of the largest seaport towns are able, on the new mode, to furnish members sufficient to constitute a house." [42]

At every turn, political, judicial, and economic developments gave continuing emphasis to Thomas Allen's prophetic warning that "it concerned the People to see to it that whilst we are fighting against oppression from the King and Parliment that we did not suffer it to rise up in our own Bowels, that he was not so much concerned about Carrying our Point against Great Brittain, as he was of having Usurpers rising up amongst ourselves." [43] To such, the return to King William's defective charter was precipitate and "directly contrary to the Instructions given to their Representatives." [44] "We have," they complained, "gradually and insensibly been departing from our once happy government, by the practices of those, whose interest it was to

40. *Province Acts, 1769–80*, p. 1275; Smith, *Pittsfield, 1734 to 1800*, p. 334.

41. St. 1775–76, chs. 3, 26; MA, CLVI, 192ff; *Province Acts, 1769–80*, pp. 542, 543; *Massachusetts Spy*, Jan. 16, 1777; Sullivan to J. Adams, May 9, 1776, T. C. Amory, *Life of James Sullivan* (Boston, 1859), I, 76; J. S. Barry, *History of Massachusetts, Colonial Period* (Boston, 1855), p. 514.

42. "A Centinel," *Massachusetts Spy*, Jan. 16, May 29, 1777.

43. Sermon in Richmond, Feb. 18, 1776, MA, CXXXVII, 77, 78.

44. Pittsfield Memorial (1775), MA, CLXXX, 150.

filch away the liberties of the subject . . . Power in the hands
of the people was diminishing, in the same proportion, as individuals became great and wealthy, in the administration of
public justice." [45]

This hostility was not passive only. Allen rapidly gained converts as he heatedly preached that "it was by no means best to
suffer it . . . that it was the Duty of the People to oppose it,
and that he had rather be without any Form of Goverment than
to submit to this . . . he had often Seen the Tears of those who
were oppressed by it, and that they had no Comforter, that on the
side of the oppressors was Power. . . . He said . . . that although the Continental Congress had advised to the assumtion
of this form of Government, yet they were . . . failable Creatures . . . and that if the People . . . Judged that they (the
Congress) had abused their power they were to be opposed in the
same manner as the King and Parliment ought to be opposed." [46]
Although some of the most radical of all, like Asa Douglas of
Hancock, fought any measure to restrict local autonomy, more
generally debtor farmers looked to the immediate adoption of a
popularly approved constitution for a cure to their ills.[47]

But those who lacked the sense of urgency that came from the
pressure of the tax collectors and the threat of foreclosure were,
for one reason or another, anxious to put off the day of decision.
The more prosperous farmers, also aggrieved by the representation of 1776, were nevertheless dubious of the gains to come from
a constitution produced by a legislature elected under that system, and found waiting tolerable so long as prosperity removed
the compulsion for change. The Province Charter gave merchants
of whatever rank and condition as much power as they were likely
to have under any constitution. From these groups came demands
for a more gradual evolution. To frame a new form of government at once would lead to "the greatest anarchy, as it would
leave the people for a time without any rulers." The issues bound
to arise would create disunity and disrupt the war effort. Furthermore, the absent soldiers would have no share in shaping the
government they fought to create. Such slogans awakened some
measure of response from every element in the state except from
the intransigent farmers made impatient by debt.[48]

45. "Cosmopolitan," *Massachusetts Spy*, May 3, 1776.
46. MA, CXXXVII, 77–78.
47. MA, CLXXXI, 201, 206. See also introduction to *The Popular Sources of Political Authority*, ed. Oscar and Mary F. Handlin (Cambridge, Mass., 1966).
48. Amory, *James Sullivan*, I, 76, 77, 96; "O.P.Q.," *Massachusetts Spy*, May 18,

Everywhere, those determined to retain a hold upon the soil engaged in a bitter struggle with the more prosperous for control over policy. In many parts of the state the balance shifted from time to time; but in Berkshire and in Hampshire, the western-most counties, debtors early secured and retained power. There, sight of specie was rare, the weight of taxes ruinous. There, the expenses of building roads and bridges, of settling the wilderness, were heaviest. There, were "no Rich farmers . . . But few of the midling Sort" and "no Very Rich Traders." [49] A number of in-habitants of Jericho (Hancock), opposing incorporation which would increase the power of the poor, explained: "This place is the out Skirts of the Provinces and has been under no proper Regulation . . . it has proved an Assalum for many Poor People, that had no whare Else to go, who have Settled upon the un-granted Lands, who greatly Swell our Numbers, but are not like to Increase our Abilities, many of whom being Ignorant of the manner and Duty of an incorporated Town, and Consequently have been . . . Influenced to consent to the afforsaid Petition, by a few . . . Designing men . . . to Probegate their own In-trest." [50] Furthermore, legal restrictions were hardly as formi-dable here as in the more orderly east. At the turbulent town meetings, the weight of numbers and of threatened violence, more important than respectability or property qualifications, enabled "Men of little or no Intrest" to turn out the "Substan-cial Imhabitants" guarding "the Dor against them, and not al-lowing them to Vote." The complaint came from Hancock where the division turned about the question of incorporating the town. The "Substancial" citizens opposed that step because they realized the town meeting would fall into the hands of "Men of . . . no Intrest" whose power would thus increase.[51]

Where they had control, the debtor farmers blocked the res-toration of a critical branch of government as a lever to extort a new and more satisfactory settlement. Having learned that courts could be closed in one cause, they were not slow to apply the lesson to their own advantage.

By accepting the royal new order in 1774, the judiciary had earned the hostility of patriots of every complexion who decided no judge should sit who acted under the commission of George

1776; J. Adams to Sullivan, May 26, 1776, J. Adams, *Works*, IX, 377ff; Dana to J. Adams, July 28, 1776, W. P. Cresson, *Francis Dana* (New York, 1930), pp. 31, 32.
49. See Great Barrington and Sylvester petitions, MA, CLXXXVI, 26, 43.
50. MA, CLXXXI, 102.
51. See MA, CLXXXI, 102, 198, 201, 202, 205, 206, 209, 211.

III. The committees of correspondence and the county conventions which shut down the province's tribunals opposed only the coercive parliamentary measures and urged debtors to meet their obligations. Almost at once the new state government reestablished the courts, which turned to the task of collecting the great mass of loans and enforcing contracts allowed to lapse in the interregnum.[52]

But those with concrete grievances against the "cumbrous judicial system," those whose Whigism "originated in a disposition not to pay their debts," those for whom all problems of government revolved about the necessity for saving the land from creditors were not satisfied. The debtor-dominated west by force prevented the reopening, pending a total overhauling of the judicial system in its application to debtor-creditor relations.[53] That could come only in a new government under a new constitution. Forthright petitions asking for the right to elect all officers, including judges, illuminated the connection between the two issues. "If the right of nominating to office is not vested in the people," maintained a Pittsfield memorial, "we are indifferent who assumes it, — whether any particular persons on this or the other side of the water," and pointedly added, "Upon the foregoing premises . . . the court of this county of Quarter Sessions is ordered to desist from any further sessions." [54]

These spontaneous measures raised the vivid fear that the same acts which resisted the tyranny of England might annihilate "the salutary restraint" of law.[55] Some indeed thought of solving the problems of government by sending an army to Berkshire to open the courts and suppress the "leveling spirit" and the "desire of possessing paper currency." [56] But revolutionary conditions closed

52. *Massachusetts Spy*, July 28, Aug. 25, Sept. 1, 15, 22, Oct. 6, 13, 20, 27, 1774, Sept. 29, 1775, Jan. 5, Mar. 1, June 28, Sept. 11, 25, 1776; *Journals of Each Provincial Congress*, pp. 601ff, 609–627; see also General Court Proclamation, Jan. 23, 1776, *Boston Gazette*, Feb. 12, 1776; *Province Resolves, 1765–80*, 947ff; W. T. Davis, *History of the Judiciary of Massachusetts* (Boston, 1900), p. 168; Amory, *James Sullivan*, I, 80; Smith, *Pittsfield, 1734 to 1800*, pp. 194, 195; J. R. Trumbull, *History of Northampton* (Northampton, 1898–1902), II, 345ff; Freeman, *Cape Cod*, I, 435ff.

53. See MA, CLXXXI, 42ff; Smith, *Pittsfield, 1734 to 1800*, pp. 325, 339ff, 347ff; Trumbull, *Northampton*, II, 374, 389; *Massachusetts Spy*, Oct. 2, 1776. Adjournment by the General Court was for special purposes. See res. 1773–74, chs. 73, 74; res. 1775–76, chs. 701, 743, 803, 899, 934, 935; res. 1776–77, chs. 457, 907, 916; res. 1779–80, ch. 245.

54. Smith, *Pittsfield, 1734 to 1800*, p. 345.

55. See Washburn, "Leicester," *Worc. Mag. and Hist. Jour.*, 2 (1826), 109, 110.

56. See Sullivan to J. Adams, May 9, 1776, Amory, *James Sullivan*, I, 77. See also MA, CXXXVII, 76, CLXXXI, 42ff.

that course; the British fully absorbed the attentions of whatever military force was available. In any case, control by the well-to-do, even when they were united, was not that secure; their power in their own communities rested on collaboration with other citizens who also voted at the town meeting and whose interests also had to be satisfied. Most important of all, the prospering shared the outlook and aspirations of the rest of the people, from whose ranks they stemmed, and they thought within the pattern of the same ideas. Everyone acknowledged the force of the argument that only a constitution could bring to realization the aims of the Revolution. No group could put off the decision indefinitely.

Simmering agitation began to bring results in the fall of 1776. In September, the General Court asked the towns whether they wished a constitution and, if so, whether they were willing to have the legislature frame it, subject to local approval. The response was mixed and confusing. Division and uncertainty throughout the state defeated the proposal.[57] Eight months later, the legislature without previous consultation directed the towns, in choosing representatives to the next General Court, to "instruct them in one Body with the Council, to form" a constitution, effective when approved by two thirds of the citizens voting on it.[58]

The question quickly stimulated interest in the next election, and the crisis in monetary and commodity regulation kept that interest at a high pitch. Many distant places like Pittsfield for the first time eked out the funds to send their full quota of legislators to Boston. The new frame of government, long looked forward to, was nevertheless rejected when returned to the towns for approval in 1778.[59]

Numerous structural defects stood in the way of acceptance, and a number of unfortunate but largely irrelevant issues alienated many who might otherwise have supported the new system. Wondrous dreams of the ultimate forms, clear in general out-

57. Vote by towns favored, but by head opposed, the proposal. Tabulation of the MS returns in MA, CLVI, 121–191, reveals no significant distribution.

58. See MA, CXLII, 64; res. 1776–77, ch. 1169; res. 1777–78, ch. 842; *Journal of the Convention for Framing a Constitution of Government for the State of Massachusetts Bay, September 1, 1779, to June 16, 1780* (Boston, 1832), p. 255.

59. The text of the constitution of 1778 is given in *Journal of Convention, 1780*, pp. 255–264, and is reprinted in Handlin, *Popular Sources*, pp. 190ff. MS returns are in MA, CLVI, CLX. These are reprinted, together with returns from other sources, in Handlin, *Popular Sources*, pp. 202ff. Tabulation reveals the commercial towns largely opposed, but no significant distribution of the agricultural towns.

line, were inchoate and hazy when reduced to specific details. Lack of a bill of rights and of explicit safeguards to property troubled men of all orders. Some felt any settlement premature until "the public affairs are in a more peaceable and settled condition." There were objections because not all militia officers were elected directly. A provision excluding Negroes from the suffrage seemed to others a denial of the elementary rights for which they fought. Still others, satisfied with relative freedom under the status quo, were "averse to the establishment of any more permanent government." A great many criticisms dealt with matters of detail and too many voters demanded perfection in their first trial at constitution making.[60]

Furthermore, the merchants and their supporters in the urban areas saw in the extensive powers given the small rural towns a threat not only to their immediate interests but also to their whole position in the government. These fears were most strikingly expressed by a convention of seaport towns in Essex County which drew up a closely reasoned statement of objections and of the fundamental principles upon which should rest the ultimate constitution of the state.[61] The Essex Result insisted that prerequisite to any frame of government was a bill of rights "clearly ascertaining and defining the rights of conscience, and that security of person and property, which every member in the State hath a right to expect from the supreme power." The proposed constitution was bad because it lacked separation of powers and the judiciary was not independent. The legislature was too large and too strong, representation was based only on numbers and not on property as it should have been, and the House had too much power as against the Senate. The governor had no veto, his property qualifications were too low and not designed to take account "of the fluctuation of the nominal value of money." In the face of such deficiencies, Theophilus Parsons exclaimed, "Surely a state of nature is more excellent." [62]

The same reservations carried weight among some agriculturists. In outlook on property and the bill of rights, the wealthy

60. These objections are summarized in the Spencer and Westminster returns, MA, CLX, 7, 17ff. See also "Z-A," *Boston Gazette*, May 11, 1778; Aaron Hobart, *Historical Sketch of Abington* (Boston, 1839), p. 136; Parsons, *Theophilus Parsons*, p. 359; Smith, *Pittsfield, 1734 to 1800*, pp. 356, 357.

61. Parsons, *Theophilus Parsons*, pp. 47, 49, 384, 385; H. C. Lodge, *Life and Letters of George Cabot* (Boston, 1877), pp. 14ff. The Essex Result is reprinted in Handlin, *Popular Sources*, pp. 324ff. See also MA, CLX, 16.

62. Parsons, *Theophilus Parsons*, pp. 54, 359-363, 384-389.

were closer to the urban moneyed elements than to the debtors about them. Substantial farmers preferred larger representation for rural areas, of course; but not all were prepared to give the vote to the poor in their midst. Many in debt also had faith in the fundamental importance of property; indeed this faith lay at the root of the fear of losing the land. Men of every rank who criticized enfranchising the clergy and disenfranchising the Negroes often did so on the grounds that the former had no property and paid no taxes, which the latter did. Once granted the justness of property qualifications, the grounds of difference were not fundamental but details of quantity and kind, and the response of purely agrarian towns like Royalston echoed the sentiments of the Essex Result.[63]

An ambiguous method of ratification turned objections to details into rejection of the whole and doomed the document to defeat. The committee which had originally proposed the project had assumed that there would be a continuing convention of the legislature which would revise and submit the frame of government over and over until it obtained a two-thirds majority. But, as presented, the instrument called for unqualified acceptance or rejection, a circumstance obviously not clear to many towns. Examination of the returns shows that many, though in favor of the scheme, voted against it for the sake of specific minor amendments, and would have accepted the basic outline had the question been put as planned. In addition, 120 towns failed to answer at all, of which a considerable number were under the impression that the continuing convention was in no hurry. With the issue thus confused, the few unqualifiedly affirmative votes counted little.[64]

This dubious defeat did not resolve the issue or put an end to political speculation. Men continued to think of a new constitution, and the persistent ineffectiveness of currency and commodity legislation in the next two years rapidly made converts to the necessity of a new frame of government. Since the outbreak of hostilities there had been no abatement in the severity of shortages or the rise in prices. The futility of an act to reduce hoarding put the seaport populations in a dangerous mood. Angry discontent and open riots showed the merchants and other urban leaders that some action was imperative; yet agrarian opposition

63. MA, CLVI, 306ff.
64. See MA, CXXXVII, 138ff; res. 1778–79, ch. 544; *Weston, Records of the First Precinct . . . and of the Town* (Boston, 1893), p. 254.

forestalled the re-establishment of price-fixing.[65] Furthermore, the currency still fell despite continued withdrawals of paper from circulation and despite the deflationary policy of finance through interest-bearing loans and heavy taxation. Creditors desperately sought a measure of protection against rapacious debtors who pursued them with payments in worthless paper. A scale of depreciation which readjusted all obligations to compensate for the fall in the value of money provided some relief. But such palliations no longer concealed the underlying evil of a government too weak to execute any policy.[66]

In any case, so long as the judiciary failed to function in parts of the state, manipulation of the statute book in Boston brought slight returns. Rejection of the constitution of 1778 had left the west with a justification for not accepting centralized government. Although the Court of General Sessions met in Springfield in 1778, a convention refused to reopen it in Berkshire County and informed the General Court that it preferred no tribunals "rather than to have Law dealt out by piece meal as it is this Day, without any Foundation to support it." With this statement came a warning that the county might secede and unite with a neighboring state which did have a constitution.[67] A committee of the legislature dispatched to inquire into these grievances was lectured at for its pains and sent back to Boston with demands for a constitution.[68] An act of 1779 which combined a general pardon for all riots and assaults with the organization of courts was equally ineffective. Three hundred people assembled at Great Barrington told the hopeful judges who came there: "It is creating a dangerous President to admit . . . the operation of Law untill there is a Constitution or Form of Government with a Bill of Rights explicitly approved of . . . by a Majority

65. St. 1778–79, ch. 31; st. 1779–80, chs. 7, 13, 15, 16; res. 1779–80, ch. 659; st. 1780, chs. 4, 7; *Province Acts, 1769–80*, pp. 1019ff, 1254–1262; *Letters*, ed. Burnett, III, 490ff, IV, 232ff, 514, 523, 526, 529, 537, V, vi, 98. See also Sewall to Jackson, Jan. 27, 1780, *Essex Inst. Hist. Colls.*, VII (1865), 195ff; Cutler to Hitchcock, Sept. 20, 1779, *ibid.*, LXXVI (1940), 375; Eliot to Belknap, Mar. 17, Oct. 20, 1779, *Mass. Hist. Soc. Colls.*, 6 ser., IV (1891), 138, 152; T. to J. Pickering, Sept. 24, 1779, Pickering Papers, V, 125; King, *Rufus King*, I, 30.

66. Res. 1778–79, ch. 628; st. 1779–80, ch. 40; res. 1779–80, chs. 134, 156, 230, 234, 765, 994; *Province Acts, 1769–80*, pp. 1034, 1338–1340; *Province Resolves, 1765–80*, pp. 351ff; *Independent Chronicle*, Apr. 27, May 11, 1780; *Letters*, ed. Burnett, I, 140, V, ix, 85; J. Adams to DeVergennes, June 22, 1780, J. Adams, *Works*, VII, 195ff; William Heath, *Memoirs*, ed. William Abbatt (New York, 1901), p. 216.

67. MA, CCXX, 462; *Province Acts, 1769–80*, p. 1028; Smith, *Pittsfield, 1734 to 1800*, pp. 358, 360ff.

68. See *Province Acts, 1769–80*, pp. 1029ff.

of the Freemen of this State." The legislature saw the futility of the attempt and surrendered by repealing the act of organization.[69]

With the courts closed, temperate elements, even in debtor communities, saw with distress the infectious growth of lawlessness. Creditors everywhere raised vigorous demands for a settlement that would re-establish state credit, restore order, and permit the opening of courts to enforce contracts and collect debts. The ineffectiveness of the Province Charter in furnishing the machinery for a workable commodity or monetary policy also increased the number who believed a new and stronger government necessary, and who agreed with John Adams that "who shall be the head, is much less important than whether we shall have any." [70]

Again, in 1779, the General Court was moved to action. Having applied for and received the consent of the towns, it asked those bodies to send representatives to a convention with instructions to frame a constitution which would go into effect when ratified by a two-thirds vote of the people.[71]

The small farmer's dream of a new dispensation was not realized in the convention which assembled in Cambridge in September. But a core of ideas, common to the whole society, and popular acceptance earned at least temporary acquiescence for the constitution that emerged.

A complex of circumstances enabled a small group of men to express on behalf of a large and representative body the views of government current in the whole society. As in 1778, some places, assured of an opportunity to discuss and ratify the plan of government in town meeting, failed to elect delegates at all. Burdensome expense also whittled down the number of those who actually reported at the start. With nothing at all happening for a month after the opening, with sessions long drawn out and frequently adjourned, attendance seemed too costly for communities fretting at taxes and requisitions. By November two thirds of the members had drifted home. When the meeting adjourned from November 11, 1779, to January 5, 1780, country people found difficulty in returning. Travel was strenuous and the

69. St. 1778–79, ch. 38; st. 1779–80, ch. 25; MA, CCXX, 456; *Province Acts, 1769–80*, pp. 1031, 1032, 1275, 1276.

70. To Mrs. Warren, Dec. 15, 1778, J. Adams, *Works*, IX, 475. See also *Independent Chronicle*, Apr. 27, May 4, 1780.

71. *Journal of Convention, 1780*, pp. 5, 6, 189ff; res. 1778–79, ch. 544; res. 1779–80, ch. 135.

winter the hardest in forty years. The convention resorted to newspaper advertisements to admonish absentees but was unable to reassemble a quorum for twenty-one days.[72] Repeated postponements and calculated delays further lowered interest.[73] In the crucial February session which debated the text, the votes cast never exceeded seventy.[74]

There was no balloting by yeas and nays; the records do not even reveal who was there and who was not.[75] But the constitution showed unmistakable evidence of its paternity. Drafted by John Adams, it followed the pattern recommended by the Essex Result, the author of which was a delegate. But the document which resulted from their efforts did not simply express the views of exceptional individuals. These leaders were aware that their work would be successful only if they won the approval of the people in the towns on issues which had already passed through six years of vigorous discussion.

In some respects the constitution of 1780 remedied the defects of its predecessor of 1778. A bill of rights assured to each citizen "the security of his person and property" as an unassailable condition to the social contract.[76] A strong executive with extensive veto powers,[77] an independent judiciary appointed for good behavior,[78] and a senate representing property effectively restrained

72. See *Independent Chronicle*, Jan. 20, 1780; *Journal of Convention, 1780*, pp. 33, 49, 52, 53, 55, 63; Samuel Breck, *Recollections*, ed. H. E. Scudder (Philadelphia, 1877), p. 20; *History of the County of Berkshire*, ed. D. D. Field (Pittsfield, 1829), p. 182.

73. Among the questions thus postponed were those of property qualifications (Jan. 28), the judiciary (Feb. 7), the Council (until Feb. 10), the governor (Feb. 5), and the extension of the common law (Jan. 31, Feb. 8, 25, 28) (see *Journal of Convention, 1780*, pp. 61, 66, 81, 85, 87, 98, 99, 142, 145). After some delay the thorny problem of representation was settled secretly in committee of the whole (*ibid.*, pp. 118–122). The effect of such delays was shown in the vote on the governor's veto. On Feb. 21 the proposal to give such power to the chief executive was defeated 44–32. Two days later it was carried 44–24 (*ibid.*, pp. 126, 133; see also below, n. 83). For the narrow margins in some of the most crucial votes, see Appendix A, below.

74. Appendix A; also *Journal of Convention, 1780*.

75. Attendance was taken at three sessions only, Nov. 8, 1779 — 93 present, 207 absent; Jan. 26, 1780 — 50 present; Feb. 4, 1780 — 84 present (representing 62 towns). *Journal of Convention, 1780*, pp. 42, 55, 80.

76. See the first and revised drafts of art. X, Bill of Rights, in which a special clause was added to protect property against the state; also Parsons, *Theophilus Parsons*, pp. 367ff.

77. See the constitution, ch. II, sec. 1; Parsons, *Theophilus Parsons*, pp. 379ff. In the original draft the veto was absolute; in the final form it could be overridden by a two-thirds vote (see ch. I, sec. 1, art. 2).

78. Art. XXIX, Bill of Rights; ch. III of the constitution. That separation of powers was also intended to protect the judiciary may be seen by comparing art.

the house of representatives, the only popular branch of the government.[79]

balance

Consistently the constitution followed the maxim of the Essex Result that power must be distributed between two groups to ensure its exercise in "the true interest of any state." For "political honesty, probity, and a regard to the interest of the whole," one must turn to "the bulk of the people"; "for the greatest wisdom, firmness, consistency and perseverance" to the "men of education and fortune." [80] Consequently representation in the Senate rested on taxes paid.[81] The popular branch was weighted in favor of the eastern mercantile towns with the larger communities gaining at the expense of the smaller. Heavy property qualifications applied not only to officeholding but also to voting, for which requirements were actually higher than under the old Province Charter.[82] The provision that amendment could come only by a two-thirds majority minimized the possibility of casual tampering with the frame of government.[83] The convention had heeded the warning of the Essex Result that "the idea of liberty has been held up in so dazzling colours, that some of us may not be willing to submit to that subordination necessary in the freest States," and had taken adequate steps to compensate.[84]

The constitution was returned to the towns for ratification accompanied by an extremely apologetic "Address" which pointed out that "we may not expect to agree on a perfect System of Government: This is not the Lot of Mankind," and

---

XXX of the Bill of Rights with art. XXXI of the original draft. For the defense of the judiciary, see Parsons, *Theophilus Parsons*, pp. 382ff. For an attack, see, e.g., "Philelutheros," *Massachusetts Spy*, Aug. 2, 1775.

79. See Parsons, *Theophilus Parsons*, pp. 376ff, 389.

80. See Parsons, *Theophilus Parsons*, pp. 368–370. See also J. Adams to Gerry, Nov. 4, 1779, *Works*, IX, 506.

81. Ch. I, sec. 2, art. 1, of the constitution. The Essex Result proposed the idea that property qualifications should be set not in terms of specific sums of money subject to depreciation, but in terms of proportions of taxes paid (see Parsons, *Theophilus Parsons*, pp. 391ff).

82. See the constitution, ch. I, sec. 2, arts. 2, 5, sec. 3, arts. 2, 3, 4; ch. II, sec. 1, arts. 2, 3; Parsons, *Theophilus Parsons*, p. 390.

83. Ch. VI, art. 10, of the constitution. How narrow majorities and repeated postponements wore down opposition was shown in the case of the provision that made a two-thirds vote necessary for revision in 1795. Twice voted down, it was finally accepted on the very last day (*Journal of Convention, 1780*, pp. 157, 159, 165.

84. The constitution as submitted is given in *Journal of Convention, 1780*, pp. 222ff; the original draft may be found *ibid.*, pp. 192ff. See also Parsons, *Theophilus Parsons*, p. 364.

stressed the opportunity for revision in fifteen years.[85] Significantly, the form of submission differed from that of 1778. Unlike the latter, this did not ask for outright approval or disapproval. The towns were to vote on each provision separately and to propose amendments. Few towns expressed themselves for or against the constitution as a whole; most suggested improvements and, thinking in terms of a continuing convention that would incorporate these changes, accepted it conditionally. Thus Stockbridge outlined some modifications and then added: "But if there should not appear to be two thirds of the people of this state who may have Voted on the articles in Favor of such amendments, or the printed Declaration of Rights and Frame of Government . . . In such Case our Delegates in Convention Assembled be Invested with the Power to make such alterations as may be agreeable to the Sentiments of two thirds of the Votes of the People." [86]

Some amendments were trivial but many struck directly at the heart of the document. On the issues of representation, of the independent judiciary, and of the relationship of church to state, more than one third seemed to disapprove of the provisions in the constitution and in the bill of rights. But there was no consistency among the alternatives proposed in the dissenting opinions.[87]

The convention adopted the constitution in its original form, although it could not cast up a coherent statistical account that would show just how many people were in favor and how many opposed. Attendance at the session which met to receive the results was sparser than ever and the weight of the seaboard towns correspondingly heavier. The majority rejected motions to read the returns to the whole body, and the substance of the answers never became known to the public or even to all the members. Instead, a select committee collated the responses and after several trials declared the new scheme accepted. The members of the convention ratified this decision, although they refused to vote by yeas and nays, and gave the constitution the stamp of approval.[88]

The constitution of 1780 failed to meet the desires of many groups who would continue to struggle toward their own ends.

85. *Journal of Convention, 1780*, pp. 216ff.

86. MA, CCLXXVI, 21; also Sandisfield Report, MA, CLX, 255ff; S. to J. Adams, Mar. 15, 1780, S. Adams, *Writings*, IV, 182ff.

87. Handlin, *Popular Sources*, 25ff. The returns are printed *ibid.*, 475ff.

88. *Journal of Convention, 1780*, pp. 171, 172, 175, 180, 186, 187.

But even those not favored by the detailed organization of powers could find in the document the possibility for implementing a larger purpose than the sponsors conceived. For it contained a broad vision of the nature of the state, explicitly propounded in terms that appealed to preconceptions in the minds of all Massachusetts men.[89]

The constitution formalized ideas current throughout the state. Placed against their proper background, its provisions appear as the intellectualized expression of deep-rooted and widespread sentiments. John Adams, whose role in its composition was pre-eminent, did not stand apart from the people. A product of agricultural Braintree, linked to the professional classes by training and interests, he spent his youth in frontier Worcester and gathered his political experience in the turbulent politics of Suffolk County. A varied career, residence in the west and in the east, gave him a sympathetic understanding of the diverse elements of his society, unmatched by any of his contemporaries. From his studies he acquired a love of order, of the legal process that for him constituted a government of laws. And out of his acquaintance with the long tradition of European political thought he had laid profound hold of a few ideas of the nature of government and of its relations with men. These three elements produced his conception of the state as Commonwealth.[90]

There was significance in the revival of the old Puritan designation, Commonwealth.[91] Like James Harrington, the earlier political philosopher whom he studied, admired, and imitated, Adams perceived "that the troubles of the time were not due wholly to the intemperance of faction, the misgovernment of a king, or the stubbornness of a people, but to change in the balance of property." [92] Revolutionary conditions which upset the usual relations among the diverse groups in the state had produced the struggle for power in these years.

Like Harrington, too, Adams believed that not reason nor abstract ideas but interest alone guided political action. Government de facto was "an art whereby . . . some few men, subject

89. S. to J. Adams, July 10, 1780, S. Adams, *Writings*, IV, 199ff; Samuel Cooper, *Sermon Preached before John Hancock* (Boston, 1780), pp. 8ff, 28ff.

90. Page Smith, *John Adams* (Garden City, 1962), I, 237–444.

91. For the special importance which Adams attached to the term "Commonwealth," note its use in his letters to Sergeant and Dana, July 21, Aug. 16, 1776 (J. Adams, *Works*, IX, 424ff, 429ff).

92. Henry Morley's description of Harrington in his introduction to James Harrington, *Commonwealth of Oceana* (London, 1887), p. 7. For Adams on Harrington, see, e.g., J. Adams, *Works*, IV, 427ff, IX, 376ff.

a city or nation, and rule it according to . . . their private interest."[93] Aware that his constitution lodged power in the hands of a relatively small group of propertied farmers and merchants, he counted that no objection, for he considered that people were free "in proportion to their property" and consequently that "a nobility or gentry, in a popular government, not overbalancing it, is the very life and soul of it."[94] If, as in Massachusetts, "a division of the land into small quantities" enabled all to hold property, "the multitude will take care of the liberty, virtue, and interest of the multitude, in all acts of government."[95]

But, if government among men was to rest on more than fear, "so sordid and brutal a passion," and operate on a higher plane than among beasts, it must also serve a larger purpose.[96] Behind the contending forces of the diverse interests, Adams noted a broader interest. Early he had seen in his own state that the "merchantile Interest" was "complicated with the landed Interest," and with the authors of the Essex Result he had attacked those who "have fancied a clashing of interests amongst the various classes of men."[97] The unity behind diversity came from the fact that transcending the interests of all its constituents was the interest of the society "common to all its Members" and expressed in the "body politic or State, one moral whole." The state was a Common Wealth, with an identity and interests of its own, apart from those of the groups within it.[98]

It was true that de facto governments ruled the state from time to time. But "the end of the institution, maintenance and administration of government" was "to secure the existence of the body-politic . . . [,] a voluntary association of individuals . . . [or] social compact, by which the whole people covenants with each citizen, and each citizen with the whole people, that all shall be governed by certain laws for the common good."[99] When government fulfilled that function it acquired a de jure

93. Harrington, *Oceana*, p. 16.
94. See Harrington, *Oceana*, pp. 12, 18, 22. See particularly in this connection Adams' refutation of the arguments of Turgot and Nedham that a commonwealth necessarily involved complete democracy (*Works*, VI, 6ff).
95. J. Adams, *Works*, IX, 377.
96. J. Adams, "Thoughts on Government," *Works*, IV, 194.
97. J. Adams to Warren, Oct. 20, 1775, *Letters*, ed. Burnett, I, 240; Parsons, *Theophilus Parsons*, pp. 364–366.
98. See Address of the Convention to the People, *Journal of Convention, 1780*, pp. 216ff; J. Adams, "Defense," *Works*, IV, 404.
99. Preamble to the constitution of 1780, *Journal of Convention, 1780*, p. 222.

character and became "an art whereby a civil society of men is instituted and preserved upon the foundation of common right or interest." [100]

This conception was not peculiar to Adams. It was the underlying assumption that breathed through the Essex Result, through the responses and petitions of western towns, and through the entire constitution of 1780. It was in the mind of the member of the convention who proposed unsuccessfully, but significantly, that the name of the state be changed from Massachusetts to Oceana. It accounts for the fact that the body which met as "the Delegates of the People of the STATE OF MASSACHUSETTS-BAY" produced the "CONSTITUTION of the COMMONWEALTH OF MASSACHU-SETTS." [101]

The commonwealth idea, sophisticated and abstract in the minds of Adams and his literate friends, had a meaning also for others in the state, a meaning no less real, if not so specific or so clearly defined. For the farmers and the seamen, for the fishermen, artisans, and new merchants, it spoke the aspirations of the founding fathers, it repeated the lessons they knew from the organization of churches and towns, and it embodied the wisdom of a people many decades in the wilderness. These men had learned on frontier after frontier the value of common action and knew what it meant to be "deprived of Social Compact and Society Privileges." [102] The great trial of war gave that lesson a fresh reality; the Revolution added new connotations. They had started against great odds. They had been warned "how vain it is . . . to war against *Great Britain* . . . It is greatly inferiour to the Giants waging war against *Olympus!* These had strength, but what have we? . . . Our country is without money, stores or necessaries of war! without one place of refuge or defence!" [103] Yet by 1780 they were winning. Reft by divisions, ineffective and unskilled in their government, guided often by motives of personal interest, they were nevertheless throwing back all the forces of a mighty tyrant. The Revolution was, at once, evidence of their power when united, and the repository of hopes for which, willingly or not, they had endured hardships and made sacrifices. It was the symbol of their unity, of their identity as a people.

100. Harrington, *Oceana*, p. 16; J. Adams, *Works*, V, 453.
101. *Journal of Convention, 1780*, pp. 43, 222.
102. See Ashuelot Equivalent, petition, Feb. 12, 1780, MA, CLXXXVI, 77.
103. *American Archives*, ed. Peter Force (Washington, D.C., 1832), I, 1216; W. V. Wells, *Life and Public Services of Samuel Adams* (Boston, 1865), II, 263ff.

The Revolution added a new element to the vague discussions of James Harrington and of the eighteenth-century English Whigs, as well as to the abstract aspirations for "a Government or a Body Politic" that would "be one connected system having but one common interest, and one public will." [104] The state became intensely real and immediate, not the aloof product of remote tradition or slow historical development. Having fashioned it themselves, the people were unable to conceive of it or of its interests as abstractions; and having labored to create it, they expected to participate in deciding what the common interest was in terms of "the security and happiness of the constituent individuals." [105]

With that conception went no illusions about the actual application of power to day-to-day problems. Men as individuals and in groups would still seek to satisfy their own ambitions as they had in the preceding six years. But no matter where control would rest, those in power would find their actions set within the framework of the commonwealth idea, of the broader concerns that comprehended the whole community. And before the decade was out, a major crisis would explore the uncertain frontier between the exigencies of particular interests and the changing demands of common interest.

104. E. Ludlow in *Massachusetts Spy*, Mar. 3, 1774; also *ibid.*, Sept. 25, 1776.
105. "Worcestriensis," *Massachusetts Spy*, Aug. 14, 1776; Oscar and M. F. Handlin, "James Burgh and American Revolutionary Theory," *Mass. Hist. Soc. Proceedings*, LXXIII (1961), 38ff; Caroline Robbins, *The Eighteenth-Century Commonwealthman* (Cambridge, Mass., 1959); Bernard Bailyn, *The Ideological Origins of the American Revolution* (Cambridge, Mass., 1967).

2 | Consolidation of Political Power

The settlement of 1780 established a balance that gave the merchants of the state a certain measure of dominance through control of the Senate and through property qualifications for holding office. In outright opposition to the new Constitution stood only the debtor farmers, some Baptists, and a few conscientious opponents like Joseph Hawley. Even those who had voted against ratification were willing to give the new arrangements a trial. "I stile it glorious," wrote Hawley, "altho, I humbly conceive it has several great blemishes, on account whereof it will until corrected be liable . . . to very weighty Exception; but still it remains glorious in respect of the great Quantity of excellent matter contained in it." [1]

The debtor farmers had accepted the new frame of government. But apprehensive of the effect upon them, and wary of those in office, they were by no means convinced of its finality. Although some believed the fifteen-year trial period too long, the possibility of amendment remained. In any case, acquiescence did not imply placid agreement with all the acts of the legitimate government. Contending interests would still determine what the common interest was, and misguided governments would always find that "the People fired with a just Resentment" could "rise like a Whirlwind & spurn them from the Earth and take the Power again into their own hands." [2]

1. Joseph Hawley, Statement, Oct. 28, 1780, Hawley Papers (NYPL).
2. Lenox Response (1778), MA, CLVI, 378; *Independent Chronicle*, Apr. 27, May 4, 1780.

Agitation persisted in communities whose "Distent Situation, from the metropolis . . . Renders the profits, of . . . farmes, Very Inconsiderable, to Those, of an equal Bigness, and Quality, near, the Maritime And, market Towns." [3] In Worcester, Hampshire, and Berkshire counties, debtors bluntly flouted a new law to restrict voting in town meetings and continued to have their say.[4] Conventions there demanded financial reforms, the suspension of debt collections, revision of public salaries and fees, and a tender law. Sporadic riots challenged the newly organized constitutional courts; the Lusk brothers in Lenox attempted to halt executions; and when a legislative committee of investigation failed to bring relief, discontent in the west broke out in a local revolt under the leadership of the unfrocked preacher, Samuel Ely. For a time the situation was so critical that in Boston it appeared "nothing less will do than an agrarian law & revolution." [5]

Swift action by the government dispelled the illusion that it was as powerless as its predecessors. The dissidents soon learned that the new regime was determined to exercise its functions. The attempt to close the courts led to a suspension of the privilege of habeas corpus in June 1782, the arrest of the ringleaders, and the dispersal of the insurgents.[6]

But the rioters also learned that even an unsuccessful outbreak evoked concessions; the suggestion that the people might "throw up our constitution" produced conciliatory measures. All the insurgents save Ely were pardoned, and the House of Representatives, within its own halls, hesitated to void the election of those who had questioned its authority.[7] Finally, a number of overdue reforms reached the statute books. A confessional act remedied a long-standing grievance by allowing justices of the peace to take acknowledgments of debt and to issue execu-

3. Spencer Petition (1782), MA, CLXXXVII, 412ff.
4. St. 1781, ch. 25; MA, CLXXXVIII, 23, 25.
5. Otis to Sedgwick, July 8, 1782, Theodore Sedgwick Papers, 1768–1858 (MSS, MHS), I, 741; *Salem Gazette*, May 2, Oct. 24, 1782; J. E. A. Smith, *History of Pittsfield . . . 1734 to . . . 1800* (Boston, 1869), pp. 396ff; R. E. Moody, "Samuel Ely," *New England Quarterly*, 5 (1932), 108ff; W. V. Wells, *Life and Public Services of Samuel Adams* (Boston, 1865), III, 159ff; J. H. Lockwood, *Westfield . . . 1669–1919* (Springfield, 1922), II, 48ff; *Centennial Celebration of the Town of Sheffield* (Sheffield, 1876), p. 49.
6. St. 1782, ch. 2.
7. St. 1782, ch. 30; L. S. Cushing, C. W. Storey, and Lewis Josselyn, *Reports of Controverted Elections* (Boston, 1853), pp. 9, 14, 15; Lockwood, *Westfield*, II, 58; J. H. Lockwood, *Western Massachusetts . . . 1636–1926* (New York, 1926), I, 116.

tions at low fees.[8] The tender law, approved by so legalistic a politician as James Sullivan, temporarily permitted the offer of cattle and other commodities in payment of debts. These measures promised some respite and dissipated a new threat to the troubled Springfield courts in May 1783, although the writ of habeas corpus again had to be suspended.[9]

Meanwhile, the end of military operations in the North released new forces which significantly altered the relations of everyone involved. In the aftermath of war, debt steadily leveled all agricultural communities, prosperity gradually welded together all mercantile elements, and emerging questions of economic policy cut the two groups apart.

After 1779, trading interests had flourished as commerce with the allies — France, Holland, and Spain — increased. Although business with England remained illegal until 1783, frequent violations, and the relaxation of some restrictive provisions after 1780, had mitigated the hardship caused by the severance of old ties. When the treaty of peace legalized intercourse with the former mother country and removed limitations on exports, the merchants exuberantly prepared for a flourishing trade. They also rejoiced in many new speculative opportunities. The ability to acquire government securities cheaply and the risky games played with paper that earned profits even from depreciation brought affluence and unprecedented prosperity.[10]

As the economy reverted to its normal channels, those who lived as satellites of trade also thrived. The uncertainty of the revolutionary years vanished. Men found their niches in business and adjusted to them. Some, heavily involved in government contracting, suffered temporarily, and few were as optimistic about recessions as Christopher Gore, who pointed out that "our trade I presume will decrease, & being contracted within a narrower sphere must produce advantages to those who are concerned. Many who retail tape & pins must, as they ought to have done years ago, return to labor." But in the prevailing

8. See st. 1781, ch. 36; st. 1782, ch. 21. For the confessional act see New Braintree Petition (1782), MA, CLXXXVII, 382; J. R. Trumbull, *History of Northampton* (Northampton, 1898–1902), II, 451.

9. St. 1782, ch. 34; T. C. Amory, *Life of James Sullivan* (Boston, 1859), I, 397; Lockwood, *Westfield*, II, 55, 60ff; Smith, *Pittsfield, 1734 to 1800*, p. 397.

10. See st. 1780, chs. 6, 24, 32; res. 1780, ch. 246J; st. 1781, ch. 27; res. 1781, ch. 654A; st. 1782, chs. 32, 68; res. 1782, ch. 39S; res. 1783, ch. 97S; Benson to Champlen, May 8, 1783. Letters of Boston Merchants, 1780–90 (MSS, Baker Library, Harvard University), IV, 46; Timothy Pickering, Papers, 1760–1800 (MSS, MHS), V, 268, 270, 286, XXXIII, 362.

good times there seemed to be a place for everyone. Fishermen, sailors, and those engaged in the maritime occupations resumed their callings, and the mercantile community settled down, on the whole prosperous and free of debt.[11]

The wand of prosperity did not touch the rural areas. There the effect of peace was quite different. The shift of the main battlegrounds to the South set loose all the agricultural energies of the northern and middle states while relief from the British blockade restored the coastal trade. Shortages and high prices that were the products of war vanished. Farmers now faced the unpleasant business of adjusting expanded production to contracting demand.[12]

The problem of payment for the cost of war accentuated the contrast in positions of city and country. Pleas based on the exigencies of war no longer justified postponement of redemption of the public debt. The balance of obligations was frightening. Against the Commonwealth's total nominal property valuation of $11,000,000 in 1783 stood a liability of above $4,000,000, in addition to the state's responsibility for issuing and supporting a share of continental bills. Veterans' demands further complicated the financial question. Settlement of the claims of both officers and men entailed immediate outlays.[13]

By 1786 refinancing and accumulated interest had increased indebtedness to $5,440,000 in specie with as much more owed to the Continental Congress. The consolidation of securities gave order to, but no relief from, the overwhelming burden; and with the merchants in control, with the holders of public securities pressing for full payment, it was unlikely that amelioration would come through repudiation.[14]

11. C. R. King, *Life and Correspondence of Rufus King* (New York, 1894–1900), I, 168; S. E. Morison, *Life and Letters of Harrison Gray Otis* (Boston, 1913), I, 27.

12. See A. H. Cole, *Wholesale Commodity Prices in the United States, 1700–1861* (Cambridge, Mass., 1938), I, 5, 117; V. L. Johnson, *Administration of the American Commissariat during the Revolutionary War* (Philadelphia, 1941), pp. 154ff.

13. See res. 1780, ch. 30O; st. 1781, chs. 6, 24; st. 1784, ch. 25; *Columbian Centinel*, Mar. 2, 1796; William Heath, *Memoirs* (New York, 1901), pp. 269, 337ff, 344ff; L. C. Hatch, *Administration of the American Revolutionary Army* (New York, 1904), pp. 143ff, 145; *Boston Gazette*, June 21, 28, 1784; Gerry to King, Mar. 28, 1785, King, *Rufus King*, I, 83; J. K. Hosmer, *Samuel Adams* (Boston, 1885), p. 381; Samuel Adams, *Writings*, ed. H. A. Cushing (New York, 1904–1908), IV, 303ff.

14. See res. 1782, ch. 74S; res. 1783, ch. 100S; st. 1784, ch. 24; res. 1784, ch. 42M; R. V. Harlow, "Aspects of Revolutionary Finance," *Amer. Hist. Rev.*, 35

How the cost of liquidating indebtedness would be assessed was crucial in determining its effects. The chief source of revenue remained, and seemingly had to remain, the traditional direct tax on polls and property. Yet that burden was already heavy, and growing heavier, especially after the valuation of 1784 raised assessments substantially. Rufus King, by no means a sympathizer with the underdog, in 1786 estimated that fully one third of the state's income drained into the public coffers.[15]

In agricultural areas where the proportion on polls was highest and rising throughout the period, the situation early became impossible. As always, the farmers perennially in debt grumbled. But now the formerly prosperous joined them as wartime gains disappeared with falling prices. To supplement decreased earnings, accumulated securities had to go, at a rate far below face value. Those landowners who for a time had considered themselves well off lost their savings and now acquired a fresh understanding of the grievances of those who had never known the bonanza days. With Coxhall, town after town declared, "We are allmost Ready to Cry out under the burden of our Taxes as the children of Issarel did in Egypt when they ware Required to make Brick without Straw," for "we cannot find that there is money enough in the Town to Pay." [16]

Despite occasional concessions permitting tender in paper, great sums were uncollected because even in those cases only notes of the new emission were accepted, and they were reckoned not at face value but in terms of their current worth in silver. Towns often voted as a unit not to pay, and between 1780 and 1785 one fifth of all levies remained outstanding.[17] Attempts to collect in hard money, beef, or other commodities led to countless embarrassments. Popular opposition forced the government to borrow in anticipation, to suspend the raising of funds to

---

(1929), 61ff; also st. 1781, ch. 12; st. 1782, ch. 67; T. to J. Pickering, Oct. 23, 1783, Pickering Papers, XXXIV, 251.

15. To J. Adams, Oct. 3, 1786, King, *Rufus King*, I, 190. See also Sullivan to Lincoln, Jan. 16, 1782, Amory, *James Sullivan*, II, 384; also Gerry's complaint, King, *Rufus King*, I, 84, 89ff; MA, CLXXXVII, 6, 55, 77, 94; st. 1780, ch. 43; res. 1780, ch. 6J; res. 1781, ch. 77.

16. MA, CLXXXVIII, 40. See also *ibid.*, 41, CLXXXVII, 280, 318, 327, 328, 334, 361, 369, CLXXXVIII, 107; [William Manning], "Some Proposals for Making Restitution to the Original Creditors" (MS, Houghton Library, Harvard University), pp. 5, 6.

17. See st. 1780, ch. 40; MA, CLXXXVIII, 96.

retire notes, and in periods of special stress, as in 1785 and 1787, to omit taxes even for current expenses.[18]

The direct tax alone was inadequate to the needs of Massachusetts. The imposition of 1781 elicited heavy remonstrances from all parts of the state but nevertheless failed to return enough to cover the running costs of government. Yet in addition the accretion of extraordinary expenses cast their somber shadow across the account books; in 1785, for instance, £88,112 had to be applied to the state debt and $448,854 given to Congress.[19]

Repeated desperate attempts to lay hands on money in other ways were rarely successful. Illusory schemes for the use of public lands in Maine and the West held out occasional hopes of a simple solution but were never realized. Loans were difficult to float, expensive, and no permanent cure. Lotteries had occasionally raised money to clothe the army, but they offered no secure source of revenue. Revival of the abhorred stamp tax excited acrimonious protests and in any case, despite efforts at enforcement, never yielded much.[20]

Hardiest perennial in the agitation for relief from direct taxation was the demand that the merchants bear a larger share of the financial burdens. An enabling clause in the constitution of 1780 had cleared the way for enactment of a tariff. Not slow to take advantage of this possibility, the farmers insisted on a radical alteration of the tax structure and incidentally raised the whole question of the ultimate place of commerce in the economy. A good many objected to the nature of trade with England, which brought profits to the seaboard but seemed inevitably to produce an unfavorable balance and a glut of imports, drained away money, and subjected the state to foreign influence. Some went beyond that, inveighed against any kind of commerce, and attacked trade to justify taxing it. Agriculture, manufacturing, and the fisheries, the prime elements of the Commonwealth's strength, they claimed, had to be encouraged against cheap foreign competition at any cost, "either by *bounties* or putting it out of the power of the importer, by *duties* on their importa-

18. MA, CXXXVII, 368, CLXXXVII, 188, 197, 202, 239, 259, 294, 391, 393; res. 1781, ch. 321; st. 1782, ch. 16; res. 1786, ch. 113S.

19. J. B. Felt, *Historical Account of Massachusetts Currency* (Boston, 1839), p. 200; King, *Rufus King*, I, 134.

20. See st. 1780, chs. 12, 15, 28; st. 1781, ch. 30; res. 1781, ch. 515; st. 1782, ch. 16; st. 1784, ch. 75; st. 1785, ch. 18; res. 1785, ch. 2O; st. 1786, ch. 24; st. 1787, ch. 51; "A.B.," *Independent Chronicle*, Apr. 8, 1784.

tions, to distress or injure the manufacturer." Though the initial expense might be heavy, the labor supply made available by the end of the war could profitably establish industry in Massachusetts.[21]

Demands for an outright impost on imports in order to reduce the direct tax were completely unacceptable to the merchants. They considered this threat to their profits "a partial tax," pointing out that "the general maxim of these burdens being borne by the consumer, does not hold in the present state of our trade, when it is notorious that most imported commodities are vended below their cost." [22] Such a levy imposed by Massachusetts alone in the absence of agreements with other states would place competitors elsewhere at an enormous advantage. Guided by mercantile influence, Massachusetts either flatly refused to act upon the requests of Congress for the grant of an impost to the central government, or in some years conditioned its agreement upon similar action by all the other states, a proviso which inevitably brought the gesture to nought.[23]

The merchants were, however, caught on the horns of a dilemma. Their commercial interests would suffer by the proposed taxes but their creditor interests demanded "other Means than the common and ordinary Mode of Taxation" to raise funds for debt payments. A legislative committee which included many who opposed indirect taxes nevertheless conceded that only those could sustain the state's credit.[24]

The merchants were willing to accept indirect taxes as an alternative to further charges on the land. But they insisted that such levies should fall not only upon foreign but also upon domestic products.[25] A series of measures "for the purpose of Paying the Interest on Government Securities" and "for the Suppression of Immorality, Luxury and Extravagance" put into effect a curious jumble of imposts and excises on a wide range of articles manufactured in or imported into the state. While

21. "A Friend to Commerce," *Independent Chronicle*, Aug. 12, 1784. See also *ibid.*, July 29, 1784; [James Swan], *National Arithmetick* (Boston, 1786), p. v; Gerry to King, Apr. 23, 1785, King, *Rufus King*, I, 90.

22. See res. 1780, ch. 249J. For defense of trade see "A Citizen," *Independent Chronicle*, Oct. 6, 1785.

23. See st. 1781, ch. 37; st. 1783, ch. 18; King, *Rufus King*, I, 14; Amory, *James Sullivan*, I, 131, 143; E. M. Bacon, *Supplement to the Acts and Resolves of Massachusetts* (Boston, 1896), pp. 138, 139, 145–147.

24. St. 1782, ch. 33, preamble.

25. For the conceptions of direct and indirect taxes in this period see C. J. Bullock, "Direct Taxes and the Constitution," *Yale Review*, 10 (1901), 6ff.

conceding some tariffs, the merchants amply protected their own position. Except in the short-lived acts of 1782 and 1783 they secured for themselves provisions for rebates upon exports. Rebates made goods for export cheaper than those for home consumption, while the excise which taxed local native products guaranteed that imports could compete on favorable terms. Furthermore, the rebates were arranged to favor Massachusetts as against foreign merchants, and the duties on some articles like molasses were lower for the former than for the latter. Occasional exceptions lightened the burdens on importers, and all the laws provided that proceeds were to apply only to the extinction of the state debt.[26]

This legislation satisfied holders of public securities, the merchants among them; nor were the latter particularly inconvenienced as traders. But disgruntled farmers early discovered that these new exactions bore most grievously upon them. Taxed both as producers and consumers, unprotected against foreign competition with their manufactures, they were yet expected to meet the large annual levies on property. Here was no improved distribution of the cost of governing. The impositions on industry, reminiscent of English policy, were universally condemned for laying "an unequal Burden upon the People of which the poorer sort will have the heaviest part." [27]

The complete disorder which had overwhelmed the currency after 1780 intensified the deleterious effect of depression and high taxes upon the farmers' economic position. Nothing that had happened since 1774 had put a prop under the steadily falling paper. Vacillation by the Continental Congress and the activity of delinquent states like Pennsylvania, Rhode Island, and Connecticut, which continued to put forth their own notes, vitiated every corrective measure by Massachusetts. The new emission fell as soon as it left the presses, while the old con-

26. See st. 1781, chs. 17, 21, 22, 33; st. 1782, chs. 13, 33, 51, 64; st. 1783, ch. 12; st. 1784, ch. 13; st. 1785, ch. 17; st. 1786, ch. 28; res. 1783, ch. 4J; res. 1785, ch. 53J; res. 1785, ch. 134M; res. 1785, ch. 134O; Amory, *James Sullivan*, I, 131, 143. These were not protective tariffs. Protection of new manufactures and restraint of extravagant expenditures were subsidiary to the fiscal problem and appeared prominently in argument because of the patriotic connotation acquired in the previous decade. Protection, as in the case of loaf sugar, was given by simply forbidding imports (see st. 1785, ch. 41).

27. See West Springfield and Spencer petitions, Jan. 15, Feb. 11, 1782, MA, CLXXXVII, 339, 412, 413; "A Countryman," *Massachusetts Spy*, quoted in *Salem Gazette*, Jan. 24, 1782; Sullivan to Lincoln, Jan. 16, 1782, Amory, *James Sullivan*, II, 384; Lockwood, *Westfield*, II, 53ff.

tinued its downward course, reaching the amazing proportion of
1000:1 in 1781. By the middle of that year the government directed its purchasing agents to disregard the face value even of
the new currency, and soon prices in paper were "not . . . mentioned in trade." [28] To add to previous difficulties, counterfeiting became a prevalent and confusing evil.[29]

But, as before 1780, government policy still favored creditors;
it withheld the relief this inflation might have offered debtors.
Large loans, funding operations, and the acceptance of continen-
tals in payment for taxes aimed to draw paper out of circulation
as rapidly as possible, while scales of depreciation, adjusted from
time to time by the justices of the Supreme Judicial Court, compensated for the effects of the continued fall in values.[30] Freed
from the necessity of accepting paper as tender at face value,
those to whom money was due found ample protection and
sometimes actually gained from the collapse of the currency. The
same uncompromising scales trapped the debtor farmers. Readjustments quickly matched every decline of the bills; cheap
money was now powerless to wipe out obligations.[31]

With paper valueless, specie was difficult to obtain. Occasional
new supplies only added to the confusion. Hard cash brought
into the state after 1780 by trade with the British, the French
fleet, and Havana, and by seizures from prizes hardly slackened
the fall in the value of paper. The slightest showing of the rare
metal drove down the prices received by farmers, frantic to exchange their products for the feel of silver. There was still no
adequate circulating medium. At one time lack of bullion actually forced the state treasurer, despite legislative intent, to pay
out paper as fast as taxes paid it in. Efforts to cope with the
problem by setting fixed rates for coins were futile, and by 1786

28. See "Instructions," June 26, 1781, Pickering Papers, XXXIII, 391; "An
American," *Boston Gazette*, Jan. 21, 1782; res. 1781, chs. 130, 132, 142, 148, 157,
187; res. 1785, ch. 203F; Amory, *James Sullivan*, II, 383; MA, CLXXXVII, 94. See
also st. 1780, ch. 40; st. 1784, ch. 26; res. 1784, ch. 140.

29. See King, *Rufus King*, I, 87; st. 1781, ch. 10; st. 1786, ch. 15; *Boston Gazette*, July 16, 1781.

30. The whole policy was set forth in an apologetic address "To the Inhabitants of the Commonwealth," res. 1780, ch. 163J. See also st. 1780, chs. 3, 4, 12,
22, 39; res. 1780, chs. 18J, 54J, 177J, 181J, 212J; st. 1781, chs. 12, 18, 30; res.
1781, ch. 109; st. 1782, chs. 17, 67; res. 1784, ch. 125; "A Countryman," *Independent Chronicle*, Jan. 25, 1781. On the new emission see also res. 1780, chs. 10O,
179J; st. 1781, ch. 7; *Independent Chronicle*, May 11, 1780.

31. Proposals for modification of the scales of depreciation were uniformly
unsuccessful (see MA, CLXXXVI, 407ff). The only measure of relief applied to
debts for which tender for payment was made before 1777 (st. 1784, ch. 57).

Massachusetts reluctantly raised the value of hard money to stop its flight from the state.[32]

The dearth of currency and the fiscal policy shaped by the challenge of public debt contributed to an enormous growth of private debt. With the price of agricultural goods falling, with recently sprouted home industries shriveled up by foreign competition and excises, farmers were unable to shake off the unremitting taxes. Step by step large blocs of the rural community fell into the ranks of the debtors. Worcester County reflected the gravity of the situation; in 1784, in a total population of less than fifty thousand, there were two thousand actions at one time on the docket of the Court of Common Pleas. Two years later in Springfield, not the least prosperous of towns, more people owed money than did not, and in the state as a whole, it was estimated, one fourth of the polls were defendants in suits at law.[33]

The law brought the fury of impending disaster nearer. The husbandman's predicament became dangerous as the courts became more effective agencies for collecting debts and enforcing contracts. Despite occasional attacks upon it, the judiciary grew stronger through reorganization and reform in 1781 and 1782. Other acts facilitated the service of executions. Yet fees remained high and complex pleadings were long drawn out and expensive. The writings of Benjamin Austin (Honestus) and John Gardner at once reflected and stimulated discontent with the bar, and even James Sullivan (Zenas, Tully), who defended the courts, felt that some relief was necessary. The very maneuvers of the lawyers, generally astute enough to keep the legislature from acting, evoked demands "that the whole order . . . be annihilated; for . . . building themselves upon the ruins of the distressed." [34]

The depth of depression was not plumbed until 1786. A spurt of liberal, perhaps too liberal, credit expansion put off the day of

32. See *Independent Chronicle*, Dec. 21, 1780; A. to J. Adams, May 25, 1781, Abigail Adams, *Letters* (Boston, 1840), I, 162; Amory, *James Sullivan*, II, 383; King, *Rufus King*, I, 168.

33. Amory, *James Sullivan*, I, 186ff; M. A. Green, *Springfield* (Springfield, 1888), p. 308; Lockwood, *Western Massachusetts*, I, 127.

34. See st. 1780, ch. 17; st. 1781, chs. 19, 32, 41; st. 1782, chs. 5, 9; st. 1783, ch. 57; Smith, *Pittsfield, 1734 to 1800*, pp. 394ff; W. T. Davis, *History of the Judiciary of Massachusetts* (Boston, 1900), pp. 173–177; "Senex," "N.L.," and "Zenas," *Boston Gazette*, May 6, 13, 27, 1782; Amory, *James Sullivan*, I, 188, 189, II, 63; Joseph Allen, "Historical Account of Northborough," *Worc. Mag. and Hist. Jour.*, 2 (1826), 170.

reckoning. With trade re-established, a flood of imported goods swept into the interior, inundating western Massachusetts with products from Boston, Hartford, and New York. If it was difficult to get real money, thriving merchants in a speculative mood and new stores seeking business granted credit freely. By January 1785 eight to twelve months' grace was not unusual and an orgy of extravagance swept the state. Then came the inevitable contraction. By the end of 1785 complaints were heard in the land. Credit was tight, interest exorbitant. A law at the end of the year "that no man shall have a commission or hold an office till he swears he has not taken more than six per cent" was scarcely worth the paper on which it was engrossed. The number of men held in prison for debt and for nonpayment of taxes rose. Soon there appeared among the farmers in debt the old demand for a new tender law. The response of the legislature in 1786 — more stringent provisions for tax collections — involved large areas in ruin.[35]

With so much of Massachusetts encompassed by the same wretched circumstances, conflict brewed rapidly. It was not likely that the debtors, a category which now included all but the most exceptional farmers, would stand idly by and watch the seeds of revolution bring forth the withered fruits of foreclosed mortgages. United by their misery, they managed in 1786 to push through the House a new tender act and a measure regulating the profession of law. When the property-voiced Senate tore down both cherished bills, the disgruntled husbandmen turned back for relief to their primal institution, the town meeting, disregarding efforts to make property qualifications for voting there permanent.[36]

Using Article XIX of the Bill of Rights as their legal justification and revolutionary experience as their model, the towns met in county conventions in all parts of the state to condemn the legislature.[37] At first these extralegal bodies confined them-

35. Amory, *James Sullivan*, II, 384, 389ff. See Dwight to Mrs. Morton, Jan. 10, 1785, Sedgwick Papers, 2 ser., V; S. to J. Adams, July 2, 1785, S. Adams, *Writings*, IV, 315ff; H. H. Burbank, "The General Property Tax in Massachusetts" (unpub. diss. Harvard University, 1915, University Archives), pp. 82ff; Jonathan Smith, *Some Features of Shays' Rebellion* (Clinton, 1905), pp. 4ff.

36. See st. 1785, ch. 75, sec. 2; Gore to King, Nov. 7, 1786, King, *Rufus King*, I, 195; Wells, *Samuel Adams*, III, 227ff; Trumbull, *Northampton*, II, 484.

37. For the status of conventions and the nature of complaints against them see "Speculator," *Massachusetts Spy*, Oct. 16, 1776; *Boston Gazette*, June 14, 1784; S. Adams, *Writings*, IV, 305ff; *The Popular Sources of Political Authority*, ed. Oscar and Mary F. Handlin (Cambridge, Mass., 1966), p. 5.

selves to requests for such specific reforms as repeal of the excise, restrictions on courts and lawyers, lower fees and salaries, increased powers for the towns, a confessional act, a tender law, and a moratorium on all civil cases.

Absence of response had already brought to the minds of many the thought: "Was not government designed for all men — the poor as well as his neighbours?" [38] Now, unredressed grievances fanned popular hatred of the harsh rulers. Humble petitions burst into thundering demands. Before long the call came for the removal of the seat of government from Boston, for changes in the organization of the judiciary, and finally for a statewide convention to amend the constitution. Meanwhile in Maine a separatist movement threatened the integrity of the Commonwealth itself.[39]

Events soon rendered discussion, whether of fundamental or immediate issues, academic; the movement whirled out of the hands of those who had started it. A Great Barrington mob halted the courts soon after the Berkshire County Convention of August 1786, dominated by moderates, had promised to keep them open while waiting for redress. The new breakdown of law enforcement spread concern among the solid citizens who sat in these assemblies. Speaking through such organs as the *Hampshire Herald*, they deplored violence, but they could not halt it.

Impatient men throughout the state, led by revolutionary officers like Daniel Shays and Luke Day, waited no longer for slow-moving reforms and struck at the judiciary, the immediate threat to their security. As in 1774, a wave of disorder organized the discontent and halted the proceedings of the Court of Common Pleas in one county after another. The rioters at first protested that, pending legislative relief, they wished only to close the civil courts trying actions of debts. But inevitably they moved as well against the Supreme Judicial Court to forestall criminal prosecutions. Although subsequent events focused attention upon the west, these outbursts occurred everywhere — in Bristol County as well as in Berkshire, in Middlesex as well as in Hampshire.[40] Rebellion now infected not the fringe of society merely,

38. *Boston Gazette*, June 28, 1784.

39. See res. 1785, ch. 2O; Smith, *Pittsfield, 1734 to 1800*, pp. 398ff, 413; W. D. Williamson, *History of the State of Maine* (Hallowell, 1832), II, 522ff.

40. King to J. Adams, Oct. 3, 1786, King, *Rufus King*, I, 190; Smith, *Pittsfield, 1734 to 1800*, pp. 401, 402; *History of Bristol County*, ed. D. H. Hurd (Philadelphia, 1883), pp. 294, 711; *Our Country and Its People . . . Bristol County*, ed.

but the very core. By the end of the year, armed bodies of men stood in open revolt in many sections of the state, banded together "in Order for the Suppressing of tyrannical government." [41]

The implied menace to the whole organization of government was now in the open. The rulers of the state had lightly dismissed earlier warnings that the insurgents wanted *"property . . . equally divided* among all the citizens, [and] . . . all debts . . . annihilated."* They had believed that specific grievances might still be met or evaded by temporizing or by arguing over "detail reforms." But when the disturbances aimed at the very basis of control, the mobs encountered unyielding opposition.[42]

Those who held the reins of power in 1786 were still not sure of their position and were perilously near to losing their grip. The prize of 1780, so narrowly won, was in jeopardy from rebels for whom *"the Constitution itself, is the* GREATEST GRIEVANCE OF ALL."* [43] To tamper with that document was to bring again into question many doubtful issues better left unraised: representation in the Senate, the qualifications of the governor, the appointed judiciary, and the bills of rights. The disaffected would "sap the foundations of our constitution," wrote General Lincoln, and then "mold a government at pleasure and make it subservient to all their purposes." Then would come an end to public and private debts, and "the agrarian law might follow with ease." Positions and purses fortuitously won after 1774 trembled in the balance when the rioters hacked away at the major premises of political power.[44]

In this crisis, an address from the General Court to the people laid the troubles at the door of artful persons who "affected to make a Distinction between the Government & People as though their Interests were different & even opposite." Defending the state's financial policy, the legislature exhorted the citizens to more frugal living, held out the hope for constitutional revision

Alanson Borden (Boston, 1899), pp. 106ff; Aaron Hobart, *Historical Sketch of Abington* (Boston, 1839), pp. 136, 137; C. F. Adams, *Three Episodes of Massachusetts History* (Boston, 1892), II, 895ff.

41. See Lockwood, *Western Massachusetts*, I, 138ff, 149; William Willis, *Journals of the Rev. Thomas Smith and the Rev. Samuel Deane* (Portland, 1849), pp. 259ff.

42. See King to Kilham and to Gerry, Oct. 29, Nov. 5, 1786, King, *Rufus King*, I, 192ff, II, 612.

43. Judge Cushing's charge to the Middlesex Grand Jury, *Worcester Magazine*, 3 (1786–1788), 106ff.

44. Lockwood, *Western Massachusetts*, I, 144. See also, e.g., Sedgwick to King, June 18, 1787, and King to Kilham, Nov. 19, 1786, King, *Rufus King*, I, 224, II, 613.

in 1795, and warned that without obedience "the Commonwealth must break in pieces . . . and the whole" be "reduced to a state of nature." [45]

Meanwhile Governor James Bowdoin's administration took more direct steps, acting vigorously because the artisans as well as the wealthy in Boston and the other commercial towns came to its defense. The panic-stricken who tried to get the aid of a Congressional army, to be raised ostensibly for fighting the Indians, proved needlessly alarmed. In the east, reading the riot act was enough to put down dissension. In the west, the young Bostonians in the governor's militia, who set forth on their armed pilgrimage with the support of "gentlemen of property" desirous of insuring against anarchy "by advancing liberally," found opposition melting before them.[46]

As troops moved into the disaffected areas, the uprising collapsed. The malcontents seemed unable to act unitedly in their own behalf. The moderate men in the conventions had recoiled from violence against the courts and were certainly unwilling to support open rebellion. Many others, prompt to join in mobs against the judges, shrank from outright war against the government lest they weaken the state and become "easy victims to foreign and inveterate foes." Divided counsels produced hesitancy and doubts, confusion and absence of leadership. Thus the town of Rowe, unable to decide where its sympathies lay, finally recommended that its militia "join that party as they shall Judge to be in the right." [47]

Everywhere men of good will called for peace. The Baptist minister of New Salem sadly noted, "The political fathers have provoked their children to wrath, and by oppression wise men have been mad, and the children have been unruly and rebellious." [48] The yearning for an end to fighting and for restoration of harmony and unanimity quickened demands by insurgent sympathizers "that the general Voice of the People might be taken . . . and let the Majority . . . deside the controversy. We wish that immediate Stop may be Put to the further Effusion of human Blood . . . let those People of the Neutral Part (Viz).

45. *Acts and Resolves, 1786,* pp. 142ff.

46. See st. 1786, ch. 38; res. 1786, chs. 5J, 40J; Amory, *James Sullivan,* II, 390, 391; King, *Rufus King,* II, 614; Morison, *Harrison Gray Otis,* I, 30; J. K. Hosmer, *Samuel Adams,* p. 391.

47. Lockwood, *Western Massachusetts,* I, 132, 133; C. F. Adams, *Three Episodes,* II, 896–898.

48. Isaac Backus, *Church History of New England* (Boston, 1796), III, 188.

Those who have not taken an active part on either Side . . . let Government know that the major part of the People are not Content with the present Mode of Proceeding tho' they wish not to be active in the Sheding the blood of their Brethren & Countrymen."[49] After January 1787, Shays was ready to accept terms; but the government, now certain of the upper hand, was in no hurry. Those who wished to discredit the idea of constitutional revision insisted on a crushing defeat in the field to pulverize the forces of resistance.[50]

The victory was complete. While its militia by force dispersed the revolutionaries, the General Court disenfranchised hundreds to preclude the remotest chance of attaining by ballot what could not be attained by arms. A gangrenous pessimism diffused by the growing number of foreclosures struck down the debtor farmers. With no hope for relief from the state, many found the easier alternative in emigration to the more attractive regions of Maine, Vermont, Pennsylvania, New York, and Ohio. Meanwhile the erstwhile leaders scattered and lost influence.[51]

A few extremists among the merchants were still uneasy and argued that "some material change must take place in our national government." Fearing that the state was "inefficient to support the great objects of civil institutions and personal liberty and property of the subject," they sought to contrive "some plan to increase the circulation at the heart, and thereby dispense heat and vigor to the extremities." [52] In this regard they had the support of many farsighted traders who perceived that the question of commerce was not statewide but national, and who sought a commercial policy that could stand up to England. The failure of the independent efforts of Massachusetts "for the want of a co-operation of our sister States" had accented the need for more concerted action, and had led to the Annapolis and Philadelphia conventions.[53] The solution of all these questions came

49. J. Hubbard, "Manifesto," Sedgwick Papers, 2 ser., X; S. C. Damon, *History of Holden* (Worcester, 1841), p. 83; "Pacificus," *Hampshire Gazette*, Nov. 1, 1786; Lincoln to Bowdoin, Feb. 20, 1787, *Mass. Hist. Soc. Colls.*, 7 ser., VI (1907), 145.

50. See Amory, *James Sullivan*, II, 391ff; King, *Rufus King*, I, 198; Wells, *Samuel Adams*, III, 239ff.

51. G. R. Minot's contemporary *History of the Insurrections in Massachusetts* (Worcester, 1788) is still the best account of the actual fighting. See also the mortgages in Sedgwick Papers, 2 ser., X; King, *Rufus King*, II, 614.

52. King to Sedgwick, June 10, 1787, Sedgwick Papers, I, 355ff; King, *Rufus King*, I, 222, 227, II, 615.

53. See st. 1784, ch. 15; st. 1785, chs. 8, 31; res. 1785, chs. 61O, 78M, 135M, 199F; st. 1786, ch. 16; *Boston Gazette*, Feb. 11, 1782, Oct. 6, 1785; *Independent Chronicle*, Apr. 21, May 26, June 2, 16, 23, Sept. 15, 29, 1785; J. Adams to Jeffer-

at a stroke with the adoption of the federal Constitution, which transformed the problems of paper money, of excise, and of impost. Tariffs would apply equally throughout the nation. The provision against bills of credit and the abrogation of debts forestalled a revival of the currency question. Above all, federal power now stood in the way of any attempt to change the Commonwealth's frame of government by force. Indeed, John Adams' handiwork remained untouched until the separation from Maine necessitated a constitutional convention in 1820.[54]

But more immediate problems of statecraft faced the Commonwealth in the two years between the dispersal of the rebels and the entrance into office of the new federal administration. Military conquest was not enough. Those who had won wanted civil government, not the rule of a cowed population. When farmers appeared in the legislature of 1787 in numbers larger than ever before, the merchants realized they must either satisfy some of the immediate complaints of those who had followed Shays or refute their own arguments that all differences could be resolved under the constitution; and few were so far removed from memories of an agrarian background, or so secure in the possession of their own wealth, as to choose the harsher horn of that dilemma. Appeasement went hand in hand with force. "After the spirit of Rebellion is completely subdued," it was pointed out, "the business will be half done; a spirit of obedience and *industry* is to be restored which is the greatest object of Legislation." The armed uprising was ruthlessly suppressed, but reforms satisfied many rebel demands.[55]

A commission of indemnity granted 790 pardons in March 1787, and a general act of amnesty in June 1788 removed the stigma of treason from the former insurgents. Other efforts at amelioration, antedating the crisis and stimulated by it, finally culminated in legislation: a moratorium on private debts, a tender law, a reformed fee system, and relief for debtors unable

son, Aug. 7, 1785, John Adams, *Works* (Boston, 1850–1856), VIII, 291ff; Amory, *James Sullivan*, II, 389; King, *Rufus King*, I, 57ff, 67ff, 157ff.

54. For the federal Constitution see Oscar and M. F. Handlin, "Radicals and Conservatives in Massachusetts," *New England Quarterly*, 17 (1944), 350ff; Madison to Washington, Jan. 20, Feb. 3, 1788, Theophilus Parsons, *Memoir of Theophilus Parsons* (Boston, 1859), pp. 60, 62ff; S. B. Harding, *Contest over the Ratification of the Federal Constitution in the State of Massachusetts* (New York, 1896); see also Governor Adams' address, *Columbian Centinel*, June 6, 1795.

55. Cf. Pamela to Theodore Sedgwick, June 17, 1787, Sedgwick Papers, 3 ser.; Sedgwick to Dane, July 5, 1787, Sedgwick Papers, 2 ser., V; Amory, *James Sullivan*, II, 391; King, *Rufus King*, I, 614; Appendix B, below.

to support themselves in jail. Suspension of collections pledged to the public debt and appropriation of one third of the excise "for the exigencies of Government" lightened the weight of direct levies. Provisions for back payments of taxes in kind also helped, and Governor John Hancock's regime after 1787 substantially lessened the total load.[56] At the same time Massachusetts tried to alleviate the currency shortage by offering a rebate of 10 per cent to ships bringing into the state bullion equivalent to the duties, and by operating a mint.[57]

The federal Constitution ultimately eliminated the bothersome indirect taxes. But in the interim the legislature set to work untangling them. To begin with, the internal excise was separated from the impost on imports. A new measure set duties of from 5 per cent to 15 per cent on articles of foreign manufacture and limited the character of rebates allowed on goods re-exported. This and a complementary act abolished all the existing burdens on domestic products and established new ones on such luxuries "as are not the necessaries of life." [58] In addition, to conciliate the husbandman, the state embarked upon a protective policy. Chapter 48 of 1786 completely prohibited the importation of some fifty items, since it was "the duty of every people, blessed with a fruitful Soil, and a redundancy of raw materials, to give all due encouragement to the agriculture and manufactures of their own Country." On the other hand, raw materials like molasses, wool, dyes, raw lead, tin, iron, and salt, carried in American ships, were to be duty free, and the impost of 1 per cent on imported hemp went to encourage the raising of that plant in Massachusetts. Special exemptions from time to time further aided native industry.[59]

These steps restored a measure of stability to Massachusetts society. Only four years after Shays' Rebellion, General Lincoln exulted, "There never was a moment since I knew the state when so much happiness reigned in it as at this period." [60]

Yet it would be wrong to imagine that those who had emerged

56. See st. 1786, chs. 39, 47, 73; res. 1786, chs. 101J, 122J; New Braintree Instructions, *Worcester Magazine*, 3 (1786–1788), 132ff; King to Gore and Dane, and Gore to King, Feb. 11, June 19, 28, 1787, King, *Rufus King*, I, 201, 225, 227.

57. St. 1786, ch. 32; res. 1785, ch. 201F; res. 1786, chs. 14A, 90J, 125J; res. 1787, ch. 1M.

58. St. 1786, chs. 48, 49. Duties were raised and extended by st. 1787, ch. 63. See also res. 1785, ch. 2F. All these measures were repealed after the adoption of the federal Constitution and assumption of state debts.

59. St. 1787, ch. 63; res. 1787, ch. 33F. See also res. 1785, ch. 3O.

60. To Sedgwick, Jan. 5, 1791, Sedgwick Papers, II, 13.

as victors in the long struggle found much joy in their victory. On the contrary, in the next two decades a note of pessimism, a gloomy foreboding of evils yet to come, ran through the thinking of the merchants, their squire allies, and their intellectual spokesmen. "Whether the government will long outlive me is doubtful," wrote a governor of Massachusetts. "I know it is sick, and many of the physicians say, of a mortal disease . . . Yet, I confess, if we should . . . get out again into the open sea, we shall have . . . a lease for years, — say four or five, — not a freehold, certainly not a fee simple." [61]

Underestimation of the value of property reflected an uneasiness about the future that prompted the choleric Henry Van Schaick to threaten to move from the state.[62] There was a consciousness that independence had awakened mighty popular forces, that these could not be beaten down and ultimately would have to be placated. Shortly the French Revolution, which stimulated so many hopes at first, aroused most earnest forebodings "of the tendency of their form of government to degenerate into licentious democracies." [63] Unconfident newcomers, wielding unaccustomed power and uneasy over the methods by which they had earned it, saw levelers still a majority in the state. The possessors of wealth cautioned the public creditors to be patient, pointing to the irritations from measures which cause "a great fluctuation of property & . . . transfer it from the poor to the rich." [64] The merchants had won in an arduous struggle, but whether the fruits of their winning would be sweet to their taste was still uncertain.

Yet for the time being the issue of control had been settled and the opposing sides reconciled, if not satisfied. The constitution, challenged, remained unamended. All subsequent changes would have to come within the framework of government set up in 1780 and consolidated in the next seven years. The test of rebellion reaffirmed faith in the Commonwealth. The terrifying crisis in which man had turned upon man remained a monument in the memory of society, a mark of the appalling alternative to preservation of the structure of the polity. The farmers learned that the ultimate weight of numbers in a de-

61. W. H. Sumner, *Memoir of Increase Sumner* (Boston, 1854), p. 15.
62. To Sedgwick, Jan. 22, 1795, Mar. 7, Apr. 14, 1796, Sedgwick Papers, II, 721, III, 97, 165.
63. *Monthly Anthology and Boston Review*, 7 (November 1809), 334.
64. Higginson to Hamilton, November 1789, *Jour. of Econ. and Bus. Hist.*, 3 (1931), 685.

mocracy would speak for them within the law. The merchants came to the realization that the state could not operate on their behalf alone, that they could not simply write their own interests into the interpretation of the common interest. Nor could any group gain for itself advantages the price of which the whole community would pay. A vigilant society would weigh special privileges in the scales of the common welfare. These compelling restraints conditioned the application of the prevailing conception of the role of government to the economy of the new state.

3 | To Encourage Industry and Economy

The momentous period that had opened in 1774 bequeathed to Massachusetts a many-sided legacy. The commonwealth idea, the belief that "the forces of a state should compose one body & be animated by one soul," influenced governmental policies for decades to come. That fundamental assumption was particularly relevant to the developing productive system.[1]

With independence came a yearning for a place of power and prestige in the universe, a desire to emulate and surpass the old nations of the Old World. Americans now had an interest of their own "to augment and defend"; they had "an empire to raise and support." [2] To develop fully Massachusetts needed a strong and aggressive economy operating for the welfare of all. Correspondingly, all looked to the Commonwealth, the guardian of the common interest, to breathe new life into the productive system. The growth of agriculture, commerce, and industry would invigorate the whole state; and the strength thus gained would suffuse the entire community with well-being.

Ultimate power rested with the people and was to be used for their welfare. It followed that political interference was not to serve the special ends of special groups. That understanding was not a bar but a stimulus to direct action by the government. Despite the possibility of corruption, error, or tyranny, the men

1. Charles Sumner, "Commonplace Book" (MS, 1829, Harvard University Archives), p. 9, quoting Gibbon.
2. Noah Webster, *Collection of Essays* (Boston, 1790), p. 36.

of this period were not "frightened . . . from the pursuit of
. . . common interest by the words arbitrary power." They
thought "it would be folly" not to encourage "kinds of production . . . eventually useful to the community and profitable to
the concerned, but which could not otherwise be undertaken
without loss in the beginning, and therefore, would not be spontaneously undertaken at all." [3]

Constitutional provisions imposed few restrictions upon action. The organic charter of Massachusetts in 1780 specifically
enjoined upon the state the obligation to supply "rewards and
immunities, for the promotion of agriculture, arts, sciences,
commerce, trades, manufactures." [4] The guarantee of property
rights in the same document was narrow, and the reservation
that property could be taken for public use left room for latitude of interpretation.[5] The federal Constitution, which took
away the power to issue paper money and to interfere with contracts and with interstate and foreign commerce, was not yet a
serious encumbrance to state action. Broad spheres remained in
which competence to legislate was unquestioned.

Massachusetts observers conceived of the beneficent hand of
the state as reaching out to touch every part of the economy.
The Commonwealth would make its influence felt in every aspect of production, readily adjusting assistance to the needs of
changing industrial, agricultural, commercial, and communication systems. The organization of education, the public works
undertaken, codes of law administered, and the type of taxes
imposed, as well as more direct guidance, all would shape the
enterprise of the region.[6]

These measures were, or could be, good. Those who supported
them sometimes reasoned that the intercession of the state was
absolutely desirable and had made European nations great, and
sometimes contended that peculiar American conditions justified the retention of practices pernicious in Europe. But whatever
argument brought them to it, they agreed on the conclusion.
They found "manifestly erroneous" the notion that industry
should be left alone, that the people individually, and not the

3. "Publicola," J. Q. Adams, *Writings*, ed. W. C. Ford (New York, 1913–1917),
I, 92; Willard Phillips, *Manual of Political Economy* (Boston, 1828), pp. 193–195,
200.

4. Ch. V, sec. II of the constitution.

5. Bill of Rights, Art. X.

6. See Phillips, *Manual of Political Economy*, pp. 195, 209, 210; also Willard
Phillips, "Review," *North Amer. Rev.*, 47 (1838), 89ff.

government, "are the judges of their interests, and consequently should be allowed to regulate them unobstructed." That principle was "subversive to the end and aim of all governments; and . . . utterly impracticable." [7]

In acting, the state was not to be niggardly. Nor was it to construe production narrowly. All projects except those bearing a moral stigma, such as prostitution and the slave trade, were important and useful. There was faith in the future potentiality of each fledgling activity if fostered with care, and every request for assistance was to be considered liberally.

Special interests would, of course, seek the aid of the state. Where they got it without examination of the common interest, "the present or permanent interest of one class . . . at variance with that of the whole" might produce what Adam Smith called "odious monopolies." [8] But not all privileges, grants, or monopolies were odious. "A connecting chain" among "all the various employments of mankind" established a common, general interest which permeated the specific interests "of the different classes of the industrious." [9] So long as that general interest of the community was the object in view, aid to special groups was beneficial to all. "It is for the present interest of every class, as well as every individual, to obtain a grant from the government, but no class or individual thinks of asking it, unless he can give some reason, and if he can give a good reason, it is as much for the interest of the community to make the grant, as for his to receive it." [10]

Manufacturers therefore had a high claim to protection and encouragement; agriculture, commerce, and the fisheries also deserved patronage; and aid to each would bring profits to all, bound together as they were by an "indissoluble community of interest." [11] Most men sincerely believed that under a wise govern-

7. "Public Interests," *Boston Commercial Gazette*, Sept. 23, 1819. See also Ames to Minot, May 29, 1789, Fisher Ames, *Works* (Boston, 1854), I, 49; J. Adams to Richmond, Dec. 14, 1819, John Adams, *Works*, ed. C. F. Adams (Boston, 1850–1856), X, 384; Oscar Handlin, "Laissez-Faire Thought in Massachusetts, 1790–1880," *Tasks of Economic History* (December 1943), pp. 55ff.

8. Phillips, *Manuel of Political Economy*, pp. 181–183.

9. See J. Q. to J. Adams, Oct. 19, 1790, J. Q. Adams, *Writings*, I, 63; Phillips, *Manual of Political Economy*, p. 181; "An American," *Independent Chronicle*, Apr. 21, 1785; Governor Strong's address, Jan. 8, 1807, *Resolves of 1807*, p. 4.

10. Phillips, *Manual of Political Economy*, pp. 181–183, 209. See also [W. Phillips], "Statistical Annals," *North Amer. Rev.*, 9 (1819), 219ff, 231.

11. Edmund Quincy, *Life of Josiah Quincy* (Boston, 1868), p. 100; W. V. Wells, *Life and Public Services of Samuel Adams* (Boston, 1865), III, 326; Samuel Adams, *Writings*, ed. H. A. Cushing (New York, 1904–1908), IV, 386ff; answer of the

ment which would direct and aid these pursuits with an equal hand, the people could "divide themselves into different professions . . . in which their private advantage and that of the public will concur." [12] And the few who were cynical nevertheless mouthed the doctrine of inseparable interests to capitalize on the deep popular attachment to the ideal.[13]

The internal structure of the state stimulated these aspirations and also shaped them into a living reality. The nature of political control, economic insecurity, and a pervasive public debt conditioned the reduction of theory to practical legislation. The political balance established in the aftermath of Shays' Rebellion persisted. The common interest still had different meanings to different men. But with the character of the Commonwealth established, division, which in the formative period had occurred over the most fundamental issues involving the very nature of the state, now took place only at the level of the application of policy. The frame of government remained unaffected by later developments. In 1795, the vote for amendment fell short of the necessary two thirds, and though a majority actually asked for revision the question aroused no bitterness, and the matter ended there. Again in 1811, proposals for alteration raised no excitement, and the convention of 1820 left the basic structure unchanged.[14]

The merchants still held tenaciously to their position of dominance, refusing offices and privileges to those who had not "sided with the government in the late insurrection." [15] But they failed

---

House, Jan. 22, 1796, *Acts and Resolves*, pp. 515ff; Governor Sumner's message, June 6, 1797, *Acts and Resolves*, p. 651; *Eastern Herald*, Feb. 1, 1802; Governor Strong's address and answer of the House, *Annals of the Times* (Kennebunk), Jan. 20, 27, 1803; Governor Gore in *Resolves of 1809*, p. 305, and *Boston Patriot*, June 10, 1809; Governor Gerry's speech and answer of the House and Senate, *Salem Gazette*, June 12, 15, 19, 1810.

12. Governor Strong's address, *Annals of the Times*, Jan. 20, 1803.

13. See, e.g., Van Schaick to Sedgwick, Jan. 24, 1793, Theodore Sedgwick Papers (MSS, MHS), II, 405.

14. See Andrews to Sedgwick, Feb. 12, 1795, Sedgwick Papers, II, 776; *Columbian Centinel*, Jan. 24, June 20, 24, 1795; *Boston Gazette*, May 30, 1811; S. E. Morison, *History of the Constitution of Massachusetts* (Boston, 1917), pp. 28–38; L. A. Frothingham, *Brief History of the Constitution and Government of Massachusetts* (Cambridge, Mass., 1916), pp. 60ff.

15. See, e.g., correspondence of Jonathan Jackson and John Welsh, May 16, 20, 1790, Lee-Cabot Papers (MSS, MHS); Dwight to Sedgwick, Mar. 14, 1790, Sedgwick Papers, I, 771; Sullivan to King, Feb. 25, 1787, T. C. Amory, *Life of James Sullivan* (Boston, 1859), II, 391; L. S. Cushing, C. W. Storey, and Lewis Josselyn, *Reports of Controverted Elections* (Boston, 1853), p. 23; Sedgwick to King, July 26, 1799, C. R. King, *Life of Rufus King* (New York, 1894–1900), III, 71ff.

to shake off the contingent nature of their control. Property qualifications soon became a dead letter and almost disappeared in 1820.[16] The democratic basis of the state, the reminder that the majority of the people could resume command if they wished, set limits beyond which the merchants dared not use their authority. "You see good men in high office here," complained George Cabot, "but those men hold their powers upon the sole condition that they will not use them." [17] Compromise and acceptance of the will of the majority became "inseparable from a social, connected state." [18]

The constitution which left the towns free to send delegates or not strengthened the balance. The General Court, center of political gravity through these years, more than confirmed Bagehot's dictum that "every large assembly is . . . a fluctuating body; it is not one house, so to say, but a set of houses; it is one set of men to-night and another to-morrow night." [19] Enormous fluctuation in representation showed, in general, that the state tolerated merchant control and only bestirred itself sporadically to protest under special circumstances.[20]

The political parties that emerged in the middle of the last decade of the eighteenth century hardly affected this balance. Developing in Massachusetts out of divisions over foreign policy, they focused primarily upon national subjects until well in the nineteenth century. The groupings around Hancock, Sullivan, the Adamses, and the junto slowly acquired coherence and the ability to act in a disciplined fashion.[21] But these evolving align-

16. Gore to King, Dec. 27, 1820, King, *Rufus King*, VI, 370; S. E. Morison, *Life and Letters of Harrison Gray Otis* (Boston, 1913), II, 235, n.2.

17. To Pickering and King, Feb. 14, Mar. 17, 1804, H. C. Lodge, *Life and Letters of George Cabot* (Boston, 1877), pp. 343–345.

18. W. E. Channing, *A Sermon Preached in Boston, August 20, 1812* (Boston, 1812), p. 5.

19. Walter Bagehot, *English Constitution* (New York, 1924), p. 177; Morison, *Harrison Gray Otis*, I, 300.

20. Dwight to Sedgwick, May 25, 1790, Sedgwick Papers, I, 826; *Wiscasset Telegraph*, Oct. 23, 1798; *Boston Gazette*, May 30, 1805; J. Q. to L. C. Adams, June 1, 1806, J. Q. Adams, *Writings*, III, 143; see below, pp. 249ff.

21. See the discussion in Ames to Pickering, June 4, 1798, Ames, *Works*, I, 228–229, and Everett to Ingersoll, Sept. 2, 1828, Edward Everett Papers (MSS, MHS), LXIII, 105ff; *Jenks' Portland Gazette*, Apr. 28, 1800. See also *Columbian Centinel*, Apr. 6, 1794; *New-England Palladium*, Jan. 28, 1812; A. H. Everett, *Defence of . . . Jefferson* (Boston, 1836), pp. 10ff; Oscar and M. F. Handlin, "Radicals and Conservatives in Massachusetts after Independence," *New England Quarterly*, 17 (1944), 343ff; Joseph E. Charles, *Origins of the American Party System* (Williamsburg, 1956); Paul Goodman, *The Democratic-Republicans of Massachusetts* (Cambridge, Mass., 1964); Anson E. Morse, *Federalist Party in Massa-*

ments had only slight relevance to the problems of economic policy; a careful examination reveals that party affiliation had very little influence upon the significant state issues. Looking back at this period and comparing it with events in 1831, a veteran Boston politician wrote, "I have known the time when . . . the very foundations of our little community were, almost broken up by the unrelenting violence of conflicting partizans, upon some great questions of national policy; but . . . I have never, before, seen . . . any *citizen* . . . *thus* baldly, denounced, on account of any honest, conscientious opinion which he may have conceived, or avowed, upon any matter appertaining, exclusively, to the affairs of his own State." [22] "The substantial yeomanry of the State," who voted for Jefferson, also elevated the merchant Federalist Caleb Strong to the governorship.[23]

Charges and countercharges arrayed Jacobin against junto in legislative hall and in partisan journals. But moderate men probably agreed with Thomas Cushing of Salem, who noted in the margin of a newspaper, "Whether Mr. Strong, or Mr. Gerry should be chosen, we shall have a good Governor. Thank God! He always does right." [24] Whatever their effect upon national questions, the parties failed to upset the equilibrium created by 1789. As the government became stabilized, dissenters were more and more satisfied. With the tolerant acquiescence of the rest of the Commonwealth the merchants, whether members of one party or another, retained and wielded control. So long as this balance appeared to offer assurance of equal access to the bounty of the Commonwealth, government action seemed no menace.[25]

The economic background against which these political forces operated also kept alive the concept of the state as a positive directing force in the economy. Neither peace nor the establishment of the new federal government healed the wounds inflicted upon Massachusetts by the violent outbreak of 1774. Trade was the fulcrum upon which all productive activities rested; upon it

chusetts (Princeton, 1909); David H. Fischer, *The Revolution of American Conservatism* (New York, 1965).

22. George Blake to Bigelow, Nov. 4, 1831, J. P. Bigelow Papers, 1723–1865 (MSS, Houghton Library, Harvard University). See also *Boston Commercial Gazette*, Jan. 21, 1819.

23. Alden Bradford, *Biography of the Hon. Caleb Strong* (Boston, 1820), p. 19; *Boston Gazette*, Apr. 30, 1801; Sedgwick to King, May 11, 1800, King, *Rufus King*, III, 238ff.

24. *Eastern Herald*, Apr. 13, 1801 (HCL copy).

25. See Lincoln, Thomas, and Dwight to Sedgwick, Jan. 12, 15, 1791, Jan. 23, 1795, Sedgwick Papers, II, 44, 45, 733; J. Q. Adams, *Writings*, I, 61ff.

depended the prosperity of agriculture and handicrafts as well as of commerce. Yet the Commonwealth's old position in the British imperial system was gone, never to return. The West Indies had once supplied the precious commodities for export. Lacking that link, business fell off. With abolition of the traffic in slaves in 1788 another ingredient of the old order disappeared.

Something new, either from within or without the state, had to compensate. There were repeated efforts to develop the scrubby New England hinterland. The results were meager and, at any rate, were often nullified by competition from New York City, the superior attractions of which lured ever larger areas to its markets. As long as the China trade rested on the export, via the Cape of Good Hope, of lumber, grain, and meat from the interior, Yankees failed to break the English hold on the tea business or to make openings in Latin America and Europe. The exotic but uncertain Eastern commerce began to thrive only when its course shifted to channels that could utilize Northwest furs acquired by barter with the Indians. But British goods and British specie were essential in this traffic and the Commonwealth's dependence on a place in the commercial system of the Empire continued a reality. The unattainable alternative was discovery of a formula that would enable the poor back country to produce the exports, lifeblood of an extensive independent trade.[26]

There was, of course, Brissot de Warville's aspiration to give the United States a place in the rival French system.[27] Merchants like Higginson were willing to "play one off against another," at least until Jay's Treaty sketched a blueprint for sharing England's business.[28] The French, moreover, lacked the credit facilities and the colonial outlets Massachusetts men demanded, while restrictive trade laws hampered the operations of the Americans. At best, a Gallic connection meant Gallic leadership, with Yankees playing second fiddle.

26. See, e.g., Gorham to Hamilton, Alexander Hamilton, *Industrial and Commercial Correspondence*, ed. A. H. Cole (Chicago, 1928), p. 65; William Bentley, *Diary* (Salem, 1905–1914), II, 84; [James Bowdoin], *Opinions Respecting the Commercial Intercourse between the United States of America and the Dominions of Great-Britain* (Boston, 1797).

27. See J. P. Brissot de Warville, *Nouveau voyage dans les États-Unis* (Paris, 1791), vol. III.

28. Higginson to Adams, July 1786, *Amer. Hist. Assoc. Annual Report, 1896*, I, 738, 739; Andrews to Sedgwick, Apr. 9, 1794, Sedgwick Papers, II, 519. For the importance of Jay's Treaty in this respect, see *Columbian Centinel*, July 29, Aug. 15, 19, 1795.

Every other expedient devised by ingenuity and enterprise
was a stopgap, nothing more. Neutral shipping and privateering
in the quarter-century struggle of the British and French em-
pires, the Russia trade, and the ice trade failed to make up for
what had been lost in the Revolution. None offered a secure
foundation for commerce. Successful merchants who felt that
they had had enough and retired before they reached the age of
thirty bore witness that there was something wrong with the business life of the state. The impediments to commerce imposed
before and during the War of 1812 by the exigencies of national
policy affected the Commonwealth so severely because its trade
was already moribund. There was danger that commerce would
flicker out unless revived by drastic remedies.[29]

But for many years a false bloom of seeming health covered
over the sickly countenance of the state's economy. Despite an
inherently weak position, many merchants clung to and enlarged
what they had. Shifting from one expedient to another, grasping
the likeliest chance, they frequently came through with unimpaired and often augmented fortunes. Money acquired during
the Revolution by foresight, fortune, or public favor was always
available for further speculation. Its owners assumed heavy risks
precisely because there were no firm and stable channels for investment. They took plunges in the public lands and speculated
in the public stocks. Trade itself was a gamble: a two-year voyage
to the Hongs might return 250 per cent or nothing; a hazardous
passage through the English blockaders or an encounter with
Napoleon's cruisers could as easily make as lose a fortune. The
chance was worth taking.[30]

New people continued to find places in trade. A train of suc-
cessors followed the outlanders who had moved in during the
Revolution. Though some young men from the country met disaster, other recent arrivals prospered; in three short years William
Appleton pyramided five thousand dollars to sixty thousand.[31]

29. See, e.g., Nathaniel Silsbee, "Biographical Notes," *Essex Inst. Hist. Colls.*,
XXXV (1899), 25; J. Q. Adams, *Memoirs*, ed. C. F. Adams (Philadelphia, 1874–1877),
II, 194ff; Oscar Handlin, *Boston's Immigrants, 1790–1865* (Cambridge, Mass.,
1959), pp. 3–10; S. E. Morison, *Maritime History of Massachusetts, 1783–1860*
(Boston, 1921), pp. 30ff.

30. See, e.g., T. to J. Pickering, Mar. 31, 1872, Timothy Pickering Papers
(MSS, MHS), V, 257; J. Q. Adams to J. Adams, Sept. 21, 1790, J. Q. Adams, *Writings*,
I, 58.

31. "Memoir of Hon. William Appleton," *Mass. Hist. Soc. Proceedings*, VI
(1863), 435; Bentley, *Diary*, IV, 41, 47; Gore to King, Mar. 26, 1806, King, *Rufus
King*, IV, 511ff.

But if the rewards of good fortune were lavish, they were accompanied by a driving insecurity, an enervating uncertainty. In their search for stability the merchants often looked with envy upon the tillers of the soil. Even during the Revolution, some traders had shown attention to farming. Timothy Pickering was curious about the prospect of raising Siberian wheat in New England; and, from time to time, interest in the soil led other gentlemen into agriculture. Like Theodore Sedgwick they noted that the plowman who labored for a small pittance was the happiest of all men for he could "lye down in peace and no one to order him here & there & everywhere." [32]

Yet whatever security agriculture appeared to enjoy came from a continuous elimination of the insecure. Emigration in the aftermath of Shays' Rebellion had liquidated the unruly and economically unstable elements in Berkshire County. But there the process by which debt led to mortgage and mortgage to foreclosure and consolidation continued to the end of the century and beyond.[33] Small farms gave way to larger and more profitable estates which were sometimes operated by hired labor or tenants and which produced surpluses of wheat and cheese for markets in Boston, Hartford, and, most of all, in New York City, via Troy, Albany, or Kinderhook, and the Hudson.[34] The Connecticut River towns found in the South and in the West Indies a profitable market, which, however, depended upon and fluctuated with the fortunes of trade. Nearer the coast, reviving commercial cities absorbed the farmers' products. Here the traditional independent yeoman dug a subsistence out of his own fields, found a ready outlet for his surplus in the nearby maritime towns, and enjoyed a modest competence. In central Massachusetts, smaller, self-sufficient units continued to be the rule;

32. Theodore Sedgwick to Theodore Sedgwick, Mar. 20, 1795, Sedgwick Papers, II, 800. See also T. to J. Pickering, May 8, 1781, Pickering Papers, V, 209; *Massachusetts Agricultural Repository and Journal*, 3 (1813–15), 27ff, 32ff.

33. See, e.g., Bowdoin to Sedgwick, May 19, 1789, Sedgwick Papers, I, 539; and the mortgages and transfers of land to the Sedgwicks by E. Kingsley, Apr. 20, 1790, A. Hull, Nov. 5, 1792, M. Ashley, Nov. 5, 1792, D. Culver, Aug. 20, 1793, E. Parsons, Aug. 30, 1793, A. Hopkins, Sept. 15, 1793, E. W. Thayer, Nov. 30, 1793, E. Edwards, Nov. 6, 1794, J. Deming, W. Thayer, Feb. 9, 1810, H. Lynch, May 17, 1813, Sedgwick Papers, 2 ser., VI, VII.

34. See "Statement of the Merchants of Berkshire," *Stockbridge Western Star*, Oct. 11, 1791; Morton to Sedgwick, Dec. 10, 1794, Sedgwick Papers, II, 631; Keyes Danforth, *Boyhood Reminiscences* (New York, 1895), pp. 37ff. For evidence of tenant farming see Egleston and Blossom to Hill, May 24, 1800, July 12, 1803, Willard Phillips Papers (MSS, MHS), and the contract of William McKnight and Theodore Sedgwick, Apr. 17, 1791, Sedgwick Papers, 2 ser., VI.

embargoes and commercial crises had little effect on them. With the aid of the household industries these farmers got by.[35]

Agriculture everywhere got by, but it did not boom. Farmers were content, but they were not flourishing. The cruel soil that exhausted labor on relatively small plots stood in the way of profitable expansion. It could, after a fashion, take care of those already there, but not of their children. The rocky hills and dry gullies drove off the sons of the farmers. Even now the flow of emigration that ultimately depopulated great areas of rural New England carried away the most enterprising and the most ambitious. In 1786 the current was already discernible. Augmented by Shays' Rebellion, it soon swelled into a vigorous stream that sometimes slackened but before the Civil War never halted. The sea took some, trade others. Most inviting of all, fertile trans-Allegheny acres turned many a rural town into "a great tavern house, where fathers and sons have rested for a few years, on their way . . . to the West." Their own land failed to contain them, for Massachusetts held little hope for men who wanted to do more than make ends meet.[36]

Farmers on Cape Cod and elsewhere who combined offshore fishing with agriculture were better off than those who relied on the soil alone. But the fisheries, for many towns "the one grand source of our subsistence," also lacked the essential elements of organic growth. Again independence altered circumstances. The most profitable market of all, the British West Indies, was now foreign as were the swarming banks themselves, and despite the formal protection of repeated treaties Yankee fishermen faced formidable obstacles there, to say nothing of the handicaps imposed by mounting costs and by French and British competition. After 1790, as restored fleets put to sea with the aid of federal bounties, the cod fishery grew steadily if not spectacularly, until it suffered another setback in the War of 1812. But here too possibilities were unexciting; here too the ambitious had to ferret out new vents for their energy.[37]

An alternative appeared after the turn of the century in the

35. *Senate Docs.*, 1854, no. 7, p. 13. For evidence of prosperity see *Columbian Centinel*, Nov. 14, 1795; Dwight to Sedgwick, July 13, 1790, Sedgwick Papers, I, 878.

36. J. G. Holland, *Western Massachusetts* (Springfield, 1855), II, 457; *History of the County of Berkshire*, ed. D. D. Field (Pittsfield, 1829), p. 178; J. E. A. Smith, *The History of Pittsfield . . . 1800 to . . . 1876* (Springfield, 1876), pp. 21ff; Brissot de Warville, *Nouveau voyage*, I, 149.

37. See *Salem Gazette*, June 23, 1801; *Columbian Centinel*, Dec. 19, 1795; Higginson to Adams, Dec. 30, 1785, Mar. 24, 1790, *Amer. Hist. Assoc. Annual Report*,

quest for the "mottled mackerel" of "steel-dark fin." But shortly that activity also ceased to expand and in the smaller towns fell off seriously. More glamorous was the pursuit of the great leviathan, for the sake of whose lucrative oil hardy skippers roved from the Straits of Magellan to those of Bering. But the whale fishery too suffered by wartime losses of ships and by peacetime loss of the English market and, like the China trade, brought immense profits to a few without furnishing a substantial basis for the economy of the state as a whole.[38]

The position of the urban artisans in these years is obscure. Some undoubtedly did well, particularly those who catered to the new luxurious tastes of prospering merchants. But the industries promising large employment did not thrive; the boom in shipbuilding along the Merrimack in the 1790's, for instance, was transitory. Fuller growth failed to come until the 1840's in spite of the development of trade.[39]

In Massachusetts few were certain of prosperity. The shifting sands upon which fortunes, great and small, rested necessitated a continuous search for new enterprises and new activities. In these circumstances, the aid and guidance of the state were of immense importance; no one was secure enough to demand a limit to state action who on the morrow might also need assistance. The tenuous economic status of every group constantly reaffirmed the general belief in the Commonwealth as an active force in the economy.

One pervasive threat, a heritage of war, menaced the aspirations for a vigorous state sustaining and sustained by the prosperity of its citizens. For forty years the specter of overwhelming public debt haunted the people of Massachusetts in their pursuit of an expanding economy aided and directed by government. As long as old obligations ate away the accustomed revenue, new expenditures meant new taxes, and none forgot how the whole structure of society had trembled under the shock of such exactions at the time of Shays.

A basic assumption in the society, a tacit agreement that property taxes would have to fall, affected every political and eco-

---

1896, I, 729ff, 779ff; Enoch Pratt, *Comprehensive History . . . of Eastham, Wellfleet, and Orleans* (Yarmouth, 1844), p. 135.

38. See [James Swan], *National Arithmetick* (Boston, 1786), p. 12; Shebnah Rich, *Truro — Cape Cod* (Boston, 1883), pp. 426, 438ff; F. R. Hart, "New England Whale Fisheries," *Col. Soc. Mass. Publications*, XXVI (1934), 72ff; Daniel Ricketson, *History of New Bedford* (New Bedford, 1858), pp. 106ff, 302ff.

39. See, e.g., *Columbian Centinel*, June 24, 1795.

nomic issue and resulted in the remarkable circumstance that the state tax for current expenses remained fixed at $133,000 for the quarter-century 1795–1820.[40]

Nor was there a disposition to solve fiscal problems by loans. Popular weariness with the problem built up a distaste for borrowing so overpowering that even those who accepted the economic soundness of the English theory of a fixed government debt would not venture the attempt to apply it.[41]

Limited to a fixed and inflexible income, the Commonwealth found a substantial segment diverted to the service of its old liabilities with little left for anything else. Despite the grievous exactions of the 1780's and their attendant agonies, the amount outstanding actually had grown in that decade. Assumption of almost half the state debt by the federal government relieved some of the pressure, but not to the extent anticipated in Massachusetts.[42] A comparison of expenditures of 1794 with those of 1786 (shown in the table) reveals that the relief afforded by assumption yielded a decline in interest charges but not a corresponding rise in other outlays.

Massachusetts Expenditures [43]

	1786	1794
Salaries	$ 57,300	$ 54,100
Miscellaneous	16,400	46,200
Interest	278,700	114,900
Total	$352,400	$215,200

Although the Commonwealth's finances were in order and funding operations under way by 1795, a considerable load

40. See, e.g., *Independent Chronicle*, Oct. 26, 1780; *Stockbridge Western Star*, Apr. 6, Aug. 31, 1790; *Columbian Centinel*, Jan. 20, 1798; C. J. Bullock, *Historical Sketch of the Finances and Financial Policy of Massachusetts* (New York, 1907), p. 16. For merchants' attitude toward taxes see, e.g., Samuel Breck, *Recollections*, ed. H. E. Scudder (Philadelphia, 1877), p. 186; for farmers' attitude see [Manning], "Proposals for Making Restitution to Original Creditors," pp. 14, 15.

41. See J. Q. Adams to Monroe, Apr. 9, 1816, Jan. 29, 1817, J. Q. Adams, *Writings*, VI, 8, 154.

42. See Lincoln and Henshaw to Sedgwick, Jan. 27, Feb. 7, 20, 1790, Sedgwick Papers, I, 708, 731, 745; J. Q. Adams to J. Adams, June 28, 1789, Mar. 19, Apr. 5, 1790, J. Q. Adams, *Writings*, I, 41, 48, 50; *Stockbridge Western Star*, Jan. 5, 19, Feb. 9, Mar. 23, Apr. 20, 1790; Cabot to Hamilton, Mar. 4, 1793, Lodge, *George Cabot*, p. 73; Higginson to Adams, Mar. 1, 1790, *Amer. Hist. Assoc. Annual Report*, 1896, I, 775ff.

43. Data from Bullock, *Finances of Massachusetts*, p. 20. For attitudes toward funding see King to Sedgwick, June 10, 1787, Sedgwick Papers, I, 355ff, and Sewall to Sedgwick, Feb. 19, 1796, Sedgwick Papers, III, 77.

remained, often eating up half its total expenditures. Early in the nineteenth century obligations due the state probably offset its liabilities for a time, but loans during the War of 1812 restored the deficit. Not until the sale, in 1821, of bank stocks and federal securities hoarded to that end were the voters freed from the necessity of reckoning with the consequences of debt in every calculation.[44]

The existence for four decades of an enormous charge for the payment of interest and principal conditioned the reactions of government in every sphere which involved the expenditure of more money and threatened either new taxes or new debt. Frugality was a fixed principle. Torn constantly between the desire to act and unwillingness to increase expenses, the state occasionally flatly chose between saving or spending. More often it compromised and sought its ends by indirection.[45]

Penny-pinching finance and a political balance that made citizens vigilant about the use of privilege left the members of the General Court slight latitude for action. At first they turned to the body of practice and law at hand in 1780 to implement the ideals of government activity in the economy. Old statutes based on English and colonial precedents persisted to some extent; wartime legislation had frequently revived earlier provisions, the constitution of 1780 provided for continuity, and even in 1783 blanket measures extended the life of many expiring acts.[46]

But ancient forms were not automatically acceptable. The Revolution and interregnum marked a break that permitted, indeed often forced, a re-examination of policies. The state's unwillingness to assume additional expenses prevented it from using public contracts to further enterprise as the French did. Until 1789 Massachusetts tried to protect the glass, woolen, and loaf-sugar industries by prohibiting imports and remitting duties on the raw materials they utilized. But after that date federal control made embargoes and tariffs unavailable to it.[47] Other bounties, franchises, and regulatory legislation, when adopted, soon displayed unexpected variations in application. The forces

44. Bullock, *Finances of Massachusetts*, pp. 25, 26.

45. For the need of paying the debt see Governor Strong's address, Jan. 8, 1807, *Resolves of 1807*, p. 4; also *Salem Gazette*, Jan. 27, 30, 1801.

46. Constitution, ch. VI, art. 6; st. 1781, ch. 2; st. 1782, ch. 35; st. 1783, chs. 7, 31. See also James Sullivan, *History of Land Titles in Massachusetts* (Boston, 1801), p. iii.

47. Phillips, *Manual of Political Economy*, pp. 200ff; st. 1784, chs. 14, 22; st. 1785, ch. 41; st. 1786, ch. 48; res. 1787, ch. 33F; st. 1789, ch. 30.

that were the product of these critical years found no adequate expression in the derivative patterns of an older society. Novel economic and political conditions worked upon customary techniques, sometimes transposing them intact into new contexts, sometimes refashioning them entirely.

Massachusetts drew freely upon the normal legislative power, a power to which it recognized no limits but those set by feasibility and utility. It accepted the task of setting up codes to regulate many commodities. The maintenance of uniform standards through inspection was a matter of considerable importance to those whose products, destined for distant markets, passed through the hands of several middlemen. Such laws lent assurance against adulteration and prevented "discredit to a whole class of men by the frauds of a few." [48] Merchants to far-off ports, responsible for wares they purchased from others, also approved of acts which guaranteed quality and added the prestige of state approval to their goods. In their own dealings they knew the value of such governmental regulation; Lee and Cabot thus instructed their agents in other states to buy only flour that was strictly inspected. Eager for similar controls at home, they hoped that the export of country produce, encouraged by warranty, would make a place for Massachusetts in the West India trade and generally extend its markets abroad.[49]

The state looked for guidance to colonial practices of long standing when it established systems of inspection. But as postrevolutionary legislators turned to the process of re-enacting provincial legislation on the subject, they uncovered a tangled skein. Time had added all manner of accretions. Intertwined with the inspection laws were survivals of medieval assizes, of old guild regulations, and special provisions contrived for forgotten special circumstances. To incorporate the undigested whole at first offered the line of least resistance.

The most primitive form of regulation, a simple setting of standards, served in certain spheres for a long time. An act of 1800 to foster the manufacture of boots, leather, and shoes provided for a maker's stamp "as a warranty that the article stamped is merchantable, being made of good materials and well manufactured." The same law imposed a fine for fraud. In 1803 the

48. Governor Strong's address, *Annals of the Times*, Jan. 20, 1803.

49. K. W. Porter, *Jacksons and the Lees* (Cambridge, Mass., 1937), I, 443; Hamilton, *Industrial and Commercial Correspondence*, pp. 297ff; *Dame* v. *Baldwin* (1812), 8 Tyng 518; Higginson to Adams, Dec. 30, 1785, *Amer. Hist. Assoc. Annual Report, 1896*, I, 731; "Statement by David Townsend," MA, 1792, ch. 73.

cutting of brads, now an important and useful manufacture, received similar legislative encouragement and regulation.[50]

A more effective procedure provided for inspection to guarantee standards. Some sturdy standbys of Massachusetts exports and the first articles thus regulated furnish a good example of the haphazard application of old rules. Blanket laws of 1783, 1784, and 1785 dealt with the inspection of lumber, flaxseed, pot and pearl ash, beef and pork, pickled and dried fish, tobacco, butter, onions, and lime. Sworn officials, some chosen by the towns, others appointed by the governor, were to inspect quality and packing to prevent "damage to merchants and much loss to the interests of the Commonwealth" from "diminished . . . value at foreign markets." Specifications covered all products in great detail, but some applied only to articles for export while others applied to goods offered for sale in any town. Many specific requirements also differed according to the destination of the item. In addition, to confound confusion, there was no provision for traffic by land, although the term export at the time applied to interstate as well as to foreign shipments. Without regard for consistency, these measures simply re-enacted customary and often contradictory practices.[51]

Sooner or later, altered conditions called for new departures. When the article regulated was itself changing, the law kept pace with technology and trade by a tedious evolution. There was hope for reform through the creation of increasingly specific regulations for each product. More detailed rules were applied to pot and pearl ash in 1791, to stone lime in 1794 and 1795, to beef, butter, and lard in 1800, and to pork in 1802.[52] Sometimes pressure from producers unwilling to be cut off from potential markets developed new categories with lower standards. In beef, butter, and pork, for example, refuse ultimately became Grade

50. St. 1799, ch. 63; st. 1802, ch. 103.

51. St. 1783, chs. 15, 54; st. 1784, ch. 30; st. 1785, ch. 25. Amended in details of specifications by st. 1786, ch. 46; st. 1787, ch. 19; st. 1791, ch. 11. For precedents see, e.g., st. 1695–96, ch. 5; st. 1710–11, ch. 7; st. 1743–44, ch. 22; st. 1762–63, ch. 5. Commercial rivalry with Connecticut and New Hampshire before 1789 accounted for some details of the laws (see "Order for Committee to Consider Commercial Regulations of Connecticut, June 20, 1784," MA, 1784, ch. 30).

52. For pot and pearl ash see st. 1791, ch. 8; st. 1792, ch. 73; st. 1821, ch. 55; Higginson to Adams, Dec. 30, 1785, *Amer. Hist. Assoc. Annual Report, 1896*, I, 730; T. J. Kreps, "Vicissitudes of the American Potash Industry," *Jour. of Econ. and Bus. Hist.*, 3 (1931), 635. For lime see st. 1793, ch. 65; st. 1794, chs. 22, 54; st. 1796, ch. 16; st. 1802, ch. 121; st. 1809, ch. 62; st. 1810, ch. 128; also *Columbian Centinel*, Mar. 21, 1795. For beef, butter, and lard see st. 1799, chs. 69, 84; st. 1800, ch. 28. For pork see st. 1801, ch. 78.

No. 3. Later measures required dating and the reinspection of beef and pork imported from other states.[53] Similarly, regard for the Irish and Scottish customers adjusted requirements in the flaxseed laws.[54] Finally, some merchants, like Higginson, objected to the feature which often, though not always, left inspection in the ineffective hands of town officials, since that emphasized local interests and served "to conceal and encourage frauds of every kind." Demands for a thorough reform to end parochial rivalry and to centralize responsibility led to the appointment of state officials answerable to shippers for bad goods.[55] By 1816, when an act was passed requiring returns to the secretary of state, the governor appointed inspectors of pot and pearl ash, of pork and beef, nails, butter and lard and pickled fish, each with a retinue of deputies.[56]

The laws regulating nails illustrate the pattern of elaboration and detail, the manner in which government decisions affected fabrication, packaging, and shipping. Nail making was still largely a household industry carried on by farmers all over the state who spent their winters thus supplementing their agricultural earnings. A short-lived act of 1790 and a more careful measure the following year had set standards of number and weight enforced by local officials who branded the casks of nails with the name of the town in return for fees from the sellers. In 1795 an official in Boston, chosen by the governor, became responsible for the selection and demeanor of inspectors. The new measure also dealt with the casks and their construction and provided that only approved nails properly packed might be exported. An amendment in 1796 provided that the inferior nails might be shipped out if marked "of the second sort." By 1803 the categories of grade rose to three, and other classes appeared as the process of manufacture became more complex and as more producers sought the seal of government approbation without the drawback of circumscribed sales.[57]

53. St. 1800, ch. 59; st. 1803, ch. 139; st. 1804, ch. 121; st. 1815, chs. 9, 114; st. 1820, ch. 34; st. 1822, ch. 62. See also *Revised Statutes of the Commonwealth of Massachusetts* (Boston, 1836), ch. 28, secs. 44–58.

54. St. 1786, ch. 35; st. 1789, ch. 20.

55. Higginson to Adams, Dec. 21, 1789, Mar. 24, 1790, *Amer. Hist. Assoc. Annual Report, 1896*, I, 769ff, 778; Higginson to Hamilton, *Jour. of Econ. and Bus. Hist.*, 3 (1931), 683ff. For opposition by local interests see, e.g., MA, 1791, ch. 8, petitions of Watertown and William Hunt *et al.*; MA, 1792, ch. 73, petition of John Austin *et al.*

56. St. 1815, ch. 38.

57. MA, 1789, ch. 36; st. 1790, ch. 41; st. 1794, ch. 52; st. 1795, ch. 77; st. 1799,

After 1800 frequent laws extended inspection to new products and continually altered details.[58] Because the inspection system involved no expense to taxpayers there was no resistance to its spread. Enforcement cost nothing, for it generally rested entirely on the initiative of the parties concerned. Cases could reach trial on information by a citizen, the traditional informer, who received for his virtue part of the fines imposed. Fines, in fact, often produced an income for government; the proceeds of many offenses helped support the poor.[59]

Appointed officers received no salaries but relied on specific fees from the purchasers or sellers and on a share of reward from prosecutions. More important than such income was an indirect privilege arising from the office. Some coopers acquired a favored place in the trade because their activities as inspectors gave them an informal advantage in handling the goods they examined. By granting these officials a monopoly in packing the branded articles, occasional laws confirmed what was almost inevitable in practice. Henry Purkitt, a cooper and inspector of pickled fish, and Francis Wright, a tobacconist who was first inspector of tobacco and then spread his activities to include butter and lard, were models of the lucrativeness of these offices. Best known was John Bray who, as culler of fish, acquired Spear's wharf and with a staff of eighteen subordinates earned $750 each month from fees alone.[60] These "places" thus bore a marked resemblance to some of the Elizabethan monopolies where "the power granted . . . was not so much that of exclusive production or sale as of exclusive 'searching and sealing.' "[61] A readiness to raise fees reflected a frank recognition of the quasi-monopolistic nature of these positions, and also of the fact that their holders deserved to benefit. Naturally these were political plums of some importance.[62]

---

ch. 64; st. 1802, ch. 103; st. 1806, ch. 10. See also *Columbian Centinel*, Nov. 25, 1795; Bowdoin to Temple, Oct. 10, 1789, *Mass. Hist. Soc. Colls.*, 7 ser., VI (1907), 196; Higginson to Adams, Dec. 30, 1785, *Amer. Hist. Assoc. Annual Report, 1896*, I, 730.

58. See, e.g., *Boston Commercial Gazette*, Jan. 19, 1818; st. 1803, ch. 54; st. 1813, ch. 51; *Revised Statutes*, ch. 28, secs. 60–68; *Franklin Herald*, June 20, 1815; st. 1804, ch. 81; st. 1813, ch. 192; MA, Senate, 8024A.

59. See, e.g., st. 1785, ch. 25; st. 1816, ch. 26, sec. 13.

60. See st. 1802, ch. 20; MA, 1801, ch. 18; J. T. Buckingham, *Annals of the Massachusetts Charitable Mechanic Association* (Boston, 1852), pp. 28, 47, 124; *New-England Palladium*, Mar. 19, 1805.

61. J. P. Davis, *Corporations, A Study of the Origin and Development of Great Business Combinations* (New York, 1905), I, 217.

62. See, e.g., advertisement of David Rush, culler of fish, *Independent Chron-*

Although such measures failed to cope with the fundamental weakness of trade, the low volume of exports, there was a general belief that inspection added prestige to Massachusetts goods in foreign ports. The officials thought of the perquisites of office, but also of "the interest and reputation of this Commonwealth, agriculturally and commercially"; like Stephen Bunce they advertised their packing facilities, but also published long instructions on marketing.[63] Despite inefficiency, corruption, and evasion, the utility of these regulations was taken for granted; poor results led not to abandonment but to reform and elaboration. The amendments, based on no general principle save expediency, constantly tailored the laws to the exigencies of the market and the demands of exporters in the interest of the wider distribution of the state's products.[64]

The inspection system set up categories of goods which could not be sold and thus placed in a privileged position those the state judged fit. This was only one example of the government's wide use of legislative power to encourage desirable activities. The same selective principles prevailed in the licensing of favored individuals to do as a special privilege that which was prohibited without a franchise. To stimulate worthwhile endeavors, special provisions made exemptions from the operations of the laws against gambling, against interference with the public ways and waters, and against monopoly.

Permission to raise money by lottery thus served as a form of state aid for many years. Although English law in 1699, colonial laws twenty years later, and the state laws of 1785 and 1801 declared unsanctioned lotteries illegal, such undertakings, prototypes of the numbers game, flourished throughout the period.[65] But these lacked sanctions and were not likely to command public support and confidence. The countenance of the government guaranteed that the objective was worthy, that the drawings, often supervised by state-appointed managers, would be

icle, Dec. 3, 1807; also *Salem Register*, Nov. 1, 26, 1804; *New-England Palladium*, Jan. 11, 1805; MA, 1792, ch. 73; Buckingham, *Massachusetts Charitable Mechanic Association*, p. 48; Bentley, *Diary*, III, 68.

63. See, e.g., *Castine Journal*, Sept. 19, 1800; *New-England Palladium*, Sept. 6, 1805; *Repertory*, Nov. 8, 1811.

64. For later calls for reform see, e.g., Governor Strong's address, June 17, 1806, *Resolves of 1806*, p. 3; *Repertory*, June 20, 1806; also *Salem Gazette*, Jan. 27, 1801; Ames to Gore, Mar. 5, 1800, Ames, *Works*, I, 277.

65. St. 1719–20, ch. 8; st. 1732–33, ch. 14; st. 1785, ch. 24; st. 1800, ch. 57. See also st. 1817, ch. 191; st. 1819, ch. 140; *Salem Gazette*, Jan. 27, 1801. For colonial lotteries see C. H. J. Douglas, *Financial History of Massachusetts* (New York, 1892),

honest, and that, in the event of fraud, the courts would entertain suits. On the other hand, lotteries cost Massachusetts nothing and furnished a ready alternative to grants in cash. Indeed the state itself used that method to replenish its own purse.[66]

Improvements in communications — roads and bridges, to bind the Commonwealth together — were thus favored by the state, particularly in periods like the war years when towns and other local agencies, overwhelmed with debt and subject to many unusual charges, could not raise money more directly. In 1780 a $200,000 lottery financed roads in Berkshire and Hampshire counties. The next few years saw similar schemes to bridge the Chekebee River on the Springfield-Hadley Road, and the Agawam River in West Springfield, and to repair bridges in Essex County, in Watertown, Westfield, Winchendon, and Lancaster. In 1796 the roads of Gloucester received the same privilege, as, in 1811, did the Hatfield Bridge.[67]

This form of public support came to the rescue at special disasters, as when fire destroyed the Boston North Mills in 1783. But such grants were by no means limited to extraordinary circumstances; they answered as a matter of course whenever the state wished to give aid: in 1782, for instance, to build a paper mill in Milton, and in 1783 for a foundering glasshouse in Boston.[68]

The lottery fever reached a climax in 1790 and gave grounds to the complaint that these devices would "withdraw the people's attention from industry, & . . . distract them with the hope of gain by chance & accident. They also . . . [laid] a very unequal tax upon the people at large; the indigent, & embarrassed . . . being . . . generally the greatest adventurers." [69] Although the state gave the Beverly cotton factory seven hundred tickets in its own lottery in 1791, it exercised much more caution in the next few years and rejected a project to aid the development of Sa-

pp. 98ff. For English lotteries see D. R. Richards, "Lottery in the History of English Government Finance," *Economic History*, 3 (1934), 57ff, 74.

66. See MA, CLXXXVII, 293 1/2; Amoskeag Canal Papers (MSS, Boston Public Library); st. 1789, ch. 47.

67. See st. 1782, chs. 18, 28, 37; st. 1783, chs. 1, 2; st. 1784, ch. 5; st. 1795, ch. 28. See also MA, CLXXXVII, 293 1/2, CLXXXVI, 206; res. 1779–80, chs. 438, 469; Hill to Quincy, Oct. 18, 1809, Willard Phillips Papers, 1769–1836; *Weston Records* (Boston, 1893), pp. 359, 385.

68. St. 1782, ch. 45; also st. 1781, ch. 39; MA, 1782, ch. 48, petition of R. Hewes, repealed by st. 1787, ch. 13. See also st. 1789, ch. 55.

69. Governor's address, *Acts and Resolves of 1791*, p. 572; Bentley, *Diary*, I, 139.

lem Harbor.[70] Thereafter the yield fell off. By 1812 Plymouth realized less than $10,000 from a project which broadcast about $900,000 worth of tickets. Proposals for a Boston and New York canal and special licenses for drawings within and without the state reflected a continued disposition to regard this as a legitimate, often a necessary, form of government assistance. But distrust of the social consequences, occasional mismanagement, and poor returns combined to limit the use of the lottery in the nineteenth century.[71]

Without charge to itself the state also aided enterprisers through another franchise, the toll, which gave an individual the freedom to convey goods or travelers along or across a public stream and to collect fees for his services unhampered by the interference of competitors. Whatever the origin and character of that liberty, its value depended upon the recognition of government and the willingness of the courts to uphold it by excluding rivals. Lacking such security no one would undertake extensive and expensive projects.[72]

A general law of 1796 confirmed colonial practice by licensing anyone who applied to keep a ferry on condition that he accept a fixed schedule of charges and the obligation, enforceable by fine, of constant service to travelers.[73] The liberty to take toll over a bridge, construction of which involved greater expense and more permanent establishments, came in a direct grant either to a single proprietor or a group of proprietors.[74]

The legislature frequently rendered vested rights nugatory by yielding to requests for new ferries and new bridges. A grant to a bridge builder thus almost invariably impaired the franchise of an existing ferry, which received compensation or not at the discretion of the state. Whatever the weight of personal influence, the government made each decision in terms of evidence concerning the public necessity of the new project and the inability of the old to accommodate the community. In weighing

70. *Salem Gazette*, Mar. 8, 1791; Bentley, *Diary*, I, 138; Lodge, *George Cabot*, pp. 43ff. See also st. 1789, ch. 57; st. 1790, ch. 13; res. 1790, chs. 11M, 157J.

71. See *Columbian Centinel*, Jan. 28, 1792; MA, Senate, 4685; *Repertory*, Mar. 11, 1806; res. 1807, ch. 81; Amoskeag Canal Papers; *Journal of the House of Representatives . . . of Massachusetts . . . 1808* (Boston, 1808), pp. 53, 221, 231, 302.

72. Sullivan, *Land Titles*, pp. 125ff.

73. St. 1796, ch. 42; see also st. 1694–95, ch. 16; st. 1726–27, ch. 14; *Revised Statutes*, ch. 26; W. H. Sumner, *History of East Boston* (Boston, 1858), pp. 5, 11.

74. St. 1786, ch. 25; st. 1792, ch. 75; st. 1812, ch. 138; *Columbian Informer*, May 13, 1802.

these factors the Commonwealth acted within a wide area of choice. Its rulings became precedents for denying or acceding to similar petitions. But the accumulated judgments in the statute book left little doubt about Massachusetts' intention to hasten the renovation of the transportation system through the use of this franchise.[75]

The same appraisal of cases warranting infringement upon existing interests for the common good was basic to the grant of the privilege of using the public ways and public waters. License to erect a bridge correlatively meant license to interfere with navigation and fishing. Aqueduct builders needed the same immunity and were willing to promise services in return, as did Calvin Whitney in 1796 when he received permission to lay pipes under the Dedham streets provided that he supply the town with water to fight fires.[76]

This franchise entered most significantly into the mill law. The mill site had always been a subject of communal concern. To develop facilities for grinding their grain and sawing their timber, towns and town proprietors had granted away the privilege of exploiting water power, often adding other inducements as well.[77] As industry conceived more complex uses for the abundant energy of ubiquitous streams, it became apparent that new establishments interfered with three communal rights: the dam flooded adjacent lands, it obstructed the passage of fish up the stream, and it diverted water from natural channels. Without the state's tolerance, builders faced unlimited responsibility for damages.

To encourage industry, the government generously dealt out franchises to protect the millowners. An act of 1796 regulated procedure in respect to flooding on the basis of colonial precedents which had never envisaged the extensive damage that would come with the advance in production. Millowners received the liberty to raise a head of water by inundating adjacent fields and were free to pay no more than an annual charge set by the courts, despite the protests of landowners who wanted the full value of their property returned at once. That the millers were bound to keep weights and measures and were limited

75. See, e.g., st. 1792, ch. 65.
76. St. 1796, ch. 12.
77. See, e.g., Holland, *Western Massachusetts*, II, 43, 44, 330, 431, 432; Emory Washburn, "Topographical and Historical Sketches of the Town of Leicester," *Worc. Mag. and Hist. Jour.*, 2 (1826), 96. J. E. A. Smith, *The History of Pittsfield . . . 1734 to . . . 1800* (Springfield, 1869), pp. 140ff.

by maximum tolls in return for the privileges was poor consolation to those who had lost valued meadows. But the state made the final decision.[78]

The interaction of mill privileges and fishing rights was far more complex. Farmers, to whom the inland rivers yielded valuable crops of salmon, shad, and alewives to grace their tables and enrich their fields, accepted any obstruction with reluctance. Yet the promise of thriving local industry dulled the edge of outright hostility and made compromise attractive. Sometimes, as with reference to the Taunton River in 1792, a simple division into specified periods for each use of the water settled the matter.[79] But usually no general act comprehended all the minutiae of contending claims or set up blanket principles to cover every problem. Instead, a well-nigh endless succession of special enactments regulated the dams on scores of streams. Amended and altered, repealed and re-enacted, these measures reflected constant pressure from confused local interests, as the towns to which the fishing rights belonged, the riparians, and the millers engaged in continual wranglings over details. The Merrimack River alone needed seventeen distinct laws between 1783 and 1820.[80]

One example among many illustrates how hundreds of these laws drained legislative energy. In Milton and Dorchester on the Neponset River a series of chocolate, grist, saw, and powder mills interfered with the passage of shad and alewives to their spawning grounds in Stoughton, Stoughtonham, and Walpole ponds. An act of 1782 provided for sluiceways of specific size, built and maintained by the three towns interested in the passage of fish, and regulated by a committee representing all five. An amendment in 1784 reduced the size of the sluices and the time they were to remain open and provided preference for the gristmill if there was not enough water for all. A year later, on the plea that the fisheries were suffering, the sluices were enlarged. Yet it was not long before a new law shifted the burden

78. See st. 1795, ch. 74; st. 1797, ch. 63; st. 1799, ch. 78. St. 1814, ch. 173, further simplified procedure on damages. The whole question was discussed in 1829, *American Jurist and Law Magazine*, 2 (1829), 25ff.

79. St. 1791, ch. 23.

80. See. st. 1783, ch. 21; st. 1785, ch. 14; st. 1787, ch. 57; st. 1789, ch. 51; st. 1792, ch. 78; st. 1793, ch. 62; st. 1802, ch. 51; st. 1803, ch. 158; st. 1804, ch. 134; st. 1806, ch. 28; st. 1811, ch. 175; st. 1812, ch. 84; st. 1817, ch. 16; st. 1819, chs. 4, 20; st. 1820, chs. 22, 70. For other quarrels over fishing and mill privileges see, e.g., C. W. Jenkins, *Three Lectures on the Early History of . . . Falmouth* (Falmouth, 1889), p. 96.

of maintenance to the millowners in return for enlargement of the period in which they had full use of their dams. This solution was no more durable than its predecessors. In 1797 another act vested control of the fish in a committee chosen by the towns and control of the water in a committee of three disinterested freeholders selected by the county court of General Sessions, with the charges of maintenance apportioned by a complicated formula. Again amended two years later, this measure lasted until 1810 although in the interim supervision of repair of the dams fell to a committee of the General Court.[81] Constant amendment stuffed the chinks of the general acts in the effort to adjust the effects of the mill franchise upon antecedent rights to the fisheries.

The interference of the mill privilege with the similar rights of others to a flow of water also called for government supervision. By the common law, the owners of sites could use the river upon which they fronted but not to the extent of interrupting the share of those lower down. The diversion of water from its natural channels in the absence of state consent infringed upon the inalienable privileges of riparians and invited suits for heavy damages. Even in the case of Richardson's River, Woburn, where all concerned agreed, legislative approval was requisite to any deflection.[82] The same question was of special importance in Maine, where waterways also carried logs to market.[83]

As in flooding and the fisheries, each change from the status quo, whatever its equivalence, marked an intercession by the government in the interests of expanding industry. When sawmills joined gristmills, and then shared space with slitting, and powder, and paper mills, when looms harnessed to power grew into factories, the dams grew higher and absorbed an ever greater proportion of flowage. Only active state encouragement, through the mill franchise, leveled the obstacles of vested rights.[84]

All franchises included an element of privilege, permitting to a few, as special assistance in a worthwhile enterprise, what was forbidden to all others. Long before the Revolution the restrictive feature of the franchise had become its most impor-

81. St. 1782, ch. 15; st. 1783, ch. 63; st. 1784, ch. 71; st. 1790, ch. 45; st. 1796, ch. 83; st. 1798, ch. 53; st. 1809, ch. 46.
82. See st. 1787, ch. 25; *Stowell* v. *Flagg* (1814), 11 Tyng 364; W. S. Holdsworth, *History of English Law* (London, 1903–1938), VII, 338ff.
83. See, e.g., *Eastern Herald*, Apr. 19, 1802.
84. See MA, 1793, ch. 27.

tant attribute. Adapting the practice to more general uses, the government declared certain activities illegal with the explicit intention of licensing a limited number to practice at an advantage. Here, as in other phases of state assistance, special groups sought the device to serve their own ends and to secure their own positions. But no grant was forthcoming without justification in terms of the interests of the state as a whole.[85]

In America now, as in England earlier, taverns, particularly necessary to meet the needs of transients along developing routes of travel, deserved encouragement by licenses which protected them against competition. In addition, of course, the license served the purposes both of those convinced that innkeepers were unproductive disseminators of extravagant habits and of those anxious to control rural social centers which had been the focus of revolutionary disturbances.[86]

Immediately after Shays' Rebellion, revision of colonial legislation provided for a limited number of annual licenses by the county courts at the recommendation of the selectmen. In return, the innkeepers swore to support the government, resist conspiracies, and maintain certain moral standards, promised to furnish food and lodging, and undertook to collect the current excise. Severe penalties, including stripes, punished violations. Later acts permitted appeals directly to the courts when the selectmen refused to certify, allowed licensing by justices of the peace outside incorporated districts, and extended the same measures to confectioners and victualers in Boston.[87] Whatever rationale motivated the grants from time to time, the principle of exclusive privilege in return for service to the community remained unchanged.

Application of licensing to the profession of law in this period exposed starkly the rudimentary character of that privilege. For thirty-five years voluntary bar associations in Boston and elsewhere had regulated legal practice, fixing fees and defending the guild against attack. An attempt to put government sanctions behind these agreements had achieved limited success in 1785, only to be abandoned in a few years as a result of protests.[88]

85. See the general recapitulation by Judge Parker, *Portland Bank* v. *Apthorp* (1815), 12 Tyng 256.

86. See, e.g. [J. Swan], *National Arithmetick*, p. 21; C. F. Swift, *History of Old Yarmouth* (Yarmouth Port, 1884), p. 186.

87. St. 1786, ch. 68, amended by st. 1794, ch. 23; st. 1796, ch. 21; st. 1812, ch. 134.

88. St. 1785, ch. 23; st. 1789, ch. 58. See also regulations at a meeting "of the Gentlemen of the Law," May 18, 1781, Sedgwick Papers, I, 125; regulations "At

Nevertheless, until 1805 the complexity and technicality of procedures in themselves generally winnowed out nonconforming outsiders. In that year Story's work on pleadings expounded in simple terms the essentials of arguing a case, and enabled "some men to get a living in the character of lawyers, whose knowledge and whose moral delicacy are far removed from being subjects of commendation." [89] Fearful that the book would simplify the mysterious science, the lawyers demanded licensing. Almost at once, the Supreme Judicial Court set up rules for practice, including formal examinations and a three-year apprenticeship with a barrister or councilor.[90]

Licensing also protected two occupations important to the smooth flow of trade. Auctioneers had once been agents of the court acting in the sale of goods taken by execution. Though they now engaged in all types of commercial transactions, they were still public officers, taking oath and giving bond. Limited numbers at first testified not to the disrepute of the occupation but to its exclusive nature.[91] Similarly, the basic pilotage law, enacted in July 1783, set fees, regulated the size of boats, and permitted the governor and council to appoint a specified number of pilots in some ports, with discretion to extend the provision to other areas. As public officers, the pilots also took an oath and gave bond for the faithful performance of duties. They were personally responsible for losses through neglect and answered to the governor for complaints. Fees were not payments for services but obligations for the use of the port; a master who wished to take his own ship in was, with few exceptions, still liable.[92] Martha's Vineyard, which objected to a system that handed over its harbors to a chosen few, secured one concession after another and then, still unappeased, finally attained complete exemption.[93]

There was not much difference among all these franchises,

a Meeting of the Bar September Term at Lenox 1792," Sedgwick Papers, 2 ser., VI; W. T. Davis, *History of the Judiciary of Massachusetts* (Boston, 1900), pp. 320–324; J. Q. to A. Adams, Dec. 23, 1787, J. Q. Adams, *Writings*, I, 37.

89. *Monthly Anthology and Boston Review*, 2 (1805), 483.

90. W. T. Davis, *Judiciary of Massachusetts*, pp. 310ff.

91. See st. 1780, chs. 25, 30; st. 1782, ch. 66; st. 1822, ch. 87; *Revised Statutes*, ch. 29; *Commonwealth v. Clap* (1808), 4 Tyng 163; C. A. Duniway, *Development of Freedom of the Press in Massachusetts* (New York, 1906), pp. 151, 152; Pierre Rouillon, *Le Commissaire-Priseur et l'Hôtel des Ventes* (Toulouse, 1928), pp. 19ff; Marie Kröhne, *Die Grosshandelsversteigerungen* (Tübingen, 1909), pp. 2ff.

92. See st. 1783, ch. 13.

93. See st. 1783, chs. 23, 56; st. 1796, ch. 85; st. 1797, ch. 13; st. 1819, ch. 45.

the toll, the mill, pilotage, as well as others, and the deliberate grant of an outright monopoly as an instrument of state policy. If monopoly had acquired unfortunate connotations in the struggle with the East India Company, it had by no means lost favor. The constitution of 1780 explicitly recognized its legitimacy and set up standards for bestowing it in "consideration of services rendered to the public." [94]

No legal obstacles existed to the possibility of thus satisfying petitions for aid without expenditure of cash.[95] An act of 1783 granting copyright for twenty-one years to books published in Massachusetts remained in effect until superseded by the federal Constitution.[96] In 1784 Simon Willard requested, and got, the exclusive privilege of manufacturing clock jacks.[97] In the following year, on the governor's recommendation, Paul Revere and others received a similar right for the manufacture of iron by steam engine.[98] In 1788 Eliphalet and Jonathan Leonard and Adam Kinsley, inventors of a method of blistering steel, sought a monopoly and a protective tariff. Although their bill foundered on second reading, the legislature showed a disposition to look favorably upon similar pleas.[99]

The Commonwealth used this instrument among others in the course of the persistent attempts to start a factory for the fabrication of glass, that beautiful and happy invention. After a number of earlier petitions, the Boston Glass House in 1787 obtained the privilege for fifteen years, an optimistic span that failed to stretch out its brief career.[100] With the field again clear, William Phillips and his associates acquired the "sole and exclusive right of manufacturing all sorts of window and plate glass" in the state for ten years, if they employed £2,000 annually in the process. They also received a similar monopoly of hollow ware conditioned on the actual production of a specified amount

See also Louis Laurent-Toutain, *Du Pilotage maritime en France et dans les pays étrangers* (Paris, 1918), pp. 19ff, 182ff; A. A. Giesecke, *American Commercial Legislation before 1789* (Philadelphia, 1910), pp. 118ff.

94. Bill of Rights, Article VI. See also J. Q. Adams, "Publicola," *Writings*, I, 99ff; Phillips, *Manual of Political Economy*, pp. 205ff; W. B. Weeden, *Economic and Social History of New England, 1620–1789* (Boston, 1891), II, 654ff; Holdsworth, *English Law*, IV, 344ff.

95. See, e.g., MA, 1785, ch. 65, petition.

96. St. 1782, ch. 58.

97. MA, 1784, ch. 17, petition of Simon Willard.

98. MA, 1785, ch. 65, petition.

99. MA, Senate, 1081, 1081/1.

100. Hamilton, *Industrial and Commercial Correspondence*, p. 60. See also MA, CLXXXVII, 292; MA, 1787, ch. 13, petition of Edward Payne *et al.*; MA, 1788, ch. 33, petition of Jon. Amory *et al.*

of goods. With the privilege came the right to license others.[101] Finally, in 1809, Jacob Perkins, inventor of the stereotype plate, secured the exclusive power to print bank notes for a time.[102]

In an allied category belong measures which were not outright monopolies but which nevertheless, in effect, limited competition. On the statute books, for instance, appeared in 1813 an act which forbade the floating of logs in order "to prevent damage to the Bridges & Mill Dams erected across Miller's River." The law was actually passed at the behest of millers who aimed to engross the business of sawing timber, and was repealed within eight months after remonstrance from the landowners, who wished to send their pine down to a Connecticut company.[103] Similarly, in 1788, tanners and curriers had secured enactment of a law prohibiting the export of green calfskins to keep the manufacturing process within the state and "to promote the interest of the whole" when a group of merchants cornered the year's supply for export.[104]

The franchise spread rapidly throughout the period. The limited use of one form, the outright monopoly, was due not to theoretical objections but to slight economic value; with the state powerless to prevent the importation of competing products the device offered little protection within the Massachusetts market, much less outside it. That the franchise was a privilege occasioned no protest, so long as it served or seemed to serve a social purpose. If it put additional expense upon the consumer, in many cases the alternative seemed worse. Better higher prices for transportation, for glass, or for lodgings out of the pockets of those who chose to pay than taxes out of the purses of all. In the beginning, few resented such charges borne voluntarily and granted for improvements which promised benefits generally. The thrifty farmer wishing to evade the expense of the new bridge or new road could do so by ignoring it and going some distance out of his way as he had in the past. Even those who sought safeguards against, or compensation for, flooded meadows did not challenge the innovation which offered them and their neighbors security that their grain would be ground, their timber sawed, their wool fulled. Whatever fundamental

101. St. 1793, ch. 3.

102. St. 1808, ch. 99.

103. MA, 1813, chs. 33, 122, petitions of Edward Houghton *et al.*, Clark Stone *et al.*, and Josiah Bardwell *et al.*

104. MA, 1787, ch. 64, petitions of Noah Perrin, John Rogers, Mar. 10, 18, 1788; *Amendments to the Report of the Commissioners Appointed to Revise the General Statutes of the Commonwealth* (Boston, 1835), p. 43.

complaints arose, it will be seen, aimed not at the character of the privilege, but at attempts to limit it to a favored few. Those who counted such limitation an evil looked for relief not in abolition but in diffusion.

The eagerness to create favorable conditions for economic activities through franchises and inspection laws gained strength from the inadequacy of direct assistance through bounty or simple gift to individual producers. Well-established colonial usage and post-revolutionary theory had exalted the notion of aid through an immediate outlay from the state treasury. Many considered the bounty the best technique and cheapest for society as a whole because it did not lead to a rise in prices or in cost of production, because it encouraged the introduction of new processes, gave enterprisers advantages in foreign as well as in domestic markets, and tended to reduce the export of specie. Analogous activities by other states and by England at first served as a spur to keep Massachusetts from falling behind.[105]

After the failure of a blanket proposal thus to help a great many products, the legislature set about befriending some favored ones.[106] Aid to the fisheries continued until the national government relieved Massachusetts of that burden.[107] Agriculture secured the assistance of £4 for the head of each crop-destroying wolf.[108] In 1786, 1788, and 1791 laws granted a bounty for the production of hemp, important in shipping, which benefited as well the farmers who raised it, the ropemakers, and the merchants.[109] A similar subsidy went to the manufacture of sailcloth, duck, and twine in Boston in 1788 and 1791 "to enable the manufacturer to give such a price for Flax, as will induce the Farmer to exert himself." [110] In another attempt to nurse it to

105. See Weeden, *New England, 1620–1789*, II, 686ff; Giesecke, *American Commercial Legislation before 1789*, pp. 59ff; Hamilton, *Industrial and Commercial Correspondence*, pp. 242, 290ff, 294; *Boston Commercial Gazette*, Sept. 9, 1819; Jackson to Ames, Feb. 7, 1790, Sedgwick Papers, 2 ser., VI; J. Adams to King, Feb. 14, 1786, King, *Rufus King*, I, 161; *Stockbridge Western Star*, Feb. 28, 1792; MA, 1799, ch. 28, petition of Samuel Slater.

106. MA, House, 2322.

107. See [Swan], *National Arithmetick*, pp. 8–10; F. R. Hart, "New England Whale Fisheries," *Col. Soc. Mass. Publications*, XXVI (1934), 74.

108. See MA, CXXXVII, 293, 294; st. 1782, ch. 39; Richard Frothingham, Jr., *History of Charlestown* (Boston, 1845–1849), p. 114; Sylvester Judd, *History of Hadley* (Springfield, 1905), pp. 344ff.

109. See res. 1790, ch. 157J; res. 1791, ch. 1J; res. 1792, ch. 66M; Hamilton, *Industrial and Commercial Correspondence*, p. 61.

110. Shephard to Sedgwick, Dec. 16, 1791, Sedgwick Papers, II, 194; res. 1791, ch. 91J; Hamilton, *Industrial and Commercial Correspondence*, p. 60.

success, the prodigal glass manufactory in the Hub received 6*d.* for each sheet of window glass for three years if it turned out at least four thousand.[111]

Other expedients answered as variations of the bounty in cash. The state made occasional loans to enterprisers, such as that of £300 to Benjamin Shepard for the manufacture of cotton goods in Wrentham.[112] It freed from taxation the Boston glasshouses and cotton factories in Worcester and Rehoboth and elsewhere for periods of from five to ten years. Breweries which turned out one hundred barrels annually received the identical concession to encourage the production of the healthful beverage, create a product for export, and supply a market for farmers. Salt and sugar works had the same advantage held out to them for a time.[113] Sometimes either the state or the town extended the exemption to employees of the new venture. Thus the foremen of a factory in Beverly were relieved of the poll tax and the laborers at the Boston glass factory released from militia duty.[114]

But the Commonwealth was too poor thus consistently to finance its aspirations. Although acceptance of the theory, precedent, the example of other states, and personal influence, persistence, and credibility smoothed the way, the legislature was never enthusiastic about this type of aid. The lack of money always loomed larger than the insistence of merchants that "notwithstanding our losses and expences during the War, we have still such resources, as enable us ... to apply large Sums as Bounties to open new, or to extend old branches of commerce." [115] Such favors as exemption from taxation involved no direct outlay, but they too came to be recokoned poor fiduciary practice. To limit these grants was difficult, yet extended widely they would erode the base on which government income rested. The whole technique, therefore, fell into disuse. Petitions for help

111. St. 1793, ch. 3.

112. Res. 1793, ch. 32M; res. 1796, ch. 5M. For other requests for loans see *Repertory*, Feb. 28, 1806.

113. St. 1785, ch. 41; st. 1787, ch. 13; st. 1789, ch. 10; res. 1791, ch. 86J; st. 1793, ch. 3; MA, 1799, ch. 28, petition of Samuel Slater; st. 1806, ch. 92; MA, Senate, 3922. For other proposed aid see *Salem Gazette*, Feb. 6, 1810, and in general, [Swan], *National Arithmetick*, p. 17.

114. St. 1787, ch. 13; st. 1793, ch. 3; E. M. Stone, *Lecture Comprising the History of the Second Parish in Beverly* (Boston, 1843), p. 29. For other requests for tax exemption see *Repertory*, Mar. 7, 1806.

115. Higginson to Adams, Dec. 30, 1785, *Amer. Hist. Assoc. Annual Report, 1896*, I, 730; [Swan], *National Arithmetick*, pp. 48ff.

to silkgrowers failed, and between 1798 and 1804 the General Court refused to renew the bounties on duck, glass, and hemp.[116]

By the turn of the century, the conception prevailed that the direct bounty was an unusual expedient to serve only in very extraordinary cases. This attitude, surprising in view of the theoretical arguments justifying a wider use, resulted from the weight of a counterpoise which held back state action. Out of the pressing desire to lower taxation and the ever present recollection of the revolutionary crisis, sprang a reluctance to use any measure that involved a cash outlay, an "extreme of unthrifty parsimony" that often prevented grants otherwise considered beneficent.[117]

The long discussions of finance dragged endlessly on while the Commonwealth still held substantial resources to the eastward. In the District of Maine it owned great tracts of virgin land inherited from the province, which had, at the end of the seventeenth century, extinguished all confused claims deriving from early patents. But the promise of these possessions never came to fulfillment; as in economic policy in general, the balance of political pressures and the weight of debt gave a new direction to the thrust of state ambition.

Part of its territory Massachusetts used as an alternative to cash, making gifts, in accordance with older customs, for revolutionary services, military and civilian, for the encouragement of education, the ministry, and industry, for the building of roads and mills, and for the protection of beaches and harbors.[118] Yet by 1820 only one of the six million acres then alienated had been devoted to such purposes. Difficulties in marketing the products of these lands reduced the value of distant grants to the vanishing point so that such assistance, while not disdained by recipients, was of dubious worth. Moreover, the state doled out its real property as carefully as it did its tax exemptions and its money.[119]

Partly this caution originated in the consciousness that the

116. See Bentley, *Diary*, II, 28; MA, Senate, 1591/1, 2391, 2391/1, 2391/2; Governor Hancock's address, Jan. 30, 1793, *Acts and Resolves of 1793*, p. 695; *Salem Register*, Sept. 6, 1804; Phillips, *Manual of Political Economy*, p. 207.

117. See Cabot to Sewall and to Pickering, Feb. 6, 1797, Dec. 20, 1815, Lodge, *George Cabot*, pp. 116, 566ff; Governor Strong's address, *Annals of the Times*, Jan. 20, 1803; Phillips, *Manual of Political Economy*, p. 157.

118. There is a summary of land legislation, *Senate Docs., 1836*, no. 4, pp. 6–13; for specific grants see, e.g., res. 1807, ch. 107; res. 1812, ch. 89; *Stockbridge Western Star*, June 21, 1791. See also MA, 1782, ch. 26.

119. See *Eastern Herald*, Feb. 8, 1802; *House Docs., 1859*, no. 302, pp. 1, 2.

basic function of the land was to contribute to the development of the state in quite another context. All who wrote on economic affairs in these years agreed that agriculture was the fount of the country's wealth and that encouragement was necessary and desirable; not a few gave farming, "this original and natural employment," higher rank in social utility than commerce.[120] It seemed logical to devote the forests and fields to the husbandmen seeking new grounds, for "the opening the Wilderness and Turning the Desert into Wheatfields" was "of great advantage to the publick." Furthermore, if, as James Swan and John Hancock pointed out, the real riches of the state were its population, deeds to settlers on easy terms would, by increasing production, ultimately increase wealth and "afford a resource for taxes far exceeding what the value of the lands have been estimated at." [121] As farmers began to move westward, many voices called for immediate and liberal grants to halt the exodus.[122]

Political considerations underpinned the economic argument. To parcel out the soil in workable lots would also quiet the prevalent fear of large holdings. A proposed constitution in 1779 had planned to restrict the amounts held by individuals lest they "denominate their landed estate, manners or lordships, as has been practised in other parts of the world." [123] And the failure in 1780 to set such limits was severely criticized.[124]

Overcasting the objective of settlement, however, always loomed the temptation to find in this ready asset, land, relief from the government's precarious financial position. Massachusetts persistently attempted to dispose of its treasure at a price. In this it was not alone; local communities were also busily engaged in selling town property to liquidate debts and to increase revenue.[125]

For a time the state yielded to the demand that it sell primarily

120. See *Massachusetts Spy*, Oct. 2, 1776; *Boston Gazette*, Feb. 9, 1784; Adams to Calkoen, Oct. 27, 1780, J. Adams, *Works*, VII, 309; [Swan], *National Arithmetick*, pp. 6, 7; *Stockbridge Western Star*, Apr. 6, 1790; Governor Hancock's address, Jan. 30, 1793, *Acts and Resolves of 1793*, p. 695; Caleb Strong, *Patriotism and Piety* (Newburyport, 1808), pp. 69, 70; [James Sullivan], *Path to Riches* (Boston, 1792), p. 8.

121. See [Swan], *National Arithmetick*, p. 65; *Acts and Resolves of 1790*, p. 550.

122. See *Boston Gazette*, July 5, 1784.

123. *Boston Gazette*, July 19, 1779. See also J. Adams, "Defence of the Constitutions," *Works*, IV, 359.

124. *Boston Gazette*, June 19, 1780.

125. See, e.g., *Boston Gazette*, Mar. 19, 1801, Mar. 4, 1802; Governor Adams' address, *Columbian Centinel*, June 6, 1795; Pratt, *Eastham, Wellfleet, and Orleans*, p. 134.

in small quantities, establishing a land office in 1783 and a survey in 1784.[126] Yet despite some interest in mill sites and water privileges, there were few takers. A gigantic lottery in 1786, which held out the inducement of a fifteen-year tax exemption, failed ignominiously. By 1790 total receipts did not cover administrative selling costs.[127]

When the policy of small sales failed to attract settlers, much less earn a profit, the General Court turned not to free grants, as Swan had suggested, but to an alternate program, the disposal of large tracts to speculators. The Commonwealth would then receive an immediate return and could rely on the landowners to inveigle settlers. The purchasers would profit, of course, but only by inducing farmers to take up their offerings. The state's experience in selling its possessions outside its borders to Gorham, Phelps, and others commended this method of redeeming the public debt to a hard-pressed government, and, no doubt, to the speculators themselves.[128]

Toward the end of 1791 Massachusetts shed the early reluctance to make large grants. As a sensational boom turned men's minds to the prospect of getting rich from stocks and land, as the merchants looked about for new channels of investment, the government, like its colonial predecessors, began to seek out venturesome customers. In 1791 it alienated almost two million acres, on paper at least, and sales continued heavy in the next few years. Through a big auction in 1797 it planned to dispose of much of the remaining domain at a minimum of one dollar an acre. The complaints of squatters, of Indians edged out, and of moralists who shuddered at the effects of such gambling upon the state's economy were of no avail.[129]

Although thus granting away vast tracts, with liberal concessions to boot, the legislature, sometimes acting through governor and council and sometimes through agents, retained a miserly control over the disposition of the land. Although it failed to reserve mast rights as the Crown had done, it directly regulated other minutiae of possession. Above all, it continued to impose

126. See *Boston Gazette*, Feb. 4, 1782; st. 1784, ch. 16.
127. St. 1786, ch. 40; R. E. Shikes, "Lottery in American History to 1850" (unpub. diss. Harvard University, 1938, University Archives), p. 47; Bullock, *Finances of Massachusetts*, p. 21.
128. See st. 1784, ch. 60; st. 1788, ch. 23; Gorham to Sedgwick, Jan. 27, 30, Mar. 14, 1790, Sedgwick Papers, I, 702, 716, 779; *Commonwealth History of Massachusetts*, ed. A. B. Hart (New York, 1927–1930), III, 353ff.
129. *Columbian Centinel*, Jan. 28, 1792, Sept. 19, 1795, Mar. 16, 1796, June 14, 24, 1797; st. 1786, ch. 40; st. 1788, ch. 17; res. 1790, ch. 28J; res. 1791, ch. 130J.

requirements for colonization as it had previously done in smaller grants.[130] In larger conveyances it conditioned clear title upon the settlement, within a limited period, of a specified number of persons, usually forty for each township. While the legislature almost invariably extended the time and often commuted the requirement into cash payments or road building, uncertainty of tenure persisted.[131] Bingham's two million acres, forfeited in 1807, fourteen years after they were purchased, were granted and regranted and not finally written off the books until the 1830's. Confusion about terms and doubts about ownership led to complex litigation throughout the District of Maine for many years, discouraging those who might have filled up the speculators' holdings and depressing the value of all land.[132]

Political inability to deal definitively with squatters likewise vitiated the ultimate objective of settlement and the immediate one of financial gain. The land law had always taken account of "a special right to be supported from occupancy," and Massachusetts consistently recognized the settlers' equity in their improvements.[133] There was, however, no willingness on the part of government to welcome unauthorized entrants by pre-emption. But there was also no willingness to clear the way for applying the enunciated state policy by driving off recalcitrants. In practice, after 1785 the state from time to time allowed those long on its domain to obtain one hundred acres at a nominal sum. The stubborn continued to work and wait, scoffed at perennial gubernatorial edicts to leave, and got the reasonable terms they wanted.[134]

Those who, by accident of location, squatted on lands already granted away had to deal with businessmen instead of with a government easy with concessions. Without provisions for reasonable quieting of claims or for just prices for improvements, the settlers were at the mercy of "proprietors who will plague

130. See, e.g., st. 1782, chs. 26, 27; res. 1807, chs. 21, 26; [Swan], *National Arithmetick*, p. vi; st. 1783, ch. 22; also P. J. Treat, "Origin of the National Land System," *Amer. Hist. Assoc. Annual Report, 1905*, I, 235.

131. See, e.g., res. 1807, ch. 28; res. 1808, ch. 209; res. 1809, chs. 244, 246, 282, 288; res. 1810, ch. 98; res. 1813, ch. 45; res. 1814, ch. 151.

132. See, e.g., *Thompson v. Bright* (1848), 1 Cushing 420, and the discussion, *Boston Commercial Gazette*, Feb. 15, 1816.

133. Sullivan, *Land Titles*, pp. 193ff; *Kennebeck Intelligencer*, Mar. 20, 1798.

134. See st. 1784, ch. 60; res. 1806, ch. 35; res. 1807, chs. 62, 129, 136, 167; res. 1809, ch. 273; Henry Tatter, "State and Federal Land Policy during the Confederation Period," *Agricultural History*, 9 (1935), 18off; *Repertory*, Mar. 18, 1806, Feb. 19, 1808; A. C. Ford, *Colonial Precedents of Our National Land System* (Madison, 1910), pp. 138ff.

. . . [them] like the despots of Europe, one set or company after another." The farmers who had pitched upon the soil remembered that "it was land and liberty that we fought for," yet they "did not murmur" when the government resolved to replenish its treasury by selling instead of freely giving its territory away. However, when the legislature disposed of vast tracts to speculators for a pittance, and confirmed ancient patents without charge, the squatters tauntingly demanded, "what right the Court has to give it away, in such a way as the State shall never be the better for it." "It is a thousand to one," a leader declared, "but blood will be shed" when a "poor man, though he ventured his life to conquer the land, shall have none of it." [135]

Troubles on the Waldo patent in the 1790's started a long series of riots which drove the state to a succession of unavailing compromises to make good the titles of legal holders while placating the illegal settlers. Resistance by armed farmers to the service of ejectment notices led first to a hysterical call for the militia, then to a qualmish recall, and finally to the "betterment law," which gave squatters the option of taking up their land at fixed sums or of accepting compensation for improvements if they chose to depart.[136] Disputed interpretations resulted in repeated amendments, and the whole question remained nettlesome until 1813 when commissioners allowed those who had settled before 1789 two hundred acres for $10 and offered others land at the rate of 30 cents per acre. On the islands disputes dragged on until 1820.[137]

Although squatters thus never received carte blanche, they were obstacle enough to the full enjoyment of titles to deter speculators from venturing into Maine. The state's proclivities to compromise showed investors that their interests would not always receive protection. Yet few wished to see the issue openly joined. Those especially who were also politicians hesitated at

135. [Samuel Ely], *The Deformity of a Hideous Monster Discovered in the Province of Maine* (n.p. [1797]), pp. 3, 10, 11; Ford, *Colonial Precedents of National Land System*, pp. 119ff.

136. See R. E. Moody, "Samuel Ely," *New England Quarterly*, 5 (1932), 117ff, 124ff, 128ff; W. C. Hatch, *History of the Town of Industry* (Farmington, 1893), pp. 83ff; *Eastern Herald*, Mar. 15, 1802; Caleb Strong, *Patriotism and Piety*, pp. 25, 61, 149; *Repertory*, June 20, 1806, Feb. 5, 1807, Jan. 29, Feb. 9, 12, 26, 1808; proprietors' petition and "Standing Laws," *Boston Gazette*, Jan. 28, Feb. 1, 1808; Amory, *James Sullivan*, II, 271–278.

137. *Resolves of 1813*, pp. 181–208; see also res. 1810, ch. 159; res. 1814, ch. 181; res. 1819, ch. 144; "Report of the Land Commissioners," MA, res. 1820, ch. 24; *Salem Gazette*, Feb. 6, 1810; *Repertory*, Feb. 8, 1811; *Portland Gazette*, Feb. 1, 1813.

unpopular actions from uncertainty of political position if not from scruples.[138]

All this while, new and more fertile lands promised quicker and more secure gains. Not long after hostilities ended, New Englanders made their way into the distant regions of the Empire State. Massachusetts' sale of its New York property deflected attention away from its eastern offerings. Western Pennsylvania also absorbed Bay State interests. And beyond lay the welcoming Northwest Territory sucking in the richest energies of old New England. In the train of Mannasseh Cutler, of Phelps, and of Gorham, merchants like Higginson and Cabot sent their money westward, setting in motion a process which continued until the Civil War.[139] In vain the Commonwealth cast its influence against any liberal national land policy that might increase competition with its own holdings.[140] Continued efforts by agents and legislative committees notwithstanding, sales in Maine slackened after the first flush of speculative excitement, and the promise of substantial revenue faded.[141]

At the close of the Revolution Maine possessed a number of advantages over the more fertile, but less known, Indian-ridden and inaccessible West — close water communications with the eastern seacoast, an established government, and an advanced degree of settlement.[142] But Massachusetts policy impeded development. The $896,281 cleared by the state between 1785 and 1820, when Maine became independent, was poor compensation for the failure to appropriate the lands to the services of wider production and full settlement. Vacillation and compromise and the wish to profit in cash stood in the way. By favoring speculators to whom most of the land went at an average price of 2.75 cents an acre, the Commonwealth antagonized new farmers. By

138. See Parker to Sedgwick, Feb. 18, 1806, Sedgwick Papers, IV, 761.

139. See Orasmus Turner, *History of the Pioneer Settlement of Phelps' and Gorham's Purchase* (Rochester, N.Y., 1851), pp. 131ff, 136ff; Porter, *Jacksons and the Lees*, I, 468; Everett to Parks and Duncan, Oct. 24, 1836, Everett Papers, LXVII, 108, 109; L. K. Mathews, *Expansion of New England* (Boston, 1909), pp. 103, 140ff, 158ff.

140. See King to Mason, Feb. 20, 1819, [G. S. Hillard], *Memoir and Correspondence of Jeremiah Mason* (Cambridge, Mass., 1873), pp. 220ff; Ford, *Colonial Precedents of National Land System*, pp. 88ff.

141. See *Repertory*, Feb. 19, 1808; *Portland Gazette*, June 14, 1813. For later land policy see, e.g., MA, 1815, ch. 131, extended by MA, 1818, ch. 116; st. 1819, ch. 36; res. 1820, ch. 24; st. 1830, ch. 98; *Revised Statutes*, ch. 10; *Boston Commercial Gazette*, Feb. 1, 1816.

142. See King to King, Mar. 5, 1819, King, *Rufus King*, VI, 218; J. H. St. J. Crèvecoeur, *Letters from an American Farmer* (London, 1783), p. 182.

protecting squatters and by withholding clear title for many years, it discouraged investors. Dissatisfied, both groups found better opportunities elsewhere.[143]

The problem of the Massachusetts domain illustrated in a graphic sense an inconsistency in the application of economic policy in this period. The Commonwealth that was to be the instrument of ambitious aspiration found itself fettered by debt and constricted by a political balance that limited its ability to follow a consistent line. But the pattern became clear only in retrospect. For several decades the great mass of people, conservative in affairs involving risk of taxes, blocked action that depended on state expenditures and eagerly espoused any alternative method of achieving the Commonwealth's ideals. They were hopeful that the indirect measures of franchise and inspection, spread widely, would realize their objectives. And they found additional cause for optimism in another technique, already in use and mounting in importance, that promised to play a vigorous part in the new system of production.

143. J. W. Fleming, "Maine: Studies in Resources, Finance, Local Government, Economic History" (unpub. diss. Harvard University, 1938, University Archives), p. 138; Bullock, *Finances of Massachusetts*, p. 24; *Senate Docs., 1859*, no. 302, p. 2.

4 | The State in Association

Assistance and guidance for a thriving and expanding productive system flowed through many channels. To achieve a desired end, Massachusetts often extended its resources or the force of its laws to a person or group. Seeking in its own history and in the experience of other countries for examples of the available means, the Commonwealth used, from the very start, a variety of traditional administrative agencies to further its objectives. These organs of government, evolving from the past and adaptable to the future, furnished the framework of a new technique for implementing the role of the state in the economy.

Oldest of the intermediaries and strongest in internal structure were the towns. Familiar from the very beginnings of settlement, these bodies by 1780 had developed into powerful and flexible local organizations. The Act of 1785 confirmed long-standing colonial practice when it recognized, in addition to other prerogatives, the right of these agencies to make contracts, to hold property autonomously, and to enjoy certain other privileges.[1] Many towns, on their own initiative, offered bounties and otherwise supported local agriculture and industry. Exercising a monopoly of the river fisheries within their limits, and, where geography permitted, of the shellfish and bait off their shores, they either set up general conditions for taking or farmed out the concessions.[2] Similarly, the urban communities retained the

1. St. 1785, ch. 75, secs. 7, 8; *Revised Statutes of the Commonwealth of Massachusetts* (Boston, 1836), ch. 15, secs. 8, 11.

2. See, e.g., st. 1780, ch. 34; st. 1783, ch. 4; st. 1785, ch. 26; st. 1790, ch. 45; st. 1791, ch. 63; st. 1796, chs. 83, 91; st. 1797, chs. 69, 71; st. 1801, ch. 59; st. 1811, ch.

medieval right to control and organize markets, regulating in great detail the conditions of sale.[3]

Parochial considerations, always crucial in town meetings, frequently rubbed against the limits of broader state policy. The towns were independent, but only concerning matters that had not yet fallen within the orbit of the state government. Occasionally, appeals from conflicting interests within or between towns elicited positive choices by the General Court.[4] More frequently, the Commonwealth selected its own fields for legislation, laying down wide, comprehensive programs and charging the local agencies with administration.

The state always required the towns to act as its tax gatherers. Needing the service of intermediaries armed with coercive power, it urged charters on districts which lacked the requisite status and which consequently had no right to collect.[5]

All manner of economic functions judged desirable by Massachusetts became duties of the towns. They were go-betweens in licensing inns, scales, and chimney sweeps, and in the construction of private drains and sewers, activities in which discretion rested upon neighborhood judgments.[6] They regulated the rules of travel and were often agents in the payment of state bounties and the enforcement of inspection laws.[7] It was incumbent upon them to register "marks of creatures" for farmers who used brands as identification, to keep a pound for stray beasts, and to appoint reeves and drivers to pick them up.[8] These communi-

129; G. W. Chase, *History of Haverhill* (Haverhill, 1861), p. 482; Solomon Lincoln, Jr., *History of the Town of Hingham* (Hingham, 1827), p. 3; Enoch Pratt, *Comprehensive History, Ecclesiastical and Civil, of Eastham, Wellfleet, and Orleans* (Yarmouth, 1844), pp. 82, 133; C. W. Jenkins, *Three Lectures on the Early History of the Town of Falmouth* (Falmouth, 1889), p. 94.

3. MA, 1783, ch. 29; MA, 1784, ch. 37; Edmund Quincy, *Life of Josiah Quincy* (Boston, 1868), pp. 398ff; Charles Shaw, *Topographical and Historical Description of Boston* (Boston, 1817), pp. 178, 180ff; st. 1823, ch. 147; *By-Laws and Orders of the Town of Boston* (Boston, 1818), pp. 36–42.

4. See, e.g., MA, 1784, ch. 37.

5. See [James Swan], *National Arithmetick* (Boston, 1786), p. vii; W. C. Hatch, *History of the Town of Industry* (Farmington, 1893), p. 83; MA, 1784, ch. 54, Parsonsfield petition.

6. *Revised Statutes*, ch. 27; st. 1796, ch. 88; st. 1816, ch. 26; Chase, *Haverhill*, p. 473; *By-Laws of Boston*, p. 19.

7. St. 1781, ch. 25; st. 1783, ch. 15; st. 1784, ch. 31; st. 1785, chs. 25, 52, 75; st. 1786, ch. 81; st. 1791, ch. 58; st. 1796, ch. 67; st. 1799, ch. 60; st. 1809, ch. 62; st. 1811, ch. 9; st. 1824, ch. 102; st. 1834, ch. 184; *Revised Statutes*, ch. 15, secs. 33–40; also st. 1782, ch. 39; "A Citizen of Boston," *Columbian Centinel*, Feb. 3, 1796; John Bacon, *Town Officer's Guide* (Haverhill, 1825), pp. 62, 63.

8. St. 1788, ch. 65; st. 1834, ch. 184; *Revised Statutes*, ch. 19, secs. 19–24; C. M.

ties were also responsible for laying out and maintaining roads and highways, ferries and bridges, and they were liable for damages through neglect.[9] The adaptability and efficiency of these local bodies inspired frequent proposals that the Commonwealth yoke their coercive power to new burdens, the manufacture of potash, the cultivation of a fuel supply, and the issue of currency, for instance.[10]

By 1780 the state could also reach out for and utilize the services of a number of more specialized organs that had evolved from the town in a long process of definition and redefinition of governmental prerogatives. A homogeneous population had, at the beginnings of settlement in New England, dealt in a single meeting with all manner of activities, religious, economic, political, and educational. But a century and a half of development divided interests and destroyed homogeneity. Thus, as the religious uniformity of the first settlers vanished, church was distinguished from parish and parish from town, each with its own set of rights and obligations.[11]

At its inception in 1780, the Commonwealth found even narrower agencies fully established; new problems arising from complex conditions in the larger towns had brought into being bodies entrusted with fragments of the power to govern. The Overseers of the Poor in Boston had acquired the right to administer independently relief for the provincial metropolis. Similarly, the marine societies in Boston, Salem, Marblehead, and Newburyport had taken over the authority to make charts and soundings, to build beacons, to recommend suitable pilots for

and Alexander Hyde, *Lee* (Springfield, 1878), p. 188; *History of Bristol County*, ed. D. H. Hurd (Philadelphia, 1883), p. 449.

9. St. 1759–60, ch. 21; st. 1764–65, ch. 31; st. 1785, ch. 75; st. 1786, chs. 67, 81; st. 1796, ch. 42; *Revised Statutes*, ch. 15, secs. 16, 33, 82–84, ch. 26, secs. 7–9. Districts which were not towns lacked the taxing power and needed special enabling acts to build roads (see, e.g., MA, 1784, ch. 12; st. 1796, ch. 58). In Maine, therefore, the state often acted directly or gave aid by grants (see res. 1807, chs. 38, 68; res. 1810, chs. 148, 153, 158).

10. *Columbian Centinel*, Oct. 21, 1797; *Eastern Herald*, Dec. 18, 1797; *New-England Palladium*, Jan. 1, 1805; *Boston Gazette*, Jan. 31, 1805; T. J. Kreps, "Vicissitudes of the American Potash Industry," *Jour. of Econ. and Bus. Hist.*, 3 (1931), 637ff.

11. See st. 1786, ch. 10, sec. 3; st. 1833, ch. 83; *Revised Statutes*, ch. 20; Peter Thacher, "Rights of Protestant Churches in . . . Boston," *Monthly Anthology and Boston Review*, 3 (1806), 635ff. The whole subject of parish status received intensive investigation as a result of the Unitarian controversy. See *Baker* v. *Fales* (1820), 16 Tyng 488; *Stebbins* v. *Jennings* (1830), 10 Pickering 172; *Decision of the Supreme Judicial Court of Massachusetts . . . Relating to the Sacramental Furniture of a Church in Brookfield* (Boston, 1832), pp. 6–39.

licensing, and to carry on a wide range of other activities approximating those of Trinity House in England.[12]

Another offshoot, malleable to the ends of the state, had arisen from a partition of economic functions. Originally, the residents of a district were all proprietors, sharing its property and governing the undivided land, as they did other matters, through the town meeting. But as newcomers appeared, the primeval owners strove to retain the common lands, differentiating their rights from those of the other inhabitants. A long-drawn-out struggle had forged a distinction between town and town proprietors, with exclusive privilege to the common fields arrogated to the latter. Recognition of the proprietorship not only barred outsiders, but also gave the new collective body power to govern its members.

This form had also spread during the eighteenth century to landowners with clear titles, who, though unconcerned with the problem of excluding interlopers, nevertheless perceived the advantages of the capacity for compulsion. In questions of joint improvement of marshes and meadows, a majority had frequently wished to vote expenditures and to impose a share of the cost upon an uncooperative minority. A recognized procedure had given that power to tenants in common, that is, to those who held land together but by different titles. Acts of 1692 and 1713 authorized such proprietors to alienate land by a majority vote, entering into the property rights of the minority.[13]

By 1780 both types were known as proprietors of common fields, and the essential nature of their status, the power to coerce for some desirable end, was generally recognized. A petition, in 1782, for permission to organize in this manner noted

12. St. 1771–72, ch. 21; st. 1773–74, ch. 5; st. 1777–78, ch. 8. The Marblehead Society was rechartered by st. 1798, ch. 44. A short history with extracts from the minutes and by-laws may be found in the notes to *Province Acts, 1769–80*, pp. 188ff, 354, 823ff. See also L. W. Jenkins, "Marine Society at Salem," *Essex Inst. Hist. Colls.*, LXXVI (1940), 1ff, 200ff; W. H. Bayley and O. O. Jones, *History of the Marine Society of Newburyport, Massachusetts* (Newburyport, 1906), pp. 19, 24, 36–43, 48, 53, 60, 88, 200. For Trinity House see [Adam] Anderson, *Historical and Chronological Deduction of the Origin of Commerce* (Dublin, 1790), II, 35, 502, 503.

13. James Sullivan, *History of Land Titles in Massachusetts* (Boston, 1801), pp. 122ff, 171; st. 1712–13, ch. 9. Significantly, first mention of common fields was in a general act regulating towns, st. 1692–93, ch. 28. For the conflict of town and town proprietors see R. H. Akagi, *Town Proprietors of the New England Colonies* (Philadelphia, 1924), pp. 2–33, 55, 60, 74, 79ff, 291; F. J. Turner, "First Official Frontier of the Massachusetts Bay," *Col. Soc. Mass. Publications*, XVII (1914), 268ff; S. E. Morison, "Comment," *ibid.*, XVIII (1915), 69ff; Chase, *Haverhill*, p. 75.

that, while all the landholders did not agree, "perfect Unanimity is not to be effected in such Cases, nor ordinarily so general an agreement as in the present, and Society in General and this Government in particular has been established by the Influence of that indisputable Maxim. That Individuals should yield private Opinions to Considerations of public Utility, and the Minor submit to the Major, a Principle by which all Communities are regulated, and which applies to the present Case in its full Extent." [14]

The Commonwealth continued to create these bodies for such objects of public utility as the drainage of swamps and the reclamation of lands. Familiarity with the form and its apparent usefulness early promoted the enactment of a general law for the constitution of such bodies. An act of 1784 provided that any five, or the majority, of the proprietors of a common or general field could call a meeting through a justice of the peace and organize with the power, like towns, to pass by-laws, assess taxes, elect officers, and sue and be sued. The law permitted vote by proxy and held forth the rights to raise assessments upon members in proportion to interest and to sell the lands of deliquents. The entity was to endure as long as land remained undivided; at its expiration the records went on file with the town clerk.[15] Formation under the general law was easier but brought the same privileges and duties as special acts, thereafter resorted to only under unusual circumstances: in Southwick and Orleans where the land crossed state or town lines, in Cambridge where only a part of the tract was included, in Rowley and Ipswich where the privilege of building dikes and interfering with the fisheries was important, and in Ossipee where a mine was to be worked.[16]

These pliant, handy organs of government were regarded in a matter-of-course fashion by 1780, and they continued to serve various uses thereafter. The proclivity toward association, in this characteristic form, entered into every phase of Massachusetts life. People who shared common interests normally formed

14. MA, 1782, ch. 3. See also Akagi, *Town Proprietors*, p. 226.

15. St. 1783, ch. 39; st. 1785, ch. 53, further amended by st. 1818, ch. 11; st. 1820, ch. 1; Sullivan, *Land Titles*, pp. 167ff.

16. MA, 1789, ch. 16; MA, 1791, ch. 56; MA, 1796, ch. 17; MA, 1797, ch. 81, petition of Joseph Gay *et al.*; MA, 1799, ch. 50; st. 1799, chs. 5, 43, 79; st. 1800, ch. 63; st. 1812, ch. 138; st. 1813, ch. 64; st. 1814, ch. 179. See also Parsons' argument, *Ellis* v. *Marshall* (1807), 2 Tyng 274; Sullivan, *Land Titles*, p. 196. For other common fields see, e.g., st. 1791, ch. 56; st. 1792, ch. 84; st. 1794, ch. 71; st. 1795, ch. 6.

groups to work for a common end. The bond of union was a contract voluntarily entered into by the members who agreed to obey the rules. In this respect such bodies repeated in microcosm the essential structure of the state itself. Sanctified by theology, tested by the ever recurrent contest with the frontier, proved by the trial of war, and formally embodied in constitutional government, cooperative group associations were the accustomed way of meeting problems in the Bay State.

But towns, marine societies, the Overseers of the Poor, and the proprietors of common fields had acquired a critical attribute that differentiated them from voluntary organizations. The latter, formed by voluntary compacts, had no power to enforce decisions. Obedience to their dictates was optional; a member who disagreed with the collective judgment was always free to secede and to withdraw his share of the property.[17] Only the state had the authority to make laws sanctioned by force. For reasons of its own it could, however, delegate some of its political powers. Associations like the town and its offshoots, granted that privilege, were political entities, little republics in Blackstone's language, or bodies politic. Contemporaries knew such societies as "corporations" and assumed that the basic intent, the purpose, of all corporations was for better government, either general or special.[18]

The corporate mechanism for applying the power of the government to special areas of group action was not peculiar to nor original with Massachusetts or America. Its customary use reached back into the feudal background of western Europe, and its application to business fields in the interest of national policy was characteristic of the seventeenth century. Indeed, as such a device it was intimately familiar to the people of the Bay State. Their own history had started in a chartered trading corporation, a form to which many thought they were returning in 1780. The new constitution, which envisaged the Commonwealth as a body politic and corporate, whose citizens were related to it as stockholders, reflected the common currency of the idea and

17. Cf. *Warren* v. *Stearns* (1837), 19 Pickering 73.

18. Those who feel that the essence of the corporation rests in the contract among its members rather than in the government decree reach that conclusion because they fail to distinguish, as the eighteenth century did, between the corporation and the voluntary association; see, e.g., A. A. Berle, Jr., *Studies in the Law of Corporation Finance* (Chicago, 1928), p. 23. Historically, the voluntary association antedated the corporation, but the peculiar corporate qualities were derived from the state. See, e.g., the dedication, Sullivan, *Land Titles*, p. vi–a.

encouraged by analogy the conception of more specialized activities in terms of more specialized corporations.[19]

The constitution of 1780 spelled out a tendency long in maturation when it provided that corporations could not arise spontaneously. A century and a half of development in the New World had determined that only the state could create them. Some corporations, it was true, lacked charters because of a confusion in status in the early years of settlement. In the period when control from Boston was tenuous — to say nothing of control from London — many, like the proprietors of common fields, had assumed corporate powers without explicit grant. Furthermore, until 1691 Massachusetts was itself merely a creature chartered by the Crown, without sovereignty and powerless by the common law to create other corporations. The Bay Company could not incorporate towns and churches without incurring royal disfavor. Indeed, the ultimate ground for the revocation of the Massachusetts Bay Charter had been the incorporation of Harvard College.[20] The Board of Directors, the General Court, simply organized such bodies and endowed them with coercive power without naming them bodies politic. But whatever their origin, whether in a permissive act or in the independent arrogation of prerogatives, all acquired their legitimacy and effectiveness only by the willingness of the government to accept and enforce their decisions. Through the seventeenth century the legislature amply recognized the town's corporate status in one aspect after another. Ultimately, these quasi corporations, differing only in manner of conception, were treated in law like all other corporations.[21]

After the imposition of royal government in 1691, there was no question that the legislature had the right to incorporate common fields and towns. The only limits came from royal reluctance to increase local autonomy in the province. By 1776 the corporate character of these associations, whether by prescription or by charter, was universally and openly accepted.[22]

The Revolution and its aftermath emphasized that acceptance.

19. See James Wilson, *Works* (Philadelphia, 1804), I, 305, II, 425ff; also *Journal of Debates and Proceedings in the Convention to Revise the Constitution of Massachusetts, 1820* (Boston, 1853), p. 272. Herbert L. Osgood, "The Corporation as a Form of Colonial Government," *Political Science Quarterly*, 11 (1896), 502ff.

20. See Thomas Hutchinson, *History of the Colony and Province of Massachusetts-Bay* (Cambridge, Mass., 1936), I, 145ff.

21. See V. F. Barnes, *Dominion of New England* (New Haven, 1923), p. 184.

22. See Hutchinson, *Massachusetts-Bay*, I, 148.

The course of the struggle with England occasionally brought forth the claim that the town was "an incorporated republic." [23] The constitution of 1780 reaffirmed and regularized the position of this body; it, not its members, had a right to representation in the General Court.[24] And an act passed soon after confirmed the ancient privileges of suing, of levying taxes, and of making by-laws.[25] By 1801 contemporary lawyers ascribed those attributes to all bodies politic: "Our towns and parishes are all corporations." [26] All "these communities . . . may claim corporate rights both from *prescription* and by *implication* from acts of the colony . . . They may do all legal acts, which may be done by other artificial persons." [27]

Paradoxically, the same slow development which had endowed the corporation with status had also curtailed its autonomy. The growing strength of the colony that was the outcome of the new relation to the Crown after 1691 had subjected all bodies politic to the central government. The development of settlement, the transformation of stray clearings in the wilderness into substantial communities, had rendered the privilege more valuable. The legislature, desirous of bringing all activities in Massachusetts under its own control, had recognized as new corporations only those it had created by charter. And even the old had become uneasy; indeed, on the very eve of the break with the Empire the Proprietors of the Long Wharf in Boston, who had acted as a corporation for many years, had obtained a charter in the interests of security.[28]

The Revolution gave the central government absolute sovereignty and increased its power over the corporation. The same constitution which reaffirmed the towns' position also established over them the state's supremacy, derived directly from the people who had ratified the fundamental frame of government. The paramount place of the Commonwealth applied, as a matter of

23. J. K. Hosmer, *Samuel Adams* (Boston, 1885), p. 2.

24. See L. S. Cushing, C. W. Storey, and Lewis Josselyn, *Reports of Controverted Elections in the House of Representatives of the Commonwealth of Massachusetts, from 1780 to 1852* (Boston, 1853), pp. 198ff.

25. St. 1785, ch. 75, sec. 7; John Adams, *Works*, ed. C. F. Adams (Boston, 1850–1856), V, 495.

26. Sullivan, *Land Titles*, p. 196.

27. Thacher, "Rights of Protestant Churches in Boston," *Monthly Anthology and Boston Review*, 3 (1806), 632. For the status of common fields see, e.g., the arguments and decision in *Proprietors of Monumoi Great Beach* v. *Rogers* (1804), 1 Williams 121ff. See also *Dillingham* v. *Snow* (1807), 5 Tyng 547, 548; J. S. Davis, *Essays in the Earlier History of American Corporations* (Cambridge, 1917), I, 5ff.

28. See E. B. Greene, *The Revolutionary Generation* (New York, 1943), p. 57; *Journal of Convention, 1820*, p. 375.

course, to all other bodies politic. Herein Massachusetts repeated the experience of the former mother country two centuries earlier.[29]

The Commonwealth consciously strove to direct the existing corporate bodies and to establish, in fact as well as in law, its authority over them. To this end it increased immensely the power of the county. That unit, merely a judicial subdivision under the province charter, had acquired vitality and influence in the revolutionary interregnum.[30]

The strength of the county derived from its utility in offsetting the influence of the convention, which, acting through and for the towns, in some regions had actually challenged the legislature in Boston. In fact, a suggested constitution in 1779 had proposed to make the convention a permanent organ of state government. But adoption of the new frame of government in 1780 and the suppression of Shays' Rebellion discredited these organs as illegal assemblies and blocked off that road to decentralization.[31]

Instead, the legislature strengthened the position of the county courts. These agencies, frequently reorganized, gave those who wielded state power under the constitution an instrument for checking the towns and guiding their activities into proper channels. The counties served the central government where the town was deficient. Their courts could, for instance, overcome reluctance to spend money on roads not obviously helpful to local interests, yet considered necessary. An act of 1786 permitted an appeal to the judiciary from the decisions of the selectmen in laying out or discontinuing highways. The collapse of Shays' Rebellion gave heart to those who demanded more stringent measures. The court received the right to overrule the town on the question of the necessity of a road and, in the absence of local cooperation, to build and to collect costs from the recalcitrant corporations.[32]

The county court superintended the licensing of liquor dealers by selectmen.[33] It also licensed ferries, and it could force the towns to maintain them if "no person shall appear to keep the

29. H. A. Cushing, *History of the Transition from Provincial to Commonwealth Government in Massachusetts* (New York, 1896), p. 275; H. J. Laski, "Early History of the Corporation in England," *Harvard Law Review*, 30 (1916–1917), 562ff.

30. See Hutchinson, *Massachusetts-Bay*, I, 379. For the county in general, see st. 1811, ch. 75; *Revised Statutes*, ch. 14, sec. 5.

31. *Boston Gazette*, July 19, 1779.

32. St. 1785, ch. 75, sec. 7; st. 1786, ch. 67.

33. See, e.g., res. 1806, ch. 5; *Revised Statutes*, ch. 14, sec. 31.

same for the stated profits thereof." [34] Similarly, the county had
extensive power over bridges, operating them directly or requiring localities to do so — in either procedure financing the
projects by charges which ultimately rested upon the towns. In
at least one case a court took advantage of an alternative method
of financing, when Middlesex County appointed an agent for the
River Parker, with the power to charge tolls that would accumu-
late in a fund for repairs. [35] Through the county courts, too, the
state influenced another creature, the proprietors of common
fields, giving the tribunals jurisdiction over improvements of
many kinds either through the power to partition lands held in
common or through the right to appoint commissioners of
sewers who could assess damages and costs. [36]

Corollary to its efforts at aggrandizement, the Commonwealth
insisted, after 1780, that new corporations come into existence
only by a direct grant. Any future attempt by an association to
arrogate such powers exposed it to stinging charges of disloyalty.
The Cincinnati aroused distrust because they presumed to pass
laws, raise funds, and act as an "imperium in imperio." [37] Similarly, reprobation of popular societies and approval by Massachusetts writers of the conviction of the Philadelphia journeymen rested on the grounds that they constituted themselves into
"communities, enacting by-laws, and sanctioning them by the
severe penalties of ignominy and ruin" without the approbation
of government. Unincorporated bodies of all kinds having no
legal means of enforcing their by-laws often depended upon
secrecy for sanctions and were thus further objectionable. [38]

Hostility to the use of the power to govern by unauthorized
associations reflected a consciousness of the value of the right to
mark out a sphere for regulation, to make rules, to coerce and
tax members, and to exclude outsiders, and, above all, reflected
the determination by the state to reserve these privileges for
approved bodies working toward approved ends. Liquidation of
royal authority had removed the fear of possible restrictions on
the grant of charters; petitioners would now address not "an

34. St. 1796, ch. 42.
35. See, e.g., st. 1792, ch. 59; st. 1794, ch. 30; st. 1797, ch. 47.
36. See st. 1783, ch. 41; st. 1795, ch. 62; st. 1822, ch. 71.
37. *Salem Gazette*, Apr. 1, 1784; st. 1805, ch. 102.
38. See *Columbian Centinel*, Aug. 27, Sept. 3, 1796; *Monthly Anthology and
Boston Review*, 3 (1806), 609, 610; the regulations of the Newburyport Marine
Society, *Province Acts, 1769–80*, pp. 823ff. Walter Austin, *William Austin* (Boston,
1925), pp. 20, 21; Oscar and Mary Handlin, *The Dimensions of Liberty* (Cambridge, 1961), pp. 115ff.

enthroned Tyrany" but "a Government consisting of Men, who are in such stations & private walks of Life, as will enable them to judge of our feelings." [39]

At the same time, the Revolution had increased the wants the Commonwealth could not directly satisfy. Financial difficulties prevented the government from doing what was expected of it at the very time when it became the instrument for the realization of restless ambitions. Incorporation offered a ready alternative, for, as Governor Gore pointed out, Europe's history and America's experience proved that state assistance in every sphere "may be more advantageously applied, through societies established under the countenance of government, than in any other way." [40] While employing the techniques of bounty, franchise, and inspection and utilizing the old corporations, Massachusetts also launched a great variety of new bodies to do what had to be done.

In 1781 the Commonwealth chartered the Massachusetts Medical Society to regulate and encourage a desirable and worthy, but suffering, profession. Depreciated revolutionary currency had worked great hardships on Bay State physicians as on all professional men. During the war the doctors of Boston, for their own protection and for the maintenance of economic standards, had met as a club in the Green Dragon Tavern to fix fees payable only in hard money. Incorporation put sanctions behind such activities. The society received the sole right to license a limited number of practitioners. Subsequent acts regulated examinations and assessed fines upon its officers if they were tardy or unwilling to administer the tests, but the essential monopoly of the group over the practice of medicine remained unchallenged for more than twenty years.[41]

Financial exigencies that barred direct aid also drove the state to seek indirect channels for assistance to agriculture. Massachusetts always recognized the importance of farming and its versatile, if paradoxical, utility in developing both self-sufficiency and products for export. When the Commonwealth established the American Academy of Arts and Sciences, it hoped to create

39. Charlestown Petition (1785), MA, 1784, ch. 53.
40. *Boston Patriot*, June 10, 1809.
41. "Dr. Ephraim Eliot's Account of the Physicians of Boston," *Mass. Hist. Soc. Proceedings*, VII (1863), 181; st. 1781, ch. 15; st. 1788, ch. 49; st. 1802, ch. 123; *Revised Statutes*, ch. 22, secs. 1, 5, 6; S. A. Green, *History of Medicine in Massachusetts* (Boston, 1881), pp. 5–11, 87ff; Richard H. Shryock, *Medical Licensing in America* (Baltimore, 1967), pp. 20ff.

a body that would find resources to aid all the arts, including agriculture.[42] But that society early diverted its attention to other concerns. Although the state's interest in the academy and in other literary and scientific societies continued through the second decade of the nineteenth century, the field was open for another group guided primarily by the interests of the husbandmen.[43] As early as 1786 James Swan ardently wished that the legislature would "grant a charter, or act of incorporation, to a number of persons who shall form a society for the promoting of agriculture and the manufactures." This, he believed, "would, undoubtedly . . . remove those obstacles in the way of encouraging them, which arise from the poverty of the State Treasury."[44] To meet the need, the General Court in 1792 incorporated the Society for Promoting Agriculture "to make experiment themselves and invite others thereto" by the offer of premiums.[45]

To achieve the ends delegated to them, these bodies, like the towns and the common fields, had the power to levy assessments on their members. But it was at once clear that problems would arise in the case of expensive projects. Whether the state could or could not force an unwelcome task upon a body of individuals as a corporation was soon brought to the test of law.[46] Yet the legal right, even were it established, would be worth little. Experience with town road building had shown that to force the autonomous association to tax itself was difficult and ineffective, with results niggardly. There was little hope that these weak reeds would support vast projects commensurate with the Commonwealth's ambitions.

When neither the central government nor any extant body politic was willing or able to execute a desirable but costly function, the state held out to a new corporation inducements in the shape of a promise of profits. Such a promise became credible and attractive if fortified by the grant of a valuable franchise. Tolls, lotteries, or monopolies, and the prestige that came from state sponsorship, underwrote the expectation of gain and acted as an enticement for which the members would tax themselves and manage the coveted enterprise efficiently.

42. [Swan], *National Arithmetick*, pp. 31–33.

43. *Boston Commercial Gazette*, Jan. 18, Feb. 8, 12, 1816.

44. [Swan], *National Arithmetick*, pp. 32–35, 43, 44.

45. MA, 1791, ch. 49; "First Annual Report, Board of Agriculture," *Senate Docs., 1854*, no. 7, pp. 10ff.

46. See Otto von Gierke, *Das deutsche Genossenschaftsrecht* (Berlin, 1868–1913), III, 460.

The incentive to make money through a franchise in return for a valuable service was, of course, also extended to individuals and to noncorporate groups. The coercive power of assessment, however, gave the corporation a more efficient fund-raising mechanism; and the usefulness of connecting corporateness with the grant of a monopoly or some other special privilege was already known from European models tied to the state, either as agencies, as instruments for raising money, or through partnership with the king.[47]

Here lay the opportunity for the new merchants, in whose hands a surplus of capital accumulated as the Revolution drew to a close. A contracting public debt in the next three decades added to available funds and prepared these men, for a consideration, to assume the burdens of the Commonwealth. Government sponsorship would lend the newcomers, insecure and unsure of their position, the prestige of participants in enterprises operating not only for personal but also for communal ends. In the name of Massachusetts could come privileges that would underwrite risky ventures and guarantee profits in the hazardous course of postrevolutionary business.[48]

Between 1784 and 1789 the state granted charters for five significant corporations. Small coteries of merchants centering around Thomas Russell and George Cabot used the device to further one enterprise in banking, three in transportation, and one in manufacturing. Special considerations, in each case, gave grounds for an argument that the charter would help both those who received it and the whole Commonwealth.

To Russell and Cabot, incorporation thus seemed the key to the solution of the fiscal problems of Massachusetts. A chartered bank, they anticipated, would finally bring order to a distressed currency and also be advantageous to its promoters.

Emission by the state government had proved a miserable failure, and the fate of the continental was not more calculated to lend confidence in the ability of the United States directly to maintain a sound circulating medium. On the other hand, many like John Adams hesitated to give private banks the right of issuing notes, with all the economic power attached to it. Nor was there hope in the alternative of bullionism; the scarcity of specie, a consequence of the character of Massachusetts trade, and the commonly accepted idea that a fixed fund was needed for commerce closed that road of escape. But whatever the theory or immediate facts, few failed to recognize that money was merely a representation of property and that a paper currency properly managed was useful and desirable. As early as 1776 there were demands that the state create "a bank of paper money." [49]

The Commonwealth's first step was an outgrowth of continental action. Congress, upon which had rested the ultimate responsibility for the conduct of the war and for revolutionary finance, had encouraged a voluntary association in Philadelphia to raise funds in a "bank" for supplying rations to the army and in 1782 had incorporated it as the Bank of North America.[50] Although Massachusetts representatives had been suspicious at first, the state recognized the institution, endowed it with a monopoly of banking business in the Commonwealth for the duration of the war, and made its notes receivable for taxes.[51]

The progress of the company aroused great interest. But the end of the war jeopardized its status; Pennsylvania repealed the charter, and the monopoly provision of the Massachusetts law expired. To replace the Philadelphia firm, to create an agency that would issue a secure currency, and to keep at home the rich proceeds of local banking, the General Court in 1784 chartered the Massachusetts Bank.[52]

The title was significant. This was a state bank like the Bank of England or the Bank of Scotland, or the Bank of North America, and it was actually referred to as "the State Bank." [53] Like its predecessors, it enjoyed the right to issue notes that carried the prestigious Commonwealth name and bore the Common-

49. See Thomas Weston, *History of the Town of Middleboro, Massachusetts* (Boston, 1906), p. 578; W. I. Budington, *History of the First Church, Charlestown* (Boston, 1845), pp. 244, 245; John Adams, *Works*, IX, 638; [William Manning], "Some Proposals for Making Restitution to the Original Creditors" (MS, Houghton Library, Harvard University), pp. 10, 11; [Swan], *National Arithmetick*, p. 27; Henry Knox in *Kennebec Gazette*, March 17, 1803; James Sullivan, *Path to Riches* (Boston, 1792), pp. 10–14.

50. See Gerry to Morris, June 11, 1780, Schuyler to Washington, June 18, 1780, *Letters of Members of the Continental Congress*, ed. E. C. Burnett (Washington, D.C., 1921–1936), V, 205, 224, 235; Lawrence Lewis, *History of the Bank of North America* (Philadelphia, 1882), pp. 44–73.

51. St. 1782, ch. 17; res. 1782, ch. 127; J. B. Felt, *Historical Account of Massachusetts Currency* (Boston, 1839), pp. 193ff.

52. See *Salem Gazette*, July 31, 1783; st. 1783, ch. 25; M. H. Foulds, "Massachusetts Bank, 1784–1865," *Jour. of Econ. and Bus. Hist.*, 2 (1929–1930), 256ff.

53. See Gore to King, Aug. 7, 1791, C. R. King, *Rufus King* (New York, 1894–1900), I, 401.

wealth seal. The government protected the bank's currency as it did its own coins, punishing counterfeiters with confiscation of property, confinement in the pillory, and loss of civil rights.[54] The corporation was fiscal agent for Massachusetts, holding its deposits and making loans to it. Above all, this was the only chartered bank, and, while the loosely worded act establishing it contained no explicit provision to that effect, the precedent of previous institutions of the same type warranted the deduction that it would remain alone in the field.[55]

The investors naturally expected to profit from their privileged position. But "the Interference of the Legislature" was "cheerfully afforded" because, in the words of the petitioners, the bank would be "beneficial to the Public in general" by maintaining the legal rate of interest, setting standards of punctuality and credit, and supplying a place of safe deposit. It would help Massachusetts just as the Bank of North America had helped Pennsylvania.[56]

The Commonwealth's concern with an impasse in the improvement of transportation, a duty hitherto placed upon the towns, quickened the creation of three other corporations. Bridges, extremely expensive yet indispensable in carrying a growing traffic, were most burdensome. The obligation to build and maintain was clearly incumbent upon communities which still reeled from the shock of oppressive revolutionary debts and taxes. Additional charges were repugnant and, where possible, evaded. Coercion rarely brought results, and occasional assistance from lotteries failed to prime aggressive action.[57]

When the river lay between two towns, the task of allocating expense, which often seemed insoluble, might defer any expenditure at all. Yarmouth and Dennis wrangled for years over a span for the Bass River, resorting to one expedient of delay after another. And then should not adjacent towns, not bordering the stream but benefiting by the crossing, bear the cost as well?[58]

54. St. 1783, ch. 53. See also st. 1786, ch. 15; res. 1790, ch. 164J; N. S. B. Gras, *Massachusetts First National Bank of Boston, 1784–1934* (Cambridge, Mass., 1937), p. 85.

55. See Robert Rantoul, Jr., *Memoirs, Speeches and Writings* (Boston, 1854), p. 527; also A. M. Andreadës, *History of the Bank of England* (London, 1909), pp. 83, 123; Scott, *English, Scottish and Irish Joint-Stock Companies to 1720*, III, 253ff; W. S. Holdsworth, *History of English Law* (London, 1903–1938), VIII, 189.

56. MA, 1783, ch. 25, petition of William Phillips *et al.*; res. 1787, ch. 91M.

57. See, e.g., res. 1810, ch. 135.

58. See C. F. Swift, *History of Old Yarmouth* (Yarmouth Port, 1884), pp. 180, 186, 249, 251. For other examples see as follows: Newton and the Great Bridge

The strengthened county might discipline the localities, might even act directly. But that agency too lacked funds. Whatever the existing means of effecting the improvement, at root was the inescapable fact that this unwelcome load would ultimately fall upon the taxpayers. Although expenditures were unpalatable, the prospect of transforming many a town into a bustling metropolis was nevertheless exciting. The alternative was to grant enterprisers the right to collect tolls in return for building the bridges. Such franchises would stimulate internal trade without the use of public funds, and the tolls would tax only the users.

Three great rivers between the capital and the New Hampshire line obstructed the flow of traffic by land. The crossing of the Charles, the Mystic, and the Merrimack was a requisite and precedent condition to any serious attempt by the Commonwealth to build a home market and tap the source of goods for its commerce. Rival towns eager for these facilities rallied to the cause of rival groups of capitalists led by Russell and Cabot in the struggle for control of this line of travel.

For the crucial span across the Charles, the syphon through which all northern traffic into Boston would flow, the Cabots sponsored a route via Lechmere's Point, Cambridge, while Russell proposed one via Charlestown. With the support of Medford, Charlestown, and Boston, Russell's Charles River Bridge corporation, following the course of the existing ferry, won out in 1785. Against those who opposed any structure that might impede navigation, the favored communities argued that the bridge would "promote the general Accommodation of the Public," help the towns' development, and at the same time assist them to "pay the heavy Debts . . . incurr'd the last War." [59]

At the petition of Malden, which sought an improved outlet to markets and which urged the grant of adequate inducements to the investors, the legislature set up the Malden Bridge over the Mystic River in 1787. During the same year the Cabot group secured the incorporation for seven decades of the Essex Bridge from Salem to Beverly with the support of North Shore towns like Manchester, which pressed the measure in the interests of the widows who "from a train of misfortunes, during the late

over the Charles at Cambridge, st. 1780, ch. 41; Concord and Lincoln, st. 1783, ch. 20; Weston and Waltham, *Weston Records* (Boston, 1893), pp. 359, 395, 506ff.

59. MA, 1784, ch. 53, petitions of Charlestown, Boston, Cambridge, Medford, and of Cabot. The early history of these bridges emerged in the famous Charles River bridge case (1829), 7 Pickering 377, 378.

War, too melancholy to relate" earned their livelihood by working up materials procured across the river in Salem. In both cases the places which had been passed by fought the projects, but both opponents and sponsors reasoned in terms of "general utility to the good people of the Commonwealth *at large*." [60] In each case, the charter and franchise were suitable encouragement for a public association working for the general good and, incidentally, for its own.[61]

A substantial addition to the patronage of these bridges, it was hoped, would come from the carriage of the products of fresh industries nurtured and guided by the state. In the New World, manufacturing had always borne a public aspect from the necessity of utilizing mill sites for power. The demands of a frontier society had emphasized the importance of the production of finished goods and in the colonial period had already stimulated government interest. Such enterprises then seemed normally to partake of a social, almost charitable, nature; the will of Thomas Hancock, for instance, had left a bequest of £200 to help develop better methods in the linen factory in Boston. In addition, the desire for autarchy in the struggle with the former mother country during the Revolution and after endowed manufacturing with a patriotic quality and again stressed its public character. As late as 1799, the importation by Benjamin Austin, Jr., of English ropemaking apparatus occasioned considerable adverse comment.[62]

Finally, the postrevolutionary economy of the state placed industry, progressing enormously, in a crucial position. By 1789, the Commonwealth made 1,000 dozens of wool and cotton cards a month, and the town of Lynn alone turned out 170,000 pairs of women's shoes a year. In addition, the production of sailcloth, paper hangings, and glass made tentative beginnings.[63] These

60. MA, 1786, ch. 69, petitions of Chelsea and Medford; MA, 1787, ch. 27, petition of Manchester.

61. MA, 1787, ch. 27; Lee-Cabot Papers (MSS, MHS), Jan. 8, 1788; K. W. Porter, *Jacksons and the Lees* (Cambridge, Mass., 1937), I, 468; H. C. Lodge, *Life and Letters of George Cabot* (Boston, 1877), p. 13; Edward Gray, *William Gray of Salem* (Boston, 1914), p. 25.

62. See res. 1785, ch. 26F; A. M. Schlesinger, *Colonial Merchants and the American Revolution* (New York, 1918), pp. 65, 109, 123; Samuel Rezneck, "Rise and Early Development of Industrial Consciousness in the United States," *Jour. of Econ. and Bus. Hist.*, 4 (1932), 786ff; W. V. Wells, *Life and Public Services of Samuel Adams* (Boston, 1865), I, 417ff; C. M. Andrews, "Boston Merchants and the Non-Importation Movement," *Col. Soc. Mass. Publications*, XIX (1917), 197ff; *Russell's Gazette*, Mar. 11, 1799.

63. See Bowdoin to Temple, Oct. 10, 1789, *Mass. Hist. Soc. Colls.*, 7 ser., VI

were significant in the local markets, but potentially even more significant in the foreign. The merchants of Massachusetts, struggling to find a new place in the commercial world and increasingly aware of their exposed position in competition with Europeans, hoped to develop an industrial hinterland to supply the exports that failed to come from the meager agricultural back country. To overcome the handicaps resulting from political assistance to European manufacturers, they demanded that "new manufactories be erected, and fostered by the . . . government." Premiums, franchises, bounties, and inspection laws were helpful. But special corporations, similar to the successful English ones administering these aids, would furnish more unified direction and control and result in an ever increasing volume of commodities.[64]

Cabot's Beverly associates saw opportunities in the expansion of population and of agriculture for stimulating the manufacture of cotton, silk, hemp, flax, and wool. New processes, they thought, once introduced, would spread generally to the benefit of the state as a whole. In return for the expense of innovation they requested in 1788 "some peculiar favors to the first Adventurers" through incorporation, with such immunities and benefits as the legislature might consider necessary.[65]

Just what assistance the promoters had in mind was not clear. To Brissot, who knew them, it seemed they asked for a *privilège*, which implied some measure of exclusiveness.[66] The charter, however, was not explicit in the matter, although it gave the corporation the power to levy fines up to £50, an unusually high sum, and the right to label its products with the corporate seal backed by the prestige of the state's name. In the light of such English precedents as the Winchelsea Cambrick and Lawn Company, and of the existing condition of household industry, it may be surmised that the merchants connected with the Beverly Company planned some scheme to control local production in

(1907), 195; J. Q. to J. Adams, Oct. 19, 1790, J. Q. Adams, *Writings* (New York, 1913–1917), I, 62; W. B. Weeden, *Economic and Social History of New England* (Boston, 1891), II, 855.

64. Samuel Deane, *A Sermon Preached before . . . Samuel Adams . . . May 28th, 1794* (Boston, 1794), p. 25; "A Friend to Commerce," *Independent Chronicle*, June 2, 1785.

65. MA, 1788, ch. 43. See also W. T. Davis, *New England States* (Boston, 1897), I, 119, 120. W. E. Rappard, *Les Corporations d'affaires au Massachusetts* (Paris, 1908), pp. 20ff.

66. J. P. Brissot de Warville, *Nouveau voyage dans les Etats-Unis* (Paris, 1791), II, 310. For the meaning of *privilège* to a Frenchman, see Cole, *Colbert*, II, 135.

the interests of their foreign markets. Certainly they hoped that their gains would come more from the impetus to manufactures that would create an exportable surplus than from direct profits on products made to sell close to cost. At any rate, the Commonwealth stood behind them, making up a slight loss after four years of operation by a gift of land and a lottery.[67]

In this first decade the Commonwealth had thus set to unfamiliar service a versatile and trusty form. The forces for change implicit in the economic condition of a state emerging from an attenuating war dictated the resort to the corporation. That reaction was not far different from the response of European governments under similar circumstances — Elizabeth's England earlier, liberated Prussia later.[68] But, almost at once, the nature of the Massachusetts polity imposed variations that would gradually transform the essential character of the technique and its usefulness to the state.

67. Res. 1790, ch. 96. See also R. S. Rantoul, "First Cotton Mill in America," *Essex Inst. Hist. Colls.*, XXXIII (1897), 1ff.; Cabot to Hamilton, Sept. 6, 1791, Alexander Hamilton, *Industrial and Commercial Correspondence*, ed. A. H. Cole (Chicago, 1928), pp. 61–64; Lodge, *George Cabot*, pp. 45, 46; Anderson, *Origin of Commerce*, II, 548.

68. See, e.g., Kurt Bösselmann, *Die Entwicklung des deutsche Aktienwesen im 19.Jahrhundert* (Berlin, 1939), pp. 12ff; Karl Lehmann, *Die geschichtliche Entwicklung des Aktienrechts bis zum Code de Commerce* (Berlin, 1895), pp. 5ff; Davis, *Corporations*, I, 24ff.

5 | Commonwealth and Corporation

The public purpose which justified extension of government powers to a bank, to bridges, and to a factory soon comprehended a wide and ever widening circle of enterprises. The Commonwealth's concern with the entire productive system, its solicitude for the welfare of many diverse activities, all interdependent and all adding to the strength of Massachusetts, quickly put the corporate form to the use of many new ventures. The political balance deflated any notion of keeping the device exclusive; the expansive thinking, the excited spirits of the young state, brooked no casual denial. Charters in steadily mounting volume clothed with living tissues the skeletal hopes for an economy to serve the common interest.

The promoters of all manner of projects saw in the new examples opportunities for achieving ends of their own as agencies of the state. The lumbermen who had, without success, attempted to control the flow of logs at the head of tide on the Androscoggin River, in 1788 asked for and secured incorporation as a "Body Pollitick, with all the Power & Authourity that other Bodies Pollitick do Enjoy," on the grounds that thereby "the Publick as well as private may bee greatly favoured." The town of Topsham, in support of the petition, pointed out that the only regular way to assure the benefits of the boom to those who used the river was "to apply to Coart for a bill of Incorporation," and annexed at the same time a schedule of rates it thought proper.[1]

1. MA, 1788, ch. 60, petition of Topsham. A similar boom on the Merrimack was incorporated a year later (cf. st. 1789, ch. 41).

Soon many small communal organizations, formed to lay pipes for carrying water, sought charters as aqueduct companies. They defended their requests for franchises to open roads and cross the lands of others by the utility of the service and the promise of free help to towns in fighting fires. The seventeen incorporated in all parts of the state between 1795 and 1798 took as models the proprietors of common fields, as did the general act of 1799 which simplified the chartering process. These bodies sometimes involved just four or five neighbors and sometimes organized such large enterprises as the Salem & Danvers and the Jamaica Plain aqueducts. But central to all was the grant of power to assess and to govern their members.[2]

After the precedent set by the Charles River and Essex bridges, a general act of 1787 gave the operators of existing private ways and bridges some powers of assessment for the purpose of making repairs.[3] But this limited authority did not satisfy those who looked enviously upon the broad prerogatives of the chartered spans. The immense profits from such structures accelerated demands for new ones. Dividends were high and investors often gained by connection with the enterprises; Lee and Cabot sold the timber for building the Essex, and the sponsors of the South Boston Bridge of 1804 benefited from the rise in real-estate values.[4] Competition for likely sites, dissatisfaction with existing ferries, and the prospect of indirect advantages from the stimulus to trade and the integration of the internal market led to twenty-three incorporations between 1792 and 1800. Nor did the process slacken after the turn of the century.[5]

Charters for bridges which ultimately cost as much as $100,000

2. See, e.g., st. 1795, ch. 70; st. 1796, ch. 76; st. 1797, ch. 73; MA, 1798, ch. 10; st. 1798, chs. 3, 21, 27; also MA, Senate, 2338, 2338/1; res. 1797, ch. 74aJ. See also Charles Shaw, *Topographical and Historical Description of Boston* (Boston, 1817), p. 300; G. W. Chase, *History of Haverhill* (Haverhill, 1861), p. 471; "History of Salem and Danvers Aqueduct," *Essex Inst. Hist. Colls.*, II (1860), 106ff; Edward Gray, *William Gray of Salem* (Boston, 1914), p. 25.

3. St. 1787, ch. 17, extended by st. 1801, ch. 80; *Revised Statutes of the Commonwealth of Massachusetts* (Boston, 1836), ch. 25, secs. 34–43.

4. See MA, Senate, 3326/1–16; "Building of the Essex Bridge," *Essex Inst. Hist. Colls.*, XXX (1893), 93, 94; K. W. Porter, *Jacksons and the Lees* (Cambridge, Mass., 1937), I, 466, 467; Lee-Cabot Papers (MSS, MHS), Oct. 1788; *Boston Gazette*, Jan. 9, 1804; Helen Reisinger, "Christopher Gore" (unpub. diss. Radcliffe College, 1942), pp. 301–303.

5. St. 1791, chs. 35, 56; st. 1792, chs. 52, 63, 71; st. 1793, chs. 20, 35, 52, 69; st. 1794, chs. 3, 32, 33; st. 1795, chs. 36, 63; st. 1796, chs. 19, 24, 68, 74, 81 (also st. 1799, ch. 72); st. 1797, chs. 17 (also st. 1811, ch. 155), 19, 48, 49 (also st. 1804, ch. 29); st. 1800, chs. 40, 53; st. 1801, ch. 33; st. 1807, ch. 49. See also *Eastern Herald*, Apr. 5, 1802; Chase, *Haverhill*, p. 459.

or as little as $5,000 all contained the essential power to levy assessments and the lucrative franchise to take toll. In return the legislature imposed well-defined conditions: completion in a limited period and construction in accordance with specified plans, the slightest change in which needed the consent of the General Court. All the corporations except those chartered in 1794 received a limited life term after which their spans were to revert to the Commonwealth, which also retained the right to lower tolls after a number of years, usually forty. The patron state, having set up these rules, was, however, indulgent in administration. When the original tolls seemed insufficient to sustain dividends, it often made gifts of land, raised the rates, extended the building time and the duration of the franchise, modified onerous obligations, and permitted the laying out of feeder roads.[6]

The urge for improvement also led to considerable canal building. The inland communities valued better water communications to bring farmers nearer markets and to facilitate transportation of lumber. Merchants everywhere sought easier navigation on the great interstate rivers, and they looked to the experience of the Connecticut, which during the Revolution had become a vital internal artery, linking the interior of Massachusetts, New Hampshire, and Vermont with the port of Northampton and indirectly with Boston. In Newburyport and Boston elaborate plans aimed to convert the Merrimack to the service of northeastern New England; elsewhere less ambitious schemes envisioned similar benefits from turning sluggish streams into much traveled channels of trade.[7]

To stimulate such developments, towns gave privileges of many kinds to individuals who undertook to dig small canals, and occasionally they acted themselves, as Eastham did in 1804. But all the factors which kept local agencies from bridge building operated even more heavily in this new sphere.[8]

A flurry of activity between 1791 and 1797 created twelve

---

6. See, e.g., MA, 1792, chs. 21, 35; st. 1795, chs. 44, 49, 64, 79; st. 1796, ch. 36; st. 1798, chs. 30, 39, 40; st. 1799, chs. 16, 22, 40, 74; MA, 1799, ch. 54; st. 1801, chs. 46, 52, 63; st. 1803, ch. 18; st. 1806, ch. 57; st. 1808, ch. 33; res. 1809, ch. 300; st. 1810, ch. 107; st. 1812, ch. 1; res. 1813, ch. 3; st. 1815, ch. 63; st. 1824, chs. 15, 29.

7. [James Swan], *National Arithmetick* (Boston, 1786), p. 19; MA, 1791, ch. 32; MA, 1792, chs. 11, 13. See also Henshaw to Sedgwick, June 13, 1798, Theodore Sedgwick Papers (MS, MHS), III, 465; Loammi Baldwin, *Thoughts on the Study of Political Economy* (Cambridge, Mass., 1809), pp. 20ff.

8. See Shebnah Rich, *Truro — Cape Cod* (Boston, 1883), p. 200; Enoch Pratt, *Comprehensive History . . . of Eastham, Wellfleet and Orleans* (Yarmouth, 1844), pp. 86, 87, 93.

canal corporations to execute these tasks. The charters regulated the constitutional first meeting and granted the power to make by-laws and to levy fines. They also bestowed the privilege of taking land with damages assessed as on highways, but under exceptionally liberal conditions. Wide discretion in choosing routes, vagueness about responsibility for flowing adjacent lands, and the requirement that the aggrieved bring all suits within a year freed these companies from heavy burdens. Tolls were collectible for a specified period and were conditioned upon completion of the projects in a stated number of years.[9]

Incorporation was easy to come at when it seemed to serve the interests of Massachusetts, but only in such cases. The legislature opposed projects that operated to the advantage of out-of-state ports, refusing, for instance, to charter John Brown's Blackstone Canal in 1796 lest it draw trade to Providence.[10]

Almost always unprofitable, the canal ventures shortly beset the government with requests for higher and more permanent tolls, for permission to construct tributaries and to hold mill seats, for longer building time, for alterations in route, for grants of Maine land, of tax exemptions, and of lotteries, and for other privileges.[11] The Commonwealth willingly conceded help which cost it nothing directly but refused to assume any substantial burden that might raise the tax rate. Occasionally, therefore, worthy designs never went beyond the blueprint; Knox's canal to the Hudson, the Cape Cod Canal proposed by the legislature in 1776 and in 1791, and that planned in 1802 from Boston to the Connecticut River to be paid for by a lottery got nowhere.[12] Often limited state aid failed to rescue those finally built. Some like the Middlesex languished for a long time; charges too high for the farmers who shipped produce to Boston kept that corporation from prospering until the building of Lowell gave it a new kind of traffic.[13]

9. See MA, 1795, ch. 23; st. 1791, ch. 7; st. 1792, chs. 11, 13; st. 1793, ch. 21; see also *House Docs., 1860*, no. 100, pp. 21–26; M. T. Parker, *Lowell* (New York, 1940), pp. 61, 62. The Roxbury Canal alone was free of toll (st. 1795, ch. 65).

10. Israel Plummer, "History of the Blackstone Canal," *Colls. Worc. Soc.*, I (1888), 41.

11. See st. 1792, chs. 39, 67; st. 1793, ch. 13; st. 1794, ch. 67; st. 1795, ch. 27; st. 1797, ch. 6; st. 1798, ch. 16; st. 1799, chs. 35, 58; st. 1801, ch. 48; st. 1802, ch. 98; st. 1803, chs. 102, 126; st. 1804, chs. 79, 98; st. 1808, ch. 2; st. 1809, ch. 19; st. 1810, ch. 53; st. 1811, ch. 111; st. 1812, chs. 113, 115; st. 1814, ch. 100; st. 1817, ch. 152, sec. 12; MA, Senate, 4831, 4831/1.

12. See st. 1817, ch. 152; st. 1823, ch. 75; Frederick Freeman, *History of Cape Cod* (Boston, 1869), I, 493; *Boston Gazette*, Mar. 11, 1802.

13. See "Q," *Boston Commercial Gazette*, Mar. 24, 1825; Christopher Roberts, *Middlesex Canal* (Cambridge, Mass., 1938). For political influence in canal legis-

That the Commonwealth would stand by and allow misfortune to fall upon the canals was not yet apparent by the turn of the century. Failure in one project merely diverted energies to others; it did not dampen enthusiasm for internal improvements.

Efforts to speed communications by land ran parallel to those to develop the waterways. On the eve of the Revolution, William Goddard had attempted to set up a regular post between the leading commercial towns, and the exigencies of war had underlined the necessity for better communications.[14] Less than a year after peace, coaches plied the route from the Hub to New York via Worcester, Hartford, and New Haven. Travel between New Haven and Boston, served by two stages in 1786, required fully twenty by 1794. Localities became aware of the dignity and practical importance of becoming stations on the through lines and struggled over the location of post roads by the federal government.[15] As Connecticut and Rhode Island took steps "with an intent to turn the western Travel that way," and as New York cut into the trade of Vermont, it became a matter of self-protection for Massachusetts to better her roads. Everywhere arose the clamor for more suitable highways.[16]

But serious obstacles hindered the transformation of twisting backwoods paths into wide, smooth thoroughfares. Road building had always been a function of the towns, which in theory approved the benefits but in practice did little to attain them. The road tax was particularly onerous and was often paid in labor — inefficient and halfhearted labor. It was one thing to vote assessments in town meeting and another to get farmers to sweat out their shares. Yet as late as 1826 the attempt in some places to adopt the alternative, a money tax, was bitterly and successfully resisted. As it was, existing highways required con-

lation see Henshaw and Dwight to Sedgwick, Jan. 7, 1793, March 18, Dec. 13, 1794, Sedgwick Papers, II, 365, 499, 643.

14. See *Massachusetts Spy*, Mar. 17, 24, 1774.

15. See Andrews, Ely, Dwight to Sedgwick, Mar. 4, Dec. 26, 1794, Feb. 11, 1795, Sedgwick Papers, II, 481ff, 673, 771; *Columbian Centinel*, Aug. 12, 1795, June 24, 1797; B. T. Hill, "Beginnings of the Boston and Worcester Railroad," *Colls. Worc. Soc.*, XVII (1901), 532–534; Henry Wansey, *Journal of an Excursion to the United States* (Salisbury, 1796), pp. 71ff.

16. MA, 1796, ch. 5, petition of Levi Pease *et al.*, Feb. 5, 1795; MA, 1798, ch. 85; MA, 1799, ch. 54, petition of Elisha Murdock, and the towns of Mendon, Holliston, Sherborn, and Boston; J. P. Brissot de Warville, *Nouveau voyage dans les Etats-Unis* (Paris, 1791), I, 164ff; Governor Adams' message, Jan. 19, 1795, *Acts and Resolves of 1795*, p. 616; *Columbian Centinel*, Oct. 21, 1797; Ames to Gore, Mar. 5, 1800, Fisher Ames, *Works* (Boston, 1854), I, 277; *Salem Gazette*, June 23, 1801.

tinual maintenance, and new ones, which inevitably involved not only immediate expenditure but the certainty of perpetual obligations, were exceedingly unpopular and grudgingly laid out. These charges absorbed every financial windfall and drove the hard-pressed communities to many expedients to shift the burden elsewhere.[17]

Under these circumstances roads which passed through several towns invariably engendered bitter quarrels over the allocation of expenses and led to frequent recourse to the cumbersome agency of the county court. But here too the mere existence of an administrative device solved no difficulties. The state could, if it wished, force action, no matter how offensive to independence and pocketbooks, but it had early learned that to try to draw cash out of empty purses was neither efficient nor salutary.

Generally unable to bear the expense directly, or to induce others to do the job, the towns therefore were eager to relinquish the task to bodies politic which would make the improvements in return for a toll. In the same financial situation as its subdivisions, Massachusetts freely granted charters for a purpose which it highly approved but could not directly finance.[18]

Stagecoach proprietors like Levi Pease and merchants like Henry Lee were prepared to furnish the necessary capital. The First Massachusetts Turnpike Corporation received a charter in 1796 to improve a circuitous and mountainous road between Palmer and Western, the expense of which "would be much greater than ought to be required of the said towns under their present circumstances." [19] Twelve other companies developed in the next five years, all in the west, all bearing the state's name, all espoused by towns exhilarated by the prospect of relief. Thirty more came into being between 1801 and 1806, and by then the advantages of the new form were also apparent to the

17. F. A. F., duc de La Rochefoucauld-Liancourt, *Voyage dans les Etats-Unis* (Paris, 1799), V, 189; Isaac Goodman, "History of Sterling," *Worc. Mag. and Hist. Jour.*, 2 (1826), 49; Pratt, *Eastham, Wellfleet, and Orleans*, p. 98; C. W. Jenkins, *Three Lectures on the Early History of . . . Falmouth* (Falmouth, 1889), p. 98; *Old Records of Fitchburgh* (Fitchburg, 1898–1913), I, 302, II, 49.

18. These arguments will be found in the memorials of towns supporting petitions for turnpikes (see MA, 1796, ch. 5, petition of Levi Pease, Feb. 5, 1795, and the towns of Ware, Palmer, Western, Wilbraham; MA, 1798, chs. 84, 85; MA, 1799, ch. 21, petition of Pelham, Hardwick, Holden; MA, 1799, ch. 48; MA, 1800, ch. 16). See also *Stockbridge Western Star*, Feb. 14, 1792; "A Farmer," *Columbian Centinel*, Jan. 27, 30, Feb. 3, 1796.

19. St. 1796, chs. 5, 31; st. 1798, ch. 48. See also O. W. Holmes, "Levi Pease," *Jour. of Econ. and Bus. Hist.*, 3 (1930–31), 241, 245, 257; Porter, *Jacksons and the Lees*, I, 468.

east. The Ipswich Turnpike from Beverly to Newburyport, the Boston and Worcester, and the half-million-dollar Newburyport Turnpike linked the major cities of the state, and in 1814 the Boston & Roxbury Mill Corporation embarked upon a grandiose scheme to build a pike on a dam across the Back Bay. Not without cause did the chief executive boast in 1809 that the state's roads were capable of commanding "an increasing travel for centuries yet to come." [20]

In return for the toll and the right to take land, to cross public roads, and to bridge streams, turnpike charters imposed a number of obligations. The enterprisers were to build within a limited period, with the location of gates and the width of the road specified in the act of incorporation and alterable only with the consent of the legislature. The corporation had to guarantee passage, subject to penalties for delays or defects in the road, and to allow churchgoers, militiamen, and farmers on their way to market to pass freely. The state could lower the tolls set forth in the charter after twenty years and could dissolve the corporation as soon as the body had earned its costs plus an average annual return of 12 to 15 per cent. The early acts put the settlement of disputes into the hands of the courts, the later ones, into those of ad hoc commissioners appointed by the governor.[21]

Few pikes profited. Dividends everywhere were low and the eastern superhighways early met financial difficulties. The Newburyport's attempt to save itself by edging into the hotel business only deepened its embarrassment. Gains here seemed to go primarily to the stagecoach companies, which contracted for their tolls at rates ruinously low for the road. To make matters worse, many companies had lightheartedly assumed the debilitating duty of maintaining bridges on their routes. Again calls for aid rose up to the legislature. Again the Commonwealth benignly smoothed the way by enacting special laws regulating passage, by permitting changes in route, in construction, and in the location of gates, by extending building time, by adjusting

20. *Patriotic Proceedings of the Legislature of Massachusetts, 1809* (Boston, 1809), p. 21; *Acts and Resolves of 1809*, pp. 236ff. See also st. 1814, ch. 39; st. 1796, chs. 72, 78; st. 1798, chs. 84, 85; William Bentley, *Diary* (Salem, 1905–1914), III, 71; E. B. Crane, "Boston and Worcester Turnpike," *Colls. Worc. Soc.*, XVII (1901), 585, 593; "Newburyport and Boston Turnpike," *Essex Inst. Hist. Colls.*, XLII (1906), 113, 115, 123.

21. See, e.g., st. 1799, ch. 71; st. 1801, chs. 51, 63; st. 1802, ch. 97; st. 1803, ch. 10; *Essex Inst. Hist. Colls.*, XLII (1906), 118, 123.

tolls, and by allowing the roads to abandon unprofitable sections.[22]

In internal improvements, incorporation spread rapidly and without serious conflict. Successive grants did not substantially derogate from the value of those already made; each new charter added a beneficent link that reinforced the chain of communication girdling the state.

However, in another field, banking, there were sharp clashes of interest which nevertheless failed to impede the diffusion of charters. Vociferous demands for a share in the privilege deadened the voices of those who questioned the public worth of multiplying these corporations.

The original Massachusetts Bank had received a mandate to act as issuing agent for the Commonwealth and through its notes to supply an element of order to a disordered currency. The withdrawal of state and ultimately of continental money settled the difficulties arising from revolutionary finance. But almost immediately a new problem revived the quest for a more fluid medium of exchange. Commerce after independence necessarily involved the export of specie, either to England for manufactures or in the operations of the triangular trades. Those short of cash could not see the necessity; they saw only the drain of precious metals. Some accused the English, others ascribed the losses to transactions with India and China. But whatever the immediate object of suspicion, dissatisfaction was ubiquitous. The threat of a pamphleteer in 1790 who preferred the mass bankruptcy of the mercantile community to the continued flow of specie from the state revealed widespread ill feeling against the "few men of grate Influence" who controlled the issue.[23]

The same shortages also created unrest within the marts of trade. Merchants countered the charge that foreign commerce drained away specie with the complaint that the supply of precious metals available for overseas operations was insufficient. This dearth, they claimed, limited their buying abroad "because

22. St. 1797, chs. 8, 66; st. 1798, ch. 22; st. 1799, ch. 27; st. 1800, chs. 3, 4, 30, 34, 35, 48, 56; st. 1801, chs. 63, 72; st. 1802, ch. 66; st. 1803, chs. 13, 23, 90; st. 1804, chs. 36, 72, 96; res. 1806, ch. 16; st. 1810, chs. 30, 39; st. 1811, ch. 68; st. 1813, ch. 41; st. 1814, ch. 37; st. 1815, chs. 20, 113; st. 1817, chs. 21, 31; st. 1818, ch. 73; st. 1819, chs. 34, 63; st. 1820, ch. 26; st. 1822, ch. 67; st. 1823, chs. 54, 109.

23. See, e.g., *Columbian Centinel*, Feb. 14, 1795; [James Bowdoin], *Opinions Respecting the Commercial Intercourse between the United States . . . and the Dominions* (Boston, 1797), p. 33; [William Manning], "Some Proposals for Making Restitution to the Original Creditors" (MS, Houghton Library, Harvard University), pp. 21ff, 28ff; Robert Rantoul, Jr., *Memoirs* (Boston, 1854), pp. 528ff.

We are desirous of having some Cash come home at all events" to lay in a supply for subsequent voyages. They eagerly accepted the idea, later formalized by the theorists, that bank money released hard money for export.[24]

The new supplies did not come from the Massachusetts Bank. The early operations of that institution failed to earn it the countenance of the state at large or of the merchants of Boston. The forcible reduction in the number of stockholders the very year after incorporation left behind an ulcerating fear that monopoly position and control over the currency, originally bestowed for public ends, would serve only the selfish interests of a few. The speculative panic of 1791 fostered other doubts concerning the adequacy and impartiality of the bank's service and led influential men to challenge its freedom. A law of March 1792 limited obligations to twice the capital held in specie, forbade the issue of notes in denominations of less than five dollars, and restricted speculation in stocks. James Sullivan, unappeased by the amendment, demanded repeal of the charter, or, to eliminate the privilege which made incorporation valuable, an issue based only on metal.[25]

Such attacks left unsolved the question of who would furnish a satisfactory circulating medium. Stephen Higginson and other traders, already flirting with the federal government for different kinds of help, saw the alternative in the Boston branch of the Bank of the United States. If that establishment kept in the Hub a reserve of hard money large enough to maintain confidence, the men around Higginson expected that the Massachusetts Bank, unable to compete, would "soon dwindle, and after a while fall through." [26]

But few would accept the notion of vesting control of the state's currency in an institution dominated from Philadelphia. The legislature, refusing to subscribe to its stock, insisted on "having a bank under their patronage & having a continuance of this badge of Sovereignty, the emission of money, & the interest

24. Instructions to Capt. Ellinwood, Mar. 20, 1787, Lee-Cabot Papers; *Boston Gazette*, Jan. 26, 1804; below, pp. 164ff.

25. St. 1791, ch. 65. See also *Stockbridge Western Star*, Mar. 6, May 1, 1792; James Sullivan, *Path to Riches* (Boston, 1792), pp. 54ff.

26. Higginson to Hamilton, Feb. 23, 1791, *Amer. Hist. Assoc. Annual Report, 1896*, I, 784; C. R. King, *Life and Correspondence of Rufus King* (New York, 1894–1900), I, 401; Reisinger, "Christopher Gore" (unpub. diss. Radcliffe College, 1942), pp. 294ff; J. O. Wettereau, "The Branches of the First Bank of the United States," *Tasks of Economic History* (December 1942), p. 74; J. T. Holdsworth, *First Bank of the United States* (Washington, D.C., 1910), p. 22.

of the Commonwealth & the Bank will be made to combine, that the pride and avarice of these two corporations may be gratified." [27]

There was constant talk of a new Massachusetts company, more pliable to the needs of the Commonwealth.[28] In June 1792 the General Court, dissatisfied with its old creature, set up another bank, the Union, to have headquarters in Boston and branches anywhere in the state. The act of incorporation avoided the pitfalls that had beset the Massachusetts Bank. Shares were low-priced with par between four and eight dollars, and one fifth of the funds were set aside for loans of from one hundred to a thousand dollars "wherein the Directors shall wholly and exclusively regard the agricultural interest." The state reserved the right to borrow at a favorable rate, forbade a directorate interlocking with that of any other corporation, and required rotation in office. As in the case of its predecessors, the Union's total liabilities were not to exceed twice its capital. To increase issue and to stimulate the confidence that came from actual participation, Massachusetts made the bank its depository, subscribed $200,000, and elected a proportional number of directors. The capital investment involved no outlay in cash; a loan at a rate of interest lower than the dividend rate fortuitously brought a profit into the public treasury through the transaction.[29]

Though the relation of bank and Commonwealth was close in the next ten years, the Union was unable to keep its favored position. It too failed to satisfy demands for credit and currency, neglecting to set up the branches contemplated in the charter. Failures after a wave of speculation in 1793 led to complaints that the new as well as the old institution abruptly called in loans and by impolitic measures drove business out of the state. Meanwhile merchants in other seaboard cities, aspiring to independence from Boston, staked out claims for chartered enterprises more sensitive to local needs. Eight new banks created between 1795 and 1803 were the outcome.[30]

27. Gore to King, June 13, Aug. 7, 1791, King, *Rufus King*, I, 399, 401; *Stockbridge Western Star*, June 21, July 5, 1791.

28. See, e.g., Sullivan, *Path to Riches*, pp. 56, 60ff.

29. See st. 1792, chs. 6, 50; "A Statement of Facts," MA, House, 5287. For loans see res. 1794, ch. 114M; for investment, res. 1795, ch. 25M; for origins, *Stockbridge Western Star*, Mar. 6, 1792.

30. J. Q. to J. Adams, Feb. 10, 1793, J. Q. Adams, *Writings* (New York, 1913–1917), I, 133; Bentley, *Diary*, II, 4, 6; *Columbian Centinel*, Apr. 18, 1795, Apr. 8, 1797; Gray, *William Gray*, p. 12; MA, 1799, ch. 4, petition of Jos. McLellan *et al.*

While the idea of a central bank for the entire state thus vanished, the Commonwealth still carefully allocated banking facilities, permitting only one institution in each town except Boston. The legislature remained reluctant to grant new charters, partly from fear that competition would lower the returns on the Commonwealth's own investment, mostly because it regarded such corporations not as business enterprises but as special agencies set up to create a currency. It rejected petitions for competing banks in towns already supplied. More important, to reaffirm the favored position of the houses it could not avoid chartering, it excluded unincorporated associations from the field and declared their notes void in 1799.[31]

Soon, however, the banks' exclusive position, even within their respective communities, disappeared. The supply of paper, as always gravitating to the seaboard, was still low, and loans were still hard to get, a circumstance particularly irritating to traders when the European war opened new opportunities. Nor were the country regions satisfied. In 1803 a Lenox farmer complained, "money Never was scarcer hear," and a legislative committee suspiciously investigated the affairs of the Union Bank to determine whether a due proportion of its loans was serving the agricultural community. Everywhere, mercantile and rural towns joined in inveighing against the lack of credit.[32]

Demands for more facilities seemed to most people prima-facie evidence of the need for more banks. The *National Aegis* declared, in an article described as "the soundest . . . on the subject," that "no injury has hitherto arisen from the increase of these institutions" and that a petition for incorporation was sufficient justification for granting it. Such arguments squeezed the existing firms into a quandary. They were unwilling to expand. The Union pointed out frankly in 1802, when the renewal of its charter was first discussed, that to add capital would lower the high rate of profits and force stockholders to share their position with newcomers.[33] Yet, once having refused to supply the new facilities themselves, the holders of privilege found it politically impossible to forestall multiplication. Thirteen years later a commentator recalled, "It was thought to be

31. St. 1799, ch. 32; MA, 1799, ch. 37; st. 1804, ch. 58; st. 1823, ch. 101; *Russell's Gazette*, Jan. 23, 1800; *Boston Gazette*, Mar. 3, 1803; Bentley, *Diary*, III, 74.
32. See Blossom to Hill, July 12, 1803, Willard Phillips Papers, 1769–1836 (MSS, MHS); Bentley, *Diary*, III, 71.
33. MA, House, 5287; see also *Columbian Informer*, July 1, 1802; *Salem Gazette*, June 18, 1802.

an unexpected measure that the Boston Bank should be granted; more so, that the New-England Bank should be granted; and yet more so, that the Manufacturers' and Mechanics' Bank should be granted: But these latter institutions were not opposed, because it would have seemed hard and invidious in preceding stockholders to oppose future incorporations." [34]

After 1803 the state granted bank charters more liberally, despite the advice of a few skeptics like the Adamses, father and son, ever dubious about the virtue of institutions that deluded "the many for the interest of a few." [35] Some incorporations went to farm areas, others to groups with artisan support, and still others to merchants. By 1812 more than a dozen new ones had come forth from the legislature.[36]

Peculiar disorders, consequences of the very dispersion of these institutions, failed to check the process. The notes of the country banks, following the routes of internal commerce, accumulated in Boston and seldom found their way home because of physical difficulties in redemption. The issuers, rarely pressed for payment, profited from a balance of exchange always in favor of the metropolis. But the Boston merchants who thrived from the trade in commodities suffered from the flow of the currency and often found their drawers glutted with paper difficult to redeem instead of with the specie which alone was valuable for their foreign dealings.[37] The provincial banks were poorly managed, lacked resources, and issued notes "not in proportion to their capital but to the utmost stretch of publick credulity." In addition, the circumstance that the directors everywhere were frequently the chief borrowers was unlikely to lead to caution in assuming risks.[38]

Anarchy in the currency followed as a matter of course.

34. *Boston Commercial Gazette*, Dec. 2, 1816. See also *Kennebec Gazette*, Mar. 17, 1803. For the special political considerations in the charter of the Boston Bank, see S. E. Morison, *Life and Letters of Harrison Gray Otis* (Boston, 1913), I, 260, 261.

35. See J. Adams to Sullivan, Wolcott, Vanderkamp, Rush, and Taylor, Sept. 17, 1789, June 21, 1799, Feb. 16, 1809, Aug. 28, 1811, Mar. 12, 1819, John Adams, *Works* (Boston, 1850–1856), VIII, 660, IX, 562, 608ff, 635ff, X, 375ff; J. Adams to Mrs. Adams, Jan. 9, 1793, *Letters of John Adams Addressed to His Wife*, ed. C. F. Adams (Boston, 1841), II, 117; J. Q. Adams, *Writings*, III, 10, 302ff.

36. See, e.g., J. T. Buckingham, *Annals of the Massachusetts Charitable Mechanic Association* (Boston, 1853), pp. 79, 130, 131.

37. See "A Merchant," *Boston Gazette*, Apr. 26, 1804; *ibid.*, Mar. 26, 1807; "Adventures of a Bank Note," *New-England Palladium*, Jan. 1, 1805.

38. See *Boston Patriot*, Sept. 6, 1809; *Monthly Anthology and Boston Review*, 7 (1809), 192, 193.

Money became not a guide but a snare for the unwary. The bills of each bank had their own market value and passed from hand to hand to the accompaniment of cautious consultations of cabalistic discount tables. Bewildered people, in town and in country, complained that they no longer "know what money to receive & what to reject, & debtors can purchase money which will embarass their creditors & the poor have their pay in money which will not answer their occasions." [39]

Massachusetts now confronted a problem it never satisfactorily solved, for multiplying banks to increase the supply also weakened control of the currency. General measures regulated the process of issue, ordered uniform printing to prevent counterfeiting, limited the volume of notes in terms of capital, prohibited loans to directors, ensured rotation in office, required periodic reports, and permitted inspection by legislative committees; but these hardly coped with the crux of the matter — the failure of the circulating medium to circulate and the consequent inability to test the value of notes by redemption. [40]

Remedies concocted for the specific disease sometimes soothed but never cured. An act of 1799 which forbade emission in denominations of less than five dollars by all but the Nantucket Bank, in order to stimulate redemption, merely created a serious shortage for everyday transactions and led to the circulation of larger bills at odd figures, of out-of-state currency, and of private scrip. [41] Ameliorating laws between 1805 and 1812 permitting limited issue of small notes and forbidding the circulation of foreign paper increased again the flood of bills to Boston. [42]

Other machinery, sanctioned by the state to restore the balance of country and city currencies, achieved no greater success. The Boston Exchange Office, chartered for that purpose, aimed to use its power of receiving deposits and making discounts to force

39. Bentley, *Diary*, III, 452–455.

40. See "Banquo," *Boston Patriot*, June 17, 1809. See also st. 1802, ch. 132; st. 1804, ch. 120; st. 1805, chs. 24, 111; st. 1808, ch. 99; st. 1812, ch. 140; *Columbian Centinel*, Feb. 8, 1797; *Repertory*, Feb. 4, Mar. 14, 18, 1806; Lieutenant-Governor Lincoln's address, Jan. 25, 1809, *Acts and Resolves of 1809*, p. 229. For grants to suppress counterfeiting see, e.g., res. 1809, ch. 308.

41. See st. 1799, ch. 32, sec. 3; st. 1801, ch. 71; also William Willis, *Journals of the Rev. Thomas Smith and the Rev. Samuel Deane* (Portland, 1849), p. 388; *Russell's Gazette*, Jan. 23, 1800; *Boston Gazette*, Mar. 14, 1803.

42. St. 1805, ch. 24; st. 1808, ch. 99, secs. 3, 4; st. 1809, ch. 38; st. 1812, ch. 56; extended to Maine by st. 1808, ch. 20. All notes for fractions of a dollar were forbidden by st. 1809, ch. 37. Proposals to put teeth into these measures and to prevent the flow of notes outside the county where they had been issued failed, however (MA, House, 6639). See also "Candidus," *Boston Gazette*, Jan. 16, 1804.

all banks to stand behind their bills. But its Sisyphean labors were in vain. The brokers who dealt in country notes countered its uphill thrust by encouraging a ruinous discount rate. Unscrupulous western firms, cynical about the feeble penalties, arbitrarily set limits and conditions to the redemption of their obligations. By 1807 the premium on Boston money reached 4 per cent, to the loss of the merchants compelled to accept depreciated notes in trade and of the Boston banks which saw their own paper driven out of circulation by the cheaper issue.[43]

Voluntary efforts could dam the flood no more than legislation could limit the damage it caused. When the collapse of Andrew Dexter's scheme to corner the state's circulating medium dragged down the Berkshire and Bangor banks in 1809, a tremor of disbelief passed through all New England. A quoted discount of 5 per cent on out-of-Boston notes reflected but slightly the general unwillingness to have any truck with such paper.[44] With the aid of an act that compelled payment on demand under penalty of interest charges of 2 per cent a month, the long-suffering merchants protected their own interests in the crisis by raising a fund of $10,000 to call on delinquent houses for specie. But this forerunner of the Suffolk System provided no additional safety for humbler billholders. On the contrary, to the extent that the Boston capitalists emptied shaky firms of gold and silver, they lessened the chances of redemption for the casual possessor of a note.[45]

Only the government had the capacity to control the issue by concentrating the privilege in a responsible body, a step at no time politically feasible. There was occasional recognition "that distant Country Bank Bills should not again get into circulation." But no plan projected in this period, whatever the shade of opinion, section, or interest represented, dared openly recommend withdrawal of the right to print paper.[46]

Those who suggested central banks accepted the perpetuation

43. See Letter to the President and Directors of the Banks in Boston, Appendix C, below; also, *Boston Gazette*, Mar. 14, 1803; "Mentor," *ibid.*, Sept. 17, 1807; *Boston Mirror*, Aug. 5, 1809.

44. See R. C. Winthrop, "Memoirs of Hon. Nathan Appleton," *Mass. Hist. Soc. Proceedings*, V (1861), 284; J. E. A. Smith, *The History of Pittsfield . . . from . . . 1800 to . . . 1876* (Springfield, 1876), pp. 182ff; also *Independent Chronicle*, Jan. 5, 1809; *Salem Gazette*, Feb. 6, 1810.

45. Winthrop, "Nathan Appleton," *Mass. Hist. Soc. Proceedings*, V, 285; Original Bank Circular, 1809," *Mass. Hist. Soc. Proceedings*, XI (1870), 307; st. 1809, ch. 38; *Brown v. Penobscot Bank* (1812), 8 Tyng 444; "A Broker," *Boston Patriot*, Aug. 19, 1809.

46. *Boston Patriot*, Sept. 2, Oct. 28, 1809.

of independent companies as a permanent feature of the whole system. William Tudor did not exclude them in his scheme for a new corporation modeled after the Bank of England. Under government supervision a nuclear institution in Boston "with branches in four or five principal commercial towns" would regulate its circulation at the optimum level. In return for its patronage, the state would derive "an annual income or a *bonus*" large enough to reduce dividends to a nominal rate that would attract principally "corporate bodies, annuitants, or great capitalists" more interested in safe than in high returns. With the profit motive minimized, the bank would operate safely and set standards for others.[47]

The central state bank was not exclusively a merchants' idea or a federalist idea; James Sullivan, whose *Path to Riches* was reprinted in 1809, had early advanced the concept of a similar institution capitalized at twenty million dollars, and from time to time other proposals cropped up in the legislature. The conception drew support from men of all parties. But the Republicans, under pressure of defending an unpopular foreign policy, took advantage of a wave of business failures, commonly ascribed to the unwillingness of banks to discount as usual, and converted the question into a party issue. This turn of events antagonized some, like Harrison Gray Otis, who had for a time favored the project.[48]

The State Bank, incorporated in 1812, acquired strong connections with the government. But although it probably was "founded on the determination to abolish those already existing," the capital and prestige added by Massachusetts never gave the company the pivotal position anticipated by those who hoped for a better controlled currency.[49] The politics surrounding the bank's genesis cast the shadow of partisanship over its operations. Compromises with opponents achieved the objective of a charter, but only at the price of sharing advantages with others. The old firms, rechartered at the same time, received identical powers and identical provisions for Commonwealth participation. The

47. See *Monthly Anthology and Boston Review*, 7 (1809), 192ff.

48. See Hill to Quincy, Feb. 22, 1811, Phillips Papers; J. T. Austin, *Elbridge Gerry* (Boston, 1828–1829), II, 339; T. C. Amory, *Life of James Sullivan* (Boston, 1859), II, 211ff. *Independent Chronicle*, Feb. 23, Mar. 12, 1807; *Boston Gazette*, Feb. 4, June 24, 1811; *Salem Gazette*, Aug. 12, 1811; *Journal of the House of Representatives of . . . Massachusetts . . . 1807* (Boston, 1808), pp. 19, 62, 65, 66; *Repertory*, Feb. 12, 1808.

49. See the hostile answer of the House, May 28, 1813, *Acts and Resolves*, p. 233; st. 1811, ch. 84.

State Bank became just one of many; it did not even lay hold of a monopoly of the business of lending to the very government of which it was the pet creature.[50]

In 1812 the Commonwealth held a substantial place in a banking system to which it had contributed one million of eight million dollars of capital and from which it drew important revenues by taxation. The conception of close ties between the government and its financial agencies persisted, but practice never gave substance to the theory. The requirement for regular reports at frequent intervals perpetuated a hypothetical, not an actual, control that permitted transgressors to cover real delinquency by a show of correctness and to mislead the public by an appearance of supervision which really did not exist.[51]

Whatever its policy at any time, the legislature could not count on these bodies to execute its orders. The inability to bind any single institution to the state increased the frequency and the width of the divergencies between the objectives of the government and the intentions of the investors. Indeed some banks refused to make the loans required by their charters, casually turning the state away from their counters, as they would any other customer, with the polite suggestion to apply elsewhere.[52] Its contribution in capital made Massachusetts merely one of several partners, and it was not long before there was talk of terminating that relation.[53] The failure to establish more direct control grew out of the very character of the technique of issuing money through grant of the prerogative of acting as a body politic. The Commonwealth stumbled into a labyrinth of diffusion and never established a grip over financial operations precisely because the charter carried with it a privilege which the government could not confine to a favored few.

The process of multiplication, so pronounced in banking, had no parallel in manufacturing for almost twenty years. The hectic pursuit of incorporation did not immediately extend into the

50. See, e.g., st. 1812, ch. 40; res. 1812, ch. 50; res. 1813, ch. 157.

51. "Banquo," *Boston Patriot*, June 17, 1809; res. 1814, ch. 185. For the bank tax see st. 1812, chs. 32, 40, sec. 9; *Revised Statutes*, ch. 9, secs. 1–3; *Boston Commercial Gazette*, June 20, 1816; for earlier tax proposals see *Boston Gazette*, Mar. 7, 1803; *Salem Gazette*, June 8, 1802; *Eastern Herald*, Mar. 14, 1803; *Eastern Repository*, June 30, 1803. The courts upheld the constitutionality of the tax, *Portland Bank* v. *Apthorp* (1815), 12 Tyng 252; *Waltham Bank* v. *Waltham* (1845), 10 Metcalf 334; *Tremont Bank* v. *Boston* (1848), 1 Cushing 142ff.

52. See res. 1814, chs. 79, 193; *Boston Commercial Gazette*, Feb. 15, 1816.

53. See res. 1814, ch. 122; *Salem Gazette*, Feb. 6, 1810; *Eagle of Maine*, Feb. 21, 1816; *Boston Commercial Gazette*, Feb. 19, Nov. 18, 1816.

fields of industry because the legislature was unable to bestow in charters to manufacturing enterprises the exclusive features which alone would have made the grants valuable. The incorporation movement did not gain way in this area until two decades later, and then only when stimulated by the state for the sake of implementing a public policy.

Cabot's Beverly factory corporation had been conceived for the purpose of raising a flow of exports. But the growth of Boston trade with the Orient after 1790, the opening into the British system offered by Jay's Treaty, and the gradual emergence of the new triangular routes removed some of the urgency for creating home manufactures to fill the holds of outbound vessels.[54]

Ultimately the deleterious effects upon commerce of the embargo of 1807 converted some merchants from passive indifference to open hostility. The prospect that domestic industry, stimulated as a result of the halt of trade, might cut into the home market for imported goods showed the dangers of the older policy of encouraging native production. Not a few businessmen now discovered the evils of manufacturing cities and asked, "Would the existence of our present form of government be compatible with such a populace as exists in Lyons, Manchester, or Birmingham?" [55] They also became aware, for the first time, of limits to the powers of the state in the economy. "In these cases," they gravely explained, "the interference of government is always mischievous," citing the unavailing efforts at industrialization during the Revolution and contrasting the freedom and prosperity of England with the restrictions and backwardness of France. Premiums only taxed one group for the benefit of another, and the tariff displayed a hideous aspect, hitherto concealed.[56]

Not all merchants thought alike on these questions. Many never surrendered their enthusiasm for a thriving back country; interest and sentiment continued to point to the goal of an expanding industry. And those who objected in theory did not in practice forgo new opportunities for profitable investment.

54. See Cabot to Goodhue, Mar. 16, Apr. 6, May 5, 1790, H. C. Lodge, *Life and Letters of George Cabot* (Boston, 1877), pp. 33ff, 36ff; Alexander Hamilton, *Industrial and Commercial Correspondence*, ed. A. H. Cole (Chicago, 1928), pp. 61, 312, 313; Wansey, *Journal*, pp. 84ff; C. F. Ware, *Early New England Cotton Manufacture* (Boston, 1931), pp. 62ff.

55. *Monthly Anthology and Boston Review*, 3 (1806), 609; 5 (1808), 382ff; 6 (1809), 50.

56. *Ibid.*, 6 (1809), 49, 50.

In addition, other people with a stake in manufacturing never let the idea die. Local storekeepers and traders were constantly on the lookout for enterprises in their neighborhoods. The owners of mill privileges were eager to sponsor projects to exploit the resources of water power. Mechanics and tradespeople everywhere attempted to form societies not only for fraternal and charitable but also for manufacturing ends, particularly in periods of unemployment as in 1791.[57]

Industry also interested farmers. It grew rapidly as an adjunct to agriculture and furnished an ever larger part of rural income, even when much of the production was for consumption at home. The household system spread from the time-tried textiles, shoes, and nails to new fields. Though still dependent on the traditional grist, saw, slitting, and fulling mills which supplied the intermediate processes of domestic fabrication either by the yard or on shares, the farmers also envisaged efficient new plants clamoring for raw materials and encouraging agricultural production. In Hampshire County "Geneva Distilleries" were projected to "furnish a vent for that surplus of inferior grain which the farmer has not heretofore known what to do with." [58] The first cotton factory in Worcester County aimed primarily to "give encouragement to the agriculturalist, affording a ready market for all his surplus produce." [59]

John Adams, James Swan, Levi Lincoln, and Elkanah Watson, among others, spoke of aid to manufacturing as aid to agriculture, and rural towns gave their blessings to any kind of industry that might keep a restless population at home. Recognizing the desirability of manufactures for the state as a whole, these communities zealously strove for the immediate benefits deriving from the location of plants in their own neighborhoods. Many, indeed, discounted the professions of interest from some merchants, were suspicious of plans involving mercantile control, and thought that the real leadership in building manufactures

57. See Samuel Rezneck, "Rise and Early Development of Industrial Consciousness in the United States," *Jour. of Econ. and Bus. Hist.*, 4 (1932), 789; Samuel Breck, *Recollections* (Philadelphia, 1877), p. 178.

58. See MA, Senate, 6118/2; Thomas Weston, *History of the Town of Middleboro* (Boston, 1906), p. 377; *Boston Commercial Gazette*, May 23, 1816; Smith, *Pittsfield, 1800 to 1876*, pp. 36ff, 158ff, 166ff; 172ff, 177, 180; Dwight to Sedgwick, Mar. 16, 1792, Sedgwick Papers, II, 259; Dana to Cabot, July 26, 1790, Cabot to Coxe, Jan. 24, 1791, Gorham to Hamilton, Oct. 13, 1791, Hamilton, *Industrial and Commercial Correspondence*, pp. 54, 56, 66.

59. See C. P. Crosby, "History of West Boylston," *Worc. Mag. and Hist. Jour.*, 2 (1826), 195ff; J. H. Temple, *History of North Brookfield* (North Brookfield, 1887), pp. 266, 268ff.

would have to come from country gentlemen, struggling "against the opposition of importing merchants." [60]

These entrepreneurs were, however, no more eager than the traders to challenge the position of the Beverly as the only corporation in the state. The charter and the brief experience of that company demonstrated that the kind of aid Massachusetts extended was hardly worth the trouble of petitioning for incorporation. George Cabot pointed out his difficulties in 1790 when he turned unsuccessfully to the federal government for assistance: the state was unable to make up losses when rival enterprises in other towns copied the machines at lower cost and pirated the skilled artisans trained in Beverly.[61] Yet Massachusetts could not supply the requisite remedy by following the model of European manufacturing corporations. Monopoly was acceptable for such branches of industry as glassmaking, where the expense and complexity of a highly desirable process not adaptable to household production rendered emulation improbable. But no group had weight enough in the legislature to secure the kind of exclusive privileges that would eliminate competition and make incorporation valuable in the fabrication of textiles and nails, shoes and hats — activities that busied numerous farmers, artisans, and their middlemen throughout the state.

The demands for incorporation between 1789 and 1807, all phrased in terms of the worth of an innovation and all granted, were the products of new and unusual contingencies. Because of exceptional circumstances, these enterprises sought wide powers of assessment to cope with peculiar problems of expansion and development and expected to find the prestige of state approval, through the charter, of value in contact with the law or with public opinion.

The Newburyport Woolen, the Calico Printing, and the Amesbury Nail companies seemed interested primarily in the

60. Lincoln to Sedgwick, Jan. 12, 1791, Sedgwick Papers, II, 44; J. Adams to Coxe, May, 1792, *Mass. Hist. Soc. Proceedings*, V (1860–62), 311; [Swan], *National Arithmetick*, pp. 13, 16ff; W. C. Watson, *Men and Times of the Revolution; or, Memoirs of Elkanah Watson* (New York, 1856), pp. 425ff, 452, 454ff; Keyes Danforth, *Boyhood Reminiscences* (New York, 1895), pp. 11, 14ff; Governor Adams' address, Jan. 19, 1795, *Acts and Resolves of 1795*, p. 616; Caleb Strong, *Patriotism and Piety* (Newburyport, 1808), pp. 70ff; Crosby, "West Boylston," *Worc. Mag. and Hist. Jour.*, 2 (1826), 201.

61. See Cabot to Goodhue, Mar. 16, Apr. 6, May 5, 1790, Lodge, *George Cabot*, pp. 33ff, 35ff; Hamilton, *Industrial and Commercial Correspondence*, pp. 61, 312, 313; Wansey, *Journal*, pp. 84ff.

power of assessment, although the first of these later asked state help not "for private emoluments for themselves" but as "an object worthy of the Public encouragement" and because "the discharge and dispersion of the workmen would be a public detriment." The others sought some special privilege. The Salem Iron Works became incorporated to help a group of merchants retain a mill franchise in return for maintaining and repairing a bridge. Bridgebuilding for the public welfare was similarly a condition for the formation of the Salem & Danvers Iron Works, and the Fitchburgh Cotton Manufactory asked for a fourteen-year tax exemption.[62]

Finally, the proprietors of the mills on the Charles River wanted both the right of assessment and the prestige of incorporation. They had bickered with the meadow owners without benefit of a charter for more than thirty years, but they hastened to secure one when their rivals did, to be sure of sharing any "immunities, privileges & advantages which may be granted" and to raise money for defense of their rights.[63]

These exceptional instances did not reflect any inadequacy in the practical application of more traditional ways of carrying on manufacturing. The older methods continued to serve the most important projectors of new ventures, like the Schofields, throughout the period. Cooperative efforts, often motivated by community spirit, built the factories. The various participants — local shopkeepers, mechanics, farmers, and millowners — supplied capital, labor, land, and skill in return for shares in the enterprise. The sponsor of the Globe cotton mill of Fall River, organized in 1811, contributed the land in return for forty shares, and gave forty to a carpenter, ten to three yeomen, and ten to three mechanics who erected and equipped the factory. In that respect, manufacturers merely applied to new spheres — shoes, textiles, paper — old techniques already worked out with regard to saw and grist mills.[64]

Liberal franchises and changes in the mill law facilitated the operation of these enterprises. The same joint ownership that

62. MA, 1793, ch. 27; MA, 1795, ch. 58; st. 1797, ch. 77; MA, 1799, ch. 80; MA, 1803, ch. 61; MA, 1804, ch. 139; MA, 1807, ch. 33; st. 1808, ch. 100. See also MA, Senate 2396, 2396/1; *Danvers Hist. Soc. Colls.*, XI (1923), 87–91, XVI (1928), 50, XVIII (1930), 51ff; F. B. C. Bradlee, "Salem Iron Factory," *Essex Inst. Hist. Colls.*, LIV (1918), 98ff, 112ff.

63. MA, 1797, ch. 45; also st. 1808, ch. 8.

64. See W. R. Bagnall, *Sketches of Manufacturing Establishments in New York City* (Washington, D.C., 1908), III, 1861ff; Weston, *Middleboro*, pp. 383, 384; Bradford Kingman, *History of North Bridgewater* (Boston, 1866), p. 37.

made these undertakings possible sometimes created complications. In the absence of the power to assess or to coerce the membership through by-laws, a small group within the body could retard improvement or development; a majority could not vote away the property rights of the minority. A partial remedy for those "discouraged by many doubts and disputes" came in the act of 1796 which gave all mills the power to levy certain assessments: the majority of the proprietors of "any mill worked by wind or water," the underworks or appurtenances of which needed repairs, could order the work done and collect from the remainder. In the normal operations of steadily expanding business this form was satisfactory and continued to serve industry for many years.[65]

As long as no further privilege accompanied the charter, there were no widespread demands for more grants. The manufacturing corporation spread only when political developments again emphasized its role as an instrument of state policy.

When relations with Great Britain became critical, the United States approached a break with the former mother country, first on the commercial level with Jefferson's embargo, and then in open war. The effect upon shipping in Massachusetts was serious and immediate. Governor Sullivan, shrewd in estimating the situation, was not convinced of the soundness of national Republican policy. To mitigate the harsh effects of the embargo upon the Bay State, and indirectly upon the future of his party, he turned to industry as an alternative to commerce. Sullivan wished to encourage the development of manufacturing as proof of the economic independence of the Commonwealth and as a means of demonstrating the correctness of his party's conduct of foreign affairs. He gained support from those, like Thomas Allen of Pittsfield, who had long campaigned for stimulus to home manufactures and who considered the interruption of trade a positive virtue. Still more backing came from flushed enthusiasts who buoyantly expected the new workshops to cure all the currency ills, to restore declining real-estate values, and to open up Elysian fields to capital redeemed from moribund commerce.[66]

65. See MA, 1795, ch. 74, secs. 5, 6; James Sullivan, *Land Titles in Massachusetts* (Boston, 1801), p. 123.

66. See *Monthly Anthology and Boston Review*, 5 (1808), 382ff; "A Broker," *Boston Patriot*, Aug. 23, 1809; "Answer of the House and Senate," *Salem Gazette*, June 15, 19, 1810; *New-England Palladium*, Jan. 14, 1812; Austin, *Elbridge Gerry*, II, 372ff.

Manufacturing thus became a political instrument in the war against England, and self-sufficiency in industry acquired a patriotic quality reflected in the attempt to establish a "Public Factory" for munitions in 1808, as well as in the charter, a year later, of the Massachusetts Association for the Encouragement of Useful Inventions.[67] The government's desire to dramatize the crisis and stimulate production also took the form of extensive incorporation. New bodies with the prestige of the Commonwealth's name and with the implication of public usefulness and government approval were to mobilize opinion and activity in the rural areas. The wish to diffuse the same activities throughout the state precluded special privileges to favor any single corporation against its competitors; all would share the general attributes and receive the benediction of political support.

To further this program, Acting Governor Lincoln suggested in 1809 that, in addition to bounties and tax exemptions, the state help "by extending the principles of our laws, respecting the overflowing of lands by grist and saw mills, to cotton factories and other labour saving machines." [68] The compliant legislature went even further than the chief executive had contemplated. It extended a sweeping invitation to all who would to request charters. A general law laid down the conditions under which the state was ready, on petition, to organize manufacturing corporations.[69] Immediately the General Court created seven new bodies — almost as many as in its whole previous history. Feverish imitation from town to town in the six war years that followed added fully 121, many financed by people "willing to cast in their mite" to aid the Commonwealth "amidst the embarrassment of our Commerce abroad." [70]

The expansion of home markets with the interruption in the flow of British imports facilitated development but did not cause it. The experience of the preceding decade, which had already witnessed the multiplication of industries but not of corporations, revealed that growth, normal or accelerated, would not alone evoke a desire for charters. Occasional enterprisers still had special ends in view. The Waltham Company wanted to unite a banking scheme with manufacturing, and the Boston

67. *Journal of the House of Representatives of . . . Massachusetts . . . 1808* (Boston, 1808), p. 225; st. 1808, ch. 50; also *Boston Patriot*, Mar. 3, 1809; *Columbian Detector*, Jan. 13, 1809; *New-England Palladium*, Feb. 28, 1809.
68. *Acts and Resolves of 1809*, p. 229.
69. St. 1808, ch. 65; MA, House, 6597.
70. MA, 1810, ch. 10, petition of Ebenezer Atwood *et al.*

hatters associated "into companies for the purpose of manufacturing & vending American hats on an extensive scale, and adopted such regulations as will prevent imposition, by establishing a uniformity of price." [71] But in manufacturing, with the possibility of linking privilege to the grant limited from the start, and fast becoming vestigial, the spurt in incorporation awaited the moment when political policy needed the services of these bodies for achievement of some social end. A change would soon come, but even in 1812 the provisions of a proposed general law incidentally related corporations to towns and revealed clearly the persistence of thinking in the old terms of the body politic as an agency of government. [72]

In internal improvements and in banking, as in manufactures, incorporation had come first in connection with the grant of some privilege by the state. In another sphere, insurance, ultimately regarded as similar, the demand for a charter originated in charitable motives and involved only the request for the power of internal government and the prestige of state sponsorship.

Despite the fact that marine underwriting was a complex business involving large amounts of capital, and despite the fact that this activity had expanded rapidly during the Revolution, it did not lead to the development of chartered companies. Corporations appeared first in the field of fire insurance where the eleemosynary aspects were most important. Incendiary disasters which left in their wake poverty and destitution were a problem for government; relief made demands upon towns as well as upon private benevolent organizations. That circumstance justified the sponsors of the Massachusetts Fire Insurance Company in seeking incorporation in 1795. [73] If its title reflected the desire for a close link to the state, this association was doomed to disappointment, for the emergence of a new plan of mutual insurance in New York led to imitation by the Massachusetts Mutual Fire Insurance Company three years later. [74]

71. *Boston Patriot*, Sept. 27, 1809; Ware, *Early New England Cotton Manufacture*, pp. 148ff.

72. MA, House, 7289.

73. MA, 1795, ch. 22. See also T. H. Perkins, *Remarks Made at the Laying of the Corner Stone of the Boston Exchange, August 2, 1841* (Boston, 1841), pp. 10, 11; Pratt, *Eastham, Wellfleet, and Orleans*, p. 87; Buckingham, *Massachusetts Charitable Mechanic Association*, p. 144.

74. St. 1797, ch. 67; *Columbian Centinel*, Jan. 4, 1797.

The troubled times that fell upon trade after 1795 furnished the Massachusetts Mutual with an excuse for extending its functions from the fire to the marine field. The limited life of the corporation with the implication of legislative review at the end of the period, the requirement of public reports, and the regulation of such matters as the payment and investment of capital and the nature of risks furnished guarantees attractive to customers.[75] To protect their competitive position, the older groups of underwriters in turn began to seek the same status. By 1800 corporations existed in Boston, Newburyport, Salem, and Portland, all promising to furnish in return for their charters "a security and facility to Commerce highly important to the landed as well as mercantile part of the Community." As in the case of banks, the restriction of one institution to a town soon broke down, and the number of concerns grew rapidly after 1800, many combining both fire and marine business. Dispersal of the privilege spread the advantages of government approval and supervision to many bodies, so that no single one could claim a unique relation to the state.[76]

A similar widening process cut into the influence of the regulating corporations in the fields of medicine, agriculture, and shipping. Complaints that the Massachusetts Medical Society raised costs coincided with the organization of a medical department at Harvard University. In 1803 the Cambridge corporation won the right to bestow degrees which automatically carried the license to practice, a privilege later extended as well to the chartered Berkshire Medical Institute of Williams College.[77] Although the petition for foundation of a rival association of physicians failed of enactment, the original society fell off in strength; it gave up the right to limit the number of its members, degree holders swelled the roll of practitioners, and the fee-fixing power slipped into the hands of informal local cliques.[78]

75. See, e.g., st. 1795, ch. 22; st. 1798, ch. 46; st. 1803, ch. 115; st. 1805, ch. 47; also MA, House, 6435, 6603, 6609, 6631; *Little* v. *Obrien* (1812), 9 Tyng 423.

76. MA, 1798, ch. 50; st. 1798, ch. 46; MA, 1799, ch. 42; st. 1802, chs. 106, 110, 126; st. 1803, ch. 89; st. 1814, ch. 9; MA, House, 4922; Porter, *Jacksons and the Lees*, I, 467, 468; Morison, *Harrison Gray Otis*, I, 297.

77. See William Manning, *Key of Libberty* [1798], ed. S. E. Morison (Billerica, 1922), p. 26; st. 1822, ch. 43; st. 1826, ch. 101; "Dr. Ephraim Eliot's Account of the Physicians of Boston," *Mass. Hist. Soc. Proceedings*, VII (1863), 183, 184; Smith, *Pittsfield, 1800 to 1876*, pp. 352ff, 373.

78. The Massachusetts society still received state land as aid, however. See res. 1810, ch. 86; Governor Gerry's address, Jan. 8, 1812, *Resolves of 1812*, p. 281;

The incorporation of the Kennebec Agricultural Society in 1801 challenged the exclusive position of the Massachusetts Society for promoting Agriculture, which thereafter lost ground to other county corporations. The energetic activities of Elkanah Watson that popularized the fairs and exhibitions of the Berkshire organization earned these more specialized bodies the support of annual state bounties after 1817.[79] Interest in marine societies also grew and spread in the 1790's. As earlier, these associations amassed dues into funds, made rules punishable by fines, heard complaints, and judged the conduct of their members. The Newburyport and Boston societies gained complete control over pilotage in those towns, a new group appeared in Portland, and the Salem association revived many earlier activities although finding a competitor in 1799 in the East India Marine Society.[80]

By 1815 the corporation had developed tendencies unforeseen thirty years before and had spread into many new fields.[81] But the state still continued to judge which activities deserved encouragement, and it passed upon proposals for incorporation, even in new spheres, in terms of the primordial concept of common interests. It thus judged worthy the desire to cope with the problem of making economic provisions against death. Insecurity in that respect menaced the families of all but the very wealthiest and threatened the government with the charge of supporting the helpless. The ineffectual efforts of many friendly societies had failed for lack of both funds and actuarial systems. When Bowditch's tables solved the second difficulty, the government established the Massachusetts Hospital Life Insurance Society, allocating one third of its net profits to the General

Joseph Bartlett, "Historical Sketch of the Progress of Medical Science," *Mass. Hist. Soc. Colls.*, 2 ser., I (1814), 113, 116; S. A. Green, *History of Medicine in Massachusetts* (Boston, 1881), pp. 99–116.

79. See *Kennebeck Intelligencer*, June 6, 1800; MA, 1800, ch. 46; "First Annual Report, Board of Agriculture," *Senate Docs., 1854*, no. 7, pp. 11, 12; H. B. Hall, "Description of Rural Life and Labor in Massachusetts at Four Periods" (unpub. diss. Harvard University, 1917, University Archives), pp. 62ff; Watson, *Elkanah Watson*, p. 422; P. W. Bidwell, *Rural Economy in New England* (New Haven, 1916), pp. 340ff; P. W. Bidwell, "Agricultural Revolution in New England," *Amer. Hist. Rev.*, 26 (1921), 686ff; Basil Hall, *Travels in North America* (Edinburgh, 1829), II, 75ff.

80. See Bentley, *Diary*, I, 144, 145; st. 1785, ch. 29; st. 1795, ch. 66; st. 1796, ch. 85; st. 1813, ch. 164; W. D. Dennis, "Salem Charitable Mechanic Association," *Essex Inst. Hist. Colls.*, XLII (1906), 2; Walter M. Whitehill, *The East India Marine Society* (Salem, 1949), pp. 3ff.

81. See, e.g., Exchange Coffee House, Boylston Market Company, st. 1807, ch. 31; st. 1809, ch. 66; st. 1813, ch. 36.

Hospital, which had earlier received the exclusive life-insuring privilege.[82]

Because savings banks had a similar value, the Commonwealth rewarded the efforts of the philanthropic Deacon Elisha Ticknor with a charter for the Provident Institution in 1817. They furnished a place where the poor could keep whatever funds they had and thereby contributed to social mobility. Such banks aided in the accumulation of small stores of capital which would otherwise have been squandered or kept idle and also prevented the hoarding of paper and specie. Above all, those worthy institutions encouraged thrift among people who might in a crisis pauperize the government.[83]

The areas of economic activity into which the corporate technique did not reach in this period throw further light upon the presumptions essential to grant the privilege. Those who thought of land corporations, for instance, thought of agencies already familiar — the towns and the proprietors of common fields.[84] To put the enterprises of land speculators into these forms would have raised innumerable complications concerning the status and power of proprietors, settlers, and other extant corporations with overlapping jurisdictions. Decades of struggle with residents who tried to tax the unimproved lands of absentees showed the folly of introducing such questions, with no compensating advantages, into a type of business harried by so many other difficulties.[85]

Notwithstanding the precedent of European practice, well known in 1780, commerce also witnessed no incorporations. At the existing stage of development the only privilege of value to it — monopoly — was beyond the scope of state action after 1789, while a proposed constitutional amendment and the furor over the Bank of the United States indicated that the federal government, which did assist with navigation laws, was not trusted with the incorporating power. Most important, the fact that trading operations were already well established and spread

82. St. 1817, ch. 180; st. 1823, ch. 51; N. I. Bowditch, *History of the Massachusetts General Hospital* (Boston, 1872), pp. 1off, 62, 71. See also st. 1810, ch. 94; st. 1813, ch. 158; Buckingham, *Massachusetts Charitable Mechanic Association*, pp. 6ff; *Journal of House, 1808*, p. 210.

83. Willard Phillips, *Manual of Political Economy* (Boston, 1828), p. 158; Francis Bowen, *Principles of Political Economy* (Boston, 1856), pp. 110, 113ff, 312.

84. See, e.g., *Acts and Resolves of 1790*, p. 550.

85. See, e.g., MA, CXXXVII, 354. See also *Boston Gazette*, July 9, 1781; L. R. Paige, *Address at the Centennial Celebration on Hardwick, Mass.* (Cambridge, Mass., 1838), p. 15.

wide among many individuals, partnerships and joint-stock companies made it difficult to justify special privilege for a single group. Unlike the activities which involved innovation or some special public service, incorporation in the field of trade seemed to close rather than to open new opportunities. The corporation could not extend into this area so long as the Commonwealth purpose was primary, the private interest secondary.[86]

Even in manufacturing and banking, where the process of multiplication was well advanced, projects failed, from time to time, to meet the test of public usefulness; not every petition yielded an act of incorporation. Much later, enterprises in new spheres, like hotels and stagecoach companies, had no success in their applications for the privilege.[87]

Sometimes the charter was withheld because of intrinsic deficiencies, sometimes because it met the opposition of hostile groups in control of the government at the moment. The mechanics of Boston, for instance, had developed a plan in 1794 for a corporation to license apprentices and to prevent masters from employing "any bound apprentice, who shall have left the person he was bound to, without . . . consent." Though the artisans were properly respectful and conciliatory, the merchants feared the effects of rising labor costs and defeated the scheme when it came to the legislature. The members continued as a voluntary social body, the Massachusetts Charitable Mechanics Society, and in the next few years more specialized associations of coopers (1801) and of housewrights (1804) appeared, also attempting to regulate prices and conditions of labor. Unincorporated, these groups faced countless difficulties in enforcing by-laws and collecting dues. New requests for a charter stressing the charitable aspects of these organizations failed in 1799, 1803, and 1805.[88]

But the balance in control of government permitted persistent groups ultimately to have their way. No interest was powerful

86. See, e.g., agreements by Lee and Jackson with William Pratt, G. G. Lee, S. G. Gardner, John Lowell, and T. Lee for the voyages of the brigs *Charon* and *Gipsy*, Lee-Cabot Papers, May 1, 21, June 13, 18, 30, 1810. Piers to serve the needs of commerce were, however, incorporated after the model of common fields. See st. 1797, ch. 34; st. 1819, ch. 110.

87. See, e.g., MA, House, 7083, 7132, 7386, 7610; MA, Senate, 5384, 6118, 6145, 6703, 8182.

88. Buckingham, *Massachusetts Charitable Mechanic Association*, pp. 3–16, 50, 52, 54, 57, 69, 80, 84ff, 91–93, 99; MA, Senate, 2490, 2490/1; MA, House, 4519, 6445, 7131; *Stockbridge Western Star*, Aug. 23, 30, 1791; R. G. Silver, "Boston Book Trade," *Bulletin of the New York Public Library*, 52 (1948), 494ff.

enough permanently to engross the machinery of state agency in behalf of its own conception of the common interest. The same forces that produced a dispersal of corporate privileges in the old spheres led to their extension into new ones. The mechanics finally secured an act of incorporation. Although their charter expressly limited their activities to charity, and the legislature at first denied a request for money, eventually the corporation received the proceeds of the auctioneers' tax in the city of Boston.[89] A kindred group in Salem imitated their example, obtaining a charter and enacting by-laws to expel "any member who shall take into his service an apprentice . . . who left his master without . . . consent." Similar societies followed in other places, foreshadowing a time when the privilege would be accessible to all who sought it.[90]

Four decades of development had wrought many changes in the body politic. A privilege originally conceived as selective and exclusive had spread to many spheres and had been dispersed among many holders, under pressure of the pervasive opinion that the favors of the government ought not to be "partially bestowed, and the advantages of the laws unequally distributed." [91] Already in 1807, Otis complained, "though a great deal is accumulated, yet as Paddy would say, still more is distributed, and every reservoir has many aqueducts." [92] Seven years later old John Adams, as ever distrustful of moneyed institutions, grumbled to John Taylor that "the few are craving and the many mad for the same thing . . . democrats and aristocrats all unite . . . in urging these monopolies and incorporations." [93]

Such diffusion had a profound effect upon the place of the corporation in the state and would ultimately transform the very conception of the association. But in 1815 the time had not yet come. The body politic remained a special public body until the law caught up with the practice and imparted new connotations to later diffusion.

89. Buckingham, *Massachusetts Charitable Mechanic Association*, pp. 55, 94ff, 98ff, 157, 168, 172, 183, 185.

90. W. D. Dennis, "Salem Charitable Mechanic Association," *Essex Inst. Hist. Colls.*, XLII (1906), 4ff, 12ff; st. 1822, ch. 46.

91. Sullivan, *Path to Riches*, pp. 6, 53.

92. To R. G. Harper, Apr. 19, 1807, Morison, *Harrison Gray Otis*, I, 283.

93. John Adams, *Works*, VI, 508.

6 | The Law of Private Rights in a Commonwealth

Directly or indirectly, the activities of the Commonwealth extended into all the affairs of the people of Massachusetts and inevitably affected their personal concerns. To maintain that the Commonwealth worked in behalf of all its members was not to deny that it might conflict with individual interests. The government was powerful: it granted money or favors, built or regulated, utilizing its full strength to attain its aspirations for an expanding economy. Yet the citizen was not powerless; standing between him and overreaching coercive political authority was a body of rights derived from "eternal and immutable laws of justice and morality . . . paramount to all human legislation." [1] These rights received formal statement in constitutions, but they acquired firmer sanctions from a deep popular faith in the validity of ideas generated in the matrix of the Revolution. Experience with specific problems in the first decades of the Commonwealth's history defined and developed this system of ideas, reflected and then formalized in law, which created a barrier of private rights around the power to govern. [2]

Uncertainty in the legal system, left fluid by the Revolution, increased the weight of practical influences. The solution of new questions did not follow pure principle, not only because many issues were unprecedented, but also because the very sub-

1. J. Q. Adams, "Publicola," *Writings* (New York, 1913–1917), I, 70. See [John Davis], "Thoughts Read at a Forensic Disputation," Davis Papers, 1747–1846 (MSS, MHS); W. E. Channing, "Justice," *Memoir* (Boston, 1848), I, 316, 317.

2. J. Q. Adams, *Writings*, I, 93ff.

stance of the law was but imperfectly known. The most careful of attorneys lacked a thorough knowledge. In America formal legal education did not exist for a long time; those who wanted such training had to go to London.[3] Colonial laws were inaccessible; they were not reprinted until 1801, and then incompletely, as an appendix to a compilation of recent legislation.[4] Statutes passed since the Revolution were available, but their loose construction placed a premium on interpretation.[5] Yet there were no printed Massachusetts decisions for citation. With no published judicial records until after the turn of the nineteenth century, lawyers and judges alike faced the necessity of working from notes or more often from materials which rested only in memory. In the absence of accepted rules about precedents, jurists continued to "pursue the easier, but more dangerous course of deciding all questions according to the impressions on their own minds, at the moment; and then [proceeded to] substitute their own private opinions in the place of law." [6]

Furthermore, the law was low in popular esteem. The role of the loyalist judges in the revolutionary crisis cast suspicion on the whole judiciary and kept fresh the dangers of a legal system free of popular control. Nor were the activities of the bar in the debt-collecting years after 1780 likely to win it approval. The use of offices as political plums and the expense of proceedings deepened the distrust. Miserly salaries kept promising men off the bench; in 1783, for instance, Strong declined an appointment to the supreme court because it entailed heavy financial loss. Finally, the common law seemed to many too closely related to the British tyranny so recently thrown off to be serviceable in a free republic.[7]

3. See Walter Austin, *William Austin* (Boston, 1925), pp. 34ff. For legal education in general see W. W. Story, *Life and Letters of Joseph Story* (Boston, 1851), I, 119; J. A. Krout and D. R. Fox, *Completion of Independence* (New York, 1944), pp. 279ff.

4. See *Perpetual Laws of the Commonwealth of Massachusetts, 1780 to 1800* (Boston, 1801), III, 135ff; J. Smith, "Review," *Monthly Anthology and Boston Review,* 3 (1806), 139, 149; *Laws of the Commonwealth . . . 1780 . . . 1800* (Boston, 1801), II, 961ff.

5. For compilations of Massachusetts laws see *Senate Docs., 1855,* no. 10, pp. 2, 3.

6. Smith, "Review," *Monthly Anthology and Boston Review,* 3 (1806), 139, 146ff; Joseph Story, "Review," *Monthly Anthology and Boston Review,* 5 (1808), 329ff.; James Sullivan, *History of Land Titles in Massachusetts* (Boston, 1801), pp. iv, 340ff; *Monthly Anthology and Boston Review,* 2 (1805), 482ff.

7. J. Q. to J. Adams, Mar. 19, Apr. 5, 1790, J. Q. Adams, *Writings,* I, 49, 52; H. C. Lodge, *Memoir of Caleb Strong* (Cambridge, Mass., 1879), p. 8; see also Gardiner and "Fabius," *Stockbridge Western Star,* Feb. 9, Mar. 2, 1790; "Curtius,"

The slim foundation upon which all rights rested appalled the able group of lawyers who entered the profession in the 1790's. Impressed with the necessity for strengthening the bulwarks around property, almost all turned their attention to the defense of the common law as the first stage in the elaboration of an efficient system.[8] In these early years legal arguments involved, more often than not, tortuous appeals to remote precedents, which could be twisted the more easily to the support of special arguments because but dimly known. However, verdicts once rendered, even when not overwhelmingly logical, seemed essential links in extending the chain of law. "It is not for us to question the judgments of the supreme tribunal of the commonwealth, delivered by judges of great personal and professional respectability," acknowledged Joseph Story. "They have pronounced and declared the law of the land." Indeed, jurists studied diligently the decisions in other states to bring their own into conformity and to create the concept of a fixed body of principles.[9]

The bar also campaigned for and secured the appointment of an official court reporter in 1803, a significant step toward formalization. Reforms in the judiciary and tightened regulations concerning practice accompanied the attempt to strengthen the independence of the courts by limiting the scope of legislative removals and by establishing fixed salaries.[10] Party feelings sometimes led to changes in the personnel of the bench but produced no questioning of the utility of an autonomous judiciary. Regardless of party, the lawyers fiercely resisted occasional efforts to tamper with their autonomy, with the form of pleadings, or with the rules of procedure. In fact, some proposed that

---

Boston Gazette, Jan. 3, 1803; debates in the House (Jan. 20, 1795), quoted in *Columbian Centinel*, Jan. 24, 1795; "a Country Lawyer," *ibid.*, May 20, June 6, 1795; Richard D. Birdsall, *Berkshire County* (New Haven, 1959), pp. 220ff.

8. See W. P. Cresson, *Francis Dana* (New York, 1930), p. 354; Sullivan, *Land Titles*, pp. 13, 17ff; "The Berkshire Sentimentalist," *Stockbridge Western Star*, Dec. 7, 1790.

9. See the review of Tyng, *Monthly Anthology and Boston Review*, 4 (1807), 437; also Judge Isaac Parker's review of Dallas, *Monthly Anthology and Boston Review*, 5 (1808), 159ff; Sullivan, *Land Titles*, pp. 355ff; Gerald T. Dunne, "The American Blackstone," *Washington University Law Quarterly* (1963), 321ff.

10. James Sullivan had earlier reprinted a few scattered cases in *Mass. Hist. Soc. Colls.*, 1 ser., V (1798), 45ff. See also *Monthly Anthology and Boston Review*, 2 (1805), 483; J. Story, "Review," *Monthly Anthology and Boston Review*, 4 (1807), 436; W. D. Williamson, *History of the State of Maine* (Hallowell, 1932), II, 596; J. Q. Adams to Knox, Feb. 14, 1803, J. Q. Adams, *Writings*, III, 12; *Monthly Anthology and Boston Review*, 4 (1807), 20ff; *Annals of the Times*, June 16, 1803; Story, *Joseph Story*, I, 131.

the state itself be subject to law and capable of being sued.[11] Capping these efforts, the appointment of Theophilus Parsons brought to the bench a vigorous mind imbued with conservative spirit and convinced of the pressing need for legal regeneration. Although heterogeneity of opinion and "many eccentricities of practice . . . from local circumstances" still persisted, these developments established the basis for an effective system of stable law in the first two decades of the nineteenth century.[12]

Few wished consciously to go as far as the lawyers in fortifying the judiciary. But imperceptibly, often involuntarily, the varied elements in Massachusetts society found themselves enlisted in the cause of the gentlemen of the bar. "Our people," wrote James Sullivan, "have all property and they want laws and government to support and protect it." [13] In a state where almost all artisans, farmers, and fishermen, as well as merchants, were preoccupied with possessions there was no alternative. The courts were the citizen's only citadel; in them he sought safety for his invaded rights. The protagonists in each case saw only the immediate interests at issue in the concrete conflict. Yet the resulting decisions built up and strengthened a body of principles and precedents and, whether the people willed it or not, formalized the law.

A deficiency in the judicial system hastened that formalization. Distrust of old English forms and insistence upon a jury trial guaranteed by the constitution led to persistent rejection of the pleas of lawyers and business people for an equity jurisdiction. In 1808 and again in 1812 proposals to remedy this situation, most onerous upon the trustee process and partnership in business, got nowhere.[14]

11. J. T. Austin, *Life of Elbridge Gerry* (Boston, 1828–1829), II, 323ff, 339ff, 343; J. Q. Adams, *Writings*, IV, 331; *Boston Gazette*, June 24, 1811; *Weekly Messenger*, Apr. 10, 1812; Parker to Sedgwick, July 25, 1811, Theodore Sedgwick Papers (MSS, MHS), IV, 947; Theophilus Parsons, *Memoir of Theophilus Parsons* (Boston, 1859), pp. 162ff; *Columbian Centinel*, Feb. 24, 1796; "Livy," *ibid.*, Mar. 23, 1808; Ames to Gore, Feb. 24, 1803, Fisher Ames, *Works* (Boston, 1854), I, 321; Cresson, *Francis Dana*, pp. 350ff. But see also Sedgwick to Otis, Feb. 7, 1803, S. E. Morison, *Life and Letters of Harrison Gray Otis* (Boston, 1913), I, 259.

12. Parsons, *Theophilus Parsons*, pp. 193ff; Smith, "Review," *Monthly Anthology and Boston Review*, 3 (1806), 150; *Letter of the Justices of the Supreme Judicial Court to His Excellency the Governor* (Boston, 1804), pp. 12ff.

13. To R. H. Lee, Apr. 11, 1789, T. C. Amory, *Life of James Sullivan* (Boston, 1859), II, 392; also William Manning, *Key of Libberty* [1798], ed. S. E. Morison (Billerica, 1922), p. 13.

14. See Bill of Rights, Art. XV; Sullivan, *Land Titles*, pp. 215, 216; Sedgwick to Story, Jan. 5, 1807, Sedgwick Papers, IV, 851; MA, House, 6265, 6413, 7232.

Niggardly compromises from time to time gave existing tribunals limited authority in equity, and the legislature through special act sometimes granted relief for special contingencies unforeseen by general law. As a result, after 1780 there was an enormous increase in such legislative business, which in the whole century before that date had generated only 102 private acts of all sorts.[15] But despite frequent proposals to create an equity jurisdiction, no court acquired blanket power to consider unusual cases. The inability to adapt "the form of . . . judgments to the various rights of parties" occasionally left wrongs without remedies. Exceptional cases could not come to trial as exceptions. If they were adjudicated at all, it was "by a rigid adherence to rules of decision," which did violence either to the rights of the contending parties or to the amorphous general principles which the same courts yet hoped to establish as permanent and inflexible.[16]

The absence of courts of chancery and the uncertain condition of the law left many questions on the brink of settlement. This indecision, the very need for decision, seemed intolerable in an atmosphere suffused with memories of heated revolutionary debates concerning the security of rights and of property against interference by government. Under the Commonwealth the agencies of government had actually become more numerous and more vigorous. The capacity for exercising political power rested in many hands. And if any given corporation held only a fragment, the sum was foreboding, for these organs of the state extended their activities into the very vitals of the economy and affected the welfare of all the citizens of Massachusetts.

All bodies politic had contact with property. In towns, common fields, and churches, well-established regulations, differing in detail but essentially the same, controlled such matters as membership, finance, and administration. These rules often carried over to the institutions established after 1780. But when corporations that held out profits as incentive to investors multiplied and spread, the practical management of their affairs raised new and exceptional problems difficult to solve by an appeal to naked principles. An attorney thus explained in 1810 that he

15. See *Acts and Resolves of the Province of the Massachusetts Bay*, Vol. VI, Appendix Vol. I, *Private Acts, 1692–1780* (Boston, 1896); also Sullivan, *Land Titles*, p. 101; W. S. Holdsworth, *History of English Law* (London, 1903–1938), XI, 326ff.

16. MA, House, 6265, 7232; Story, *Joseph Story*, I, 138, 139; *Boston Commercial Gazette*, June 16, 1817; Joseph Story, "Address before the Suffolk Bar, 1821," *American Jurist and Law Magazine*, 1 (1829), 21ff.

could find no precedent for the action he sought because "corporations were anciently not common, and the necessity did not exist." Proliferation beyond all former examples threatened individuals with injuries and necessitated additional remedies.[17] Many adversely affected by the power of the new bodies over property strove to set up limits, stressing the dissimilarity to the older types whose competence to act seemed beyond question. The incorporators themselves, who had sought the privilege of identifying themselves with the state, often found it essential in protecting investments to draw novel distinctions between their enterprises and the older corporations they emulated. None foresaw the ultimate result, but specific interpretations in case after case gradually undermined and transformed the law.

Although both English and American law recognized that "it was optional with the proprietors, whether they would or would not take the benefit of" the charter as a whole, a minority of the members had no discretion once the majority accepted the grant.[18] The legislature fully controlled the details of the acts of incorporation. It set town boundaries and transferred citizens from one jurisdiction to another without consent despite the effect on such matters as taxes and valuation. Common fields, too, included individuals and their property whether they willed it or no; indeed the subjection of a minority to a majority was often the very motive for organization. Finally, the General Court laid down conditions for participation in newer corporations; in the case of the Boston & Roxbury Mill Dam, for instance, it specified that three sevenths of the shares be available to all comers and that no more than fifty go to a single holder.[19] While the government rarely made public subscription a condition for charter and sometimes excepted recalcitrant individuals from the operations of common fields, there was no challenge to the state's power over membership until after the turn of the nineteenth century.[20]

The principle itself buckled under a heavy attack in 1807.

17. W. M. Richardson, of counsel for plaintiff, *Riddle* v. *Proprietors of the Locks and Canals on Merrimack River* (1810), 7 Tyng 180; also James Sullivan, "Opinion of the Attorney-General," MA, Senate, 2597; below, Appendix D.

18. *Riddle* v. *Proprietors of the Locks and Canals on Merrimack River* (1810), 7 Tyng 184.

19. St. 1814, ch. 39, secs. 7, 8.

20. See, e.g., st. 1785, ch. 10; petitions, J. Sprague *et al.*, Henry Bailey *et al.*, Elijah Dunbar and Nathaniel Fisher *et al.*, MA, 1797, ch. 81; *Boston Gazette*, Mar. 3, 1803.

Three years earlier the legislature had chartered the Front Street Corporation to improve real estate in Boston by building a new avenue that would raise the value of members' property. After the manner of common fields, the act had included all the owners of land involved. But when one of those who had not petitioned for the charter objected to an assessment, the courts held that the government could not impose association upon the unwilling.

This decision rejected the arguments of the corporation's attorneys, Theophilus Parsons and Samuel Dexter. These pillars of the law urged that the Front Street company was like any other common field which exercised similar powers "daily, and who ever heard it objected to, as an infringement of the rights of the citizens as secured by the constitution and the bill of rights?" Despite the evidence to support this position, Justice Isaac Parker accepted the flimsy authorities brought forth by opposing counsel, rendering a verdict less significant for its logic than for its reflection of a growing consciousness of difference.[21]

Sturdy precedents governing finance also withered when transplanted to the new fields of corporate activity. The powers of existing bodies politic at first carried over to new ones. Turnpike, bridge, boom, and manufacturing companies could, in fact, impose fines for infractions of by-laws.[22]

Clearly, also, the corporation controlled its own purse, drawing funds from members obliged to contribute. The general law confirmed the right of common fields to assess taxes, and even steps toward partition failed to diminish responsibility: owners permitted in 1796 to fence off their portions remained liable for their shares of the expenses of the whole. At every stage of their existence, the associations retained the power to raise funds "to support their incidental charges, and to bring forward the settlement and improvement of their lands."[23]

Every chartered body enjoyed the same fiscal authority. Thus the proprietors of the Neponset Mills had power to appoint collectors to assess "for protecting, defending or recovering their common rights" in the same manner "as town officers of like

21. *Ellis* v. *Marshall* (1807), 2 Tyng 268ff; also *Perry* v. *Wilson* (1811), 7 Tyng 393. The English cases cited all affirmed that a corporation was free not to accept grants or charters but did not touch upon the rights of a minority or of individuals in the corporation.

22. See st. 1802, ch. 97; st. 1786, ch. 69; st. 1801, ch. 63; st. 1788, ch. 60; st. 1789, ch. 41.

23. St. 1785, ch. 53, sec. 3; st. 1796, ch. 13; Sullivan, *Land Titles*, p. 172. See also MA, 1814, ch. 179.

description." [24] But the explicit enabling provision was not essential. All corporations assumed the same prerogative to raise funds, if they raised any at all, since few organizing acts provided for a share capital. In many companies there seemed no limit to the number or size of the levies. The Middlesex Canal called for fully one hundred. Despite voluntary limitations of the total by the members, the expenses of the enterprise sometimes forced demands beyond the contemplated amount; the Salem & Danvers Aqueduct collected $265 on shares initially set by agreement at $100.[25]

Fixed stock values, which appeared in the charters of banks after 1791 and of insurance companies later to secure the payment of capital, created some uncertainty about the limits of assessment.[26] There were grounds for the belief that a prescribed figure did not preclude further levies. As late as 1822 enough support for that belief lingered to convince some incorporators of the wisdom of inserting specific provisions in their charters fixing the par as the maximum. But the idea nevertheless gained currency that the same limit existed in the absence of explicit clauses to that effect.[27] In Massachusetts the question never came to issue, however, and the courts never ruled directly upon it because another related problem early overshadowed the matter.

Unless the corporations, effectively armed by the state, could compel their stockholders to disgorge amounts beyond the market price of the share, the mere power to vote taxes was irrelevant. The legislature had implemented the capacity to assess with the right to recover unpaid sums by seizing and selling the members' property. Delinquencies were rare in towns or in common fields where the land involved was more valuable than any single imposition. Nor did the contingency arise so long as a unique position and the relation to the state promised security through profits or public gifts to make up losses.

The nature of the problem changed as multiplication injected uncertainties about values and as experience showed that good returns would not always follow as a matter of course. Not all

24. St. 1797, ch. 77, sec. 2; st. 1808, ch. 100, sec. 1.
25. See [Caleb Eddy], *Historical Sketch of the Middlesex Canal* (Boston, 1843), pp. 22ff; "History of Salem and Danvers Aqueduct," *Essex Inst. Hist. Colls.*, II (1860), 107, 108.
26. See, e.g., st. 1795, ch. 22.
27. See, e.g., st. 1822, ch. 59. See also st. 1817, ch. 152, sec. 9. By 1824 a charter even included the rule that assessments could be imposed only by a two-thirds vote (see, e.g., st. 1823, ch. 95).

enterprises could adjust the amount of taxes to the members' willingness to pay. Turnpikes in particular entailed very heavy expenses before income started to come in, and, in addition, these enterprises were subject to unpredictable costs from suits for damage. Under such circumstances shareholders sometimes preferred to forfeit their stock rather than to lay out more cash. The corporations, in this instance more eager to stress than to obscure their origins, claimed that the matter did not end there; within the terms of the general act of 1804, which applied precedents from towns, they attempted to seize the delinquents' other property when the sale of shares failed to yield the full amount due.[28]

But the courts interpreted the provisions of the 1804 law very narrowly. In 1808 Chief Justice Parsons already spoke, incidentally, as if a turnpike company had no recourse when sale of its stock did not net the amount of the assessments.[29] A year later he held unequivocally that, despite the analogy to town procedure in the statute, the corporation could make collections only by the sale of the delinquents' shares.[30] These decisions permitted the seizure of other property only in the case of an explicit agreement to pay.[31] But subsequent rulings whittled away that residual power by reinterpreting ever more stringently what was a definite contract.[32] Ultimately the court decided that an accord to take one tenth of the shares after the members had estimated the total expense and had determined the amount chargeable to each was still not sufficiently specific to warrant any action beyond the sale of the defaulter's portion. Later cases declared the promises not binding on such grounds as alterations in the route of the road or the failure of the association expressly to ratify a stockholder's commitment.[33]

Thus in the most significant aspect of finance a persistent line

28. St. 1804, ch. 125; *Revised Statutes* (Boston, 1836), ch. 39, secs. 1–15.

29. *Tippets* v. *Walker et al.*, 4 Tyng 595.

30. *Andover & Medford Turnpike Corporation* v. *Gould* (1809), 6 Tyng 43; *Worcester Turnpike Corporation* v. *Willard* (1809), 5 Tyng 84.

31. See *Worcester Turnpike Corporation* v. *Willard* (1809), 5 Tyng 80ff.

32. *Gilmore* v. *Pope* (1809), 5 Tyng 491; *Andover & Medford Turnpike Corporation* v. *Hay* (1810), 7 Tyng 102.

33. See *New Bedford & Bridgewater Turnpike Corporation* v. *Adams* (1811), 8 Tyng 137; *Middlesex Turnpike Corporation* v. *Locke* (1811), 8 Tyng 367ff; *Middlesex Turnpike Corporation* v. *Swan* (1813), 10 Tyng 384; *Middlesex Turnpike Corporation* v. *Walker* (1813), 10 Tyng 390; *Essex Turnpike Corporation* v. *Collins* (1811), 8 Tyng 291. See also *Taunton and South Boston Turnpike Corporation* v. *Whiting* (1813), 10 Tyng 326. For application to other corporations see *Franklin Glass Company* v. *White* (1817), 14 Tyng 285; MA, Senate, 6031.

of thought split apart two kinds of corporations. The exact line of demarcation was still unclear; in the very cases that created the differences the judges often referred to all types, including towns, as similar. But they argued strenuously on the crucial matter of assessment that somehow a distinction existed between the old and the new bodies politic: in the former unlimited taxation did not violate the property rights of members, in the latter it did.[34]

A divergence equally striking arose in the government of the corporation. The position of officers was at first obscure. Some principles specifically detailed in the charters, such as the requirement for an oath and a bond, carried over from the practice of towns and common fields. But other characteristics of corporate officers, not spelled out in the acts, became subjects of doubt when the legislature, in occasional situations, began to deviate from precedent.

Town functionaries were not personally liable for the consequences of their actions as agents of the body politic. Most new charters remained silent on the applicability of this rule. But in financial institutions the General Court early drew distinctions between the new and the old bodies for the purpose of checking the extensive power of officials over the property of others. To protect both the stockholders, otherwise personally liable, and the creditors, Massachusetts after 1792 explicitly fixed responsibility upon directors for certain illegal operations which weakened the corporation's ability to pay — in banks for issuing obligations exceeding double the amount of paid-in investment, and in insurance for assuming risks after losses had lowered the capital stock. The seriousness of such liability became clear when the collapse of the Berkshire Bank led to the ruin and imprisonment for debt of its administrators. A bill in 1809, passed by the Senate but referred by the House, would even have made bank authorities personally accountable for bills not paid when presented.[35]

Where the charters said nothing about the accountability of officers, many people assumed that precedents derived from analogy with the earlier forms applied. One aspect of the question was adjudicated in 1808. The courts then supported the

34. See also below, pp. 155–157.
35. See, e.g., st. 1791, ch. 65; st. 1798, chs. 46, 50; st. 1802, ch. 126; st. 1804, ch. 8; MA, House, 6639; J. E. A. Smith, *The History of Pittsfield . . . 1800 to . . . 1876* (Springfield, 1876), p. 183. For English precedents see Holdsworth, *English Law*, VIII, 203.

contention that directors lacked the immunities of selectmen and, in doing so, attempted to fasten upon those charged with the business of the new companies a special responsibility for their conduct. Parsons thus rejected Dana's argument that officials contracting in behalf of a turnpike corporation but failing to use the common seal had the same status "as public agents . . . acting in a public capacity, and not as individuals." The chief justice pointed out: "A case of this kind is not like a contract made by an agent for the public, and in the character of an agent, although it may contain an engagement to pay in behalf of the government. For the faith and ability of the state in discharging all contracts made by its agents in its behalf, cannot, in a court of law, be drawn into question." [36] This particular decision dealt with a narrow point, but it reflected the broad tendency toward differentiation.

In these years the ability to pay, upon which Parsons rested the distinction between turnpike and town officers, entered into prominence in another context. The multiplication of profit-seeking corporations and the loss of security that came with the disappearance of the unique position of any of them raised serious questions concerning who was answerable for the debts of the body politic. The law had always recognized a distinction between personal and corporate obligations. But until the end of the eighteenth century the line between participant and association was still unclear, and the former was still privately responsible if the company was unwilling or unable to pay; each man in the group was "lyable by himself for the whole." [37]

On occasion, the legislature used limited liability as a special concession to accompany the charter for a special purpose. In Massachusetts a measure of exemption appeared first in mutual fire-insurance companies where all the creditors were also members.[38] In rare contingencies the General Court bestowed similar grants on other bodies to meet exceptional needs; a supplementary law thus permitted members of the Exchange Coffee House to raise a mortgage "without personal responsibility." [39]

36. *Tippets* v. *Walker et al.* (1808), 4 Tyng 594ff. By contrast, see the ruling for public agents in *Brown* v. *Austin* (1804), 1 Tyng 208.

37. Thomas Hobbes, *Leviathan* (London, 1651), p. 120; see in general, Oscar and M. F. Handlin, "Origins of the American Business Corporation," *Jour. of Econ. Hist.*, 5 (1945), 8ff; J. P. Davis, *Corporations* (New York, 1905), I, 26. See also the validity of returns against a member for the acts of a corporation (*King* v. *Rippon*, 1 Comyns 87, 1 Ld. Raym 563, *English Reports*, XCL, 1267, XCII, 973).

38. See, e.g., st. 1797, ch. 67.

39. St. 1807, ch. 78.

But no Bay State corporation received the blanket privilege by charter.

The question of liability did not arise so long as the power of unlimited assessment gave the corporation access to the resources of its members. Under these circumstances the problem might emerge only when an intransigent group refused to make levies. Creditors would then face difficulties; having contracted with the association, they were unable at law to sue stockholders not parties to the agreement. According to the principles laid down in the case of *Dr. Salmon v. the Hamborough Company*, the litigant in England and in many American states could get directly at the individuals through an action in equity to force the corporation to tax its members.[40] The absence of a broad equity jurisdiction in Massachusetts interposed difficulties to the application of the Hamborough rule and, from time to time, led to haphazard procedural remedies.

The issue hardly presented itself to the consciousness of legislators in the first twenty years after the Revolution, a period which saw not a single creditor loss from corporate activity to give reality to random speculations about what might happen in the event. For two decades the problem remained purely hypothetical.

The point became a subject for serious thought only when changes in the internal organization of the corporation — the new rules of membership, assessment, and government — put practical obstacles in the way of holding investors liable. The same trends that freed individuals and their property from the collective body also relieved them of responsibility for its debts. With the power of assessment shattered, resourceless corporations were helpless to levy upon their members for the satisfaction of creditors. Yet the latter found the courts unwilling to entertain actions against stockholders unless there was a specific enabling provision in the charter.

After 1800 the difficulties of turnpike creditors in securing payment for injuries showed that implications in the law, no matter how strong, were not enough. The general act regulating

40. American courts upheld those principles as late as 1828, although soon after there were divisions of opinion about whether the responsibility of the stockholder was direct, primary, and total, or indirect, secondary, and proportional through liability to the body politic. See *Slee* v. *Bloom* (1821), 19 Johnson (New York) 456; *Hume* v. *Winyaw and Wando Canal Company* (1828), *Carolina Law Journal*, 1 (1831), 217; *American Law Magazine*, 1 (1841), 106; *ibid.*, 4 (1845), 362ff, 368, 372; Holdsworth, *English Law*, VIII, 204ff; Samuel Williston, "History of the Law of Business Corporations before 1800," *Harvard Law Review*, 2 (1888), 162.

those roads had expressly provided for payment of damages in the manner already established for county highways. The lower courts accepted this law at its letter, ruling that, by the failure of the corporation to pay, individuals were subjected to the same personal liability as county residents in such cases.[41] But the courts of appeal hesitated to hold shareholders thus responsible. In 1809 Parsons settled beyond question a principle he had suggested parenthetically a year earlier, that "private property of the individual members cannot be taken in execution to satisfy a judgment against the corporation."[42] The chief justice deplored the absence of an adequate procedure. But he reversed the decision of the inferior tribunal, denying that an analogy existed between a turnpike and a county road, damages for which "may be recovered . . . by a warrant . . . levied on the personal estate of any inhabitant." The difference, he thought, originated in the absence of the power to force the payment of assessments and "in the want of a remedy for a corporator, whose estate may be taken . . . against the corporation; whereas an action is expressly given to the inhabitant of a town . . . against the town."[43]

The basis of this decision was procedural, the lack of redress for what seemed a wrong to the very judge who delivered the verdict. Although the courts would take no action under such circumstances, even against the fraudulent transfer of shares, the underlying assumption of individual liability remained unaffected. Those who suffered appealed to the legislature for relief or sought protection from this hostile current of opinion by contracts in which all the stockholders covenanted to be bound personally for the corporation's debts.[44]

But ten years later the growing freedom of the members from responsibility for the acts of the collective body produced an explicit, if tangential, judgment in favor of limited liability. Two significant decisions in 1819 dealt with the right to sue the former participants in a dissolved bank for the amount of bills still outstanding. Wishing to do justice to both the creditors and the stockholders, the bench ruled that relief could come only through equity. That jurisdiction alone could spread the cost evenly among all the investors, a necessary condition since each

41. St. 1804, ch. 125.
42. *Tippets* v. *Walker*, 4 Tyng 595.
43. *Commonwealth* v. *Blue Hill Turnpike Corporation* (1809), 5 Tyng 420ff.
44. See MA, House 6689, 7192; see also petition of John Vinson *et al.*, January 1816, MA, Senate, 5875, 5875/1; *Tileston et al.* v. *Newell et al.* (1816), 13 Tyng 406.

was responsible for no more than the amount he had put into and ultimately withdrawn from the capital of the defunct institution. To sustain this contention, the judges made a critical assumption concerning the nature of liability in a going corporation. They argued that the charter created whatever accountability existed, and that the absence of specific provision in the act of incorporation limited the commitments of the stockholder to his contribution to the joint stock.[45] In documenting this dictum, the court appealed not to precedents in English or American law but to a vague recollection of "the public opinion, that individuals were not answerable by the principles of the common law." The shocked editor of the reports commented: "Surely public opinion ought not to be quoted as law." [46]

This decision was a landmark in the transformation of an immunity growing out of the unfortunate deficiency in procedure to an immunity based on abstract doctrine. Some vagueness concerning the scope of liability persisted. As late as 1825 a canal company, the charter of which was silent on the question, secured a declaratory law to make sure that the stockholders would not be accountable. A year later the members of the Massachusetts Charitable Mechanics Association were uncertain, until reassured by Judge Jackson, about their personal liability if the corporation erected a building. And the question continued to crop up from unexpected sources.[47] The concept that individuals were not responsible for corporate debts in the absence of express provision had nevertheless imperceptibly become accepted; Dane in 1824 and Angell and Ames a decade later thought it a matter to be taken for granted.[48]

The direction of legal opinion conformed with a change in the general conception concerning liability. Eventually even those corporations that had charters which contained procedural statements specific enough to saddle them with the continued burdens of unlimited liability found relief. The problem of

45. *Vose* v. *Grant* (1819), 15 Tyng 505ff; *Spear* v. *Grant* (1819), 16 Tyng 9ff. The creditor in this case ultimately found relief in the federal court of equity: see *Wood* v. *Dummer* (1824), 3 Mason 308, *Federal Cases*, XXX, 435ff; *American Law Magazine*, 1 (1841), 101ff; ibid., 4 (1845), 371ff. See also S. M. Israeli, *Nature of the Liability of Shareholders* (Philadelphia, 1901), pp. 3ff.

46. *Spear* v. *Grant*, 16 Tyng 13.

47. St. 1825, ch. 11, sec. 2; J. T. Buckingham, *Annals of the Massachusetts Charitable Mechanic Association* (Boston, 1853), p. 211; S. A. Johnson, "Genesis of the New England Emigrant Aid Company," *New England Quarterly*, 3 (1931), 99.

48. Nathan Dane, *A General Abridgement and Digest of American Law* (Boston, 1824), I, 472; J. K. Angell and Samuel Ames, *A Treatise on the Law of Private Corporations Aggregate* (Boston, 1832), pp. 349ff.

remedies had occasionally come before the legislature, which had included in some acts of incorporation provisions to smooth the way of creditors made particularly rough in Massachusetts by the absence of equity. Such clauses, like the clauses detailing almost every other attribute of the body politic, appeared in some charters and not in others, without consistency and without any particular pattern.

With personal accountability unquestioned at the beginning, restatement in the statutes came only in oblique references incidental to other matters. The general laws regulating towns and parishes merely set up a procedure for enforcement in connection with suits for damages, providing for the levy of an execution against the collective body on the individual property of a member.[49]

Similar mention appeared quite casually in other charters. In the case of insurance, the act of incorporation stipulated expressly how to assess stockholders beyond their investment to meet all the losses the company might legally incur.[50] In the case of canals, there was a formal statement of responsibility in relation to damages; executions could be levied "against the property only of the Corporation, or of any individual belonging thereto." [51] A provision in the general statute for aqueducts dealt with dissolution, which by common law ended all liability, and with the peculiar difficulties of collection in corporations accommodating their own members, where "it would not be for the benefit of any other Person to purchase a Delinquent's share." [52] The manufacturing law of 1809 set up a mechanism, copied from a number of earlier grants to industry, by which an officer serving a writ or execution against a corporation was free to levy "the same writ or execution upon the body or bodies, and real and personal estate or estates of any member or members." [53] An identical clause had already appeared in the charter

49. *Chase* v. *Merrimack Bank* (1837), 19 Pickering 564; Dane, *Digest of American Law*, V, 158. For common fields see, e.g., st. 1794, ch. 38.

50. See st. 1795, ch. 22; st. 1798, ch. 50; st. 1802, ch. 126; also MA, Senate, 4938/1, 6108.

51. St. 1791, ch. 57; st. 1792, ch. 13; also MA, Senate, 3622.

52. MA, Senate, B 2636. For the problem of dissolution see *American Law Magazine*, 1 (1841), 96ff, 106ff; Williston, "Law of Business Corporations before 1800," *Harvard Law Review*, 2 (1888), 163ff; Stewart Kyd, *Treatise on the Law of Corporations* (London, 1793–1974), II, 516; William Blackstone, *Commentaries on the Laws of England* (London, 1793–1795), I, 484.

53. See st. 1808, ch. 65, sec. 6; also st. 1807, ch. 33, sec. 8; st. 1817, ch. 183; st. 1821, ch. 38.

of the Exchange Coffee House.[54] The absence of such explicit provisions for enforcing the claims of creditors against the stockholders of banks produced difficulties after 1810 and ultimately led to a law reaffirming the liability of the latter for the legal limit of indebtedness — twice the capital.[55]

For towns, these provisions remained binding through this whole period and beyond. But with the emergence of the doctrine limiting liability in the absence of specific declarations, the vestigial clauses that implemented full accountability in some old charters took on the aspect of aberrations. The broadening interest in the new types of corporations created resistance to legislative action to demolish the immunities marked out by the courts and eventually freed also the companies to which liability was clearly fastened.

The trend was early evident in banking. Sullivan's violent attack upon the Massachusetts Bank in 1792 had sounded the alarm that establishment of director accountability for misdeeds might by implication grant stockholders an unprecedented, uncommon freedom from responsibility. The charge served originally to prove the iniquity of the first institution and helped open the field of banking to many imitators. But as multiplication converted attackers into participants in privileges, the embryonic evil gradually became a positive virtue, and criticism of a vice turned into defense of a possible source of advantage. Meanwhile the doctrine that fixed par values circumscribed assessments produced the impression that the member bound himself to no more than the specified contribution and ultimately led to the belief that only the absence of a capital provision was compatible with liability, although the courts had never ruled on this matter.[56] Banks retained the provision for double liability of stockholders, but efforts to extend shareholder responsibility to cover new and unforeseen kinds of losses from speculative expansion and from the broadening deposit business

54. St. 1807, ch. 31, sec. 7.

55. In this period, notes were the only important liabilities of banks and those were limited by the charter to 150–200 per cent of capital. Directors were personally responsible for excess issue (see above at note 35). For limited liability in banks see James Sullivan, *Path to Riches* (Boston, 1792), p. 59; MA, Senate, 4069; *New-England Palladium*, Feb. 26, 1805; *Salem Gazette*, Feb. 6, 1810; *Boston Gazette*, Sept. 16, 1811; res. 1810, chs. 87, 88, 89. For the question in England see [Adam] Anderson, *Historical and Chronological Deduction of the Origin of Commerce* (Dublin, 1790), VI, 221.

56. See, e.g., st. 1817, ch. 180, sec. 2; *American Law Magazine*, 1 (1841), 100, 103ff; *ibid.*, 4 (1845), 369.

came to nought in the face of the trend toward freedom from accountability.[57]

That trend finally affected manufacturing too. Here for a while personal responsibility for corporate debts had actually become broader and heavier. With the merchants hostile to industry after 1815, and with others lukewarm once the pressure of war waned, the failures in manufacturing evoked measures to prevent stockholders from evading liability.[58] But those very failures dramatized the utility of limitation to potential investors in hazardous ventures. The possibility of industrial expansion, more attractive to the mercantile community after 1824, raised fears in the legislature lest perpetuation of full liability drive business and capital to other states. And as the favored position of other corporations became clearer, the incongruity of this invidious distinction became more striking. The efforts of Governor Lincoln helped secure a modification in 1826 and, in another four years, the final grant freeing stockholders of accountability.[59] Occasional movements in the next two decades to reverse the trend gained little support. Some questions later arose from loosely worded charters but did not negate the clearly accepted principle.[60]

The development of the concept of limited liability, eventually so prominent an attribute of corporateness, was but one facet of the general process that differentiated the old from the new associations. Beyond the changes in internal structure that protected the property rights of individuals from the coercive power of the collective body was a further transformation in the relation of the body politic to the Commonwealth which had chartered it.

57. See MA, Senate, 6787, 6787/1; *Boston Commercial Gazette*, June 20, 1816; F. H. Chase, *Lemuel Shaw* (Boston, 1918), p. 86.

58. See st. 1817, ch. 183; st. 1822, ch. 109; *Marcy v. Clark* (1821), 17 Tyng 330; *Boston Commercial Gazette*, Jan. 24, 1822.

59. See st. 1826, ch. 137; *House Docs., 1829-30*, no. 1, pp. 24-27; "Manufacturing Corporations," *American Jurist and Law Magazine*, 2 (1829), 92ff; W. E. Rappard, *Les Corporations d'affaires au Massachusetts* (Paris, 1908), pp. 24-28. For the arguments of an old-line merchant against limited liability, see William Sturgis, *Boston Daily Advertiser*, Feb. 19, 1830; for favorable comments, cf. *ibid.*, Jan. 13, 19, 30, Feb. 19, 1830; *Springfield Gazette*, Jan. 24, 1844.

60. See *Senate Docs., 1837*, nos. 18, 27; *Address of the Democratic Members of the Legislature of Massachusetts . . . 1843* (Boston, 1843), pp. 13, 14; *Boston Daily Advertiser*, Jan. 25, 1844; Webb to Sumner, Dec. 3, 1855, Charles Sumner, "Letters Received" (MSS, Houghton Library, Harvard University), XXVIII, 106; also *Revised Statutes*, ch. 38, secs. 27-37.

As the corporations increased in number and flowed over into new channels, strange problems emerged, the solution of which altered the original status and created a distinctive pattern of autonomy.

That autonomy did not exist to begin with. Public function took precedence over private rights.[61] The Commonwealth was master of its creatures, particularly since Massachusetts after 1780 no longer recognized the constituent powers of prescription, and embryonic organizations could not evolve to the higher corporate status without charter. The government prescribed the character and conditions of duties in return for the grant, delegating to its agencies what powers and privileges it wished for the better service of its own interests. It alone could terminate the existence of a corporation or relieve it of obligations.[62] Bodies politic could not voluntarily dissolve, although special provisions allowed common fields to do so by dividing their lands according to a formal, supervised procedure.[63] The duration of corporate life was also discretionary with the state, terminable at will in the absence of express time limits; a perpetual charter was merely *capable* of indefinite duration, not irrevocable.[64]

Incorporation was, like any other legislative act, subject to repeal or amendment by the enacting body.[65] The General Court had always felt free to replace one grant or franchise by another, creating bridges, for instance, to take the place of ferries, with or without compensation.[66] The state assumed as a matter of

61. See argument of the plaintiff in *Foster* v. *Essex Bank* (1819), 16 Tyng 254ff, 263ff; above, pp. 93–94.

62. See *Commonwealth* v. *Union Fire and Marine Insurance Company in Newburyport* (1809), 5 Tyng 230; and *Riddle* v. *Proprietors of the Locks and Canals on Merrimack River* (1810), 7 Tyng 183ff, which rejected the argument of the defendants to the contrary, *ibid.*, 175ff.

63. See st. 1785, ch. 53, secs. 8, 13; Sullivan, *Land Titles*, p. 175. For cases in Lenox and New Marlborough see, e.g., Willard Phillips Papers, 1769–1836 (MSS, MHS), Oct. 9, 1787; see also, e.g., st. 1822, ch. 60; *Mansfield* v. *Hawkes & al.* (1817), 14 Tyng 439. On the power of voluntary dissolution see C. J. Holt in *Butler* v. *Palmer* (1700), 1 Salk 191, *English Reports*, XCI, 172; *American Law Magazine*, 1 (1841), 97ff; Holdsworth, *English Law*, IX, 64ff. Per contra, cf. James Wilson, *Works* (Philadelphia, 1804), II, 428, on the basis of 3 Burr 186; an unclear reference, possibly *Mayor of Colchester* v. *Seaber* (1766), 3 Burr 1867, *English Reports*, XCVII, 1140.

64. See Davis, *Corporations*, II, 121; Blackstone, *Commentaries*, I, 467ff, 474; Wilson, *Works*, II, 427.

65. Sullivan, *Path to Riches*, pp. 57, 58; Blackstone, *Commentaries*, I, 44; [David Henshaw], *Remarks upon the Rights and Powers of Corporations* (Boston, 1837), pp. 5ff.

66. See, e.g., st. 1787, ch. 27; st. 1791, ch. 35; st. 1792, chs. 63, 71; st. 1800, ch.

course that it would adjust its agencies to the needs of changing conditions and aspirations, often stating that intention explicitly in the organizing act.[67] But with or without such reservations, the Commonwealth between 1792 and 1812 repeatedly modified charters, holding with Blackstone that "acts of parliament derogatory from the power of subsequent parliaments bind not." [68] While those affected, like the Massachusetts Bank in 1812, exerted "themselves by every fair & honorable mean in their power" to prevent the passage of unfavorable legislation, they failed to appeal to the judiciary.[69] The government that had made the corporation retained the power to alter or unmake it.

Even when there was no change in the specific charter, each additional act of incorporation in any field inevitably, if indirectly, impaired the rights and privileges of those already granted. The process of multiplication reduced the banks' sphere of influence from a statewide to a town level and then eliminated any monopolistic element altogether. New turnpikes opened alternative routes and diminished the business of the old, with compensation in only one case.[70]

The whole issue arose very clearly with regard to traffic over the bridges north of Boston. In 1791 the legislature favored the revived plan for the West Boston Bridge in the face of opposition from Harvard and from the Charles River Bridge, which claimed an exclusive right to the whole line of travel. Although the state compensated the old corporation and also the Essex-Merrimack when it chartered the Newbury Bridge, that did not serve as a compulsive precedent in other cases. The South Boston and West Boston bridges thus received nothing when the South Boston Free Bridge and the Mill Dam destroyed monopolies. The Charles River Bridge itself found its old advantage of slight assistance against new competitors; in 1805 it built a new street over the Mill Pond to forestall another rival. Spans at Lechmere and Prison Point in 1807 and 1816 further revealed the extent

---

40; and the arguments in the Charles River Bridge case (1829), 7 Pickering 390ff, 413, 471, 483ff, 516ff.

67. See, e.g., st. 1807, ch. 33, sec. 9; st. 1807, ch. 139, sec. 8; st. 1812, ch. 40, sec. 5.

68. Blackstone, *Commentaries*, I, 89. For a specific case see st. 1791, ch. 65; N. S. B. Gras, *Massachusetts First National Bank of Boston* (Cambridge, 1937), pp. 217ff.

69. Gras, *Massachusetts First National Bank of Boston*, pp. 219–221, 407, 408; st. 1812, ch. 33.

70. Alford & Egremont paid one fifth of its receipts to the Twelfth Massachusetts Turnpike (see st. 1805, ch. 96).

of legislative power to charter new corporations and to order payments of compensation or not at its discretion. The Commonwealth adjusted the degree to which any franchise covered a line of traffic, holding the common interest in improved communications more important than the individual advantage of the corporation or its members.[71]

Much of the thinking on the question of the dependence and independence of the body politic revolved about consideration of the length of its life. As Massachusetts strove to induce enterprisers to enter new economic spheres, it was willing to hold forth various attractions to secure the status of the property involved in the new companies. Corporations early asked to have specified a definite number of years within which to make collections, a precaution to give substance to the promise of a return on investments.[72] Other associations obtained similar safeguards to assure them of their privilege for a determinate period of time. To that extent the legislature committed itself to abstention from interference with its creatures. What the nature was of an omnipotent state's commitments, in this or in any other respect, was irrelevant so long as the Commonwealth honored them to lure capital into the enterprises it sponsored.

After 1800, however, the defenders of companies under attack put forth the argument that an express provision of time reflected not the generosity but the miserliness of the state, and that the absence of such provision implied an assurance of interminable life. By 1802 James Sullivan, for instance, confessed himself ignorant about the meaning of the charter of the Massachusetts Bank which he had himself drafted in 1784: there was no mention of time, but the certainty he had shown in 1792 that the state could dissolve the corporation vanished, shaken by the implications of that doctrine for his own investments and for the widespread holdings now involved in the new form.[73] Further growth of such holdings nurtured the idea put forth by Tudor in 1809 that the corporation was "beyond the control of the legislature." [74] Ten years later, in the Dartmouth College case, John Marshall assumed that the validity of the proposition needed no

71. The whole argument was recanvassed in the Charles River Bridge case (1829), 7 Pickering 351, 378ff, 383ff, 391ff, 411, 457, 467, 480ff. There is an excellent map, *ibid.*, 386. See also st. 1794, ch. 3; MA, 1792, ch. 65.

72. See, e.g., st. 1791, ch. 57; st. 1796, ch. 93, sec. 7.

73. See MA, Senate, 2957; Amory, *James Sullivan*, I, 146, 387; Sullivan, *Path to Riches*, p. 57. See below, Appendix D.

74. *Monthly Anthology and Boston Review*, 7 (1809), 191ff.

argument, and in still another decade, in the Charles River case, even the extreme anticorporate elements conceded that, in the absence of specific mention of duration, corporate life was eternal.[75]

Commitments concerning duration were, however, of limited importance as long as the act of incorporation, like any other act, was subject to repeal or amendment by the legislature. Continued existence was worthless without security for the privileges associated with the corporation. Investors who sought guarantees of continuance also found it necessary to fight for acceptance of the principle that promises set forth in the charters were inviolable. To sustain that contention they had to maintain that the legislature irrevocably bound itself by the act of incorporation, a notion that received legal form from the application to the relations between state and corporation of the common idea of a compact among the members of a body politic.

As the spread of corporations raised the problem of the extent of state power, the guardians of property sought to defend the rights granted by the charter through an appeal to the concept of contract, a concept which had a powerful hold on the popular consciousness. Veneration for the sanctity of contracts had deep roots in Massachusetts life and had gathered strength from the discussions of the revolutionary era. Samuel Adams had regarded contractual rights as protection against the overweening ambitions of parliament, and a Berkshire County convention in 1774 had echoed his appeal; "Any franchises and liberties . . . granted to a corporation and body politic . . . cannot legally be taken from such corporations and bodies politic, but by their consent or by forfeiture." [76] That the corporation referred to in this appeal was the state itself gave dignity to the argument when applied to new bodies. The form of the constitution of 1780 and the long discussions of the public debt had re-emphasized the importance of the concept. The inviolability of contracts written into the federal Constitution seemed for many the essential ingredient of the social order. With Fisher Ames they early perceived the necessity of fighting the belief that "compacts and constitutions are deemed binding only so long as they are liked by a majority." [77]

75. See *Trustees of Dartmouth College* v. *Woodward* (1819), 4 Wheaton 489 (Curtis); Morton in *Charles River Bridge* v. *Warren Bridge* (1829), 7 Pickering 447. See also Charles Sumner, "Lawyers' Common-Place Book" (MS, 1830, Harvard University Archives), p. 177.
76. *Massachusetts Spy*, July 28, 1774.
77. *Monthly Anthology and Boston Review*, 2 (1805), 565. Note, however, the

The application of the contract conception to the relations between state and corporation seemed, as late as 1812, "too fanciful to need any observation." [78] Yet seven years later the Dartmouth College case held unequivocally that the charter was a contract not subject to amendment by the legislature.[79] The decision represented a substantial triumph for those corporations struggling for freedom from government control, and the magnitude of the victory became apparent in the very same year when a constitutional convention asked Harvard to consent to a change affecting the university.[80] In practice, clauses reserving the liberty to alter and repeal softened the impact of the verdict.[81] The scope of corporate autonomy was yet to furnish the material for bitter struggle in the forty years after 1820. But the developments of the preceding four decades had already endowed these bodies with rights beyond the reach of the state. That new attribute reflected a significant transformation in the character of the institution and conditioned the nature of later contests.

In every phase of adaptation, novel conditions had pressed those concerned with corporations to the same recourse. Each inconvenient precedent that, in actual operation, threatened individual property rights elicited the claim that somehow a distinction existed between the old and the new, the former public, the latter private. The blundering attempts to define that difference as specific cases raised fragmentary aspects of the question testified to the persistent consciousness that all the bodies once considered public were no longer the same in essence.

At the beginning of the century, Judge Isaac Parker had rested the distinction on motive. The Front Street company, he

---

limited scope as in Noah Webster, *Collection of Essays and Fugitive Writings* (Boston, 1790), p. 41. See also "Star in the American Horizon," *Columbian Centinel*, May 30, 1795; "Retribuo," *Worcester Magazine*, 3, (1786–87), 162ff.

78. See *Brown* v. *Penobscot Bank* (1812), 8 Tyng 448.

79. 4 Wheaton 518ff (Curtis), and especially Chief Justice Marshall's decision, *ibid.*, 484ff. See also *Revere* v. *Boston Copper Company* (1834), 15 Pickering 360. Significantly, the state courts held that the contract did not preclude legislative extension of charters. See *Foster* v. *Essex Bank* (1819), 16 Tyng 244. On the case in general see Handlin, "The American Business Corporation," *Jour. of Econ. Hist.*, 5 (1945), 17ff; [Henshaw], *Rights and Powers of Corporations*, pp. 5ff.

80. *Journal of Debates and Proceedings in the Convention to Revise the Constitution of Massachusetts, 1820* (Boston, 1853), pp. 72ff, 86; Josiah Quincy, *History of Harvard University* (Cambridge, Mass., 1840), II, 332. Ultimately the doctrine received legislative formulation (see Rappard, *Les Corporations d'affaires au Massachusetts*, p. 36).

81. See st. 1830, ch. 81; Rappard, *Les Corporations d'affaires au Massachusetts*, p. 45.

felt, was private because private individuals operated it "for their emolument or advantage," while common fields were public, "promotive of general convenience, and operating equally upon all citizens whose property is . . . improved by them." This distinction was unreal since common fields and wharves were also formed for the profit of their organizers. The court actually found it urgent, lest "an unnecessary alarm . . . may spread in the community," to go out of its way to reassure the public that the law for common fields remained unchanged.[82]

Theophilus Parsons, as counsel for the losing side in the Front Street case, had rejected Parker's reasoning and had denied the justice of distinguishing among various kinds of corporations. But succession to the bench brought a new perspective. The immediate compulsion for ruling on cases in which new bodies seemed to have outgrown old precedents forced him also to create two categories, although on reasoning different from his predecessors. "We distinguish," he wrote, "between proper aggregate corporations, and the inhabitants of any district, who are by statute invested with particular powers without their consent." [83]

Joseph Story perceived that the original character of the corporation stood in the way of a clear line turning on function or organization. In the Dartmouth College case he expounded a broader-based conception, first set forth four years earlier in his decision in *Trevett v. Taylor*. The distinction, he maintained, arose from the kinds of rights involved. Private corporations were those invested with private property; public, those charged only with government or administration. "A bank created by the government for its own uses, whose stock is exclusively owned by the government, is, in the strictest sense, a public corporation. So a hospital created and endowed by the government for general charity. But a bank, whose stock is owned by private persons, is a private corporation, although it is erected by the government, and its objects and operations partake of a public nature." [84]

Story's reasoning was acute enough to focus on the central significance of property rights. But bound, like his colleagues on the bench, by the exigencies of the case at hand, he broadened the meaning of private property to the point of meaninglessness.

82. See *Ellis* v. *Marshall*, 2 Tyng 268ff.

83. See *Riddle* v. *the Proprietors of the Locks and Canals on Merrimack River* (1810), 7 Tyng 186ff; Theophilus Parsons, *Commentaries on American Law* (New York, 1836), p. 378.

84. 4 Wheaton 508 (Curtis).

By holding that ownership of lands and buildings constituted a college a private corporation he created a category that contained every species of body politic, including the town.

Despite this weakness, Story's opinion profoundly influenced the American law of corporations. For decades thereafter arguments over what was public and what was private revolved about his definition. In this respect Story was more fortunate in his audience than James Wilson and Thomas Paine, who had forty years earlier ineffectually attempted to distinguish between private and public laws.[85] The difference in reception arose from the historical evolution of the business corporation in the period of origins, which created a widespread consciousness that a boundary, however defined, existed between public and private.

The people of Massachusetts could think of the corporation as public as long as it held a singular position in the state. That conception could hang on while there was some connection with a territorial unit, as long as there was only one insurance company in each county, one in each town. But the extension of privilege created bodies that competed with one another and made it increasingly difficult to identify them as public communal agencies.[86]

With the lapse of time, too, those the corporation served viewed it in a different light. Remembrance of the service rendered by the bridge or turnpike faded, but the obstructions to navigation and the burden of toll, symbols of corporate privilege and profits, remained.[87] Struggles over the assessment of damages to property and disappointment over the location of routes, overissue of notes by banks and favoritism in loans to directors further undermined faith in the corporation as a government instrument for the common welfare.[88] By 1806 a petulant editor warned his readers that they would see their "rivers blocked up with toll bridges and" their "farms cut into

---

85. See, e.g., st. 1808, ch. 65, sec. 7. For the American distinction between public and private laws, see James Kent, *Commentaries on American Law*, ed. O. W. Holmes and C. M. Barnes (Boston, 1884), I, 459; for the English, see Holdsworth, *English Law*, XI, 292ff, 613.

86. See the reasoning of the court in *Proprietors of the Kennebeck Purchase v. Crossman* (1810), 6 Tyng 458.

87. See, e.g., petition of Haverhill, MA, 1791, ch. 35. Those symbols were particularly impressive in the case of the turnpikes which merely improved old roads (see petition of Sam Jones, MA, 1799, ch. 54, and the Amherst remonstrance, MA, 1799, ch. 21).

88. See, e.g., *Jenks' Portland Gazette*, Dec. 13, 1802; MA, 1796, ch. 78; "Report of the Committee," MA, 1799, ch. 54.

inch pieces by Turnpike roads." [89] As the old aspect receded, another, always present, came more sharply into focus. The corporation, stripped of its original connotations, stood forth primarily a profit-making institution, a business vehicle serving the interests of investors rather than a public agency utilizing private capital. In this respect it had become in practice more like noncorporate businesses than like nonbusiness corporations.

The mark of the new status was the creation of a profit-making capital stock. All bodies politic started with the simple power of assessment. But in those which became known as business corporations the conduct of the venture or the terms of the charter required the accumulation of goods as an investment which would ultimately earn profits. The prevailing respect for the sacred character of property threw into the shadow every other aspect of the corporation. The individuals in it became less important as members of an association than as investors in the stock, and their relation to the body seemed best described in terms of interest in the capital. Occasional efforts to emphasize the fact that the institution had a reason for existence beyond its desire for earnings, by minimizing the weight of property in voting, were ineffective. The provision for proxies permitted large venturers to circumvent the clauses for a maximum number of votes to an individual, and thus to gain full representation for their holdings. And ultimately the law recognized what had earlier existed in fact, that the internal government of these corporations rested entirely upon interest.[90]

The property element, looming ever larger in discussions, in argument, and in thinking, transformed the legal conception of the corporation. In 1807 Judge Theodore Sedgwick parenthetically drew an analogy between stockholders and copartners in a decision that affirmed the pre-emptive right to subscribe to new stock.[91] A year later, Parsons held that the corporation received tolls in trust for members in proportion to their shares.[92] A

89. *Eastern Argus*, May 2, 1806, quoted by W. A. Robinson, *Jeffersonian Democracy in New England* (New Haven, 1916), p. 104.

90. For the development of the rule of voting, see the provisions in the following acts: st. 1692–93, ch. 28; st. 1712–13, ch. 9; st. 1783, ch. 25, sec. 7; st. 1791, ch. 65; st. 1792, chs. 6, 13, 63; st. 1793, ch. 21; st. 1795, ch. 22; st. 1817, ch. 180, sec. 3; *Revised Statutes*, ch. 36, sec. 22.

91. *Gray v. Portland Bank* (1807), 3 Tyng 382. See also A. A. Berle, Jr., and G. C. Means, *The Modern Corporation and Private Property* (New York, 1932), pp. 133, 144, 256ff; Victor Morawetz, "Pre-emptive Right of Shareholders," *Harvard Law Review*, 42 (1928–29), 186ff.

92. *Tippets v. Walker* (1808), 4 Tyng 595; see also 3 Tyng 377.

decade later, Story took up the same interpretation in *Wood v. Dummer*, elaborating a conception that entirely obscured the associational element: the capital was a trust fund, the corporation a trustee, and the stockholder *cestui qui trust*.[93]

A new idea of the very nature of the corporation thus emerged to parallel the changes that narrowed its functions and powers. The form became less a favored associational device within the Commonwealth than a mere contrivance for avoiding the inconveniences of partnership. "The true object of creating manufacturing corporations," argued an attorney somewhat later, "is to facilitate the formation of partnerships." [94]

Yet how account for the ties to the state of a technique of business management? Why the need of a charter, for instance? Ultimately, Chancellor Kent supplied the link: corporateness was not merely the capacity for acting as a body that could hold franchises; it was itself a franchise, granted, like other privileges, in return for services to the public. Here were the roots of the problems of real and fictitious personality, eventually so troubling to jurists.[95]

But practical men, after 1820 as before, did not await the outcome of legal lucubrations. Important new questions in the forty tumultuous years down to 1860 led to a pragmatic probe of the new relationship.

Whatever the later legal developments, the first four decades of operation had set the pattern. The corporation, utilized as an instrument of state activity in the economy, had fallen away from the control of those who first perceived its advantages. As forces inherent in the nature of the society pressed for multiplication, dispersal brought new attributes, and a private character

93. 3 Mason 308, *Federal Cases: Comprising Cases Argued and Determined in the Circuit and District Courts of the United States from the Earliest Times* (St. Paul, 1894–1897), XXX, 435ff. See also Story's comments in the Dartmouth College case, 4 Wheaton 51ff (Curtis); and the analogy of the counsel for the defendants in *Riddle v. Proprietors of the Locks and Canals on Merrimack River* (1810), 7 Tyng 177.

94. *Revere v. Boston Copper Company* (1834), 15 Pickering 357; also *Marcy v. Clark* (1820), 17 Tyng 333, 334; *Portland Bank v. Apthorp* (1815), 12 Tyng 257; Sedgwick in *Gray v. Portland Bank* (1807), 3 Tyng 381ff; *Franklin Glass Company v. White* (1817), 14 Tyng 288.

95. A. A. Berle, Jr., *Studies in the Law of Corporation Finance* (Chicago, 1928), p. 11. See also Parsons in *Tippets v. Walker et al.* (1808), 4 Tyng 595; E. H. Warren, *Corporate Advantages without Incorporation* (New York, 1929); E. M. Dodd, Jr., "Dogma and Practice in the Law of Associations," *Harvard Law Review*, 42 (1928–29), 977ff; Holdsworth, *English Law*, IX, 64ff; Ernst Freund, *Legal Nature of Corporations* (New York, 1929), pp. 10ff, 13ff.

replaced the public. Ties to the state became ever weaker while those to the individual shareholder became stronger.

These gradual developments lay behind the unfolding law. The exercise of governing powers that impinged upon private property rights, once justified by a public function, seemed to involve empirical injustices in the hands of groups operating for private emolument. The decisions that freed individuals from the necessity of joining a corporation, that guarded their property against the consequences of assessments and against the errors of their officers, all manifested a tendency to protect members of these associations from the vast governing powers of the body politic as originally conceived. At the same time, loss of the unique relation to the Commonwealth brought into being the belief that subjection to the state should be no more rigorous in the case of corporations than of other businesses. And the law of private rights forestalled interference with privileges originally granted to government agencies. Recognition that these bodies were not simply vehicles for state action presaged a new period in the relations of Massachusetts and its economy.

7 | Acquiescence as State Policy

Democratic unwillingness to confine the corporation to a favored few had dispersed it among many holders and that in turn had separated it from the state. Yet after four decades of development, the separation was partial and provisional only; the Commonwealth still retained the chartering power. To that extent, persistence of some connection, no matter how altered, forced Massachusetts to act as if the old presumptions continued to possess some validity.

The trend toward divorce, however, intensified after 1820. The process which multiplied the institution and the unfoldment of its private character reacted upon each other in a reciprocal, cumulative fashion. Every new grant strengthened the grounds for considering the corporation private; every new affirmation of privateness strengthened the hands of those who demanded new grants. The dissociation of government and corporation proceeded more rapidly in some economic activities than in others, but by 1850 the process had everywhere lost its provisional character. The last anachronistic attempts to shape economic policy through the bestowal of charters melted into thin air.

The body politic did not forfeit its popularity as its original qualities faded; new attributes — limited liability and security of organization — added to its desirability as a business form. The spread therefore continued without interruption, indeed, at an ever accelerating pace.

Manufacturing corporations, which enjoyed fewest corollary favors and were least dependent upon state aid, gained considerable currency in the decade of struggle with England. Steady growth persisted with enabling acts easy to come by.[1] The legislature rarely scrutinized petitions with care and showed no desire to restrict the propagation of its creatures. Requests rejected in one session were likely to pass with ease in another. The number of charters granted mounted rapidly, and their scope expanded to include the distribution of power and other peripheral activities.[2]

Charters were granted to manufacturing corporations as follows: [3]

1789–1796	3
1800–1809	15
1810–1819	133
1820–1829	146
1830–1835	100

Occasional belated demands, as in the aftermath of the panic of 1857, for a limit to the number of new companies or for guarantees of solvency as a condition of acquiring a charter met with no response. Massachusetts would take no measures to circumscribe the diffusion of the corporate form in industry. Nor did the General Court concern itself with unofficial, extralegal steps in that direction. The attempts of industrialists to concentrate control came without either active approval or disapproval by the state.[4]

In banking, which rested on the government-granted right to issue notes, the process by which the Commonwealth surrendered the capacity to limit numbers was slower and more complex. The promise of profits attracted many new venturers whose demands for a share in the privilege consistently brushed aside

1. W. E. Rappard, *Les Corporations d'affaires au Massachusetts* (Paris, 1908), p. 244.
2. See, e.g., st. 1824, ch. 26.
3. Compiled from *Senate Docs., 1836*, no. 90, pp. 7ff.
4. See *Report of the Committee of the Boston Board of Trade Appointed to Make a Thorough Investigation of the Recent Monetary Difficulties* (Boston, 1858), p. 16; Adams to Sumner, Oct. 5, 1857, and Dana to Sumner, Oct. 6, 1857, Charles Sumner, "Letters Received, 1830–1874" (MSS, Houghton Library, Harvard University), XXXV, 20, 21; E. B. Bigelow, *Remarks on the Depressed Condition of Manufactures in Massachusetts* (Boston, 1858), *passim*. See also in this context [Boston Board of Trade], *The Report of the Committee on a Resolution Submitted to the Government of the Board, February 1, 1858, by James C. Converse, on the Subject of the Branch House System* (Boston, 1858), pp. 3–17.

qualmish attempts to curb expansion. Soul-searching re-examination of policy after each periodic disorder of the currency often pointed the road to fewer charters but never induced the legislature to take it.

In 1820 the state ceased to be a participant in the banking business. Although the legislature insisted upon retaining the provisions of the acts of incorporation that permitted subscriptions by the Commonwealth, the high returns upon such investments made public contributions unwelcome. Massachusetts supplied no part of the new capital that entered finance in the four decades before 1860.[5] Without a concrete stake in these enterprises, the government no longer held the interest of a partner and relinquished the potentiality of acting through the appointment of directors. As in other branches of the economy, it exerted direct influence upon banking policy primarily through its power of granting or withholding charters.

But the critical decisions in 1812 had already implicitly circumscribed the capacity to exercise that power. Notwithstanding the bitterness of the conflict over recharter, the settlement of 1812 had substantially stabilized the Massachusetts banking system, withdrawing it from the grasping hands of a favored few. For a time thereafter, the question of currency was academic only. The effects of early disorders had passed over and the amount of paper remained stable. In fact, specie holdings, larger than circulation through the war years, permitted Bostonians to heed Nathan Appleton's advice to maintain payments when the New York institutions gave way in 1814.[6]

But accepted principles of sound finance succumbed under the strain of the economic adjustments consequent on peace. The resumption of foreign trade drew gold out of the country. The banks manipulated circulation through the period of crisis, alternately expanding and contracting the issue. These institutions generally profited thereby, but the effects upon business were unescapably bad. A severe panic and a series of failures that reached their climax in 1819 led to suspension. Widespread ruin illuminated again the stark dependence of the economy upon the course of financial policy and reopened the discussion of the wisdom of liberal grants of charters.[7]

5. See *Senate Docs., 1826–27*, no. 14; *House Docs., 1833*, no. 2, p. 23.

6. J. B. Felt, *Historical Account of Massachusetts Currency* (Boston, 1839), p. 219; Robert Rantoul, Jr., *Memoirs, Speeches and Writings* (Boston, 1854), p. 648; R. C. Winthrop, "Memoirs of Hon. Nathan Appleton," *Mass. Hist. Soc. Proceedings*, V (1861), 286.

7. See *Boston Commercial Gazette*, Dec. 10, 1818; J. Q. Adams, *Memoirs*

To the overseas merchants this and succeeding crises revealed the double-edged menace in the insecurity of the circulating medium, a direct derivative of free-and-easy incorporation. As exporters of specie in the normal course of exchange, they found interruptions in suppply restrictive if not ruinous, while the rise in the price of imports that followed the fall in the value of paper hurt dealings with the interior. The same derangements brought other calamities upon them. Though they themselves suffered, the very nature of their dealings offered a perpetual butt to those who sought a scapegoat for the difficulties of the nation's money. Adam Seybert, among others, early popularized the charge that the unfavorable balance of trade with the Orient contracted the American supply of specie, and that at the root of every stringency were the operations of foreign commerce.[8]

Apologists admitted that, in consequence of intercourse with the East, gold and silver were never available for domestic transactions. Some, including Richard Hildreth, who had his own score to settle with the banking system, argued, however, that internal credit felt no ill effects from the export of specie which in any case could not swell the American circulating medium. Others accepted the theory of a fund of money based on the quantity of metal but maintained that in the United States, by way of exception, the currency expanded with the requirements of the economy.[9] Francis Bowen went further and claimed it adjusted automatically if it was not interfered with.[10] Nevertheless, the failure of the automatic adjustments to operate during depressions led Willard Phillips, a staunch defender of commerce, to suggest government action to induce the import of specie, a tacit recognition of the link between its absence and suspension.[11]

(Philadelphia, 1874–1877), May 24, 27, 1819, IV, 370, 375, 499–501; Samuel Rezneck, "Depression of 1819–22," *Amer. Hist. Rev.*, 39 (1933), 28ff.

8. Criticized by [Willard Phillips], "Statistical Annals," *North Amer. Rev.*, 9 (1819), 224, and defended by "Public Interests," *Boston Commercial Gazette*, Oct. 14, 21, 1819. See also, e.g., "The Prospect before Us," *North Amer. Rev.*, 17 (1823), 206, 207.

9. "Prospect before Us," *North Amer. Rev.*, 17 (1823), 200ff; [Phillips], "Statistical Annals," *North Amer. Rev.*, 9 (1819), 225, 227; Daniel Webster, *Works* (Boston, 1853), II, 124; Willard Phillips, *Manual of Political Economy* (Boston, 1828), pp. 79ff, 94ff; R[ichard] Hildreth, *Letter to His Excellency Marcus Morton, on Banking and the Currency* (Boston, 1840), pp. 4, 5, 15.

10. Francis Bowen, *Principles of Political Economy* (Boston, 1856), pp. 306ff, 335ff, 355; H. E. Miller, *Banking Theories in the United States before 1860* (Cambridge, Mass., 1927), p. 61.

11. [Willard Phillips], "Plan of an Improved System," *North Amer. Rev.*, 2 (1815–1816), 369ff, 374ff.

Here was the merchants' difficulty: currency should have enough flexibility to prevent dissatisfaction with a specie-draining trade, yet not so much as to drive away that specie. Legal tender printed by the state they considered bad and, in any case, unconstitutional. The only assurance of safety and uniformity seemed to lie in a system of convertible bank notes, with the government enforcing payment as if each note were a contract.[12] But that system, experience had demonstrated, was hazardous, menaced by temptations to undue expansion beyond the point, varying with the productive resources of society, "at which advantageous accumulation [of wealth] ceases."[13] Most worrisome was the horrendous contingency that unrestrained extension might put the privilege of issue into the hands of unskilled men, giving play to speculation, to the "miscalculations and dishonesty of individuals," the true cause of depressions.[14] The merchants were not the only group concerned; they gained support from industrial interests relatively unprotected by tariffs in the 1840's and 1850's and fearful of a rise in comparative cost of production from a currency cheapened by the multiplication of banks.[15]

No one championed the cause of dishonesty. But many groups in the state displayed unflinching faith in the pump-priming faculty of looser credit and denied the possibility of locating a fixed point beyond which diffusion ceased to be beneficial. The less stable banks outside Boston, designated according to the practice of the time as "country," were not simply farmers' institutions. Some husbandmen in outlying regions sought new charters for the sake of softer money. But so did manufacturers, artisans, and even merchants who did not scruple to serve themselves through banks in the hinterland, as the examples of the Agricultural and the Fall River banks demonstrated.[16]

In truth, this was a period when money borrowers, not money

12. [George Bancroft], "Bank of the United States," *North Amer. Rev.*, 32 (1831), 34, 40, 52ff; *Boston Quarterly Review*, 3 (1840), 247.

13. Phillips, *Manual of Political Economy*, p. 95.

14. [Phillips], "Statistical Annals," *North Amer. Rev.*, 9 (1819), 228; Francis Bowen, *Political Economy*, pp. 277ff, 316, 317; Hildreth, *Letter to Morton*, pp. 6ff.

15. See [Nathan Appleton], *Examination of the Banking System of Massachusetts* (Boston, 1831), p. 17; *Senate Docs., 1858*, no. 17, p. 13; Governor Banks' address, *Senate Docs., 1859*, no. 1, p. 24; A. S. Bolles, *Financial History of the United States* (New York, 1894–1896), II, 449ff.

16. See *History of the County of Berkshire*, ed. D. D. Field (Pittsfield, 1829), pp. 177ff; J. E. A. Smith, *The History of Pittsfield . . . 1800 to . . . 1876* (Springfield, 1876), pp. 379ff; W. S. Lake, "History of Banking Regulation in Massachusetts, 1784–1860" (unpub. diss. Harvard University, 1932, University Archives), pp. 99–105.

lenders, organized such enterprises, when every would-be debtor was potentially a member of the board.[17] Community sentiment, beguiled by the magic that turned paper into gold, aspired to the dignity of a bank even when the volume of probable business was low, and thus fortified the pleas of those with special interests. The very men who agreed that "there are now too many" went on to reason, "but if Banks circulate why may not we have a Bank." [18] Soon there were calls for an institution "on every street of our city and in every town of the Commonwealth." [19] Numbers and capital both doubled in the seven years after 1822, with the new charters modeled after that of the State Bank.[20]

There was some hope that the expiration of all the grants in 1831 would offer an opportunity to review the system. Nathan Appleton in that year cautiously suggested a limit to note issue. Yet not one corporation failed of renewal under the old terms.[21] Furthermore, the legislature continued to create new companies. Committees with an over-all view of the situation repeatedly turned down petitions only to see local interests prevail in the General Court. Some projects were stillborn, but those which went into operation swelled the state's circulation.[22] The sixty-six Massachusetts banks of 1829 grew to 129 by 1837, and their capital mounted from twenty to thirty-eight million dollars.[23] The accompanying table shows the number of banks chartered during three periods between 1811 and 1835.

Bank Charters in Massachusetts [24]

	Number	Property
1811–1820	29	$12,814,000
1821–1829	51	15,534,000
1830–1835	48	40,523,000

Hostile critics ascribed this growth to the influence of bank speculators in the legislature. Proponents justified it by the need

17. See the complaint of a legislative committee looking back at this period, *Senate Docs., 1845,* no. 101.

18. Pomeroy to Sedgwick, Jan. 25, 1825, Theodore Sedgwick Papers, 1768–1858 (MSS, MHS), 2 ser., VIII.

19. "Q," *Boston Commercial Gazette,* July 4, 1825.

20. Rantoul, *Memoirs,* pp. 650ff; also, e.g., st. 1822, chs. 68, 69.

21. See st. 1830, ch. 58; *Senate Docs., 1826–27,* no. 14; [Appleton], *Banking System of Massachusetts,* pp. 3ff, 46ff.

22. See, e.g., *Boston Commercial Gazette,* Mar. 19, 1835; *Berkshire County,* ed. Field, p. 177.

23. Rantoul, *Memoirs,* pp. 650ff; Lake, "Banking Regulation in Massachusetts, 1784–1860," pp. 80–87, 90.

24. Compiled from *Senate Docs., 1836,* no. 90, pp. 47ff.

for competing with the liberal credit conditions of neighboring states like Rhode Island.[25] But at the root was the complacent feeling that these institutions hurt no one, that bank money could "never do more than displace the specie in circulation." [26] Merchants who disliked expansion in general, if not in particular, could not block it and consoled themselves with the reflection that diversification of issue stood in the way of total loss in the event of fraud or disaster.[27]

The perspicacious saw signs of a collapse before 1837, a falling ratio of specie to circulation and a decline in the interest rate that encouraged speculation and dangerous overextension. Warnings that *something must be done* to slacken note issue or "a *crash* will be the consequence" went unheeded. The ensuing panic shook every bank in the state.[28]

Governor Everett, in a strategic position, wished to use the crisis to liquidate the weaker institutions. He held off a call for a special session that might relieve the banks of tremendous penalties for failure to redeem promptly, and, when the legislature met, he recommended dissolution of firms unable to conform to the law.[29] Although some actually lost their charters, contraction of banking facilities in the immediate aftermath of panic was short-lived. Repeal of the troublemaking specie circular, an omen of good times in Boston, led to a revival of incorporation. Notwithstanding another recession in 1842, growth continued as before.[30] By 1853 there were more than fifty million dollars of bank capital in the state, yet the next year saw calls for an additional seventeen million. By 1856 there were almost sixty million, one sixth of the total in the United States. Legislative committees and governors alike pointed to the dangers but were powerless to put a stop to the process before the great crash of 1857.[31]

25. "Q," *Boston Commercial Gazette*, July 4, 1825; *ibid.*, Mar. 19, 1835; Rantoul, *Memoirs*, pp. 305ff, 374ff.

26. [Bancroft], "Bank of the United States," *North Amer. Rev.*, 32 (1831), 31, 33. See also Governor Everett's address, *House Docs., 1836*, no. 6, pp. 16ff.

27. Phillips, *Manual of Political Economy*, pp. 263, 264; Bowen, *Political Economy*, p. 352.

28. Felt, *Massachusetts Currency*, pp. 233ff; Lake, "Banking Regulation in Massachusetts, 1784–1860," pp. 133ff; see also below, p. 216.

29. Everett to Mrs. Martineau, May 10, 1837, Edward Everett Papers (MSS, MHS), LXVII, 188.

30. Cleveland to Sumner, June 3, 1838, Charles Sumner, "Letters Received," V, 8; Mason to Ticknor, July 23, 1842, [G. S. Hillard], *Memoir and Correspondence of Jeremiah Mason* (Cambridge, Mass., 1873), p. 364.

31. *Senate Docs., 1854*, no. 65; *Senate Docs., 1856*, no. 204; Governor Gardner's address, *Senate Docs., 1855*, no. 3, p. 26; *Senate Docs., 1856*, no. 3, p. 29.

Nor did the state establish any other institution to super-impose the might of government over these unpredictable creatures.[32] The merchants, though clamoring for reform, found unacceptable the safety-fund system installed in New York in 1829. They criticized it as unfair, taxing the well-managed firms in the interests of the poorly managed, and questioned the likelihood that good banks would force redemption at the expense of their own money in the fund.[33] For a time antipathy to this system earned support for the Bank of the United States, particularly while William Appleton was president of the Boston branch. But though Whig ties ensured a modicum of continuing loyalty on political grounds, Nicholas Biddle's policies in the unsuccessful struggle to keep the company alive antagonized many influential Massachusetts people.[34] More and more the conviction spread that a revived institution, even if chartered, could not remain free of politics and escape another Jackson.[35] New proposals for government banks continued to emerge, but they smacked too heavily of party affiliations and were generally too inflationary in intent to earn wide mercantile support.[36]

As earlier, the only effective efforts at control came through voluntary arrangements which rested upon the assumption that "the operations of banking contain their own check within themselves; and as long as bills are really convertible at sight, the obligation to redeem necessarily sets exact limits to the power of emission" and therefore to credit.[37] The Berkshire Bank episode had early proved that pressure upon lax institutions could keep alive the power to redeem. Soon thereafter the New Eng-

32. For other proposals for direct government action, see [Phillips], "Plan of an Improved System," *North Amer. Rev.*, 2 (1815–1816), 376ff; Bowen, *Political Economy*, pp. 335ff, 363, 369; Hildreth, *Letter to Morton*, p. 14.

33. See R. E. Chaddock, *Safety-Fund Banking System in New York* (Washington, D.C., 1910), pp. 259ff; W. B. Lawrence, "Bank of the United States," *North Amer. Rev.*, 32 (1831), 556ff; Bowen, *Political Economy*, p. 363.

34. See Lawrence, "Bank of the United States," *North Amer. Rev.*, 32 (1831), 554; [O. W. B. Peabody], "Bank of the United States," *North Amer. Rev.*, 35 (1832), 507ff; "Memoir of Hon. William Appleton," *Mass. Hist. Soc. Proceedings*, VI (1863), 450; *Boston Commercial Gazette*, Feb. 16, 1832.

35. Everett to Davis, June 28, 1839, Everett Papers, LXVIII, 290. For earlier merchant hostility, see [Appleton], *Banking System of Massachusetts*, pp. 44ff.

36. See "Facts and Arguments in Favor of a Bank of Ten Millions," *Senate Docs., 1836*, no. 30, pp. 4–16; *Proceedings of the Friends of a National Bank* (Boston, 1841), pp. 3ff; A. B. Darling, *Political Changes in Massachusetts, 1824–1848* (New Haven, 1925), pp. 135ff; Lake, "Banking Regulation in Massachusetts, 1784–1860," pp. 88, 89.

37. [Bancroft], "Bank of the United States," *North Amer. Rev.*, 32 (1831), 28ff; [J. B. Congdon], *Defence of the Currency of Massachusetts* (Boston, 1856), p. 12.

land Bank of Boston had formalized the practice of holding country houses in line by persistently presenting notes for redemption in specie and adamantly refusing to accept paper, including its own, except at a discount. Its experience taught a significant lesson to all the metropolitan banks.[38]

In 1824, as an outgrowth of this practice, the Suffolk Bank became depository of a permanent fund, subscribed to by a combination of Boston institutions and used to secure prompt redemption. The Suffolk System thrived in the 1830's and 1840's and, for a time, controlled the circulating medium of the New England states.[39]

This voluntary device, upheld as legal by the courts, functioned for thirty years but then succumbed to opposition. From the very beginning it was the target of an enveloping fusilade discharged from those in rival camps; both those who protested that it restricted and those who complained that it weakened the currency fought it.[40] An attempt in 1838 by some members of the General Court to undermine the institution petered out.[41] But the drive to freer and looser banking drew strength from every new charter and ultimately culminated in the Bank of Mutual Redemption (1855), a cooperative enterprise in which the country banks were prominent. The Suffolk System collapsed, unable to hold its own against a competitor that supplied similar clearinghouse services without as rigid control.[42]

Other financial institutions passed through the same process of corporate diffusion. By 1856 eighty-four savings banks held more than twenty-seven million dollars in deposits.[43] In insurance, automatic recharter of the old companies as their terms expired accompanied the creation of many new ones. The desire for security against losses at sea continued to grow. Protection

38. *Boston Commercial Gazette*, Feb. 15, 1816. See particularly the episode of the New York banks' notes, res. 1814, ch. 94; correspondence of King and Gore, July 11–28, 1814, C. R. King, *Life and Correspondence of Rufus King* (New York, 1894–1900), V, 397–403. See also [Appleton], *Banking System of Massachusetts*, p. 14; Felt, *Massachusetts Currency*, pp. 216–218; Justin Winsor, *Memorial History of Boston* (Boston, 1880–1881), IV, 159ff; D. R. Dewey, *State Banking before the Civil War* (Washington, D.C., 1910), pp. 79ff; see also above, p. 119.

39. See D. R. Whitney, *Suffolk Bank* (Cambridge, Mass., 1878), pp. 6–15; [Nathan Hale], "Remarks on the Banks and Currency of the New England States," *North Amer. Rev.*, 22 (1826), 467ff; [Appleton], *Banking System of Massachusetts*, pp. 15, 16; Darling, *Political Changes in Massachusetts*, pp. 13–16; Lake, "Banking Regulation in Massachusetts, 1784–1860," pp. 196ff.

40. See *Boston Commercial Gazette*, Feb. 12, 1816; Rantoul, *Memoirs*, p. 656. For a defense see [Congdon], *Defence of the Currency*, pp. 21, 22.

41. *Daily Evening Transcript*, Jan. 27, 1838.

42. St. 1855, ch. 450; st. 1860, ch. 124; Whitney, *Suffolk Bank*, pp. 57ff.

43. *Senate Docs., 1856*, no. 204, p. 5. See also *Senate Docs., 1836*, no. 90, pp. 6off.

against fire became common in even very small towns, with enterprises springing up everywhere to profit from the demand for the service.[44] In Boston the old fire insurance firms agreed to oppose the creation of new ones with a capital of less than two hundred thousand dollars, but such informal attempts to limit expansion soon broke down. Not all the charters were acted upon; in the decade before 1856 less than twenty of the sixty companies created went into business, a circumstance which further illustrates the ease with which grants were secured.[45] Easy incorporation before long became common in life insurance too; new companies destroyed the unique position of the Hospital Society, and the first mutual organization in New York provided a model much approved and much imitated in Massachusetts.[46]

The play of expansive forces upon an institution brought into being as an instrument of state policy emerged most clearly in a new branch of transportation. In the effort to reach through to the West, begun after 1815, the corporate technique was not lightly resorted to; by then the emergence of the contradictions implicit in the transformation of a special privilege into an ordinary business form had precipitated a conscious canvass of the problems of government control. But awareness of the pitfalls proved no assistance in avoiding them. The plans for a unified and coherent system of communications for the state also fell before the irresistible wave of newly chartered enterprises.

After the Treaty of Ghent, improved transportation became vitally important, promising to crowd into a few years the progress of generations and justifying almost any means of realization. Even speculation, a wasteful raiser of prices in other fields, seemed tolerable here, "since an increased productive power or facility of communication . . . augments the general resources" of the state.[47]

At the beginning merchants like Abbott Lawrence, who saw in the old Northwest, now being settled, the great American markets of the future, had the greatest stake in these develop-

44. See, e.g., st. 1819, ch. 8; st. 1822, chs. 74, 83, 91, 96; st. 1823, ch. 127; *Woburn Journal*, Mar. 20, 1852; Isaac Goodman, "History of Sterling," *Worc. Mag. and Hist. Jour.*, 2 (1826), 51; *Boston Commercial Gazette*, Feb. 20, 1837.

45. See Governor Gardner's address, *Senate Docs., 1856*, no. 3, p. 23; *Boston Courier*, Feb. 9, 1835; Winsor, *Boston*, IV, 186ff; *Senate Docs., 1836*, no. 90, pp. 62ff.

46. See D. R. Jacques, "Mutual Life Insurance," *Hunt's Merchants' Mag.*, 16 (1847), 152ff; *Boston Daily Advertiser*, Sept. 25, 1843, Feb. 8, 1844; N. I. Bowditch, *History of the Massachusetts General Hospital* (Boston, 1872), p. 71.

47. See Phillips, *Manual of Political Economy*, p. 51; Edward Everett, "Im-

ments. To secure a share as entrepôt for this rich trade, Boston needed man-made routes to the west to compete with those which nature had bestowed upon rival ports. As it was, the Massachusetts metropolis hardly felt safe in its own back country. Greedy neighbors in Portsmouth, Providence, Hartford, and most of all in New York spirited business away from the Hub. Only forceful action would protect and extend trade.[48]

To achieve their objectives the merchants turned naturally to the state. An unfriendly national administration left little hope of federal aid, and individuals were slow to take the initiative or risk. An unsuccessful petition requesting state subscription to the Gloucester Canal to Boston pointed out: "A few only of the most enterprizing citizens of Gloucester appear to be engaged in the work as proprietors, and as they are actively engaged in commerce, and prefer to employ their capital in commercial pursuits; they are desirous that the Commonwealth from the public utility of the project should bear a part of the cost." [49] The most direct and most powerful means of improvements seemed to rest in the Commonwealth. "Many things," it was acknowledged, "should no doubt be left to individual enterprize," but transportation "may and ought to receive a salutary stimulus from well timed public encouragement." [50]

General agreement about the need for government aid did not forestall tedious disagreement about its form, disagreement that delayed every positive step for more than a decade. Tentative attempts to meet the problem came early and accelerated after the Treaty of Ghent. Fears that the Connecticut River trade would drift to New York led to a demand in 1814 for a westward link. Two years later the legislature appointed Loammi Baldwin and John Farrar to report on a canal to unite the Connecticut and Merrimack rivers. In 1818 Baldwin, drawing on his experience as engineer for Virginia, suggested that Massachusetts follow the example of that state in creating a board of public works, a huge public holding corporation, to gather information, to plan, and to invest in internal improvements.[51] The Empire

portance of Scientific Knowledge to Practical Men," *Orations and Speeches on Various Occasions* (Boston, 1853–1868), I, 261.

48. See, e.g., "Message of Levi Lincoln," *Senate Docs., 1828–29*, pp. 14ff; *Boston Daily Advertiser*, Jan. 22, 1830; H. A. Hill, *Memoir of Abbott Lawrence* (Boston, 1884), pp. 10–12.

49. MA, Senate, 6882/1. See also [Phillips], "Statistical Annals," *North Amer. Rev.*, 9 (1819), 220ff.

50. [Jared Sparks], "Internal Improvements of North Carolina," *North Amer. Rev.*, 12 (1821), 17.

51. See *Boston Gazette*, Feb. 28, 1814; *Boston Commercial Gazette*, Jan. 25,

State's Erie Canal quickened interest in his proposal for a canal from Boston to the Hudson. "Enough has been executed in the State of New York," wrote an influential contemporary, "to convince the most sceptical, that Massachusetts must be intersected by canals, or the capital will suffer." [52]

But the emergence of a new factor put off action. The feasibility of the Granite Railroad, chartered to carry stone to the Bunker Hill Monument, struck a deathblow at Massachusetts canal projects, particularly since the mountains between Boston and the Hudson Valley had all along presented difficult engineering problems. T. H. Perkins' petition for a railroad to Albany and Governor Lincoln's warning that others were outdistancing the Bay State led to the appointment of a legislative committee and the review in the next few years of the various projects.[53]

Farmers, attracted by easier markets for their products, regarded the proposed road favorably at this time. In the west, local committees of correspondence organized to press vigorously for it.[54] The Blackstone Canal opening the interior business of Massachusetts to Providence added a forceful point to the arguments in favor of a railroad. Meanwhile, the growing city of Worcester, until then a village of four thousand, demanded connection with the seaboard. Impressed by the urgency, a new Board of Directors of Internal Improvement, led by Nathan Hale, recommended a railroad via Worcester and Springfield to Albany and warned that "the assistance of the Government in some manner and to some extent . . . must be given to the work." [55]

1816; *Recorder*, Jan. 24, 31, 1816; [Loammi Baldwin], "Annual Report," *North Amer. Rev.*, 8 (1818–1819), 3ff; [J. L. Sullivan], "Internal Improvements in South Carolina," *ibid.*, 13 (1821), 144ff.

52. *Bowen's Boston News-Letter*, Apr. 22, Dec. 16, 1826. See also [Patterson of N.Y.], "The New York Canals," *North Amer. Rev.*, 14 (1822), 231ff; [Major H. Whiting, U.S.A.], "Internal Improvements," *North Amer. Rev.*, 24 (1827), 1ff; "Q," *Boston Commercial Gazette*, Mar. 24, 1825.

53. "Message of Levi Lincoln," *Senate Docs., 1826–27*, pp. 7–9; "Speech of Levi Lincoln," *Senate Docs., 1826–27*, pp. 5, 13ff; st. 1827, ch. 116; [Nathan Hale], "Remarks on the Practicability and Expediency of Establishing a Railroad . . . from Boston to the Connecticut River," *North Amer. Rev.*, 24 (1827), 475ff.

54. See the correspondence from Springfield, West Springfield, Westfield, and Otis, Aug. 6, 9, 11, 31, 1827, Sedgwick Papers, 2 ser., VIII; *Senate Docs., 1828–29*, no. 2, pp. 9, 10; Smith, *Pittsfield, 1800 to 1876*, pp. 517ff; [Nathan Hale], "Report of the Board of Directors of Internal Improvements . . . on . . . a Rail Road from Boston to the Hudson River," *North Amer. Rev.*, 28 (1829), 529.

55. See st. 1822, ch. 27; st. 1823, ch. 77; st. 1825, ch. 144; st. 1826, ch. 74; *Senate*

Still, the form in which aid by the Commonwealth would best serve to modernize the communications system remained uncertain. William Jackson and Theodore Sedgwick, among others, pointed out that Massachusetts experience scarcely supported faith in the corporation as an effective instrument of public action. They suggested that the state abandon the use of intermediaries and adopt instead the alternative of building and operating directly a canal or railroad. Private capital would not venture into so hazardous an enterprise "without the pledge of more exclusive privileges than it would be expedient for the Legislature to grant." "The important interests of the people," Governor Lincoln held, "can only be preserved, and the honour and prosperity of the State promoted, by a system of Governmental enterprize." [56] The old canals and turnpikes had fallen into the hands of "speculating proprietors"; only direct state control could ensure the management of the new enterprises for the public good.[57]

Swayed by these arguments, a legislative committee in the session of 1828–1829 suggested a canal to the west, with funds to come from a state lottery. Similarly, a Boston meeting in February 1829 resolved that the towns on the route ought to sponsor a railroad, with Massachusetts subscribing at least one third of the stock. When the General Court was slow to act, a Faneuil Hall meeting asked the city of Boston to offer one million dollars toward financing a project or to undertake one alone. Again in 1829 another legislative committee recommended, although without results, that the state build a line, raising funds by a loan.[58]

A few opponents objected that direct action by the government was unconstitutional. But as a railroad man pointed out, " '*Constitutional* impediments' can be made to come and go at . . . will," and those criticisms counted little.[59] More weighty was the fear of expense to taxpayers, which for years stood in the way of substantial contributions from the Commonwealth.

Docs., 1828–29, no. 24, pp. 1–4; [Hale], "Report of the Board of Directors," *North Amer. Rev.*, 28 (1829), 528ff.

56. *Senate Docs., 1826–27*, p. 5; Berkshire [pseud.], *Brief Remarks on the Railroads, Proposed in Massachusetts* (Stockbridge, 1828), p. 14.

57. "Q," *Boston Commercial Gazette*, Mar. 24, 1825; see also MA, Senate, 8189; *House Docs., 1828–29*, no. 12, pp. 4ff, no. 42, pp. 1, 2.

58. *House Docs., 1828–29*, no. 12; *Senate Docs., 1828–29*, no. 24, pp. 6–12; *Boston Commercial Gazette*, Feb. 19, 26, 1829, May 17, June 3, 7, 21, July 15, Aug. 5, 12, 1830.

59. *Boston Commercial Gazette*, June 21, Aug. 9, 1830.

From the start there were complaints that the cost would be "little less than the market value of the whole territory of Massachusetts." [60] Self-appointed guardians of the public purse pointed in horror at the example of Pennsylvania, where a thirteen-million-dollar debt for construction required seemingly enormous exactions.[61] Against this false economy the proponents of improvement urged that the "mere poverty of the Treasury, while there is abundance in the community," ought not "to defeat . . . [a] most desirable accomplishment," that the state was free of liabilities, that its current expenses were low, and that many years had passed without a direct tax.[62] But the theory that the expanding economy of Massachusetts made deficits unimportant carried little weight against the farmers' terror of debt and the general fear of the slightest rise in taxes.[63] Cautious legislators, unassured, remained dubious.

The proposal that the government itself build and finance the road to the west threw discussions of the route into the political arena and further complicated the matter. Competing local pressures immobilized one another in fruitless indecision. In vain Governor Lincoln held out the vision of ultimate profit for all. Resentment of towns off the chosen course strengthened all the forces of opposition and defeated the scheme when it finally reached a vote in 1830.[64]

60. J. T. Buckingham, *Personal Memoirs and Recollections of Editorial Life* (Boston, 1852), II, 15.

61. See, e.g., "A Calm Observer," *Boston Commercial Gazette*, Feb. 4, 1830; also *ibid.*, Feb. 9, Mar. 5, 1829.

62. See *Senate Docs., 1828–29*, no. 2, pp. 12, 16; Governor Lincoln's addresses, *ibid., 1828–29*, no. 1, pp. 8–10; *ibid., 1829–30*, no. 1, pp. 14–17; [Sparks], "Internal Improvements of North Carolina," *North Amer. Rev.*, 12 (1821), 18; *American Monthly Magazine*, 1 (1829), 73; *House Docs., 1830*, no. 1, pp. 22ff. For taxation see C. J. Bullock, *Historical Sketch of the Finances and Financial Policy of Massachusetts* (New York, 1907), pp. 31–50, 138, 139; C. J. Bullock, *Economic Essays* (Cambridge, Mass., 1936), pp. 394ff; *Address of the Whig Members of the Senate and House of Representatives of Massachusetts* (Boston, 1843), pp. 13ff; *House Docs., 1844*, no. 27, pp. 3ff.

63. For the question of debt see Edward Everett to Lord Grenville, to the Greenfield Young Men's Association, and to E. H. Derby, July 16, 1828, June 25, 1839, Mar. 20, 1840, Everett Papers, LXIII, 49ff, LXVIII, 281, 381; Appendix E, below. For the connection with party issues see also Ticknor to Legare, Mar. 4, 1842, George Ticknor, *Life, Letters and Journals* (Boston, 1880), II, 198; *Proceedings of the Democratic Legislative Convention, Held in Boston, March 1840* (Boston, 1840), pp. 3ff; Amaziah Bumpus (pseud.), *A Series of Letters to Gov. John Davis* (Dedham, 1842), p. 25; *Springfield Gazette*, Mar. 29, 1843; *Address of the Democratic Members of the Legislature of Massachusetts* (Boston, 1843), pp. 1, 8, 9, 12, 13.

64. *Senate Docs., 1829–30*, no. 1, pp. 6, 8–12; *House Docs., 1829–30*, no. 1, pp. 5–10. See report of the debates and discussion, *Boston Commercial Gazette*, Jan. 28, Feb. 1, 4, 1830; *American Monthly Magazine*, 1 (1829), 74.

At this point railroad enthusiasts in Boston and in Worcester reverted to the use of the corporation. They induced the state to divide the undertaking between two intermediaries and to set up as separate enterprises the Boston & Worcester and the Western railroads. The less expensive and more profitable eastern venture could then go forward with lightened political pressure on choice of route and with a monopoly as security. The western section could wait for the results of the first experiment.[65]

At the same time, rail communications also pushed north into an area traditionally dependent on the metropolis for its trade. The Middlesex Canal, now paying well for the first time as a result of new industrial developments in the region, protested in 1830 against a parallel road. But the interest of the moneyed millowners prevailed in the legislature, which chartered the Boston & Lowell with a long-term monopoly. Receipts on the Middlesex Canal fell one-third when that road began its service and another third when the Nashua & Lowell opened.[66]

There was also concern over the desirability of capturing the highly competitive but profitable traffic between New England and the city of New York. Agitation for a Cape Cod canal to bring Long Island Sound closer to Boston continued but effected nothing. Attention turned instead to plans for a link by rail. The Boston & Providence, also chartered in 1830, aimed to make that connection and incidentally to draw Rhode Island into the Hub's hinterland.[67]

In the long years of discussion the legislature had envisioned a communication system with great through routes radiating out from Boston to the north, west, and south. There was an inclination to call a halt there, to oppose charters for unnecessary lines which "by dividing between two or more parties, a privilege which can be valuable only when possessed by one," wasted property and resources.[68] But, as in every other sphere, a few selected enterprises could not engross the corporation and its attendant privileges of eminent domain, of interfering with highways and

65. Stephen Salsbury, *The State, the Investor, and the Railroad* (Cambridge, Mass., 1967) gives a complete account of the railroads to Albany.

66. *House Docs., 1829–30,* no. 40; *Senate Docs., 1829–30,* no. 21; [Caleb Eddy], *Historical Sketch of the Middlesex Canal* (Boston, 1843), pp. 5, 17, 25ff; *Boston Commercial Gazette,* Feb. 4, 1830; F. B. C. Bradlee, "Boston and Lowell Railroad," *Essex Inst. Hist. Colls.,* LIV (1918), 195ff; Winsor, *Boston,* IV, 126.

67. See *Senate Docs., 1828–29,* no. 2, p. 9; *Boston Commercial Gazette,* Feb. 1, 15, 1830; also *Senate Docs., 1838,* no. 98, p. 7; "Message of Levi Lincoln," *Senate Docs., 1826–27,* p. 20; res. 1860, ch. 84; *House Docs., 1860,* no. 214.

68. See *Boston Daily Advertiser,* Jan. 6, 1847; C. G. Loring, *Argument on Behalf of the Eastern Railroad Company* (Boston, 1845), p. 14.

waterways, and of other aids. It was not long before Edward Everett wrote, "There are indeed too many of them. They interfere with each other, & many . . . are ruinous to their first undertakers." [69]

Custom and law both implemented the diffusion. Short linking travel had been normal in stagecoaches; the journey between New York and Boston, for instance, had once involved fourteen or fifteen changes. Furthermore, the early charters regarded the railroads as iron turnpikes, with anyone free to run his carriage or locomotive on the road for a price. This conception stimulated demands for branches which could, after a relatively small investment, attach themselves to a long expensive route. [70]

There was no objection to lines designed to serve purely local interests, such as the Charlestown Branch, which ran to Fresh Pond for ice and to the Fresh Pond Hotel for passengers. But firstcomers vigorously fought competing projects that menaced their incomes. [71]

From time to time, communities without rail service, seeking direct connections with the capital or with some other large city, threatened to cut into the sphere of influence of each of the great through routes. The Boston & Worcester lost some business to the Fitchburg and faced serious troubles from towns between the two roads. Thus the citizens of Watertown, who lacked any facilities, asked the legislature to charter a new line along the Charles River to Boston in 1846. Protests by both old companies eventually resulted in a compromise branch to be run by the Fitchburg, a burden which that road unwillingly shouldered to avoid independent competition. [72]

Sometimes these local enterprises burgeoned into main arteries in their own right, with slogans of general utility to the state serving as sanctions to advance parochial interests. Many communities continued to take advantage of the failure of the Western to create the long-desired through route. The rails existed, but extensive trade from beyond the Hudson still did not pass through Massachusetts. Inefficient operation and high

69. Everett to Holland, May 10, 1851, Everett Papers, XCVII, 149.

70. *Boston and Lowell Railroad Corporation* v. *Salem and Lowell Railroad Co. & Others* (1854), 2 Gray 28; F. H. Chase, *Lemuel Shaw* (Boston, 1918), pp. 220ff; see also the long legislative report, *Senate Docs., 1837*, no. 92; Oliver Holmes, "Levi Pease," *Jour. of Econ. and Bus. Hist.*, 3 (1930–31), 258; statement of facts, *Newton* v. *Thayer* (1835), 17 Pickering 129.

71. *Senate Docs., 1858*, no. 59, p. 2.

72. See st. 1846, ch. 261; st. 1847, ch. 223; st. 1849, ch. 223; st. 1851, ch. 72; *Senate Docs., 1848*, no. 59, pp. 2–8. See also *Senate Docs., 1846*, no. 110.

rates, a consequence of authority divided between two corporations, discouraged out-of-state shippers from using this channel to the seacoast. The Western's traffic remained largely local, destined for points within the state, and Boston's exports lagged behind those of the other great Atlantic ports.[73] Disappointment turned attention to more northerly routes, reviving earlier plans for a road to Brattleboro that would branch out to the west, and north into Canada.[74] T. H. Perkins and other merchants reckoned that the Fitchburg railroad combined with the Troy & Greenfield and the Vermont & Massachusetts would open a choice of routes via Buffalo, Ogdensburg, and Montreal that would lower the cost of doing business from Boston to the West. Although the Western put pressure on the legislators "to induce a tendency in their minds against the project," by 1860 all the component parts of this through line had received charters, and the state was actually subsidizing one critical link, the Hoosac Tunnel, to the extent of an issue of two million dollars in scrip, while adjacent towns added subscriptions of their own.[75] Yet even then there was no end to newer proposals for a golden passage westward.[76]

The Lowell and Providence routes fared no better than the Western so far as exclusive position was concerned. Projects for a road to Salem foundered upon the opposition of stagecoaches, turnpikes, and local interests in Chelsea and Lynn until the Eastern Railroad secured a charter in 1836 by stressing the common advantage of reaching into New Hampshire. It, too, built with the aid of state scrip. Another series of ventures combined into the Boston & Maine Railroad.[77] And the modest desire of Bellingham people in 1854 to have the Charles River Railroad

73. See, e.g., *Hunt's Merchants' Mag.*, 16 (1847), 190; below, pp. 211–212; [Otis Clapp], *Boston and the West* (Boston [c. 1851]), pp. 3, 4.

74. See *Boston Commercial Gazette*, Nov. 5, 1829.

75. Keyes to Phelps, Nov. 13, 1851, Western Railroad Corporation, "Records" (MSS, Baker Library, Harvard University), IX. See also *House Docs., 1860*, no. 185, pp. 111ff; Forbes to Bigelow, Sept. 19, 1851, J. P. Bigelow Papers (MSS, Houghton Library, Harvard University); *Boston Daily Advertiser*, May 12, 1843, Jan. 9, 25, Sept. 13, 14, 21, 1844. For struggles over routes see, e.g., *Senate Docs., 1845*, no. 25; Edward C. Kirkland, *Men, Cities, and Transportation* (Cambridge, Mass., 1948), I, 362ff.

76. See *Steam Communication between Boston and New Orleans* (Boston, 1860), pp. 3, 7. (Appeal signed by Otis Norcross *et al.* of the Boston Board of Trade.)

77. *Senate Docs., 1833*, no. 52, pp. 1–5, 13ff, 23; *Boston Commercial Gazette*, Apr. 14, 1836, Sept. 6, 1838; F. B. C. Bradlee, "Eastern Railroad," *Essex Inst. Hist. Colls.*, LII (1916), 242ff, LIII (1917), 1ff; Bradlee, "Boston and Maine Railroad," *Essex Inst. Hist. Colls.*, LVI (1920), 242ff.

extend to Woonsocket eventually strengthened propaganda for a new way to New York.[78]

Another series of local roads developed from the attempts of out-of-state ports to secure access to the Commonwealth's hinterland. Providence thus sponsored the Blackstone Canal to Worcester, completed in 1828, and sixteen years later the Providence and Worcester Railroad.[79] Hartford similarly coveted the trade of western Massachusetts. The Hampshire and Hampden Canal to Northampton and later to the New Hampshire line was an opening wedge for the ambitions of the Connecticut businessmen. Although projects for connecting railroads to Worcester and Albany were unsuccessful, the Canal Railroad ultimately reached Springfield, cutting into the traffic of the Western.[80]

Finally, attempts of competitors on parallel routes to steal one another's patronage combined with local desires for more facilities to generate still other lines. The union of a number of shorter roads into the Boston & Maine early initiated a long period of bitter competition in the northeast. The new company, on the offensive, petitioned for branches into the Eastern's territory. When it finally attained that objective through the Newburyport and Danvers Railroad, it threatened to absorb a lion's share of all travel "down east." The Eastern, at a disadvantage because its passengers entered Boston only via a ferry from East Boston, in reprisal bought the Saugus Branch and the Essex railroads, captured the South Reading, and strove to enter the metropolis directly by eliminating the cumbersome transfer. Ultimately, both lines suffered, sinking into debt to build and acquire profitless offshoots.[81]

The Boston & Maine also acted the aggressor against another adversary. Freed, by extension of its rails into the Hub, from dependence upon the Boston & Lowell, it early cast about for a share of the latter's business. The Lowell had thrived as carrier

78. See *Senate Docs., 1854*, no. 53.

79. See Israel Plummer, "History of the Blackstone Canal," *Colls. Worc. Soc.*, I (1888), 42–49; *Boston Daily Advertiser*, Jan. 22, 1844.

80. See st. 1822, ch. 59; st. 1827, ch. 128; st. 1829, ch. 50; st. 1832, ch. 47; st. 1836, chs. 199, 230; M. A. Green, *Springfield, 1636–1886* (Springfield, 1888), pp. 414, 415, 417, 488.

81. See *Senate Docs., 1845*, nos. 100, 109; *Senate Docs., 1846*, nos. 80, 85; st. 1852, ch. 164; st. 1858, ch. 18; Loring, *Argument on Behalf of the Eastern Railroad Company*, pp. 18ff; and, in general, G. P. Baker, *Formation of the New England Railroad Systems* (Cambridge, Mass., 1937), pp. 145ff; Bradlee, "Boston and Maine Railroad," *Essex Inst. Hist. Colls.*, LVI, 247ff, 259ff; Bradlee, "Eastern Railroad," *ibid.*, LII, 268ff, 272, 289ff, 309ff; H. F. Long, "Newburyport and Danvers Railroad," *ibid.*, XLVI (1910), 17ff.

for the prosperous mills. Consistently high dividends and rising stock values made it dubious about the virtues of expansion. It built a few feeders like the Wilmington, Andover & Haverhill but refused to combine with the Nashua & Lowell, its tie to the north, counting upon its chartered monopoly for security. But Boston & Maine branches, granted reluctantly but inexorably by the legislature and sustained by the courts, which ruled they did not infringe upon the legal rights of the Lowell road, undermined that favored place. In addition, the Salem & Lowell, cutting into the carriage of cotton, created a further drain. Losses now forced the original road to retaliate by building to Lawrence to suck away business from the Boston & Maine. The resultant competition depressed all stock values and dividend rates.[82]

On the line to New York City, the Boston & Worcester and the Western early became rivals of the Boston & Providence, sponsoring other routes to Long Island Sound via the Norwich & Worcester and connections at Springfield.[83] The steamship companies plying from New York also displayed interest in their land links to the Hub. The S.S. *President* and the S.S. *Franklin*, which formerly met stagecoaches at Providence, found themselves isolated from Boston when the older conveyances went out of business, since the Boston & Providence arranged its schedules to meet one favored line only.[84] The owners of the displaced vessels secured a charter and at a cost of twenty thousand dollars built the Seekonk Branch Railroad, a short spur to the Boston & Providence, the rails of which they then claimed a right to use. This maneuver failed through the united opposition of older roads and other interests adversely affected.[85]

But whatever the consequences, looseness of control, liberal incorporation, and the freedom of lines to use each other's tracks encouraged the tendency to allow all to proceed at their own risk without favoritism, that is, without direction from the government. By the end of the period the crisscrossing patterns of the Massachusetts railroad map showed that security no longer came by the fiat of the state, exercising choices through the grant of the charter. Not even government grants of credit served that

82. See *Boston Daily Advertiser*, Mar. 13, 1844; *Senate Docs., 1845*, no. 30; Loring, *Argument on Behalf of the Eastern Railroad Company*, pp. 13ff; Bradlee, "Boston and Lowell Railroad," *Essex Inst. Hist. Colls.*, LIV, 203–206, 217–219, LVI, 251ff; Baker, *New England Railroad Systems*, pp. 100–127.

83. See Everett to W. W. Rockwell, Nov. 13, 1835, Everett Papers, LXCII, 5ff.

84. *Boston Daily Herald*, Nov. 23, 1836; *Senate Docs., 1840*, no. 50, p. 9.

85. *Senate Docs., 1838*, no. 98; *Daily Evening Transcript*, Jan. 23, 1839.

purpose. Security now came only through the vigilance of each company in the pursuit of its own profits.[86]

As in manufacturing, in banking, and in insurance, struggles for control here too took extralegal forms. The through railroads found the anarchical sprouting of unprofitable lines an insuperable obstacle to uniform policy or rates. They acquired operational leases and later bought outright many smaller branches often deep in debt before the first car rolled. Between 1854 and 1858, for instance, the Boston & Maine took over the Danvers and Newburyport railroads while the Boston & Lowell laid hands on the Nashua & Lowell, the Salem & Lowell, and the Lawrence & Lowell.[87]

By 1860 few survivals of the old exclusive character of the corporate privilege remained anywhere. In railroads, in manufacturing, in banking, in insurance, the institution had spread widely and had extended, as well, into many new fields; hotels, dry docks, gas companies, theaters, newspapers, horse railroads, trading ventures, and steamship lines used the form, now a simple business device.[88]

The diffusion of corporations had been much more rapid than in the more advanced economies of Western Europe. The tendency had already been marked before 1820.[89] By then, proliferation had turned a government agency into a business form, but one available only as a franchise from the state for a desirable end. Unlimited increase thereafter had, in practice, transmuted the very privilege to act as a body politic into a right justly accessible to any competent petitioner. Incorporation was rarely a considered act of the legislature weighed in terms of utility or desirability; it was now almost invariably the expression of the wish of the enterpriser. Multiplication, begun to give fullest realization of the Commonwealth's aspirations, had ended by devouring the states' capacity to direct production through judicious bestowal of the privilege.

86. See [C. F. Adams], "State Debts," *North Amer. Rev.*, 51 (1840), 318ff; Hosmer to Sumner, Mar. 5, 1852, Sumner, "Letters Received," XVIII, 114.

87. See *Senate Docs., 1854*, no. 2, p. 67; H. F. Long, "Newburyport and Danvers Railroad," *Essex Inst. Hist. Colls.*, XLVI (1910), 21ff; F. B. C. Bradlee, "Boston and Lowell Railroad," *ibid.*, LIV (1918), 218, 326ff.

88. See, e.g., st. 1822, ch. 41; st. 1823, ch. 88; st. 1858, ch. 92. Significantly, the creation of horse railway systems took place late in the 1850's without the struggle for routes or attempts at favored position that had marked railroad development two decades earlier. For some of the issues involved, see, e.g., *Senate Docs., 1858*, no. 59, pp. 16, 17; *Senate Docs., 1860*, no. 86; *House Docs., 1860*, no. 187.

89. Oscar and Mary F. Handlin, "Origins of the American Business Corporation," *Jour. of Econ. Hist.*, 5 (1945), 3ff; Charles E. Freedeman, "Joint-Stock Business Organization in France, 1807–1867," *Business History Review*, 39 (1965), 185ff.

The seed, carefully sown and nurtured, had luxuriated beyond the control of the cultivator. But the very luxuriation, rooted in every city, in every town, touching every activity, had another effect. It obfuscated the old justification in terms of the Commonwealth idea and laid open a fair field upon which new social forces, gathering momentum in these very years, could attack the validity of the whole system of privilege through which the state had acted.

The transformation in the character of the corporation came within a context of precipitous social change that upset the structure of the old economy, tore apart traditional modes of action and of thought, and drove deep fissures into the community. By the time the Civil War intervened with its own conditioning impact, both the means and end of government action had taken on a strange aspect.

The War of 1812 had stimulated household industry to a high level of efficiency. The setback consequent upon peace and the revival of British imports did not seriously retard home manufactures.[1] Many still looked hopefully to such enterprises as a patriotic activity and as a spur to agricultural prosperity.[2] But this source failed to satisfy the ever widening native market protected by the adoption of the American system in the tariff of 1816. An adjunct to farming, dependent for low costs on spare-time labor, it lacked the capacity for growing indefinitely in the face of continued emigration of husbandmen.

If household industry would not supply the demand, another system, controlled by other people, would. The period was one

1. See, e.g., J. G. Holland, *History of Western Massachusetts* (Springfield, 1855), I, 397, 398; J. E. A. Smith, *The History of Pittsfield . . . 1800 to . . . 1876* (Springfield, 1876), p. 464; G. B. Perry, *Discourse Delivered in the East Parish in Bradford* (Haverhill, 1821), p. 10; A. H. Cole, *American Wool Manufacture* (Cambridge, Mass., 1926), I, 183.

2. *Boston Commercial Gazette*, Jan. 23, June 12, 1817. See also *Commonwealth History of Massachusetts*, ed. A. B. Hart (New York, 1927–1930), IV, 363ff.

of great mental activity in industry; inventions revamped the methods of fabrication for many articles and opened fabulous opportunities to the imaginative and venturesome.[3] The local capitalists, merchants and shopkeepers, often distributors for neighborhood products, gradually acquired control of numerous mills and mill sites, grasping the promise of new markets and new methods. Family groups like the Pomeroys and the Bordens sought out and made fresh openings, applying capital and skill to one activity after another, wool and shoes, iron and paper, power and transportation, and in the process transformed many fields of production.[4]

The tempestuous commercial policy of the decade before 1815 had also turned the attention of some merchants to the possibilities of American industry. Few regarded Jefferson's embargo with the equanimity of William Gray and John Bromfield, who found solace in the thought that the "good to the community at large" would outweigh immediate injuries.[5] Most were bitter, particularly after the failures of 1807 reduced traders brought up in affluence to "the cold courtesy of creditors." [6] Worst of all, the War of 1812 suspended some branches of overseas business; William Appleton, for instance, closed his doors for the duration. Yet, despite losses reflected in acrimonious divisions over policies, accumulated surpluses remained in the hands of enough mercantile families to constitute a problem of investment.[7]

After the war new factors continued to drive commercial capital into industry. Movement of the great American market across the Alleghenies deepened Boston's disadvantages as an entrepôt. Again, as in 1789, the merchants turned to manufacturing to offset their weakened condition. But unlike the Beverly factory, the new enterprises held forth the prospect of direct profits.

3. See D. A. Wells to Sumner, Jan. 24, 1853, Charles Sumner, "Letters Received, 1830–74" (MSS, Houghton Library, Harvard University), XXI, 21.

4. See R. K. Lamb, "Development of Entrepreneurship in Fall River: 1813–1859" (unpub. diss. Harvard University, 1935, University Archives); *History of Bristol County*, ed. D. H. Hurd (Philadelphia, 1883), pp. 314ff, 370ff, 393ff, 411; W. R. Bagnall, *Sketches of Manufacturing Establishments in New York City* (Washington, D.C., 1908), II, 1066–1071; Cole, *American Wool Manufacture*, I, 225, 229; H. H. Earl, *Centennial History of Fall River* (New York, 1877), pp. 8, 12ff.

5. Hill to Quincy, Feb. 11, 1808, Jan. 3, 1809, Willard Phillips Papers, 1769–1836 (MSS, MHS); K. W. Porter, *Jacksons and the Lees* (Cambridge, Mass., 1937), II, 829ff.

6. William Willis, *Journals of the Rev. Thomas Smith and the Rev. Samuel Deane* (Portland, 1849), p. 407; also pp. 387ff, 406.

7. See "Memoir of Hon. William Appleton," *Mass. Hist. Soc. Proceedings*, VI (1863), 436.

The success of the Waltham Company showed investors the advantage of complete factory organization. The corporate form permitted traders who acted as selling agents to participate without assuming the identity of the project and to earn dividends and commissions from the same venture.[8]

Between 1822 and 1826 men like Henry Lee and Harrison Gray Otis, without other outlets for investment, began to put into manufacturing corporations large sums released by a contracting public debt. Buying up existing concerns and establishing new ones, they developed the Boston-office factories, owned partly in the Hub by merchants and partly locally by managers. The famous Lowell plants, the Boston & Springfield Manufacturing Company, and the Greenfield Manufacturing Company early illustrated the process.[9]

New developments in transportation completed this stage of evolution. Canals, railroads, and a growing volume of coastal shipping extended markets and permitted conversion from water power to steam by lowering the price of coal. Busy factories mushroomed along the route of the Blackstone and of the successive strands in the railroad web. Low interest rates extended by numerous financial institutions further stimulated manufacturing. Finally, a new supply of immigrant labor, eager to work at any price, facilitated further expansion in these industries after 1845.[10]

The growth of factory production affected every element in Massachusetts. Although merchants were the chief beneficiaries, finding in the mills rich dividends as stockholders and even richer profits as selling agents, the rise of industry was at first a source of dissension among them. Economically the interests of investors in manufacturing clashed with those who regarded the tariff as an attempt "to enact the country into riches." [11] The decline of the East India piece-goods trade as a result of domestic

8. Cole, *American Wool Manufacture*, I, 210ff, 289ff.

9. See [A. H. Everett], "American System," *North Amer. Rev.*, 32 (1831), 127ff; Otis to Harrison, Mar. 21, 1823, S. E. Morison, *Life and Letters of Harrison Gray Otis* (Boston, 1913), II, 289; Porter, *Jacksons and the Lees*, I, 470; Cole, *American Wool Manufacture*, I, 227; Justin Winsor, *Memorial History of Boston* (Boston, 1880–1881), IV, 103ff.

10. See Israel Plummer, "History of the Blackstone Canal," *Colls. Worc. Soc.*, I (1888), 47; Barbara Vatter, "Industrial Borrowing by New England Textile Mills," *Jour. of Econ. Hist.*, 21 (1961), 216ff; Oscar Handlin, *Boston's Immigrants, 1790–1865* (Cambridge, Mass., 1959), pp. 74ff.

11. See [Edward Everett], "Debate in Congress," *North Amer. Rev.*, 19 (1824), 232ff, 252; Morison, *Harrison Gray Otis*, II, 242; *Hunt's Merchants' Mag.*, 16 (1847), 362.

competition fortified the complaint that protection would "drive capital out of commercial investments." [12]

That division was transient only. At the very start, Henry Lee perspicaciously noted that the tariff drew heavy support from the merchants, "that Class of People who are the greatest Sufferers." [13] Throughout the period, defense of the tariff policy in terms of commercial interests minimized the splintering effect of the issue. The system of protection, it was argued, was an instrument for securing concessions from England through reciprocity and an essential ingredient of triangular traffic.[14] Although the conception of limited duties, low on iron, wool, and tallow, high on woolens, gave way to a recognition that "the only security is in the union of all the friends of the protective system," the question was not disruptive. The merchants and their industries thrived whether rates went up or down, and that took the edge off the argument.[15]

Ultimate consonance of opinion on the tariff reflected a growing cohesion among the traders, or, more properly, among the trading families. In these years the great Boston merchants ceased to act merely as individuals drawn together from time to time by combinations of interests arising out of a common occupation. By now not all maintained activities in commerce; some concerned themselves with a stake in manufacturing and others lived on incomes that permitted indulgence in the learned, the legal, or the political professions. Common origins in foreign trade nevertheless became the wellspring of unity from which

12. See "The Prospect Before Us," *North Amer. Rev.*, 17 (1823), 191; J. T. Austin, "Proposed New Tariff," *ibid.*, 12 (1821), 61ff; [Joseph Story], "Daniel Webster," *The New-England Magazine*, 7 (1834), 101ff.

13. Lee to Palmer, Oct. 26, 1817, Porter, *Jacksons and the Lees*, II, 1295.

14. See Oscar Handlin, "Laissez Faire Thought in Massachusetts, 1790–1880," *Tasks of Economic History* (December 1943), pp. 57, 58; *Report of the Committee of the Boston Board of Trade Appointed to Make a Thorough Investigation of the Recent Monetary Difficulties* (Boston, 1858), pp. 4ff; *Boston Daily Advertiser*, June 7, 29, July 1, 7, 1843.

15. See Mason to Webster, May 27, 1832, [G. S. Hillard], *Memoir and Correspondence of Jeremiah Mason* (Cambridge, Mass., 1873), pp. 337ff; Everett to Holland, Sept. 25, 1848, Edward Everett Papers (MSS, MHS), LXXXVI, 3. For the attitude to the tariff of 1846 see *Boston Daily Advertiser*, Jan. 13, 1847; *Senate Docs.*, *1846*, no. 65. See also Daniel Webster, *Works* (Boston, 1853), I, lxxxvff; J. Q. Adams, *Memoirs*, ed. C. F. Adams (Philadelphia, 1874–1877), VIII, 437–443, IX, 318; Edward Everett, "American Manufactures," *Orations and Speeches on Various Occasions* (Boston, 1853–1868), II, 69ff; *Boston Commercial Gazette*, Dec. 18, 1823; E. Everett to Perkins, Lawrence, and A. Everett, Jan. 20, Dec. 23, 1827, June 28, 1828, Everett Papers, LX, 20, LXII, 193, LXIII, 18; *Bowen's Boston News-Letter*, Dec. 2, 1826; *Senate Docs.*, *1846*, no. 2, p. 8.

developed an esprit de corps that tied these people together with a coherence and solidarity transcending questions of immediate benefit. Their far-flung and diversified ventures in other fields became more important in practice but remained peripheral in their thinking. As late as 1858 William Appleton sadly recorded that he was losing money, noting that a year's mercantile business had netted a loss, and then added parenthetically that incidental investments had returned a profit of one hundred thousand dollars.[16] The absence of commercial opportunities warded off newcomers and accentuated the consciousness of homogeneity. With a measure of exclusiveness came pride of ancestry; the Adamses now shunned reminders that the father of the second president had been a shoemaker.[17]

Among the members of the first generation, among those who had made their mark in the half-century after the Boston Port Act, awareness of recent rise in status never wore off completely. Men like Edward Everett, whose brothers were debtors and farmers, did not completely put aside their origin; they maintained substantial if primarily sentimental connections with the hinterland.[18] But the sons of the merchants no longer had roots in the soil. They lacked the personal and family associations of their fathers with the back country, revolted against leveling traditions that forced them into the common schools, and toiled to master the accomplishments of gentlemen.[19]

The interests the merchants' families shared with the rest of the state waned. Trade had only a slight connection with the base in Massachusetts. Many firms shifted their activities to New York; by 1830 a good share of the China business, even when carried on ships owned in Boston, had moved to the port on the Hudson. Investments in railroads were more likely to be in the Midwest than in the Bay State. The industries also lost their ties with the countryside. The new mills, unlike the old, had little contact with the surrounding agricultural areas, drawing their raw materials from distant sources and working them

16. William Appleton, *Selections from the Diaries of Wiliam Appleton, 1786–1862* (Boston, 1922), p. 214.

17. See Everett to Blunt, Apr. 25, 1827, Everett Papers, LX, 77; also G. M. Elsey, "First Education of Henry Adams," *New England Quarterly*, 14 (1941), 683.

18. See, e.g., E. to A. Everett and to Clay, Sept. 29, 1825, Oct. 12, 1826, Everett Papers, LVI, 56, LVIII, 31; T. L. Nichols, *Forty Years of American Life, 1821–1861* (New York, 1937), pp. 83, 84.

19. See C. F. Adams, *1835–1915: An Autobiography* (Boston, 1916), pp. 21ff; also Edward Everett's letters to his son at Cambridge University, Everett Papers, CXIII, 28, 129, 161, 175.

up entirely within the factory. Meanwhile, immigration developed a distinctive proletariat that stood completely apart.[20]

Divorce from the community strengthened the consciousness of the merchants' identity as a group. By the end of the period, Theodore Parker spoke of an "organized Trading Power" controlling all things, "amenable only to the allmighty dollar" and allied with the organized ecclesiastical and literary guilds which kaleidoscopically diffused the coalescent opinions of those they served. Then Holmes's Brahmin, with two generations of gentlemen behind him, was ready to step onto the Boston scene.[21]

Other groups also found their places in the community altered. While the growth of cities increased farmers' markets a little, the negative effects were more serious. The agricultural products of the fresh lands in New York and the West, brought into competition with those of the Bay State by improvements in transportation, pushed native wheat and other grains out of their accustomed selling places. By 1833 a legislative committee complained "that a farm in the vicinity of Buffalo is worth more by the acre, to raise anything for the Boston market . . . than the same quality of land on the Connecticut River." [22] The building of the Western made matters worse; flour shipped from Albany to Boston on the road more than doubled in volume between 1842 and 1846.[23] Attempts to compensate by introducing new products like silk in Northampton and Dighton were notably unsuccessful.[24] The few branches which remained prosperous through improved methods, beef fattening, sheep raising, dairying, and lumbering, generally required substantial investments of capital and offered no easy relief to the husbandmen.[25]

The growth of factories further weakened the position of

20. S. E. Morison, *Maritime History of Massachusetts, 1783–1860* (Boston, 1921), p. 275; Winsor, *Boston*, IV, 143ff; J. T. Morse, *Memoir of Colonel Henry Lee* (Boston, 1905), p. 17.

21. See Theodore Parker, *Experience as a Minister* (Boston, 1859), pp. 92, 93.

22. *Senate Docs. 1833*, no. 29, p. 20. See also P. W. Bidwell, "Agricultural Revolution in New England," *Amer. Hist. Rev.*, 26 (1921), 684ff.

23. *Hunt's Merchants' Mag.*, 16 (1847), 325.

24. See Henry Colman, "Third Report of the Agriculture of Massachusetts," *Senate Docs., 1840*, no. 36, pp. 97ff, 104, 154ff; J. R. Trumbull, *Recollections* (Northampton, 1898–1902), pp. 156, 157; also *Whalemen's Shipping List and Merchants' Transcript* (New Bedford), June 22, 1858; Elizabeth Ramsey, *History of Tobacco Production in the Connecticut Valley* (Northampton, 1930), pp. 133–146.

25. Figures for the decade 1840–1850 may be found in the "First Annual Report of the Board of Agriculture," *Senate Docs., 1854*, no. 7, pp. 20, 24, 31–38, 81–90.

rural Massachusetts by taking away an important source of income, the domestic system. Under the impact of the new method of production, household fabrication inevitably decayed; by the 1850's even the familiar clothing industries had disappeared from the farms and moved to the cities.[26] Deprived of extra cash from these sources, the farmers found themselves without a buffer against the shocks of contracting markets. With a few fortunate exceptions, their position was economically weak and unstable. Emigration accelerated, drawing away many discontented with diminishing earnings and increasing hard work.[27] Those who remained resisted stubbornly each additional challenge to their calling. Waging a losing battle, they fought emigration to the West or to the city that sapped away their youth. Suspicious of all enticement, they condemned the academies that led boys to "quit the plough, attend . . . a few months, and become too inflated with a very little learning to return to their labors of the field." [28] Resentment of the cities and of those who lived in them mounted steadily and on occasion burst forth in angry movements of protest.[29]

The large and hitherto prosperous groups of artisans, the "workingmen," also suffered. Trade and transportation, burgeoning with the new energies of an expanding economy, brought the products of distant shops and mills into competition with those of Massachusetts. Widening markets proved a dubious boon, for they reduced producers to dependence upon mercantile middlemen. And everywhere calamitous machines seemed to put to nought the craftsman's cunning. Unable to compete in the new industrial system, many independent skilled laborers soon faced the disagreeable choice between emigration and new employment at home. Not a few ultimately adjusted well, often in managerial positions, but uncertainty and insecurity of economic status engendered continuing bitterness.[30]

Social divisions did not turn about a contrast in fortune alone.

26. Bidwell, "Agricultural Revolution in New England," *Amer. Hist. Rev.*, 26 (1921), 693–696; Cole, *American Wool Manufacture*, I, 279ff.

27. See *Boston Daily Herald*, Nov. 25, 1836.

28. *Boston Commercial Gazette*, Feb. 5, 1816. See also Albert Mordell, *Quaker Militant, John Greenleaf Whittier* (Boston, 1933), p. 12; *Springfield Gazette*, July 9, 1841.

29. See *Boston Daily Herald*, Dec. 7, 1836.

30. See O. A. Brownson, "The Laboring Classes," *Boston Quarterly Review*, 3 (1840), 472ff; O. A. Brownson, "Address of the Workingmen of Charlestown," *ibid.*, 4 (1841), 121; Robert Rantoul, Jr., *Memoirs* (Boston, 1854), pp. 222ff; *Springfield Gazette*, Dec. 18, 1844.

Other prospering groups could no more find a bond of interest with the merchants than could the depressed. Lesser traders in the outlying towns and in the Hub itself, and the new manufacturers not connected with commerce but often wealthy and powerful, discovered a wall, real and usually insurmountable, between themselves and the Boston great merchants. Differences of interest set apart aggressive outsiders, struggling with varying degrees of success for a foothold, from the long-arrived, already entrenched behind the barriers of economic power and the prestige of social position.

In an economy battered by the impact of radical innovations and disrupted by unforeseen changes in status, social fragmentation snapped communal ties and often cast individuals free but adrift. Attenuation of old responsibilities and weakening of old controls at every level, from state to family, left men to cope alone with increasingly complicated problems arising from industrialization, growth of cities, and integration into broader markets. The displaced artisan and marginal farmer frequently suffered, aggressive new manufacturers and struggling traders sometimes profited, and the great merchants usually managed to retain their wealth if not their equanimity. But whatever the experience of any group, friction at every level was a concomitant of disintegration in the community.

The contrast between these actual conditions and the society's fundamental articles of faith gave rise to the conviction that the "selfish dissocial system . . . must give way to Christianity." [31] There was still no doubt that man was naturally good and naturally progressing toward perfectibility. The social evils, poverty, crime, intemperance, and the rest, arose not from his own nature or from uncontrollable forces like excess population, but from defective human institutions capable of correction.[32] Partly this feeling sprang from a rising appreciation of the dignity of man, partly from democratic egalitarianism in a country where "the distinction of the One, the Few & the Many has no existence." [33] The revival, among some elements of the population, of evangelical Protestantism with the hopes of quick con-

31. W. E. Channing, *Memoir* (Boston, 1848), III, 38.

32. See Francis Bowen, *Principles of Political Economy* (Boston, 1856), p. 172, and the general argument against Malthus, *ibid.*, pp. 155ff. See also *Woburn Journal*, Dec. 13, 1851; John Pierce, *Brookline Jubilee* (Boston, 1847), pp. 31ff; M. P. Braman, *Discourse on the Annual Election January 1, 1845*, (Boston, 1845), pp. 12ff.

33. Everett to Kirkland, Oct. 23, 1826, Everett Papers, LVIII, 50.

version and imminent millennial regeneration, and the spread among others of an optimistic and rational humanitarianism associated with Unitarianism lent the impulse of urgency to these benevolent reveries. But whatever the source, the essential truth seemed to be that "the chief end of the social state is the elevation of all its members as intelligent and moral beings." All looked forward to a "great approaching modification of society . . . under which every man will be expected to contribute to this object according to his ability." [34]

There was faith that the democratic state would play a part in the movement to assure to each human being the opportunity for fullest development of his capacities, turning its energies to save men from the consequences of poverty, to fit them by education for the problems of citizenship and the economy, and to guard them against the temptations of dissipation, gambling, liquor, and crime. [35]

But the same aspiration for social progress through improvement of the individual subtly called the government into service in another guise. In numberless day-to-day relations the old codes of propriety decayed. The conventions of a trade, of commercial negotiations, of family behavior, of simple neighborliness grew less binding as radical change undermined the presumptions on which they rested. Faced by new circumstances, lacking the assurance of traditional ways of action, and deprived of alternative modes of redress, those who felt the need for the intercession of a superior power turned more frequently to the services of the state as an arbiter to render tempered judgments assuring equitable conditions for all. Government was thus to render impartial judgments as well as to stimulate individual improvement. Through both channels, the urge to retain the elements of human dignity and decency in an impersonalized and decentralized society broadened the conception of what the community owed its members who were unable to protect themselves.

Threads of this reform spirit ran through the patterns of thought of almost every sector of the community. This was the common heritage of a common social environment. But the application to politics, and through politics to the economic structure of Massachusetts, raised consequential differences among voters and officials.

34. Channing, *Memoir*, III, 38; see also Dickinson to Bancroft, Jan. 27, 1835, George Bancroft Papers (MSS, MHS); Theodore Sedgwick, *Public and Private Economy* (New York, 1839), I, 196.

35. See below, Chapter 10.

Certainty of progress had a millennial quality. The pervasive impression of imminence produced a generation of enthusiasts who expected through rational examination to recast existing institutions. For them immediate action was necessary and inevitable; delay or compromise needlessly put off the moment of final redemption. Zealots supplied the leadership for the endlessly sprouting causes; their following came from the fund of discontent built up by new circumstances.

The luckless farmers and handicraftsmen found solace, sometimes confidence, in the faith in a new dispensation. And for them reform had a further mission — to enable men to compete with one another on an equal footing by leveling all artificial barriers erected by the government. Each new road to the West that cut into the Massachusetts market for Berkshire wheat, each new mechanical device that lured customers away from the artisan's shop to the corporation's factory, steadily, incessantly, eroded the belief in the common interest on which had rested the old Commonwealth concept. The gradual disappearance of economic integration that had made understandable special grants to some for the benefit of all brought into question the social justification of the privileges through which the state acted. Without a common interest to cherish and defend, the General Court merely legislated for the select few, forbidding one man "to do what he has a natural right to do" and authorizing another "to do what he has not a natural right to do . . . counting itself the real owner and sovereign disposer of the individual . . . disfranchising all individuals, and then pretending to redistribute individual rights, according to its own caprice, interests, or necessities." [36] People from all strata had attempted and would continue to attempt to put government to their own service. Yet in practice each specific favor raised the protest by those adversely affected that it served the welfare only of its holders.[37] "Fanatics in freedom," indiscriminately battling "tolls, taxes, turnpikes, banks, hierarchies, governors, yea laws," meshed together the struggle for reform and the struggle against privilege.[38] The concrete concern in ending pernicious favors

36. *Boston Quarterly Review*, 1 (1838), 71, 72; O. A. Brownson, "Constitutional Government," *ibid.*, 5 (1842), 31.

37. *Boston Quarterly Review*, 1 (1838), 200–206; George Bancroft, *Address at Hartford before the Delegates to the Democratic Convention of the Young Men of Connecticut, on the Evening of February 18, 1840* (n.p., n.d.), p. 1.

38. R. W. Emerson, "Life and Letters in New England," *Lectures and Biographical Sketches* (Boston, 1884), p. 309; Theodore Sedgwick to Theodore Sedgwick, Mar. 21, 1833, Theodore Sedgwick Papers, 1768–1858 (MSS, MHS), 2 ser., IX. For the general intellectual background see Russel B. Nye, *William Lloyd*

reinforced the longing for regeneration, which in turn supplied the intellectual framework for an attack upon special advantages.

The merchants shared the abstract outlook on reform. They were in agreement on the evils of slavery, on the need for temperance. They were impressed by the movement for better treatment of criminals, of the insane, and of the diseased. And they used the identical arguments based on progress and the need for revising old institutions when they fought for changes in their own interest. Furthermore, these men, though prosperous, daily faced problems involving their own status that sensitized them to reform tendencies. Those who stood apart in a democracy but who still wished to maintain a governing position needed an effective technique, grounded in the spirit of the times, for relations with other groups.[39]

Long practice had taught the merchants how thus to operate within the democratic framework. They were aware of the close correlation between power and wealth. The final abolition of property qualifications in the state, however, reduced the formal weight of their influence and accentuated their dependence upon the cooperation of other elements in the state. Shaky in their political position, they sought sympathetic contacts to compensate for growing social and economic isolation.[40]

Generous with charity for the unfortunate and the destitute, accepting the fact that the poor would always be with them, the merchants yet perceived the danger of the existence of a class of perpetual paupers. Consequently, high wages played an important part in economic thought. Wages which reflected "the actual state of the whole community" reduced the burden of relief and preserved a measure, but only a measure, of social mobility. If the poor man is bound to his class, "himself and his heirs for ever," he "must regard the . . . society, which holds him in this condition, as an inhabitant of a conquered territory

---

Garrison and the Humanitarian Reformers (Boston, 1955); Arthur M. Schlesinger, Jr., *Age of Jackson* (Boston, 1945), pp. 132–176, 267ff.

39. See, e.g., Morse, *Henry Lee*, p. 119; Winsor, *Boston*, IV, 641ff.

40. See *Journal of Debates and Proceedings in the Convention to Revise the Constitution of Massachusetts, 1820* (Boston, 1853), pp. 309ff; Webster, "First Settlement of New England," *Works*, I, 36, 39; Francis Bowen, "Distribution of Property," *North Amer. Rev.*, 67 (1848), 126ff; *House Docs., 1840*, no. 9, p. 38; Henry Farnam to J. P. Bigelow, Dec. 10, 1850, J. P. Bigelow Papers (MSS, Houghton Library, Harvard University); E. Everett to Milmay, Jan. 26, 1851, Everett Papers, XCIX, 61ff; O. A. Brownson, "Constitutional Government," *Boston Quarterly Review*, 5 (1842), 33; Chilton Williamson, *American Suffrage from Property to Democracy* (Princeton, 1860), pp. 190ff.

looks upon a citadel of the conquerors. He is naturally, and
. . . almost . . . justifiably, an enemy of the government" as
long as the state merely guarantees "an existence of no value." [41]
Revolution and the most violent measures were then justified.
On the other hand, an equitable distribution of landed property
through proper inheritance laws and the preservation of economic opportunity would destroy both the need and the justification for revolt.[42] That very mobility would undermine the
validity of the English fund and natural-rate theories of wages.
Since the Malthusian argument was invalid in America, high
wages were compatible with and essential to high profits, which
in the last analysis depended on the country's resources.[43]

The merchants also set education to serving their purpose.
Through their thinking ran the wistful hope that schooling
would develop a respect for private rights, restrain the "pre-
dominant influence of mere numbers, check the tendency of
popular government . . . to radicalism & anarchy," and advance
"the interests of the whole people" as distinct from those of any
special group.[44] In the face of deepening divisions, they sought
to teach that there need be no conflict among all the elements
in society. Borrowing from the commonwealth idea, they reiterated the concept that all but the idle were "workingmen,"
and all "inseparably bound together in a community of interest." [45] The connection of schooling with the vestigial doctrine

41. Willard Phillips, *Manual of Political Economy* (Boston, 1828), pp. 149–
152; Rantoul, *Memoirs*, pp. 248ff; Lawrence to Sumner, Nov. 2, 1848, Charles
Sumner, "Letters Received," XII, 148; Sedgwick, *Public and Private Economy*,
III, 29ff.

42. See Bowen, "Distribution of Property," *North Amer. Rev.*, 67 (1848), 126ff,
137ff, 151ff; Bowen, *Political Economy*, pp. 493ff; Rantoul, *Memoirs*, pp. 135ff;
Webster, *Works*, I, lxiii, 34ff; Sedgwick, *Public and Private Economy*, I, 237, III,
68ff.

43. Bowen, *Political Economy*, pp. 131ff, 193ff, 201, 237ff; Phillips, *Manual of
Political Economy*, p. 159. See also J. J. Spengler, "An American Opponent of
Malthus," *New England Quarterly*, 12 (1936), 97ff. On wages and the tariff see
Springfield Gazette, Feb. 16, 1842. For a hostile view of the wage position see
Amaziah Bumpus (pseud.), *A Series of Letters to Gov. John Davis* (Dedham, 1842),
pp. 15–17.

44. Governor Briggs, *Boston Daily Advertiser*, Jan. 13, 1847; Bowen, *Political
Economy*, p. 18; Rantoul, *Memoirs*, pp. 238ff; Everett to Bates, Oct. 25, 1852,
Everett Papers, CII, 43; Phillips, *Manual of Political Economy*, pp. 153, 154; "A
Plea for the Laboring Classes," *The New England Magazine*, 9 (1835), 429ff;
Webster, *Works*, I, 41ff; Sedgwick, *Public and Private Economy*, I, 238.

45. Edward Everett, "The Workingmen's Party," *Orations and Speeches*, I,
283ff; Edward Everett, "Accumulation, Property, Capital, Credit," *ibid.*, II, 289ff;
Sedgwick, *Public and Private Economy*, I, 232; Francis Bowen, "Phillips on Protection," *North Amer. Rev.*, 72 (1851), 415.

of common interests led such men as Edward Everett to oppose Orestes Brownson's project for industrial training, fighting the idea "that there are different classes of our youth requiring different kinds of education." [46] With a body of voters trained to believe that "agriculture, manufactures, and commerce, are intimately blended and mutually dependent, and each equally connected with the permanent welfare of the community," there would be no fear of democracy or the tyranny of the majority. Universal suffrage and free elections were "in reality great conservative principles"; revolutions came from withholding those rights.[47]

Sympathizing with reform, the merchants nevertheless feared the consequences of allowing radicals to set the pace and determine the scope. An impassioned striving for newness seemed dangerous to those who knew that the gentlest current of change could suddenly debouch into an uncontrollable flood. "State Street had an instinct that" reform "invalidated contracts and threatened the stability of stocks." [48] The urge to precipitate legislation, particularly when linked to the attack upon privilege, often was heedless of the rights of property and thus antagonized the wealthy, fearful of the implications for their own holdings.

Furthermore, attacks upon special state patronage frequently became attacks upon the select group, the constant prosperity of which invited the belief that its share in privilege was excessive. Criticism of banks easily turned into fulminations against a "financial aristocracy" which lacked "fixed opinions of a moral nature." Locofocos and debt repudiators who seized control in other states, Dorrites who launched an armed rebellion, raised a terrifying specter for this minority: to weaken privilege at any point would be an entering wedge that would ultimately leave all wealth entirely at the mercy of every future legislature.[49] "Public necessity," Webster thought, under these circumstances "is apt to be public feeling, and on this rock we are in danger of making ship wreck of the bill of rights." [50] To set the proper

46. Everett to Brownson, May 16, 1836, Everett Papers, LXVII, 87; Rantoul, *Memoirs,* p. 138.

47. Phillips, *Political Economy,* pp. 125, 126; Everett to Peel, Holland, and Hallam, Mar. 23, 29, 1837, July 25, 1848, Everett Papers, LXVII, 155, 157, LXXXIV, 157, LXXXV, 221. However, Everett significantly denied the need for the secret ballot (to Denison, April 1853, *ibid.,* CII, 84).

48. Emerson, "Life and Letters in New England," *Lectures,* p. 325.

49. *Boston Commercial Gazette,* Jan. 25, 1838.

50. *Charles River Bridge* v. *Warren Bridge* (1829), 7 Pickering 441.

limits for action generated by the surging reform impulse called for an autonomous body of rights founded on the principles of natural law, "rules of conduct . . . coeval with society"; indeed many saw the fundamental problem of the period in terms of a conflict between liberty and law.[51]

Few Massachusetts men questioned the inviolability of private property and of contract. Property held "a higher and stronger title than any which society can confer"; without it "all other rights became worthless and visionary," and it alone made progress possible.[52] A compact rested upon a "principle of policy . . . essential to all tolerable governments . . . the absolute security of property." Its binding force "depends upon a law which neither kings nor people enacted or can repeal. It comes from the awful Being who created and fashioned us . . . and the united will of the whole human race cannot influence it." [53] In the most famous test of the contractual relation in this period, all parties recognized its sanctity. Even Judge Marcus Morton, a reform democrat anxious to circumscribe the application of the idea, admitted that "a contract is deemed sacred, and the constitution nowhere allows the violation of its obligations . . . for any exigency or upon making compensation . . . Any legislative act . . . having this effect, is a nullity." [54] If the radicals could put the idea of contract to the service of their own extreme proposals, that only emphasized further Chief Justice Parker's assumption that the principles themselves were no longer disputable.[55]

51. L. S. Cushing, *Introduction to the Study of Roman Law* (Boston, 1854), pp. 8, 17; Rufus Choate, "American Bar as an Element of Conservatism," *Addresses and Orations* (Boston, 1878), pp. 143–150; A. H. Everett, *Defense of the Character and Principles of Mr. Jefferson* (Boston, 1836), pp. 27, 29.

52. Bowen, "Distribution of Property," *North Amer. Rev.*, 67 (1848), 121; Bowen, "Phillips on Protection," *ibid.*, 82 (1851), 416; [B. R. Curtis], "Debts of the States," *ibid.*, 58 (1844), 145ff; Cary, "Dependence of Fine Arts on Security of Property," *Boston Daily Advertiser*, Nov. 18, 1844; Joseph Story, *Discourse Pronounced upon the Inauguration as Dane Professor of Law in Harvard University* (Boston, 1829), pp. 24ff; Sedgwick, *Public and Private Economy*, I, 14ff, II, 85ff; John Adams, *Works*, ed. C. F. Adams (Boston, 1850–1856), VI, 8ff; Bancroft to Barre Committee, July 10, 1840, Bancroft Papers.

53. [Curtis], "Debts of the States," *North Amer. Rev.*, 58 (1844), 142, 145; *New York Review*, 2 (1838), 372ff; *Boston Daily Advertiser*, Nov. 16, 22, 23, 24, 27, 1843.

54. *Charles River Bridge* v. *Warren Bridge* (1829), 7 Pickering 453, 459.

55. *Charles River Bridge* v. *Warren Bridge* (1829), 7 Pickering 506ff. See also Governor Morton's address, *House Docs.*, *1840*, no. 9, p. 5; *Proceedings of the Democratic Legislative Convention Held in Boston, March 1840* (Boston, 1840), p. 4.

There was no agreement, however, about the extent to which commitments hobbled a government prompted by supplications in the name of reform to venture into unfamiliar paths. The defenders of privilege attempted to broaden the conception of property and contract to protect previous grants from adverse legislative action, seeking to prevent the General Court from becoming sole judge of exigency in disputes to which it was a party, a role inconsistent "with all sound and just notions of private right." [56] The franchise, they reasoned, was, like other property, beyond state control. The individual owner of a licensed bridge which seriously obstructed navigation claimed successfully that there was no authority capable of forcing him to remove or alter his structure.[57]

But the failure to secure the same vantage point for the corporation left privilege teetering at the edge of disaster. The test came with the claim in 1829 of the proprietors of the Charles River Bridge that their act of incorporation was a contract by which they acquired "an incorporeal hereditament; being a valuable property, consisting in the franchise of being a corporation." The charter to the competing Warren Bridge, cheek by jowl with their own structure, was, they contended, unconstitutional as a violation of contract and as confiscation of property.[58] They vigorously asserted that their rights covered the whole line of travel between Charlestown and Boston and included the essential power "to put down injurious competition"; for, "where a thing is granted, all that is necessary to the enjoyment of it goes with it." And if the government could create as many bridges as it pleased without regard to the prosperity of the existent ones, then the splendid security of the original act of incorporation was of no value. The franchise would remain intact on the statute books but would rot away beneath an insidious attack against which the Chinese wall of contract would offer no defense.[59]

The contrary argument of the Warren Bridge that the act of incorporation referred only to the immediate termini, that there

---

56. See *Charles River Bridge* v. *Warren Bridge* (1829), 7 Pickering 399, 405, 427, 438; also C. G. Loring, *Argument on Behalf of the Eastern Railroad Company* (Boston, 1845), pp. 3, 6ff.

57. *Commonwealth* v. *Breed* (1827), 3 Pickering 460.

58. *Charles River Bridge* v. *Warren Bridge* (1829), 7 Pickering 354, 355, 356, 395, 396, 427, 436, 440. See also "Solemn Protest," *Senate Docs., 1836*, no. 83, pp. 1, 10ff; *Charles River Bridge, in Equity* v. *Warren Bridge* (1828), 6 Pickering 376.

59. 7 Pickering 432, 433, 483, 494.

was "no contract by the commonwealth, that no new charter shall be granted, which shall interfere with the business or profits of the old" drew the support of half the Massachusetts court.[60] More disconcerting was the decision of the chief justice. Parker could not reconcile what seemed valid in both positions. He saw merit in Webster's conception of an implicit guarantee, in the grant of a bridge, that there would be crossers; otherwise the franchise would have little value. But he was not certain: "This appears to me a very reasonable doctrine; but I confess I am not able to adduce any authorities in support of it. I ground it on the principles of our government and constitution, and on the immutable principles of justice." On the other hand, indirect loss by government action was a risk inherent in the possession of all private property. In opening new roads, for instance, "it will often happen, that estates upon old roads are diminished in value; the seat of business may be transferred . . . inns and stores . . . may become deserted . . . but the proprietors would have no claim . . . for redress, for it is necessarily one of the contingencies on which property is . . . held, that it is liable to be impaired by future events of this kind." The chief justice was therefore unwilling to rule.[61] Divided, the state court refused to act and threw the whole question into the federal judiciary. In Washington, Justice Story labored mightily to protect the corporation, but Taney's court, heavy-weighted with Jacksonians, turned the balance against privilege. Corporations could not count on safety in the contract idea.[62]

Other decisions further reduced the margin of security. The courts refused to hold unconstitutional those reservations in corporate charters that permitted the legislature to alter or repeal, judging that these were not judicial acts and therefore not contrary to the separation-of-powers clause in the Bill of Rights.[63] Eventually the bench laid down the broad maxim that "the whole of a franchise might be taken by the legislature for public uses . . . on payment of a full compensation, without

60. 7 Pickering 407, 412, 417, 424, 425, 454–475.
61. 7 Pickering 522, 512, 514, 519ff, 524ff.
62. *Charles River Bridge* v. *Warren Bridge* (1837), 11 Peters 420. See also Story to Mason, Dec. 23, 1831, [Hillard], *Jeremiah Mason*, pp. 336ff; *Senate Docs., 1833*, no. 52, p. 8.
63. St. 1830, ch. 81; *Creese* v. *Babcock* (1839), 23 Pickering 334; Francis Hilliard, *Supplement Being a Digest of Pickering's and Metcalf's Reports* (Boston, 1843), p. 132. Cf., however, *Charles River Bridge* v. *Warren Bridge* (1829), 7 Pickering 520.

violating the clause in the constitution of the United States, against any law which impairs the obligation of contracts." [64]

This line of decisions had not sprung full-grown from the specific issues of the cases involved. Its period of gestation reached back to the moment, decades earlier, when the Commonwealth yielded to demands for the extension of privilege. But the cumulative effect, the unmistakable trend, coinciding with the fragmentation of society and the mounting intensity of humanitarian reform, shook the merchants' faith in the judiciary as defender of vested rights. Harrison Gray Otis perceived at once that the Charles River Bridge case exposed the whole realm of private property to legislative interference.[65] The like-minded gradually withdrew into a stubborn opposition, holding with the elder Dana: "The whole modern system seems to me to be grounded on a false view of man — in his power of self-restoration & self-elevation, &, in reality, as acknowledging no God, nor the need of any . . . there is a spirit of self-confidence in it which, left to its natural tendencies, will inevitably bring a deeper & wider woe upon man than earth has ever yet known. It is my sincere belief that we are preparing for ourselves an awful rebuke to our pride. The 19th century spirit is anything rather than a hopeful one to me." [66] Broody over the turn of events, they fell in with the position of old Nathan Appleton, who pointedly lectured an ambitious young lawyer, "I believe in the law of *force* — . . . and that human nature . . . can be governed by no other — . . . I should be very unwilling to rely on simple abstract justice — without force to back it." [67]

But not many merchants drew the same intransigent conclusions or felt it necessary to choose flatly between the law of force and abstract justice. Most still looked to the General Court for measures in their own interest and found it impossible to reject the idea of state action as such. Acknowledging, in any case, the ultimate justness of reform, they temporized, hoping by private benevolence to forestall the need for government intervention

64. *Boston Water &c.* v. *Boston and Worcester &c.* (1839), 23 Pickering 360; Hilliard, *Supplement*, pp. 90, 91; *House Docs., 1843*, no. 176.

65. Morison, *Harrison Gray Otis*, II, 286. See also *New York Review*, 2 (1838), 385–398; [C. S. Davies], "Constitutional Law," *North Amer. Rev.*, 46 (1838), 135.

66. To Sumner, Aug. 16, 1853, Sumner, "Letters Received," XXII, 12. See also Choate, "American Bar as an Element of Conservatism," *Address and Orations*, p. 143.

67. Sumner, "Letters Received," IX, 60.

and, when action came, to moderate its effects upon their own concerns and upon property in general.

Litigation now became more engrossed with questions of what constituted public use and full compensation. Bickering over whether exigencies existed and haggling over the size of indemnities further strengthened the professional and technical character of the law. By 1830 the accretion of precedents and the elaboration of rules of procedure had erased any danger of interference by laymen.[68] Investigations of Roman, Continental, and English jurisprudence, heavy sales of learned treatises and journals, and the establishment of law schools were marks of rapid formalization.[69] The widening of equity powers after 1815 made it easier than before to avoid trial by jury and hastened the curtailment of lay influence.[70] Popular agitation against these tendencies met fierce resistance.[71] Proposals to codify the common law were "deemed to smack of radicalism," and Rantoul's insistence that all jurisprudence be reduced to "a positive and unbending text" to minimize the discretion of judges produced only innocuous revisions of the statutes in 1835 and 1857.[72] Dependence upon the independent judiciary as the last bulwark of life, liberty, and property quickly restored the salaries of judges when those were reduced for partisan motives.[73] The link between the law and private rights was clearly in the mind of the contemporary who wrote, on the occasion of the appointment of Chancellor Kent to the Harvard Law School, "If anything can

68. Story, *Discourse*, pp. 18ff; Everett to Denison, Jan. 13, 1851, Everett Papers, XCV, 139.

69. See Everett to Denison, Oct. 11, 1845, Everett Papers, LXXVII, 8; Cushing, *Roman Law*, pp. 179ff.

70. See *Boston Commercial Gazette*, Feb. 1, 1816; *Boston Daily Advertiser*, Mar. 1, 5, 1844; st. 1857, ch. 214; 7 Pickering 354, 358, 364, 369.

71. See *American Monthly Magazine*, 1 (1829), 369ff, 469ff; Theodore Sedgwick to Theodore Sedgwick, Feb. 6, 1833, Sedgwick Papers, 2 ser., IX.

72. Everett to Thacher and Grennell, Jan. 20, Mar. 5, 1836, Everett Papers, LXVII, 30, 40; Rantoul, *Memoirs*, pp. 48, 277. See also *Report of the Commissioners on the Revision of the Statutes, 1858* (Boston, 1858), pp. iii-vii; *Senate Docs., 1855*, no. 10, pp. 4–10; Governor Gardner's address, *Senate Docs., 1857*, no. 3, pp. 39ff; *Senate Docs., 1859*, no. 202, pp. 5ff; W. W. Story, *Life and Letters of Joseph Story* (Boston, 1851), II, 241–248.

73. Governor Washburn's address, *Senate Docs., 1854*, no. 3, p. 12. For the question of salaries see *Address of the Democratic Members of the Legislature of Massachusetts . . . 1843* (Boston, 1843), pp. 9, 10; *Commonwealth History*, ed. Hart, IV, 59–67; *Boston Daily Advertiser*, Oct. 7, 9, Nov. 7, 1843, Feb. 9, 1844; Story to Webster, Jan. 10, 1824, Story, *Joseph Story*, I, 438; *Senate Docs., 1853*, no. 5, p. 22.

retard (stop it you can not) the jacobinical torrent which is sweeping past and undermining the foundations of . . . our institutions, the barrier of sound law and conservative influences which the Harvard Law School is building up, will do it." [74]

Further to secure property, the merchants sought an alliance of all those concerned with the preservation of worldly goods and offered farmers, manufacturers, traders, and even artisans a program of change within the limits of vested rights. No opposing combination of forces held together until well into the 1850's. The artisans, as Brownson realized, could count on neither the capitalists nor the agriculturists but served merely to "swell the forces of one or the other." [75] The "poor — of whom I think more than of the rich — seem to have no hope," wrote Channing sadly. At critical moments "the middle classes will foresake them. They have no helpers." [76]

With every other element in society chaotically uncertain, the merchants found a ready tool for control in the swiftly changing party system. Among the Whigs, merchant influence was always weighty. And although Bancroft and Morton for a time harnessed the Democratic organization to "radical democracy, . . . hostility to monopolies, and [the] . . . desire to promote the intellectual and moral improvement of the whole people," their success in doing so was qualified and short-lived.[77] The merchants, manufacturers, and traders who generally guided the Democrats viewed change in the same light as other men of wealth. Moreover, the inability of the party, tied to a southern platform, to take a forthright position on the slavery issue, and the growing weight of its conservative Irish constituents cast suspicion on its devotion to reform.[78]

Neither party was radical, but both compromised and allied with extremists. The system of general ticket representation, which gave a bare majority possession of the entire slate in a

74. Silliman to Sumner, June 29, 1846, Sumner, "Letters Received," X, 70. See also *American Jurist and Law Magazine*, 1 (1829), 26ff, 378; *ibid.*, 2 (1829), 192.

75. *Boston Quarterly Review*, 3 (1840), 475.

76. Channing, *Memoir*, III, 294.

77. Morton to Bancroft, Sept. 9, 1835, Marcus Morton, "Letters, 1818–1864" (MSS, MHS), I; Morton to Henshaw, Calhoun, and Van Buren, Feb. 1, 1830, Feb. 13, 1834, Mar. 27, 1837, *ibid.*, I; Bancroft, *Address*, pp. 9ff.

78. For Morton's personal difficulties and his opinion that his program had failed, see, e.g., his letters to Niles, Bancroft, and Hildreth, Feb. 12, 1846, Mar. 24, 1848, May 11, 1849, Morton, "Letters," III, 107, 318, IV, 18. See also Orestes Brownson, "The Policy to be Pursued," *Boston Quarterly Review*, 4 (1841), 74ff, 124–126; Jeremiah G. Harris to Bancroft, 1838, Bancroft Papers.

town, deprived minorities of any voice in the legislature.[79] For every group the only alternative to permanent subordination was a program of enough compromise to command wide popular support. A Whig governor pointed out to an English prime minister, "Little is . . . gained by resisting popular reforms; . . . everything is gained by measures of conciliation, which keep the great majority in good humor." [80] With his usual insight Theodore Parker saw all the politicians as a single group, "the Parties in office, or seeking to become so. This [group] makes the statutes, but is commonly controlled by the trading power, and has all of its faults . . . yet it seems amenable to the instincts of the People, who, on great occasions, sometimes interfere and change the traders' rule." [81]

The two national political parties passed through a long chain of permutations. Every few years between 1820 and 1860, observers noted hopefully or despondently that public events were getting into new channels, that new lines were about to be traced and the old ones forever effaced. This instability of political organizations derived to a considerable measure from the impact of a succession of short-lived but significant minor parties that mirrored all the vicissitudes of social and economic maladjustment.

In the 1820's such groups as the "middling interest," composed of "men of property and men of substance," developed out of transient local incidents.[82] But after 1830 new parties, each dedicated to a single issue, became the vehicles of visionaries who aspired to lead the state toward "Reform, Improvement, Liberty." These causes gathered support from the discontented and often exerted considerable influence through combination with the older organizations. Inexorably, the challenge of aggressive platforms drove both Democrats and Whigs along the road to reform.[83]

79. See Alvord to Sumner, Aug. 21, 1849, Sumner, "Letters Received," XIII, 92.

80. Everett to Peel, Jan. 8, 1850, Everett Papers, XCI, 251. For complaints by an old Whig against compromises see Phelps to Bigelow, Dec. 26, 1842, Bigelow Papers.

81. Parker, *Experience as a Minister*, pp. 92, 93. See also Channing, *Memoir*, III, 262.

82. See *An Exposition of the Principles and Views of the Middling Interest in the City of Boston, May, 1822* (Boston, 1822), p. 5; *Defence of the Exposition of the Middling Interest on the Right of Constituents to Give Instructions to Their Representatives and the Obligation of These to Obey Them* (Boston, 1822); Morison, *Harrison Gray Otis*, II, 238–241.

83. A. H. Everett, speech quoted in *Boston Daily Advocate*, Nov. 14, 1835; Braman, *Annual Election*, p. 79. For the relation of reform to the major and minor

From time to time between 1830 and 1845 the balance of power fell into the hands of the Workingmen's party, the Locofocos, the Anti-Masonic party, and various nativist and abolitionist factions all resting heavily on the votes of the rural population and of the urban mechanics.[84] But after 1845 the splintering effects of the slavery issue on both old parties offered those primarily interested in reform the opportunity finally to seize the state government.[85] The Free-Soilers attempted to capture the Whig party in 1848 and urged the conservative, Edward Everett, to accept an independent nomination for the vice-presidency. Although they failed in both efforts, the outcome of the election that year encouraged many disillusioned rank-and-file Whigs to turn their backs upon their old party.[86]

After 1850 the reformers dominated the state, first in a coalition of Free-Soilers and Democrats and then marshaled under a nativist banner after defeat of the radical constitution of 1853 by the Irish vote. The Know-Nothings reigned until their mantle fell upon the new Republican party in 1858.[87] This culmination of the shifting political alliances steadily strengthened reform influence and threw conservatives into confusion.[88] After years of half-satisfaction through paltry concessions by the old parties, the radicals held sway without substantial restraint. The program of reform and the battle against privilege, shackled for so long, approached fulfillment. Worked up from the materials brought to hand by the experience of the past, and following the broad outlines sketched in the resolution of numerous specific issues for many years earlier, the new structure of state action took finished form in the final decade before the Civil War.[89]

---

parties see Edward Everett to Denison, Delavan, April, Sept. 30, 1853, Everett Papers, CII, 84, CIII, 71.

84. See Morton to Simpson, Pearce, Harrington, and Henshaw, Feb. 17, 20, 1834, Jan. 9, June 1, 6, 1836, Morton, "Letters," I; Everett to Shattuck, Hallett, Dec. 24, 1832, Oct. 5, 1835, Everett Papers, LXVI, 186, 291; *Springfield Gazette*, Sept. 14, 1842; A. B. Darling, "Workingmen's Party in Massachusetts," *Amer. Hist. Rev.*, 29 (1923), 81ff, 84–86; J. Q. Adams, *Memoirs*, IX, 33ff.

85. Everett to Aberdeen, Nov. 14, 1845, Everett Papers, LXXVII, 90.

86. E. to A. H. Everett, Oct. 30, 1846, Everett Papers, LXXX, 32. See also Everett to Winthrop, Kent, Hallam, Sumner, Bancroft, and Peel, Apr. 25, June 22, July 25, Aug. 4, Oct. 31, Dec. 23, 1848, *ibid.*, LXXXIV, 270, LXXXV, 226, 227, LXXXVI, 39, LXXXVII, 30, 204.

87. See Everett to Green and Clay, Nov. 5, Dec. 3, 1851, Everett Papers, XCIX, 28, 79; "S" and Stone to Sumner, Feb. 15, 1853, Mar. 15, Dec. 29, 1854, Sumner, "Letters Received," XXI, 48, XXIII, 118, XXV, 148; Everett to Fillmore, Cushing, Dec. 16, 1854, Nov. 11, 1855, Everett Papers, CIV, 55, CV, 7.

88. Everett to Capen, Nov. 6, 1858, Everett Papers, CIX, 104.

89. See Handlin, *Boston's Immigrants*, pp. 191ff; *Commonwealth History*, ed. Hart, IV, 74–82.

9 | Liberal Humanitarianism

Progressive atrophy of the ability to exercise influence through incorporation went along with paralysis of the will to act through all the aids which had once guided the enterprise of Massachusetts. Yet the media through which privilege formerly operated did not altogether vanish. The government did not cease to play a role. The social and economic disorders, which tore apart the old fabric, exposed the need for the services of the polity as a regulating agency and cut to a new pattern the outmoded materials for control. Legislation sometimes displayed a remarkable if superficial continuity, sometimes struck out into new directions, but in either case was framed in the context of different objectives. Slowly the Commonwealth gave way to a humanitarian police state which set up rules of judgment among individuals and aimed to assure equitable conditions of life and labor to all.

The state had always exercised a judicial role in private matters, settling questions of disputed rights and assessing awards for injuries by one person against another. The General Court, armed with a heritage of common law, continued to enumerate offenses and to set down principles to guide its courts. Antecedents in law molded such statutes, but the pressure of the times furnished the stuff of which they were made. Inevitably, the slowly widening conception of what was legally wrong reflected a broadening recognition of the protection demanded by those exposed to the uncertainties of the new society.

Nuisance, for instance, had early referred to any offensive

action by one person that might cause damage to another. Abatement of nuisances had motivated the regulation of dangerous or noxious trades and of fire hazards. Old laws thus set conditions for the floating of timbers on rivers, the erection of wooden buildings in cities, the storage of gunpowder, and the location of tanneries, slaughterhouses, and ropewalks.[1] Any menace to health was subject to action, as was the neglect of roads, pikes, and sidewalks.[2] These precedents offered a ready medium for protection against injuries from new devices like steam engines and railroads.[3] The conception itself also expanded to comprehend many forms of indirect damages.[4] Protests from harried companies that they were themselves "from interest disposed to do everything that can be done for the safety . . . of the public" were futile against the "officious, meddling spirit." [5]

Another fount of new legislation was the body of general rules laid down from the start by the state for the conduct of business. The government had thus established a money of account, regulated relations under the laws of agency and contract, and defined codes of conduct for masters and men, seamen and shipowners.[6] It acted as intermediary to assure an equitable distribution of assets to the creditors of an insolvent debtor, allowing the courts of probate to appoint commissioners who supervised the procedure.[7]

There were sporadic complaints that the insolvency law permitted assignment to a single creditor and thus unwittingly implemented frauds.[8] But until the 1830's the efficient bankruptcy

1. See, e.g., st. 1782, ch. 46; st. 1785, ch. 1; st. 1786, ch. 26; st. 1799, ch. 75; st. 1801, ch. 20; st. 1803, chs. 77, 120; st. 1807, ch. 137; st. 1809, ch. 44; st. 1813, ch. 143; st. 1816, ch. 26; st. 1820, ch. 47; st. 1823, chs. 125, 149; st. 1855, ch. 74; *Revised Statutes of the Commonwealth of Massachusetts* (Boston, 1836), ch. 21, sec. 49, ch. 58; *Senate Docs., 1855*, no. 116; *By-Laws and Orders of the Town of Boston* (Boston, 1818), p. 93.
2. See, e.g., st. 1809, ch. 63; st. 1814, ch. 39, sec. 5; st. 1824, ch. 16; st. 1855, ch. 391; *General Statutes of the Commonwealth of Massachusetts . . . 1859* (Boston, 1860), ch. 26.
3. See st. 1852, ch. 191; st. 1859, chs. 125, 126; for railroads see *Revised Statutes*, ch. 39, sec. 81. See also *Senate Docs., 1858*, no. 50, pp. 17, 18.
4. See, e.g., N. I. Bowditch, *Massachusetts General Hospital* (Boston, 1872), p. 176; *Boston Daily Herald*, Sept. 6, 1836.
5. *Boston Commercial Gazette*, Apr. 13, 1835; *Senate Docs., 1846*, no. 91.
6. See, e.g., *Columbian Centinel*, Jan. 7, 1795; *Senate Docs., 1826-27*, no. 3; st. 1784, ch. 19; st. 1857, ch. 139; J. B. Felt, *Historical Account of Massachusetts Currency* (Boston, 1839), p. 211.
7. St. 1784, ch. 2; st. 1789, ch. 50; st. 1821, ch. 72.
8. See, e.g., *Boston Gazette*, June 14, 1784; *Repertory*, Feb. 23, 1808; *Boston Gazette*, Jan. 31, Feb. 7, 1811; *New-England Palladium*, Jan. 3, 17, 1812; Governor Strong's address, Jan. 27, 1813, *Resolves of the Commonwealth of Massachusetts*

system deemed essential by the mercantile community failed to materialize. Vagueness about the constitutional safeguards to contracts and uncertainty about the intentions of the federal government, which shared jurisdiction in the matter, confused the question.[9] Agitation by Webster and the Society for the Promotion of the Interests of Bona Fide Creditors and for the Benefit and Relief of Insolvent Debtors brought partial reform in that decade, first by putting the process under the Supreme Judicial Court and then by allowing creditors to choose assignees to allocate dividends proportionately.[10] A new law in 1844 set down a careful procedure on these principles, and finally a total overhauling of the system twelve years later organized special courts that guarded against illicit assignments.[11]

Those who became creditors through their own manual labor asked for and received recognition of the priority of debts owed them. The manufacturing corporation act of 1851 even made stockholders personally liable to operatives for six months' wages, and a year later mechanics received a lien on all types of buildings.[12]

A similar line of legislation developed from a traditional idea that it was a function of government to establish uniform standards of value in order to assure "security of calculation." [13] Ancient laws had calculated the legal height of fences, and the assize of bread had in one form or another set the weight of loaves.[14]

... *1812* ... *1815* (Boston, 1812–1815), p. 109; *Senate Docs., 1826–27*, no. 4; *Portland Gazette*, Feb. 1, 1813.

9. See Henshaw to Sedgwick, Jan. 22, 1793, Theodore Sedgwick Papers, 1768–1858 (MSS, MHS), II, 398; Sedgwick to King, May 11, 1800, C. R. King, *Life and Correspondence of Rufus King* (New York, 1894–1900), III, 236; *Boston Patriot*, Mar. 7, 1809; *North Amer. Rev.*, 7 (1818), 28ff; *American Jurist and Law Magazine*, 1 (1829), 35ff.

10. St. 1836, ch. 238; st. 1838, ch. 136; *Boston Commercial Gazette*, Oct. 5, 1829; *House Docs., 1841*, no. 30.

11. See *Boston Daily Advertiser*, Feb. 15, 1843, Mar. 8, 11, Apr. 11, 1844; st. 1856, ch. 284; *Whalemen's Shipping List and Merchants' Transcript* (New Bedford), Mar. 31, 1857.

12. St. 1838, ch. 163, sec. 24; st. 1852, ch. 307; *Senate Docs., 1855*, no. 3, p. 29; W. E. Rappard, *Les Corporations d'affaires au Massachusetts* (Paris, 1908), p. 42.

13. See Willard Phillips, "Plan of an Improved System," *North Amer. Rev.*, 2 (1815–1816), 367.

14. For fences see st. 1785, ch. 52; also st. 1822, ch. 60; *Revised Statutes*, ch. 19, secs. 2–14. For bread see st. 1798, ch. 67; st. 1800, ch. 76; *Revised Statutes*, ch. 28; *Report of the Commissioners Appointed to Revise the General Statutes of the Commonwealth* (Boston, 1835), I, 178ff; *Amendments to the Report of the Commissioners Appointed to Revise the General Statutes of the Commonwealth* (Boston, 1835), p. 41. See also *Columbian Centinel*, May 30, June 3, 1795, Jan. 7, Nov. 22, 1797; "A Friend to the Poor and Industrious," *Boston Gazette*, May 15, 1806.

Likewise, inspection laws sometimes went beyond the objective of protecting exporters, to guard the security of domestic purchasers. To prevent fraud in the sale of such commodities as hay, wood, bark, beer, ale, and cider, statutes defined the capacity of weights and measures.[15] The number of similar enactments grew rapidly, affecting such diverse articles as gunpowder, sand, gravel, coal, grain, salt, fruits, and vegetables, each regulated with its own standards of measurement.[16] And by 1835 a complex system of checking town with county weights, and county with state, assured uniformity.[17]

In other ways, too, inspection shifted emphasis from protecting the producers to protecting the consumers, although the vested interests of old officials sometimes created difficulties.[18] The sale of corrupt food had always been a punishable nuisance. But broadening the conception to include other than deleterious commodities facilitated the application of inspection laws to domestic sales in the interest of all buyers "who have no means to essay" products themselves.[19] In 1836 the courts held that, whatever the intent of the original statutes, inspection modified the rule of caveat emptor in the interest of the purchaser.[20] Regulations for such commodities as flaxseed and tobacco, which did not fit in the new context, dropped out at the revision of the statutes in 1835.[21]

Franchises, whether held by corporations or by individuals, grew in number and changed in character. Obstinate defense of existing liberties demonstrated the urgency of rigid legislative limitations to hedge about new grants with restrictive provisions. Gaslight and horse-railroad companies thus received charters freely, but their narrow prerogatives were a far cry from the advantages inuring to the early turnpikes and canals.[22]

15. See *Revised Statutes*, ch. 28, secs. 41–43, 95–98, ch. 30.

16. See, e.g., st. 1800, ch. 75; st. 1815, ch. 18; st. 1822, ch. 103; st. 1823, chs. 117, 121; st. 1855, ch. 188; st. 1858, ch. 68; *Revised Statutes*, ch. 28, secs. 135–37, ch. 31.

17. *Revised Statutes*, ch. 30.

18. See, e.g., *Boston Daily Advertiser*, Sept. 23, 1843; *Senate Docs., 1859*, no. 161.

19. MA, Senate, 3666. For typical commodities see, e.g., st. 1808, ch. 52; st. 1809, ch. 118; st. 1810, ch. 73; st. 1823, ch. 121; st. 1830, ch. 99; *Revised Statutes*, ch. 28, secs. 44–58, 69–91, 120–132, 200–209; see also *Journal of the House of Representatives of the Commonwealth of Massachusetts, January–March, 1808* (Boston, 1808), pp. 17, 230, 252, 287, 307.

20. See *Winsor* v. *Lombard* (1836), 18 Pickering 60.

21. *Revised Statutes*, ch. 28; *Report of Commissioners to Revise Statutes* (Boston, 1835), I, 164, 189ff; *Amendments to Report of Commissioners*, pp. 35, 47.

22. See, e.g., st. 1822, ch. 41; *General Statutes*, ch. 61, secs. 15–19; see above, p.

Town grants also reflected this tendency; in the fish laws, the monopoly of supply became less important than conservation against unlimited exploitation.[23] Other old practices passed through a similar transformation; so, to safeguard the interests of farmers, a law of 1824 altered the rule for raising a head of water, and ultimately county commissioners received broad powers to order changes in dams.[24] Deviations from the letter of their grants brought the holders of franchises swift complaints and endless troubles.[25] Careful provisions for payment of damages everywhere accompanied the bestowal of the attribute of eminent domain, as in the case of railroads, where the requirement for an exact delineation of route immensely strengthened the hands of landowners and remained law despite protests by the companies.[26] The state even tried to relieve injustices arising from former concessions, proposing in 1860 to compensate sufferers for its remissness in chartering the Middlesex Canal in 1793 without adequate protection against the flooding of meadows.[27]

In conformity with this evolution, a series of judicial decisions between 1829 and 1851 restricted the interference of private interests with the navigable waters of the Commonwealth. By common law and long-established practice, the state controlled its rivers and bays and owned all the flats appertaining to them. But for two centuries the government had permitted or tolerated encroachments which edged into the streams by filling or by building wharves. An old law of 1641 had granted away the flats to the low-water mark, riparian owners thereafter had freely taken the liberty of building beyond, and in 1803 the courts held that such unauthorized extension was not a nuisance unless it interfered with the property of others.[28]

The development of shipping and the needs of larger vessels

18o. See also *Thacher v. Dartmouth Bridge Company* (1836), 18 Pickering 501; st. 1827, ch. 54.

23. See, e.g., *Revised Statutes*, ch. 55; st. 1822, chs. 21, 54, 58, 75, 97; st. 1823, chs. 97, 110, 132; st. 1824, ch. 127; see also the suggestions for the use of market space, *Bowen's Boston News-Letter*, Jan. 21, 1826, p. 59.

24. See also st. 1823, ch. 135; st. 1825, ch. 144; st. 1857, ch. 163; *American Jurist and Law Magazine*, 2 (1829), 32; *House Docs., 1841*, no. 21.

25. See, e.g., Boston & Roxbury Mill Corporation, *Senate Docs, 1856*, nos. 110, 114.

26. See *Senate Docs., 1835*, no. 64; "Rail Road Man," *Boston Commercial Gazette*, Apr. 13, 1835; *Boston Daily Advertiser*, Mar. 2, 1844.

27. See *House Docs., 1860*, nos. 29, 100 (esp. pp. 13ff, 16ff, 32ff, 46ff, 54ff), and no. 221.

28. See *Commonwealth v. May* (1803), *American Jurist and Law Magazine*, 3 (1830), 190ff; *ibid.*, 185ff; *Senate Docs., 1850*, no. 3, pp. 4ff.

revealed the dangers in this free and easy policy.[29] Reversing the earlier trend, a ruling of the Boston Municipal Court, from which there was no appeal, held in 1829 that any wharf obstructing a navigable channel was a nuisance.[30] Later decisions by the Supreme Judicial Court maintained that doctrine and upheld the validity of harbor lines marked out by commissioners under mandate of the legislature.[31]

Like the franchise, the license suffered drastic changes as courts and legislatures alike, applying the measure of "reasonableness," eliminated monopolistic implications unadaptable to the new era.[32] By 1828 Phillips wrote, "It is unnecessary, as well as prejudicial to industry, to prescribe any conditions of apprenticeship . . . or any other limitations to the exercise of any trade or profession, unless it be one of which the public cannot judge of the qualifications." [33] While the privileged attempted to demonstrate special qualifications beyond the comprehension of laymen, the solution in each case unfolded along other than abstract lines. The final decision depended on the balance between the defenders and the attackers of such exclusive advantages.

Although Chief Justice Parsons had ruled it no crime to practice medicine without a license if "with an honest intention," certification by the Massachusetts Medical Society, by Harvard College, or by the Berkshire Medical Institution of Williams College continued to bring the prestige of state approval and, in addition, special, concrete rights. Revision of the statutes in 1835 eliminated the provision that licensees alone could sue for the collection of debts in the state courts. And incorporation in 1856 of the Homeopathic Medical Society with the same advantages as the older institutions destroyed the conception that the government supported a single standard of practice. Three

29. See, e.g., *Boston Daily Advertiser*, Apr. 17, 1844; *Senate Docs., 1850*, no. 3, pp. 12–14, 49.

30. *Commonwealth* v. *Wright & Dame* (1829), *American Jurist and Law Magazine*, 3 (1830), 185ff. Here the court returned to the principle of *Commonwealth* v. *Crowninshield* (1796), *Mass. Hist. Soc. Colls.*, 1 ser., V (1798), 45ff, an unreported case which seems to have been unknown both to the judges of 1803 and to those of 1829.

31. See *Gray* v. *Bartlett* (1838), 20 Pickering 186; *Garey* v. *Ellis* (1848), 1 Cushing 306; *Commonwealth* v. *Alger* (1851), 7 Cushing 53; *Senate Docs., 1853*, no. 109; st. 1856, ch. 293. See, however, exceptions by special act, e.g., st. 1852, ch. 85.

32. See *Henry Vandine, Petitioner &c.* (1828), 6 Pickering 187.

33. Willard Phillips, *Manual of Political Economy* (Boston, 1828), pp. 134ff, 208. See also Edward Everett, "On the Importance of Scientific Knowledge to Practical Men," *Orations and Speeches on Various Occasions* (Boston, 1853–1868), I, 256ff.

years later the deletion of the remaining licensing provisions from the General Statutes seemed to acknowledge that the state would treat all manner of doctors equally.[34]

Creation of a universal right to practice was no solution to those aggrieved by the methods of auctioneers who diverted goods from normal distributive channels and upset the stability of markets by deranging prices. These abuses grew harsher after 1815. But an increase in the number of licenses would only intensify the evils arising from this technique of sale.[35] The alternative was to diminish the value of the privilege by imposing a discriminatory tax which would give relief to rival methods of distribution. After failing four years earlier, competitors who had suffered by the system combined in 1822 with farmers friendly to any new source of revenue that did not fall on their own land, and together they forced the adoption of a levy on all sales at public vendue except those by court order. While the auctioneer retained some of his attributes as a state agent, the business nature of the office steadily blacked out its public character.[36]

Other licenses also persisted, although the exclusive advantages that went with them shrank. Exemptions from the obligation to use pilots thus broadened steadily, and eventually, in 1855, the power of examination passed from the hands of the marine societies to those of a state board of pilot commissioners.[37] Licensing generally turned into an instrument of supervision for one objective or another and ceased to be a special favor in old spheres, like innkeeping, and in those new ones conducive to "bad morals," like peddling, hawking, dealing in junk, and pawnbroking.[38]

The new era resolved the quandaries of the old concerning

34. See st. 1817, ch. 131; st. 1818, ch. 113; st. 1823, ch. 136; *Revised Statutes*, ch. 22; st. 1855, ch. 411. See also R. H. Fitz, *Rise and Fall of the Licensed Physician in Massachusetts* (n.p., 1894), pp. 5–8, 11, 16, 17. Details of law were clarified by *Hewitt* v. *Charier* (1835), 16 Pickering 353; *Wright* v. *Lanckton* (1837), 19 Pickering 288; *Hewitt* v. *Wilcox* (1840), 1 Metcalf 154; Francis Hilliard, *Supplement Being a Digest of Pickering's and Metcalf's Reports* (Boston, 1843), p. 348; *Senate Docs., 1859*, no. 16.

35. See, e.g., A. H. Cole, *American Wool Manufacture* (Cambridge, Mass., 1926), I, 157ff, 215ff.

36. See *Boston Commercial Gazette*, Feb. 19, 1818; st. 1822, ch. 87; st. 1824, ch. 129; st. 1830, ch. 61; *Sewall* v. *Jones* (1830), 9 Pickering 412; *Commonwealth* v. *Harnden* (1837), 19 Pickering 482; *Jordan* v. *Smith* (1837), 19 Pickering 287.

37. See, e.g., rules in *Boston Daily Advertiser*, Nov. 15, 1843, May 2, 1844; st. 1855, ch. 421; st. 1857, ch. 214; *Public Docs., 1857*, no. 26; *Whalemen's Shipping List and Merchants' Transcript* (New Bedford), Sept. 30, 1856, Jan. 26, 1858. See also st. 1835, ch. 149; *Revised Statutes*, ch. 32.

38. See *Boston Commercial Gazette*, Feb. 26, 1835; st. 1839, ch. 53; st. 1855, ch. 121; also st. 1785, ch. 2; st. 1799, ch. 20; st. 1820, ch. 45; st. 1823, ch. 122.

the proper allocation of state resources. Without the common interest to justify special grants for the advantage of favored persons or groups, Massachusetts could indulge unrestrainedly in the urge to thrift. Uninhibited, it ruthlessly exploited its holdings in Maine, squeezing out $2,700,536 in the quarter-century after 1820.[39] Moreover, money that fell into the government's treasury from this or from any other source was not free for dissipation on special gifts. Bounties now seemed normally to meddle "with the general law of the universe," to evil effect.[40] Indirect help through tax exemption, occasionally discussed as a stimulant to the production of such articles as salt and sheep, disappeared.[41] Efforts to secure direct grants of money to encourage manufacturing never reached the point of adoption. A modicum of aid to the agricultural societies persisted.[42] But the application of such assistance to certain favored products, wheat, beet sugar, and silk, was half-hearted, ineffective, and short-lived, and it encountered the opposition of urban groups unwilling to apply their tariff arguments here.[43] After four years of trial Henry Colman, commissioner of the agricultural survey, reported complete failure and pointed to divisions of opinion about the utility and propriety of the policy. On the basis of that document a legislative committee concluded, "The farmers must be left to determine what crops are on the whole most useful, productive and profitable."[44]

But the line of propriety was difficult to draw here too. Arguments for government participation were weightier when aid went not to advance individual enterprises but to cope with an unnatural or unexpected general condition that affected all.

39. See MA, res. 1820, ch. 24; "Speech of His Excellency Levi Lincoln, before the Legislature," *Senate Docs., 1826–27*, pp. 19–23; *House Docs., 1829–30*, no. 1, p. 20; *House Docs., 1833*, no. 2, pp. 8, 9; *Senate Docs., 1836*, no. 4, pp. 13–16; *Senate Docs., 1837*, no. 14; *Senate Docs., 1840*, no. 19; *Senate Docs., 1841*, no. 8; *Senate Docs., 1850*, no. 116, pp. 4, 5; *Senate Docs., 1851*, no. 3, p. 6; *Senate Docs., 1852*, no. 7, p. 7; *Senate Docs., 1853*, no. 5, p. 10; *Senate Docs., 1854*, no. 3, p. 20, no. 9; *House Docs., 1859*, no. 302; J. W. Fleming, "Maine" (unpub. diss. Harvard University, 1938, University Archives), p. 146.

40. See Francis Bowen, *Principles of Political Economy* (Boston, 1856), p. 23.

41. See, e.g., Pomeroy to Sedgwick, Jan. 25, 1825, Sedgwick Papers, 2 ser., VIII; C. F. Swift, *History of Old Yarmouth* (Yarmouth Port, 1884), p. 190.

42. See *Revised Statutes*, ch. 42. For manufacturing see *Senate Docs., 1836*, no. 76, pp. 3ff.

43. See st. 1835, ch. 130; st. 1836, ch. 206; st. 1837, ch. 72; st. 1838, ch. 23; *Boston Commercial Gazette*, Feb. 1, 1838; *Boston Daily Advertiser*, Mar. 9, 1844.

44. *Senate Docs., 1840*, no. 48. See also *House Docs., 1840*, no. 36, pp. 7ff, 50ff, 54, 104, 154ff; *House Docs., 1839*, no. 46; *Senate Docs., 1840*, no. 28, pp. 3–5; Governor Everett's address, *House Docs., 1836*, no. 6, pp. 23, 24.

There was thus no reluctance to offer a ten-thousand-dollar bounty for a remedy for the potato rot, or to spend heavily to fight the pleuropneumonia epidemic among cattle in 1860.[45]

The sponsors of railroads also urged that the general advantage that would accrue to everyone in the state justified the same assistance to their ventures as had earlier gone to canals.[46] Construction of the roads to the north and the south had been relatively simple, and the eastern portion of the line to Albany reached completion in 1835 after four years of building. In these companies the monopoly of traffic between termini seemed favor enough to attract investors and draw the support of local communities. But the more difficult problem of crossing the mountains called for greater outlays of cash. Furthermore, this part of the road faced opposition from Worcester interests, which used every stratagem to obstruct and delay extension that would convert the town from a terminus to a way station.[47]

Work on the Western Railroad did not begin for a number of years. The city of Boston regarded the scheme as essential to its commercial prosperity and pushed subscriptions among the public in an attempt to popularize the institution. To the same end, ministers were ultimately asked to discourse "on the moral effect of Rail-roads." [48] The great business firms contributed as a popular duty but only in small amounts; merchants saw little prospect of dividends from the project, one of the most extensive theretofore undertaken in America. Slacking by the wealthy left the main burden of support on the "middling Classes," groups incapable or unwilling to bear it.[49] In this case incorporation, even with a monopoly added, failed to induce investors to risk their funds. Already in 1835 calls arose for direct government assistance to finance construction by the company.[50] A year later Governor Everett suggested that Massachusetts would surely befriend an improvement of such vast and general utility if the necessity emerged.[51]

An attempt to raise funds through a ten-million-dollar bank

45. See *Revised Statutes*, ch. 54; res. 1851, ch. 18; *Acts and Resolves, 1857*, p. 740; st. 1860, ch. 192.
46. See, e.g., st. 1822, ch. 59.
47. "Rail Road Man," *Boston Commercial Gazette*, Apr. 6, 1835, Nov. 26, 1835.
48. See Savage to Pierce, Dec. 19, 1838, Western Railroad Corporation, "Miscellaneous Records, 1829–1843" (MSS, Baker Library, Harvard University); Edward Everett, "Western Railroad," *Orations and Speeches*, II, 146.
49. *Boston Commercial Gazette*, Aug. 31, 1835.
50. *Ibid.*, Aug. 27, Nov. 23, 1835.
51. *House Docs., 1836*, no. 6, p. 23.

connected with the railroad failed.[52] But the state finally issued scrip as security for loans by the corporation. Between 1835 and 1841 Massachusetts thus allocated four million dollars of its credit, more than half of the total funds that went into the road. This form of financing incidentally won considerable merchant support; borrowing from England brought in capital and simultaneously stimulated the business of carrying iron.[53] Similar patronage helped other projects in the next twenty years. In the 1850's local communities received permission to draw upon their credit and treasuries to help.[54]

But support for this policy was not unanimous. Attacks multiplied with the grants. Artisans in Boston itself objected to a policy in which the state took the whole risk with only slight profit, for "in this case the government will be used for the special benefit of the corporators." [55] Farmers, whose enthusiasm for the new developments had early given way to misgivings, suffered from torrents of agricultural products set loose upon their markets from the West and faced at the same time the unenviable possibility of a rise in tax rates to pay for the construction costs. After a decade of trial, enemies of the Everett railroad policy complained that it "had laid every farm in the commonwealth under mortgage." [56] By 1854 a legislative committee was convinced that the proceeds of taxation ought not to pay the expenses of "trade, traffic, or speculative enterprises." [57] Assistance to the Troy & Greenfield incited acrimonious opposition and forced Governor Gardner to veto more liberal conditions in 1857. Frauds and mismanagement cast doubts on the utility of such aid in general, while divided interests fostered the conviction that the state "should not become a copartner" in any such ventures.[58]

Monopoly was an instrument of government even less suscepti-

52. *Senate Docs., 1836*, no. 16; Robert Rantoul, Jr., *Memoirs, Speeches and Writings* (Boston, 1854), pp. 353ff; *Boston Commercial Gazette*, Mar. 31, Apr. 7, 1836.

53. See *Proceedings of the Western Railroad Corporation, January 27, 1841* (Boston, 1841), pp. 3ff; *Brief Statement of Facts in Relation to the Western Railroad, Feb. 6, 1841* (n.p., n.d.); M. A. Green, *Springfield, 1636–1886* (Springfield, 1888), pp. 416, 417.

54. See Governor Everett's address, *Senate Docs., 1839*, no. 1, p. 7; st. 1852, ch. 156; st. 1860, chs. 35, 184; *Woburn Journal*, Feb. 28, 1852.

55. *House Docs., 1830–31*, no. 54; *Boston Quarterly Review*, 3 (1840), 252.

56. Everett to Ruggles, Nov. 28, 1849, Edward Everett Papers (MSS, MHS), XCI, 113.

57. *Senate Docs., 1854*, no. 28.

58. *Acts and Resolves, 1857*, pp. 746ff; st. 1859, ch. 117; st. 1860, ch. 202; *Senate*

ble of adaptation to the new purposes. Once an obvious and legitimate technique of patronage, this now seemed outside the scope of proper state action and at the root of a whole roster of evils — high prices, short supplies, and restricted markets. No new grants appeared after those to the railroads in 1830.

Hostility to monopolies comprehended as well those already established. The Charles River Bridge, which throttled northern traffic into Boston, ultimately succumbed to the attack upon its exclusive position. The argument that competition endangered the operation of railroads did not brake movements to divest those companies of their unique status. Protests against the policy of the Boston & Providence, which connected only with its own line of steamers, for a time threatened to involve the road in legal difficulties. That the legislature of 1854 seriously considered a measure to take away the monopoly of the Boston & Lowell, despite the explicit guarantee in its charter, was an indication of the strength of the sentiment.[59]

The corporation, object of the same unfriendliness encountered by monopoly, nevertheless possessed the resiliency to adjust to new circumstances and new uses. Dispersal had acknowledged the state's right to endow the institution with tolls, monopolies, and other favors. Earlier critics had accepted the propriety of these advantages; whether through the exaction of a financial quid pro quo or through the imposition of regulations, they had merely sought reaffirmation that the grants originated in and aimed at some communal purpose.

Consistently after 1800 the desire to protect the property invested in corporations had propagated the conception that they were private and therefore secure within their charters against state interference. That stand provoked embarrassing questions concerning the special advantages retained by these associations. All privileges, by whomever held, faced a challenge, but powers acquired as a public agency were particularly vulnerable. What right had simple business organizations to the attributes of a governing body? "They are *not* for the public good — in design or end," complained a moderate newspaper, "they are for the aggrandizement of the stockholders — for the promotion of the interests of the *few* . . . We wish to have public good and private speculation more distinctly separated and understood." [60]

Docs., 1859, no. 25; *House Docs., 1860*, no. 185, pp. 16ff; *Senate Docs., 1860*, no. 108; *Senate Docs., 1862*, no. 1, pp. 25–30; *Boston Daily Advertiser*, Jan. 28, 1843.

59. *Senate Docs., 1838*, no. 98, pp. 7, 43, 60; *Boston Daily Herald*, Nov. 23, 1836; *Journal of the House of Representatives . . . 1854* (Boston, 1854), p. 445.

60. *Boston Daily Herald*, Sept. 6, 1836.

Divested of its communal functions, the corporation became an anomalous creature, privileged but unprincipled, armed with power yet devoid of responsibility. A popular story recounting the conflict between a poor widow and a great corporation moralized: "But why did the Corporation of Charles River Bridge thus pursue Martha Gardner? There is but one answer, — it was a Corporation . . . The Corporation of Charles River Bridge was composed of many men well remembered now for their private and public worth. Less than five of them would have redeemed Nineveh. But unhappily the animal and the intellectual part of Corporations generally govern the body, and conscience is a non-corporate word." [61] Marcus Morton, who wished to exorcise these bodies of their anachronistic powers, put it more concretely: "The wealth of many managed by a few is more alarmingly dangerous, for it has not the same powerful restraint of self interest and individual responsibility to check the alarm of it." [62]

Hostility to corporations centered in the large and influential group of artisans whose place in the economy of New England the factory had undermined. As the new mills manned by green hands drained away the skilled workers' livelihood to the advantage of interloping financiers, the displaced directed their resentment against the device that seemed responsible for these disastrous developments. Incorporation, they objected, "puts means into the hands of inexperienced capitalists to take from us the profits of our art which cost us so many years of labour to obtain." [63]

The artisans discovered similar grievances against railroads and against financial institutions. The former had concentrated "the business and profits of general transportation into the hands of the capitalists." These "have secured and now monopolize the business which stage proprietors, wagoners, and teamsters formerly conducted, and have deposited in their pockets the profits which formerly were distributed more generally and diffusely . . . Scores of deserted villages, in various sections of the Commonwealth bear witness to the wasting and blasting effects of this growing monopoly." [64]

61. Walter Austin, *William Austin* (Boston, 1925), pp. 165, 257ff.

62. Morton to Bancroft, Sept. 9, 1835, Marcus Morton, "Letters" (MSS, MHS), I; Rantoul, *Memoirs*, p. 529.

63. "Remonstrance of George W. Cushing & Others, Journeymen Carriage Makers . . . Feby. 8 1838" (MS, HCL); below, Appendix F; *Boston Commercial Gazette*, Feb. 5, 1835.

64. *House Docs., 1843*, no. 92, p. 18.

Jackson's fight with the Bank of the United States sharpened artisan awareness of grievances against the situation in Massachusetts. The complaints were simple. An excess of banks cheapened paper, stimulated speculation, exploited workingmen without facilities for checking counterfeits, and weakened confidence in the whole currency. The system also increased the amount of indebtedness and, by raising costs, stimulated "importation . . . desirable by a merely importing community" but "fatal to domestic manufacturers." More generally, it produced fluctuations particularly hard on the uninfluential and turned business into "a lottery with many blanks to one prize." [65] Immediate relief could come through the abolition of notes under twenty dollars and ultimate salvation through a specie currency such as the subtreasury system contemplated, reforms that would extirpate the issuing power and thus reduce banks to the level of unchartered businesses. [66]

Halfway measures like taxation did not satisfy these complaints. The legislature retained the levy on bank capital throughout the period despite arguments over its incidence and despite the charge that business would flee to the friendlier countinghouses of New York. [67] Nevertheless, occasional proposals after 1820 similarly to assess insurance, manufacturing, and railroads failed of adoption although the General Court had reserved the power to assess when it had granted such charters. [68] The foes of the corporation refused to press for a tax that would implicitly justify the privilege and would "place it in the power of moneyed Institutions, to control the question" of their continuance "by the very necessity of their existence to the support and operations of the Government. [69]

The artisans' spokesmen in politics labored to restrict the

65. Rantoul, *Memoirs*, pp. 350ff, 359ff, 635, 643; also Niles to Bancroft, Feb. 23, 1840, George Bancroft Papers (MSS, MHS).

66. See *Boston Commercial Gazette*, Jan. 25, 1838.

67. See st. 1828, ch. 96, sec. 21; st. 1831, ch. 64; *Revised Statutes*, ch. 9, secs. 1–3; *North Amer. Rev.*, 19 (1824), 257ff; Phillips, *Manual of Political Economy*, p. 262; Governor Everett's address, *House Docs., 1836*, no. 6, p. 18; *Senate Docs., 1845*, no. 101; Everett to Hume, Oct. 12, 1852, Everett Papers, CII, 2; Bowen, *Political Economy*, p. 359; [Nathan Appleton], *Examination of the Banking System of Massachusetts* (Boston, 1831), pp. 23–39.

68. See, e.g., st. 1822, chs. 99, 113; st. 1823, ch. 85; *Boston Commercial Gazette*, Feb. 1, June 11, 1821; *House Docs., 1843*, no. 92, pp. 18–23; *Boston Daily Advertiser*, Mar. 17, 20, 21, 1843; *Review of the Proceedings in the Massachusetts Legislature for 1843 By the Whig Minority* (Boston, 1843), pp. 44ff; *Public Docs., 1861*, no. 10, pp. iii–v.

69. Message of Governor Lincoln, *Senate Docs., 1826–27*, p. 22. For the use of precisely that argument by defenders of the banks see, e.g., *Boston Commercial Gazette*, Jan. 25, 1838.

corporation to public communal purposes.[70] Enterprises which lacked that function had no right to the semblance of state approval by charter. Lincoln, Morton, Rantoul, and Brownson sought "a complete and *entire separation of Bank and State*." [71] Deprived of the note-issuing power and confined to deposit, discount, and loan operations, banks would then find no justification for special recognition by incorporation and would stand forth as private businesses, which they were in fact.[72] George Hull's fervent imprecation, "They will all go soon & I say — let them go," referred in the first instance to banks, but the nostrum applied as well to charters in every business field.[73]

After 1830, however, the corporation was too closely enmeshed in the state's economy simply to disappear and too widely dispersed to give serious evidence substantiating the artisans' charge of monopoly.[74] Moreover, those who condemned the chartered company in the abstract often yielded in practice to its temptations. Rantoul hoped to make the Democratic organization the instrument of the disaffected, but the members of that party showed a distressing inclination to vote for new grants when their interests dictated, even grants for banks, the most reviled of institutions.[75] Furthermore, responsibility for the panic of 1837 fell upon Jacksonian finance, discredited the conception of a specie-rooted currency, and barred any program of reform that rested on that basis. The crisis in money perpetuated the old banking ideas; charters remained as popular as ever.[76]

70. See *Boston Quarterly Review*, 3 (1840), pp. 249ff; *ibid.*, 4 (1841), 109ff, 121ff.

71. Rantoul, *Memoirs*, pp. 350ff, 519, 620ff, 635ff; Elbridge to Bancroft, Sept. 20, 1834, Bancroft Papers; *Boston Quarterly Review*, 3 (1840), 80–112; *ibid.*, 4 (1841), 103, 108; Bancroft to J. Q. Adams, Mar. 26, 1838, M. A. DeW. Howe, *Life and Letters of George Bancroft* (New York, 1908), I, 229.

72. Rantoul, *Memoirs*, pp. 519ff, 530ff.

73. To J. P. Bigelow, Mar. 26, 1840, J. P. Bigelow Papers (MSS, Houghton Library, Harvard University); also Rantoul, *Memoirs*, pp. 315, 316, 320ff; A. H. Everett, Speech, Nov. 8, 1835, quoted in *Boston Daily Advocate*, Nov. 14, 1835.

74. See Bowen, *Political Economy*, p. 227; *Boston Commercial Gazette*, Jan. 29, Feb. 5, 1835; *Boston Daily Herald*, Dec. 14, 1836; Mark Hopkins to Theodore Sedgwick, Mar. 2, 1836, Sedgwick Papers, 2 ser., IX.

75. Rantoul, *Memoirs*, pp. 666ff; *Boston Quarterly Review*, 4 (1841), 100; [Whig County Convention, 1839], *Address to the Voters, of the Fourth Congressional District* (n.p., 1839), p. 6; *Springfield Gazette*, Mar. 23, 1842.

76. See Everett to J. S. C. Knowlton, May 16, 1837, Everett Papers, LXVII, 191; Cleveland to Sumner, June 3, 1838, Charles Sumner, "Letters Received, 1830–74" (MSS, Houghton Library, Harvard University), V, 8; [Whig Legislative Convention, 1838], *To the People of Massachusetts* (n.p., n.d.), pp. 3ff; [Whig County Convention, 1839], *Address to Voters*, pp. 4ff; H. A. Hill, *Memoir of Abbott Lawrence* (Boston, 1884), p. 16. For the significant case of Congressman

The grievances of the artisans against the corporations were real and pressing but alone did not win legislative votes. The dispossessed needed an argument that would enlist wider support to give force to the attack. Practical politics pressed for compromise. The need for working through parties compounded of disparate elements induced moderation. And for the toughest reformer the chance of achieving swifter victory by indirection was an attractive lure. If this unnatural privilege, awarded by the state to sharpen the capitalists' tools and dull the artisans' skills, would not fall before a direct assault, a more subtle offensive might undermine its most valuable quality.

Those who despaired of abolishing the corporation hoped to render it innocuous by eliminating the last vestige of state favoritism. If this was primarily a business device, any token of government approval was unjust. If available at all, the capacity to act as a corporation should be available to any petitioner, with the state relegated to the minor role of registrar and deprived of any option.[77] Dangled before farmers, traders, and incipient manufacturers, that argument might suck in those indifferent to radical pleas, yet aggrieved by the operations of specific corporations or by the expense, delay, and need for political contacts inevitable as long as the General Court demanded a special act for each company.[78] Earlier proposals for repeal of the laws against unincorporated banking turned into a movement for free banking, which gathered momentum after New York's adoption of such a system in 1838. Similar programs for general laws in manufacturing and other fields also recruited many partisans.[79]

Precedents for such enactments appeared before 1800 for common or general fields and aqueducts, enterprises which then

Parmenter and the Middlesex Bank, see [Whig Convention, Mar. 15, 1837], *To the Electors of Massachusetts* (Worcester, 1837), pp. 6ff; [Whig Convention at Concord, Oct. 25, 1838], *To the Electors of the County of Middlesex* (n.p., 1838), pp. 5, 7, 9–11.

77. Rantoul, *Memoirs*, pp. 313–317, 336ff; [David Henshaw], *Remarks upon the Rights and Powers of Corporations* (Boston, 1837), pp. 7ff.

78. See, e.g., the cases of the Boyden and the Mansfield iron companies, *Boston Commercial Gazette*, Jan. 26, Feb. 26, 1835; *History of Bristol County*, ed. D. H. Hurd (Philadelphia, 1883), p. 419.

79. See *Boston Commercial Gazette*, Mar. 5, 1835; H. E. Miller, *Banking Theories in the United States before 1860* (Cambridge, Mass., 1927), pp. 144ff, 148, 160, 164; R. E. Chaddock, *Safety-Fund Banking System in New York State* (Washington, D.C., 1910), pp. 369ff; *Journal of the Constitutional Convention of the Commonwealth of Massachusetts . . . 1853* (Boston, 1853), pp. 43, 155, 251, 299, 415.

were numerous and small and rarely impinged upon the rights of outsiders. In 1811 religious schism extended the same rule to churches to prevent favoritism among sects. But an attempt a year later to secure the same concession for cotton and woolen factories failed.[80] Although special statutes engrossed an increasing proportion of all legislation, popularized lobbying and corruption, and eclipsed general business, the General Court rebuffed proposals for further dilution of its chartering prerogative.[81] It provided for limited partnerships in 1835, but it ignored the recommendations of Governor Morton in 1840 and 1843 and of its own committee in 1846 for general incorporation.[82]

After 1851, however, a new political configuration brought to power a coalition inclined to nullify the government's grip over charters. Successive acts then permitted any group of individuals to organize as a manufacturing, banking, insurance, or gaslight corporation by a simple process of registry.[83] The grant of charters by particular laws persisted through the rest of the decade — apparently the act of incorporation still carried a kind of prestige — but the form was now automatically available to all who sought to use it.[84]

The gradual elimination of privilege from the nature of the corporation did not sever the lines of control exercised by the government through regulation. Principles designed to assure the efficient operations of a state agency became rules to stimulate competition and to protect consumers. A change in outward form marked the transformation. The earliest provisions affecting internal government and external relations had appeared in the charter or constitution and had not been uniform even for enterprises of the same type. As the number of ventures multiplied, general statutes detailed the regulations which applied equally to all firms engaged in an activity. Retention of residual public favors was often the pretext that justified demands by

80. See *Revised Statutes*, ch. 40; *Boston Gazette*, June 24, 1811; MA, House, 7289.

81. *Boston Daily Advertiser*, Jan. 6, 1847; *Journal of the House of Representatives . , . 1854*, pp. 863, 1034; Huntington, "Election Sermon," *Senate Docs., 1858*, p. 33.

82. See *Senate Docs., 1832*, no. 10; *Boston Daily Advertiser*, Jan. 28, 1832; *Boston Commercial Gazette*, Feb. 2, 1835; st. 1835, ch. 48.

83. See st. 1851, ch. 133; st. 1852, chs. 9, 236; st. 1854, ch. 438; st. 1855, chs. 146, 478; also, st. 1855, ch. 290; *Senate Docs., 1855*, no. 114; Rappard, *Les Corporations d'affaires au Massachusetts*, p. 57.

84. *Senate Docs., 1856*, no. 81, pp. 3, 4; Rappard, *Les Corporations d'affaires au Massachusetts*, pp. 52, 53; *Senate Docs., 1859*, no. 33.

rival corporations as well as by anticorporate critics for widening the scope of such legislation. But more influential was the pervasive desire to guard individuals against incalculable economic disaster. Regulation of stock issue and assessment and protection of investors dwindled in importance as Massachusetts transformed canons originally developed to enable the body politic to manage itself into rules policing entire spheres of the economy in which corporations operated.[85]

Supervision of note issue was thus the fulcrum of efforts to raise banking from the slough of recurrent crises and monetary disorders. At the same time that the government succumbed to the drive for more and more charters, its concern over the safe limits of expansion developed checks to prevent a currency run wild.

Legislation had at first aimed simply at enlightening the ignorant and restraining the dishonest drawn into finance by the liberality of incorporation. The state sealed weights, fought counterfeiting, and offered a premium for the best essay on correct banking principles. To keep the privilege in the hands of those who actually had money to invest, it enacted provisions requiring payment of part of the subscriptions in specie and limiting the amount of notes to twice the capital.[86]

Such measures were ineffective. Nothing prevented banks from accumulating enough specie to pass muster at the examination before commencing operations, only to dispose of these mercurial holdings once the doors had opened. And restricting the currency in terms of capital proved as slight an inconvenience; capital was easy to come at when stockholders could invest by borrowing from the new institution. In any case, circulation even in periods of expansion fell short of the legal limit.[87]

Yet no substantial group turned at once to more rigorous gov-

85. For regulation of the corporate structures see *Revised Statutes*, ch. 38; st. 1840, ch. 83; st. 1855, ch. 290; *Senate Docs., 1855*, no. 3, p. 30; st. 1856, ch. 264; st. 1858, ch. 167; st. 1859, ch. 104; *Salem Mill Dam Corporation* v. *Ropes* (1827), 6 Pickering 23.

86. See *Revised Statutes*, ch. 36, esp. sec. 4; *Repertory*, June 20, 1806; *Resolves of the General Court of the Commonwealth of Massachusetts . . . 1806* (Boston, 1806), p. 3; *Boston Commercial Gazette*, Feb. 15, 1816. See also Adams to Tyler, Lloyd, June 24, 1819, Oct. 1, 1822, J. Q. Adams, *Writings*, ed. W. C. Ford (New York, 1913–1917), VI, 555, VII, 311; [George Bancroft], "Bank of the United States," *North Amer. Rev.*, 32 (1831), 25; [Appleton], *Banking System of Massachusetts*, p. 21.

87. See *Revised Statutes*, ch. 36, sec. 8; st. 1852, ch. 236; D. R. Dewey, *State Banking before the Civil War* (Washington, D.C., 1910), pp. 61, 62; D. R. Whitney, *Suffolk Bank* (Cambridge, Mass., 1878), p. 25.

ernment action for a solution to its problems. Those who hoped to limit or abolish paper money were not concerned with regulation except as a means toward an end. The country banks on the contrary wished complete freedom of issue. The Boston institutions wanted a sound but a flexible circulating medium. They continued to rely upon the Suffolk System to achieve through their own efforts what the state would not do; they called upon the government simply to enforce contracts when they presented notes for redemption. Whatever the attitude to the volume of circulation, there was no desire to push actively such proposals as those to limit loans to directors. And the curtailment of small notes, which had been abandoned after 1816, was never restored because of the threat of inundation by foreign and private scrip.[88]

Emphasis shifted to regulation only after it became clear that Jackson's fight against the Bank of the United States and Rantoul's struggle for reform in Massachusetts had merely increased the number of issuing houses and weakened the currency. To make matters worse, the growth of deposit banking added to the hazards of billholders who were too far away to withdraw their funds in a crisis.[89]

Various attempts to fix the volume of circulation in terms of capital seemed to some to skirt the true question, the ratio to "real money," gold and silver; conversely, the suggestion for a mandatory specie reserve seemed to others to strike too close to the core of the matter.[90] As late as 1856 a legislative committee preferred to believe that relief would come "by the natural flow of specie . . . rather than by a law obliging [banks] . . . to keep a large sum locked up." [91]

Panic a year later led to a prompt call for restraints. The twenty-eight banks of 1821 had become 173, their capital had grown from less than ten to more than sixty million dollars, while the ratio of circulation and deposits to specie had jumped from 2.80:1 to 10.33:1. Furthermore, the end of the Suffolk

88. See "Q," *Boston Commercial Gazette*, July 4, 1825; *House Docs., 1838*, no. 18; st. 1816, ch. 43; st. 1817, ch. 76; *Revised Statutes*, ch. 36, sec. 56; Rantoul, *Memoirs*, pp. 518ff, 531.

89. See Rantoul, *Memoirs*, pp. 604ff; *Senate Docs., 1855*, no. 3, p. 30. For a plea for small notes by a country banker see [J. B. Congdon], *Defence of the Currency of Massachusetts* (Boston, 1856), pp. 3ff.

90. *Senate Docs., 1826–27*, no. 14; *House Docs., 1838*, no. 18.

91. *Senate Docs., 1856*, no. 204, p. 5; Dewey, *State Banking before the Civil War*, pp. 94, 218.

System removed a check which the merchants had been able to exercise voluntarily through the Boston banks. Rigid state regulation seemed the sole remaining recourse.[92]

The failures were immediately ascribed to "the expansion of private credit extended into speculation of every kind" by bank paper. The emission was not controlled by principle or by laws but by bankers who could not be trusted: "To suppose that bank directors will have in view the public good to the exclusion of private gain, or . . . will act the part of patriots . . . is ascribing to them motives of action different from what ordinarily influence the conduct of men. The desire for large profits . . . will outweigh public interest, and often . . . even prudential consideration." A legislative committee asked the state to "exercise strict watchfulness" by measures against small notes and by establishing a 20 per cent specie reserve.[93]

In the aftermath of the crash, the activities of bank lobbies and the protests of savings banks which were depositors were unable to prevent the enactment of a law for a 15 per cent specie reserve.[94] Within three years that restraint, seemingly harsh at the beginning, appeared insufficient; stockholders became fully liable for all notes, and the banks themselves demanded more stringent action. By the end of the period the Boston Board of Trade urged a check on loans as well as on circulation.[95]

The links between insurance companies and banks and the desire to protect innocent policyholders conditioned state supervision of underwriting institutions.[96] Charters in the 1820's put a limit to the risks that could be assumed, directed the mode of investment, and in certain cases established the liability of directors.[97] These rules expanded into general regulatory laws climaxed by the law of 1856, which set down in great detail provisions to guide the operations of insurance companies of all types and also of out-of-state firms. A similar evolution took place with regard to savings banks and loan associations.[98]

92. *Senate Docs., 1858*, no. 17, p. 16. See also "The Financial Flurry," *Atlantic Monthly*, 1 (1857), 119ff.

93. *Senate Docs., 1858*, no. 17, pp. 8, 12, 17, 18, 22ff; *Senate Docs., 1858*, no. 1, pp. 11ff; *Middlesex Journal*, Mar. 20, 1858.

94. *Senate Docs., 1857*, no. 17, p. 19; *House Docs., 1859*, no. 308; st. 1858, ch. 69.

95. St. 1860, ch. 167; *Senate Docs., 1860*, no. 1, p. 15; *Report of the Committee of the Boston Board of Trade* (Boston, 1858), pp. 17–19.

96. For early regulation see, e.g., st. 1803, ch. 123; st. 1805, ch. 34; also William Bentley, *Diary* (Salem, 1905–1914), IV, 419.

97. See, e.g., st. 1822, chs. 99, 112, 113.

98. See, for insurance, *Revised Statutes*, ch. 37, secs. 1–39; st. 1852, ch. 311; st.

The widening scope and the detailed character of regulation lent a touch of anachronism to the old ad hoc provisions for enforcement. The traditional supervision of the legislature through commissioners appointed on complaint to examine specific banks was much criticized. The firms affected protested against the exposure of "private concerns to the scrutiny of the public," while the amorphous public found slight consolation in investigations which occurred only after the damage was done.[99] The abandonment of hopes for a new central bank and the panic of 1837 gave point to such charges. A board of three commissioners received a mandate to examine all financial institutions and to close the doors of transgressors, a power upheld by Chief Justice Shaw as necessary "to prevent their becoming dangerous to the public" and as not contrary to the contract in the charter.[100] The sound Boston houses approved, but those in the country fought the scheme and under cover of an economy drive secured its abolition. Continued demands for stricter supervision, however, finally brought about re-establishment of the board in 1852 with extensive authority to examine, close, and appoint receivers for commercial and savings banks.[101] Three years later a similar body got the right to oversee insurance and loan-fund associations.[102]

In railroad as in other corporations, provisions in the charter and in supplementary statutes regulated many phases of management. There were requirements for legislative consent for sale, mortgage, or lease, and until 1854 roads were forbidden to issue bonds except for construction. To guarantee solvency no line was to start building until all shares were subscribed at par. There was care to assure safety of operations both along the right of way and at crossings, and the duties of officers were clearly set forth.[103] If these laws were stricter than in other spheres, it

1856, ch. 252; *General Statutes*, ch. 58; for savings banks see *Revised Statutes*, ch. 36, secs. 76–84.

99. See *Senate Docs., 1836*, no. 26.

100. See st. 1838, ch. 14; *Commonwealth* v. *Farmers and Mechanics Bank* (1839), 21 Pickering 542; *Senate Docs., 1839*, no. 1, p. 5.

101. See, e.g., *Boston Daily Advertiser*, Feb. 13, 1843, Feb. 4, 1847; *Public Docs., 1859*, no. 6, p. 145.

102. St. 1855, chs. 124, 236; *Senate Docs., 1855*, nos. 43, 104, 193; st. 1856, ch. 252.

103. *Senate Docs., 1858*, no. 59, p. 14; F. B. C. Bradlee, "Eastern Railroad," and "Boston and Lowell Railroad," *Essex Inst. Hist. Colls.*, LII (1916), 308, LIV (1920), 197; st. 1852, ch. 203; st. 1855, chs. 290, 452.

was because these companies originated in an era already aware of the possibility that they might "become a 'power' within the State," using the resources of government in favor only of their own selfish interest.[104]

Furthermore, quarrels between rival companies led the General Court into rate-fixing. Long-standing dissension between the Western and the Boston & Worcester railroads over the relation of through to local fares drew in Massachusetts as an arbitrator. The voluntary agreement under which the two lines had worked between 1839 and 1843 had borne harshly on the Western, burdened with higher operating costs and sustained by less local traffic. Various compromises suggested by legislative committees to satisfy the demand of that road for lower through rates failed to appease the Worcester. The bickering of the two roads, each unwillingly seeking government support, continued to 1861 and beyond, while other companies brought similar complaints to the legislature.[105]

A more important function of the General Court was to make sure that the roads delivered adequate service. The state went so far as to specify the number of trains to run daily over each route and to judge the right to discontinue lines. Thus, the Harvard Branch Railroad needed permission by special act to take up its tracks.[106] The problem was most acute when through roads wished to surrender unprofitable branches originally built to lay claim to disputed territory. The town of Watertown thus objected to abandonment of service by the Fitchburg Railroad in 1857–1858, arguing that the charter was a contract to operate in return for both the franchise and the right of public domain granted in the interests of public exigency. This was, then, a new type of highway, public in nature and, like the old, not to be relinquished merely because unprofitable. The absence

104. *Senate Docs., 1858*, no. 50, p. 9.
105. See "Petition of the Nashua and Lowell to the Legislature," Nashua & Lowell Railroad Corporation Miscellaneous Papers (MSS, Baker Library, Harvard University); "Agreement of November 27, 1860," Western Railroad Corporation Miscellaneous Records (MSS, Baker Library, Harvard University), VII; *House Docs., 1845*, no. 46, pp. 30–35, 47ff; st. 1845, ch. 191; st. 1857, ch. 291; *House Docs., 1860*, nos. 18, 29. For rate policy see *Boston Daily Advertiser*, Aug. 1, 2, Sept. 13, Oct. 3, 1843; P. P. F. Degrand, *To the People of Massachusetts* (Boston, 1840). For reluctance to accept legislative interference in railroad problems see, e.g., *Proceedings of the Convention of the Northern Lines of Railway, Held at Boston* (Boston, 1851), pp. 84ff.
106. St. 1854, ch. 334; *Senate Docs., 1857*, no. 148; *Senate Docs., 1858*, no. 59, pp. 19, 20. See also *House Docs., 1852*, no. 183.

in the act of incorporation of a provision for discontinuance, it was argued, indicated that the legislature conceived it as a running road.[107]

In answer to its accuser, the Fitchburg Railroad claimed that its charter required it to build but not to operate, and it offered the free use of its tracks to anyone who wanted to run trains upon them.[108] Baffled, the legislative committee could not reach a decision, and it left unsolved, for the time being, the fundamental question whether a road could slough off the unprofitable portions of its route or whether its obligations to those it served required consideration of the line as a whole. The appointment of a board of railroad commissioners, occasionally suggested in these years, did not come until after 1861. But the trend that precipitated the issue would later supply the solution.[109]

Although the precise limits remained undefined, legislation in every area now aimed to protect individuals who could not protect themselves against the extraordinary powers of the corporation. Arguments among business firms contributed considerably to the redirection of regulatory policy against all corporations. But the reform impulse was the main source. The change was gradual. If old forms often persisted, it was because the corporation, like the license, the franchise, and inspection, was capable of adjustment to new requirements.

The forms remained, but not the substance. The logical outcome of the fight against privilege in a society cleft by the impact of rapid economic change was to deprive the government of the ability to act as a copartner in the economy, supplying direction, guidance, and the support of its resources. In the new circumstances, the state could not operate in the old way.

Yet the same forces that immobilized the government from acting in the Commonwealth tradition had drawn it into more vigorous action in the interest of humanitarian regulation. Thinkers as far apart on larger questions as Willard Phillips, Orestes Brownson, and Francis Bowen agreed that it was "not the policy of the liberal system to abstain from all regulations whatever, upon the notion that the present private interest is in all cases coincident with that of the public." [110] In a system that

107. See *Senate Docs., 1858*, no. 59, pp. 8–10, 12, 13; *Roxbury* v. *Boston & Providence Railroad Corporation* (1850), 6 Cushing 429.

108. *Senate Docs., 1858*, no. 59, pp. 11, 22–25.

109. *Boston Commercial Gazette*, Mar. 1, 1838; *Senate Docs., 1855*, no. 128.

110. Phillips, *Manual of Political Economy*, p. 210.

aimed at free competition, "government, as the organ and agent of society," was still "a positive good . . . never" to "be dispensed with." [111]

But under the new order the role of government acquired a fresh meaning. The revised conception ruled out "unnecessary, useless, and embarassing restrictions." [112] The function of legislation was not to direct but simply "to remove all casual and unnatural impediments from that path which society instinctively chooses for itself," by laws essentially "prohibitive" rather than "mandatory." [113] Statutes would prevent artificial barriers from standing in the way of natural forces inherently beneficent. Civil government was thus "an ordinance of God, for the regulation, comfort and happiness of social life," providing sanction for the free play of natural law. The state left its citizens free, in the economy as elsewhere, to carry on their affairs as they would, but it did justice between them in conflicts and prevented injuries from holding back their development.[114]

Not every issue fell into this nice category. A number of persistent problems raised a troublesome question: What criterion will tell the governor whether the regulation or the condition being regulated is the unnatural obstruction?

Imprisonment for debt ever more clearly appeared to be improper interference by the state, although it had lost many of its harshest features before 1800. Pressure from many sources limited the obligations for which jail was a penalty. Though the desire to conserve prior rights moderated the pace, progress was steady until total abolition in 1855 ushered from "the prison's brooding gloom the victims of a savage code." [115]

But did the same argument apply to the usury laws? Willard

111. O. A. Brownson, "The Laboring Classes," *Boston Quarterly Review*, 3 (1840), 475, 476.

112. Phillips, *Manual of Political Economy*, p. 210.

113. Francis Bowen, *Political Economy*, p. 23; Francis Bowen, "Phillips on Protection," *North Amer. Rev.*, 72 (1851), 419ff.

114. See Huntington, "Election Sermon," *Senate Docs., 1858*, p. 3.

115. See Robert A. Feer, "Imprisonment for Debt in Massachusetts," *Mississippi Valley Historical Review*, 48 (1961), 252ff; *Boston Gazette*, June 14, 1784; *Repertory*, Jan. 29, Feb. 8, 1811; *Journal of Debates and Proceedings in the Convention to Revise the Constitution of Massachusetts, 1820* (Boston, 1853), p. 84; Webster to Dwight, May 2, 1830, Daniel Webster, *Works* (Boston, 1853), VI, 533ff; J. Q. Adams, *Memoirs* (Philadelphia, 1874–1877), VIII, 426ff; Governor Everett's address, *House Docs., 1836*, no. 6, pp. 13ff; *Senate Docs., 1839*, no. 1, p. 12; *Hunt's Merchants' Mag.*, 16 (1847), 511; *Senate Docs., 1855*, no. 1, pp. 28, 29, nos. 113, 143, 444; st. 1857, ch. 141. See also MA, House, 7085; *Journal of the Constitutional Convention of Massachusetts . . . 1853* (Boston, 1853), p. 414.

Phillips pointed out that limiting the interest rate to 6 per cent
excluded legitimate lenders from many phases of business and
cast it "into the worst hands." [116] Again men far apart on other
issues spoke out in unison on the specific question, condemning
interference of the government through such measures, incon-
gruous in the new economy.[117] Special provisions excepted the
letting of cattle among farmers, loans on bottomry, and, in a
sense, bank transactions.[118] Moreover, the law was not strictly
enforced; contracts were held invalid only in their usurious aspects, so the transgressor had nothing to lose.[119] But, despite occasional legislative efforts to change them, the statutes remained
essentially unimpaired.[120] A residual prejudice against the prodigal spender who prevented capital accumulation by living as
"an idle drone . . . on the industry of others" buttressed the
ethical considerations in favor of such a maximum.[121] Despite
arguments to the contrary, the changing conditions could as well
justify retention of a ceiling on interest rates, for under the new
competitive economy usury "ripened into a disease that . . .
gangrened the whole course of money transactions" and was less
to be "suffered than public brothels or gambling houses." [122]

Monopoly, the simplest nuisance and the most universally
berated, fell under the pall of the same obscurity. When granted
by the government, it was easily distinguished and successfully
fought. But how far could the state act to terminate the self-
created monopoly? After a number of shifts in position the
courts tended to rule against the validity of monopolistic agreements, holding, for instance, that a bond never to carry on a
business was void as a restraint of trade.[123] But should that inter-

116. Phillips, *Manual of Political Economy*, pp. 64ff.

117. For arguments against the usury laws see Everett to Carroll, Everett
Papers, LXV, 121; *Literary Miscellany*, 2 (1806), 120ff; *Independent Chronicle*,
Jan. 29, 1807; *Repertory*, Feb. 1, 1811; A. H. Everett, "Usury," *North Amer. Rev.*,
29 (1834), 76ff; *House Docs., 1836*, no. 6, p. 19; "Memorial of the Boston Chamber
of Commerce," *Senate Docs., 1837*, no. 26; *Senate Docs., 1855*, no. 3, pp. 27ff;
Senate Docs., 1862, no. 1, pp. 22ff.

118. See *Boston Gazette*, Mar. 7, 1803; Phillips, *Manual of Political Economy*,
p. 70; st. 1783, ch. 55; st. 1788, ch. 12.

119. See *Frye v. Barker* (1822), 1 Pickering 267.

120. See *Boston Gazette*, Feb. 2, 1807; Everett, "Usury," *North Amer. Rev.*, 29
(1834), 68ff; *Revised Statutes*, ch. 35, secs. 1–4; *House Docs., 1840*, no. 33.

121. [James Swan], *National Arithmetick* (Boston, 1786), p. 11; Bowen, *Political Economy*, p. 69; Mason to Appleton, Aug. 12, 1811, [G. S. Hillard], *Memoir
and Correspondence of Jeremiah Mason* (Cambridge, Mass., 1873), pp. 48ff.

122. *Monthly Anthology and Boston Review*, 9 (1810), 194; K. F. Mullany,
Catholic Pittsfield and Berkshire (Pittsfield, 1897), p. 12.

123. *Alger v. Thacher* (1837), 19 Pickering 51; Hilliard, *Supplement*, p. 393.

diction stretch to fit combinations of workingmen, as those claimed who charged that labor unions were also intolerable nuisances in restraint of trade, restrictive survivals of the medieval guilds? The highest state court in 1842 gave a negative answer. Yet in dismissing the accusation of conspiracy against the journeymen bootmakers on the ground that it was not unlawful to do as a group what an individual could do, were not the judges clearing a path for new obstructions to the full development of the citizens? [124]

All these matters pointed to a sharpening question: How far could the state go to free some persons if in the process it constricted others? Thorough explorations of the problem would ultimately come on many levels and in reference to many activities — railroads, banks, insurance, and manufacturing. But in this period the most exhaustive examination emerged from the movement to improve the conditions of operatives through government regulation of the length of the working day. A petition of 1845 asked for standards to replace the traditional but anachronistic sunup to sundown span with a ten-hour day, at least in corporations, "creatures of legislative enactments, and . . . subject to legislative supervision and control." [125]

Hostile committees of the General Court put off this and later petitions until the enactment of a law in 1874. The opponents granted that the state ought to act "if it should ever appear that the public morals, the physical condition, or the social well-being of society were endangered." But they denied that the need existed: conditions in the mills were good, the workers were transient, not a permanent proletariat as in England, and legislation would drive to other states the industry that had "diffused comfort & prosperity throughout New England." [126]

See, however, *Vickery* v. *Welch* (1837), 19 Pickering 523, which limited the effect of this decision as well as earlier attempts to work out a standard of "reasonableness" in *Palmer* v. *Stebbins* (1825), 3 Pickering 188; *Stearns* v. *Barrett* (1823), 1 Pickering 450. For the rule that corporate by-laws limiting the transfer of stock were in restraint of trade see *Sargent* v. *Franklin Insurance Company* (1829), 8 Pickering 90. For an attempt to use the rule to limit police powers see *Commonwealth* v. *Worcester* (1826), 3 Pickering 410.

124. See Bowen, *Political Economy*, p. 228; Rantoul, *Memoirs*, pp. 21ff, 234; *Commonwealth* v. *John Hunt & Others* (1842), 4 Metcalf 111, 115, 119, 121, 127, 136; Alexander Black (for the Society of Shipwrights and Caulkers), *Boston Daily Advertiser*, May 21, 23, 1832.

125. *House Docs., 1845*, no. 50.

126. *House Docs., 1845*, no. 50, pp. 9ff; *House Docs., 1852*, no. 185; *Senate Docs., 1856*, nos. 107, 112; E. Everett to Holland, Sept. 25, 1848, Everett Papers,

These were arguments from expediency; on this as on every other issue divisions arose from the immediate effects of regulation rather than from the abstract nature of the question. For those who would gain, the statute was salutary restraint. For those who would suffer, it meddled needlessly with private concerns. But there were also traces of a broader thesis that in later decades would gain currency. The committee of 1846 warned that to pass a ten-hour law would deprive citizens "of the privilege of contract" and would "exercise a power somewhat questionable." [127] A few years later, in the course of the conflict with journeymen tailors, the clothing manufacturers went even further, maintaining that "labour is a commodity, and its value is determined by supply and demand, and should be left to regulate itself — any interference in this respect only produces disorder and confusion . . . and results in no benefit to those who would alter or modify the laws of trade." [128]

As yet, however, there was no systematic questioning of the presumptions of regulation. No one was confident enough to dispense with it entirely. The larger problem of the propriety of any state action still bore two aspects and therefore was but dimly perceived. Regulation had become important in a society which had not ceased to be concerned with the struggle against privilege. The interaction between these two aspects deprived the men of this period of the comfort of consistency. Defenders of privilege could not categorically deny the right of the government to act positively. And the attackers who questioned the right of the state to act positively through privilege found in practice that more positive governmental intervention was needed to implement their program of reform.

LXXXVI, 1. See also *Labor Laws and Their Enforcement*, ed. S. M. Kingsbury (New York, 1911), pp. 3–125.

127. *Senate Docs., 1846*, no. 81, p. 2.

128. Geo. W. Simmons, *et al.*, to J. P. Bigelow, Aug. 13, 1849, Bigelow Papers.

10 | The Reform State

A quickening impulse to reform in a changing society had sparked the drive to sever all the restrictive chains of privilege. From the same fervor came a positive program for action to free the members of the community from the unnatural hazards to self-development.

Yet there were unnatural handicaps which did not fall before regulation, areas where the insistent demands for improvement met no easy satisfaction, strained the capacities of the old ways of action, and generated new aspirations but also new doubts to trouble the future conceptions of the role of the government in the economy.

Although the constitution of 1780 had contained no specific provisions to that effect, techniques were always available for controlling the "vicious habits of men," to protect the helpless against the temptations of the environment or of their own weak natures.[1] But the sense of responsibility, growing weightier in a deranged society, pressed for a broadened conception that would disregard traditional means. The justification for any given measure was less its constitutionality or conventionality than its appropriateness to an end.

Massachusetts had customarily taken under its charge wards rendered dependent by unusual circumstances. It had extended financial assistance to Indians and, to guard against exploitation, had appointed supervising agents with power to pass on all con-

1. See *Boston Gazette*, June 19, 1780.

tracts.[2] To the same end it had designated public administrators for estates without clear titles and had assumed a general oversight of the insane.[3]

Although poor relief had always been of concern to the entire state, it had originally been primarily a corporate function of the towns, often delegated to independent agencies. Corporations or individuals "disposed to Contract to Support the Whole, or any part of the poor of the Commonwealth" for a consideration continued to serve in many places to the 1820's.[4]

Few argued that society itself was responsible for poverty. There was generally no greater disposition to blame the state for this evil than for "the prevalence of an epidemic disease." [5] But none denied the force of the obligation to limit the social consequences of the disease. After 1820 recognition of responsibility grew more immediate; this obligation was not to be shifted nor passed on but was to be assumed directly. Many municipalities followed the example of Boston, which built an almshouse in 1823 to administer to the unfortunate. Gradually the charity legitimately the function of government widened until it included a municipal hospital.[6]

After 1830 the cost of pauperism climbed steadily with the growth of immigration. That unfortunate circumstance at no time produced complaints that the state was "overcharged with inhabitants" or incited attempts to reduce the number entering, even at the height of the antiforeign agitation.[7] The only positive steps were acts for the deportation of dependent aliens incapable of self-support, for a head tax to pay part of the costs, and for bonds to guarantee the state against expense.[8]

Despite the large number of poor among the foreign-born,

2. See B. F. Hallett, *Rights of the Marshpee Indians* (Boston, 1834), *passim*; st. 1783, ch. 35; res. 1807, ch. 44; st. 1837, ch. 101; res. 1857, chs. 26, 27, 30, 40, 80; res. 1858, ch. 27.

3. St. 1839, ch. 142.

4. See res. 1791, ch. 92; st. 1802, ch. 22; *Old Records of the Town of Fitchburgh* (Fitchburg, 1898–1913), I, 343, 344; Thomas Weston, *History of the Town of Middleboro* (Boston, 1906), p. 580; *History of Bristol County*, ed. D. H. Hurd (Philadelphia, 1883), p. 495; *Our Country and Its People; a Descriptive and Biographical Record of Bristol County*, ed. Alanson Borden (Boston, 1899), pp. 509, 510; G. F. Clark, *History of the Town of Norton* (Boston, 1859), p. 365.

5. Francis Bowen, "French Ideas of Democracy," *North Amer. Rev.*, 69 (1849), 314ff.

6. St. 1822, ch. 56; st. 1858, ch. 113; *Bristol County*, ed. Borden, p. 513.

7. See Willard Phillips, *Manual of Political Economy* (Boston, 1828), p. 145; *Boston Daily Advertiser*, Oct. 2, 1843; Oscar Handlin, *Boston's Immigrants* (Cambridge, Mass., 1959), pp. 202ff.

8. See *Norris* v. *Boston* (1848), 7 Howard 283.

reluctance to discourage immigration and to condemn the helpless to the miseries of their famine-stricken homeland in practice suspended the application of the deportation laws. Such scruples increased the stake in the problem of the state government, which reimbursed the towns for the support of those without legal settlement. Practical difficulties for a long time stood in the way of changing this expensive and wasteful system. Finally, the state built its own institutions in which the recipients of charity could be partially self-supporting, placing the responsibility for administration in a Committee on Public Charitable Institutions.[9]

Elsewhere, too, the state moved inexorably into a position of greater responsibility and greater control. Massachusetts had long patronized education for its traditional, political, and economic values. But social maladjustments called for regulations that would go beyond the simple guarantee of the existence of schools to the full assurance that they would serve their purpose. As early as 1816 the employment of children in mills moved Governor Strong to suggest that the legislature require effectual measures by industry for the education of youthful employees, a service essential to equip citizens for judging and protecting their own rights. The widening use of minors in factories interested the clergy, who requested not only time off for learning but also for play so that boys and girls would be more inclined to go to church on Sunday.[10] And the laborers themselves became concerned, asking for state supervision of instruction and of hours to assure "free, intelligent, well-educated, contented and thriving workmen." [11] A law of 1836 lacked provisions for enforcement and was more honored in the breach than in the observance. A House committee explored the question in 1847, but no decisive action came until the statute of 1858 established compulsory minimum schooling for children under twelve in factories.[12]

The relation of schools to government also changed. The agencies that administered academies and colleges, sustained by

9. See Phillips, *Manual of Political Economy*, pp. 142–145, 147ff; *Senate Docs., 1858*, no. 63; *General Statutes of the Commonwealth of Massachusetts . . . 1859* (Boston, 1860), ch. 22; Handlin, *Boston's Immigrants*, pp. 118ff.

10. See Robert Rantoul, Jr., *Memoirs, Speeches and Writings* (Boston, 1854), pp. 100, 112ff; *Recorder*, Jan. 28, 1816; W. E. Channing, *Memoir* (Boston, 1848), III, 70–74.

11. *House Docs., 1842*, no. 4.

12. See st. 1836, ch. 245; st. 1838, ch. 107; st. 1858, ch. 83; *House Docs., 1842*, no. 4; *Boston Daily Advertiser*, Feb. 16, 1847; *General Statutes*, ch. 42.

fees and endowments, broke away from state dominance and asserted their independence as private bodies. But the schools at lower levels, which ministered to the mass of students, were not able alone to bear the expense. They fell under the complete control of the towns and eventually of the state, which after 1837 regulated them through a Board of Education and through the power of granting or withholding financial aid.[13]

The conception of the government's educational responsibilities also broadened. Those convinced that the heaviest impediment to farming was the failure of techniques to improve at the same pace as in industry saw no hope for a remedy in the wining and dining activities of the old societies for promoting agriculture.[14] Continued agitation for new activities bore fruit in a library, fairs, an experimental station at Westborough, and a college, all state-sponsored.[15] In addition, a Board of Agriculture after 1852 administered aid and gathered data on methods, and Massachusetts from time to time supported such scientific projects as a study of insects injurious to vegetation and a geological survey of the Connecticut Valley.[16]

The theory that education would put into the hands of workingmen the power to improve themselves and advance industry produced frequent plans for enlightenment. The training of mariners in a nautical school and of mechanics in the reform school added to the fund of skills in the community.[17] More generally, the state held with Abbott Lawrence that "there can be no enlightened and intelligent legislation without facts" and actively collected detailed information both for its own use and to guide its citizens in coping with economic matters. Early recognizing the importance of the census and of statistics, and dissatisfied with the fragmentary work of the federal government, Massachusetts made its own survey of industry in 1837 and, beginning in 1845, gathered complete sets of data every ten years.[18]

13. See, e.g., the break with Harvard, *Journal of the House of Representatives* . . . *1854* (Boston, 1854), p. 167; also Rantoul, *Memoirs*, p. 71.

14. See, e.g., *Boston Daily Herald*, Nov. 24, 26, 1836; *Woburn Journal*, Dec. 6, 27, 1851, Jan. 10, 1852; *Senate Docs., 1858*, no. 4, pp. 8ff; *House Docs., 1860*, no. 42.

15. *Bowen's Boston News-Letter*, Dec. 31, 1825, p. 20; st. 1852, ch. 142; *Senate Docs., 1858*, no. 4, p. 16; *House Docs., 1851*, no. 13.

16. See *Senate Docs., 1853*, no. 5, p. 14; res. 1858, ch. 25; st. 1859, ch. 93; *Senate Docs., 1860*, no. 1, p. 5; *General Statutes*, ch. 16.

17. See Edward Everett, "On the Importance of Scientific Knowledge to Practical Men," *Orations and Speeches on Various Occasions* (Boston, 1853–1868), I, 246ff; *House Docs., 1859*, no. 277, pp. 13ff; *House Docs., 1859*, no. 285; *House Docs., 1859*, no. 293.

18. Lawrence and Dearborn to Bigelow, Feb. 8, July 3, 1838, J. P. Bigelow

The state also acted to free the individual from the temptation of his own vices, hoping, as through education, to release him the better to pursue his own welfare. That aspiration, in the pathological conditions of a changing society, accounted for the vigor of the movement for strict laws against intemperance, against gambling, and for a day of rest.

Complaints against the "Jewish" sabbath notwithstanding, successive measures raised the penalties for violations and tightened restrictions on travel.[19] Although enforcement failed to keep pace with the statute book, as late as 1858 new enactments curbed the hedonistic inclinations of the tiny German population.[20]

To enhance the value of government-granted lotteries, early laws had voided contracts of wager and had forbidden unsanctioned gambling. By 1816, however, gambling, whatever its object, seemed in itself vicious, injurious to the individual, and "ruinous and destructive to the State."[21] It demoralized the unwary, leading them into temptation through hopes of sudden prosperity, and distracted them from the more practical tasks of immediate improvement. The defeat of a number of proposals for lotteries that year and the enactment of several stringent laws against unauthorized projects reflected the new temper. The business flourished surreptitiously, however, with an estimated volume in 1832 of one million dollars in Boston alone. In 1833 the suicide of a clerk who had lost embezzled funds dramatized the need for further legislation. The attorney general netted seventy-six indictments in Boston, and pressure by Governor Lincoln and a group of merchants led by William Sullivan and Abbott Lawrence produced a stringent law absolutely forbidding any type of lottery. Additional legislation, more restrictive as time went on, showed, however, that many men still preferred to seek self-improvement in a lucky turn.[22]

Papers (MSS, Houghton Library, Harvard University); st. 1837, ch. 199; st. 1855, ch. 467; *Journal of House, 1854*, p. 301; [Willard Phillips], "Statistical Annals," *North Amer. Rev.*, 9 (1819), 218. For corporate reports see also *Boston Commercial Gazette*, Mar. 5, 1835; *House Docs.*, 1838, no. 18; Constitutional Amendments, Arts. XII, XIII, XXI, XXII; *General Statutes*, ch. 20.

19. St. 1782, ch. 23; st. 1791, ch. 58; st. 1796, ch. 89; st. 1815, ch. 135.

20. *Report of the Legislature on the Observance of the Sabbath* (Boston, 1814); st. 1852, ch. 245; st. 1858, ch. 151.

21. See st. 1785, ch. 58; st. 1786, ch. 68; st. 1798, ch. 20; J. E. A. Smith, *The History of Pittsfield . . . 1800 to . . . 1876* (Springfield, 1876), pp. 63ff.

22. See *Boston Commercial Gazette*, Feb. 12, 15, 1816, Jan. 22, 1821; st. 1817, ch. 191; st. 1819, ch. 140; st. 1822, ch. 90; st. 1828, ch. 134; st. 1837, ch. 179; st. 1856, ch. 121; st. 1857, ch. 194; *Revised Statutes of the Commonwealth of Massa-*

The most bitter dissension in the efforts to protect individuals against their own vices arose over the regulation of the liquor traffic. Intemperance had always constituted a serious problem on the farm. Hard conditions, long winter evenings, and general unhappiness among those who did not emigrate combined to produce "an evil spirit residing in grogshops . . . to draw them away from home, to the sorrow and distress of their families." Bad enough when rural, the problem was compounded with the growth of cities and the attendant evils of crime and pauperism.[23]

The proposal of Robert Rantoul, Jr., to make intemperance a crime suffered from the taint of impracticableness, as did occasional suggestions for a tax in the interest of various worthy causes.[24] It was easier to take advantage of certain prudential regulations always attached to licensing, regulations that forbade sales to minors, servants, idlers, and excessive drinkers.[25] The temperance forces put these precedents to a new use. Licensing became legislation to restrain in the hands of "persons of approved reputation . . . pernicious trades . . . [,] upon the same principle . . . as . . . acts . . . injurious to the community" are punished as crimes.[26]

As the movement grew in strength in the 1830's, it threatened to "produce a revolution in the political affairs of the state."[27] The foes of temperance attacked the perversion of the original function of the license as interference with property rights. But the Whigs, fearful of Locofocoism, supported a law that limited the number of sellers to one for every two thousand inhabitants and restricted all sales to fifteen gallons or more. Appeal to the courts against that restriction failed. A crucial case decided that prohibition of the sale of liquor without a license was not re-

chusetts (Boston, 1836), ch. 50, secs. 12, 13; *Message of Governor Lincoln and Other Official Documents on the Subject of Lotteries* (Boston, 1833).

23. C. P. Crosby, "History of West Boylston," *Worc. Mag. and Hist. Jour.*, 2 (1826), 201; William Sturgis, *Boston Daily Advertiser*, Feb. 19, 1844; Smith, *Pittsfield, 1800 to 1876*, pp. 6ff, 390ff; Roger Lane, *Policing the City* (Cambridge, Mass., 1967), 39ff.

24. Rantoul, *Memoirs*, p. 339; N. I. Bowditch, *History of Massachusetts General Hospital* (Boston, 1872), p. 47; *Senate Docs., 1826–27*, no. 10.

25. St. 1783, ch. 38, sec. 7; st. 1786, ch. 68; st. 1818, ch. 65; st. 1819, ch. 37; *Revised Statutes*, ch. 23, secs. 70–71, ch. 79, sec. 11; st. 1855, ch. 163; *Stacy* v. *Benson* (1836), 18 Pickering 496; also *Boston Commercial Gazette*, Feb. 1, 1816.

26. Phillips, *Manual of Political Economy*, p. 135; also st. 1832, ch. 166, sec. 8; *Address by the Hampshire Convention of the Friends of the License Law* (Northampton, 1838).

27. Rand to Sumner, Oct. 3, 1838, Charles Sumner, "Letters Received" (MSS,

pugnant to the guarantees of property in the constitution of the United States or of Massachusetts.[28]

The reformers, in full control after 1850, sought more extensive legislation and finally enacted the radical Maine law in 1852. Thereafter, only town agents could sell liquor, and then only for medicinal or scientific purposes. Manufacturers needed licenses, and severe penalties punished violations.[29] A partial amendment in 1853 failed to mollify dealers who complained that the measure hurt trade and infringed upon property rights by outlawing a legitimate article of commerce.[30] A court test in 1854 ruled certain aspects unconstitutional as violations of the guarantee in the Bill of Rights (Article XIV) against unreasonable search, but it nevertheless upheld the contention that the state had power to proscribe the possession of certain types of property. "The law destroys all these for the public benefit . . . When prohibited by law, they are no longer protected as property by the constitution." [31]

The Massachusetts liquor agency set up in 1855 as sole supplier to the town agents was intended to coordinate the activities of local distributors. But the commissioners soon proved unworthy of their trust. A. S. Mansfield, appointed in 1855, left under a cloud in 1858, and his successor, G. P. Burnham, adulterated his liquor, sold illegally to persons out of the state, and charged more than the statutory 5 per cent profit allowed him. These misdeeds and difficulties in enforcement somewhat discredited the system and supported the charge that the agency was an odious monopoly.[32] Nevertheless, continued legislation

---

Houghton Library, Harvard University), V, 18; Everett to Webster, Edward Everett Papers (MSS, MHS), LXVIII, 321.

28. St. 1838, ch. 157; Clifford to Bigelow, Mar. 10, 1839, Bigelow Papers; *Senate Docs., 1839*, nos. 10, 14; *Letters to the Hon. Harison Gray Otis by a Citizen of Massachusetts Occasioned by the Petition of Himself and Others for a Repeal of the License Law of 1838* (Boston, 1839); *Commonwealth v. Jordan* (1836), 18 Pickering 228; *Commonwealth v. Blackington* (1842), 24 Pickering 352; *Commonwealth v. Kimball* (1842), 24 Pickering 359; Francis Hilliard, *Supplement Being a Digest of Pickering's and Metcalf's Reports* (Boston, 1843), p. 278. The methods of enforcement were limited, however, by *Commonwealth v. Tubbs* (1848), 1 Cushing 2ff; *Commonwealth v. Odlin* (1839), 23 Pickering 275.

29. St. 1852, ch. 322. For the agitation see, e.g., *Woburn Journal*, Nov. 15, 1851, May 22, 29, 1852.

30. *House Docs., 1852*, no. 64; Stone to Sumner, Feb. 15, 1853, Sumner, "Letters Received," XXI, 48.

31. *Fisher v. McGirr, Comomnwealth v. Albro*, and *Herrick v. Smith* (1854), 1 Gray 1ff, 17ff, 27. See also st. 1855, ch. 271; *Senate Docs., 1855*, nos. 68, 109.

32. St. 1855, chs. 215, 470; *Senate Docs., 1855*, nos. 41, 44; *Senate Docs., 1858*,

reaffirmed the propriety of such state action.[33] Although no wholly satisfactory method of regulation had emerged through three decades of experiment, few disputed in 1860 that it was a legitimate task of government to guard the welfare of its citizens by sponsoring temperance.

The assumption of such duties affected the very structure of the polity. Massachusetts no longer pieced and parceled out the administration of its new concerns among those willing to undertake the tasks for profit or privilege. The state that made the laws became directly responsible for their enforcement.

At the beginning of the century the government had often delegated the enforcement of the law to individuals or voluntary agencies, just as it delegated other functions. Every citizen was a potential informer, and in many towns vigilante societies of mutual aid kept order and recovered stolen property. The incentives of rewards and self-interest were then more potent in bringing offenders to the courts than an organized constabulary. "The business of police," said William Tudor, "is fortunately incompatible with the nature of our government, and is always clumsily and ineffectually managed; individuals succeed better, and do not endanger constitutional principles." [34] When robbery seemed a serious problem in 1804, Governor Strong would do no more than suggest bounties or prizes.[35]

Now the growing number and complexity of the laws and the strict division between private associations and public government spawned new agencies and adapted old ones to enforce the will of the state. The common fields, which were strictly speaking neither fully private nor fully public, by virtue of their ambivalence proved ever less useful and tended toward dissolution.[36] The town became purely an administrative subdivision, and an amendment to the constitution in 1820 permitted the General Court to erect cities for greater efficiency.[37] Both towns and cities were "public corporations." Their attempts

no. 90; and the long report of the investigation, *House Docs., 1859*, no. 310, especially pp. xxff. See also *House Docs., 1860*, no. 220; Everett to Delavan, Sept. 30, 1853, Everett Papers, CIII, 71.

33. See, e.g., st. 1855, ch. 215; st. 1858, ch. 152.

34. See *Monthly Anthology and Boston Review*, 7 (1809), 194; Solomon Lincoln, Jr., *History of the Town of Hingham* (Hingham, 1827), p. 11; S. C. Damon, *History of Holden* (Worcester, 1841), p. 124; *Bristol County*, ed. Borden, p. 356.

35. Caleb Strong, *Patriotism and Piety* (Newburyport, 1808), pp. 89, 92.

36. See, e.g., st. 1855, ch. 418.

37. *Journal of the Convention for Framing a Constitution of Government . . . 1780* (Boston, 1832), pp. 250–252; Constitutional Amendments, Art. II.

from time to time to assume the immunities that grew up around other chartered bodies were consistently unsuccessful. Although they tried to attain it, they never achieved the protection of the contract clause. While the state often consulted the inhabitants, it reshaped boundaries and placed its burdens where it wished.[38]

New offices also arose to administer intricate and extensive regulations. The county courts and the General Court had often designated commissioners with judicial powers not unlike those of a court of chancery to find facts and supervise the execution of orders in specific cases.[39] As their functions grew, these ad hoc bodies were formalized into permanent agencies. In 1820, when county commissioners received the powers of the courts over licensing and roads, the county became an increasingly effective instrument of centralized control. Ultimately similar agencies appeared to deal with banks, insurance, railroads, education, charities, and pilotage.[40]

The state used the services of some of these agencies in the crises precipitated by the collapse of a significant number of enterprises it had once sponsored. Private corporations were generally no longer able to manage roads, bridges, and water-supply systems at a profit without the aid of privilege. Yet those who attacked the privilege often did so in the name of more extensive services and frequently forced the government to assume such tasks directly.

Occasional new turnpikes appeared in the 1820's, but by that decade most privately owned highways languished as traffic fell off and as tolls remained inflexible. Railroad competition in the next decade killed them. Canals too suffered from rail competition. The attack upon special favors, however, precluded a rise in rates and generally blocked the adoption of any remunerative alternatives not envisioned in the original charters. Bridge corporations that did thrive were, on the contrary, suspect because they earned profits through high charges. Consequently, resentment often wiped out their incomes, as the experience of the Charles River Bridge showed.[41]

38. See *House Docs., 1830–31*, no. 54; L. S. Cushing, C. W. Storey, and Lewis Josselyn, *Reports of Controverted Elections* (Boston, 1853), pp. 634ff; *Senate Docs., 1860*, no. 68; *General Statutes*, chs. 18, 19.

39. See, e.g., *Resolves of the Commonwealth of Massachusetts . . . 1812 . . . 1815* (Boston, 1812–1815), p. 182.

40. See R. S. Van de Woestyne, *State Control of Local Finance in Massachusetts* (Cambridge, Mass., 1935), pp. 17ff; Bradford Kingman, *History of North Bridgewater* (Boston, 1866), p. 320; *General Statutes*, ch. 17.

41. See, e.g., E. B. Crane, "Boston and Worcester Turnpike," *Colls. Worc. Soc.*, XVII (1901), 597; st. 1823, ch. 81; Lincoln to Bigelow, Apr. 22, 1837, Bigelow Pa-

Canals, outmoded, sank into obsolescence; no one cared to slow the demise. The Middlesex, once channel of ingenious schemes and ambitious aspirations, ignominiously lost its charter on an information by the attorney general. The state also allowed some pikes to surrender their routes. But usually the unwillingness to abandon roads led to a search for an alternative to corporate management. In this quest, the government forced towns and county commissioners to accept turnpikes transformed into public ways, sometimes sweetening the pill by a grant of money.[42] The towns had no choice in the matter and failed to establish their independence, despite clauses in the turnpike charter specifically absolving them of future responsibility. The claim that such provisos constituted "a contract altogether beyond the control of the legislature" proved of no avail. The General Court insisted on imposing the grievous burden of maintenance, holding that "it relates to a public matter in which the whole community have an interest." [43]

The same conception of public necessity affected the disposition of bridges. Some private toll structures continued in operation throughout the period, and taxpayers remained reluctant to bear the cost directly. Yet investors grew ever more wary, and their reluctance to do the job drove local governments into building a growing number of new spans, like the Sea Street Bridge to South Boston.[44]

Furthermore, structures already in existence fell to the care of the government. The erection of the Warren Free Bridge by a private corporation created two problems. The enterprise lacked the means of continued support, and its success closed the Charles River Bridge, depriving the public of an important avenue. After a long crisis the state took over both projects, collecting tolls through an agent and eventually charging the city of Charlestown with the duty of amassing a fund to subsidize free operation.[45] In a similar fashion, Massachusetts transferred to

pers; [Caleb Eddy], *Historical Sketch of the Middlesex Canal* (Boston, 1843), pp. 6ff, 16ff, 33ff.

42. See *House Docs., 1852*, no. 182; *House Docs., 1860*, no. 100, pp. 28, 29, 54, xxiii; st. 1857, chs. 138, 257.

43. *Senate Docs., 1859*, no. 65, pp. 8, 21ff.

44. See, e.g., st. 1822, ch. 65; st. 1856, ch. 283; st. 1857, chs. 195, 223; *Bowen's Boston News-Letter*, Sept. 9, 1826.

45. See *Boston Commercial Gazette*, Apr. 13, 1835; Rantoul, *Memoirs*, p. 321; Governor Everett's address, *Senate Docs., 1839*, no. 1, p. 14; st. 1855, ch. 253; *Senate Docs., 1855*, no. 39; *Senate Docs., 1859*, no. 62; see also *Senate Docs., 1835*, no. 58.

the interested towns the private Hancock Free Bridge and others, like the Essex, which reverted to the state at the expiration of their charters.[46] Involuntarily, county and town found the burden of roads and bridges resting more heavily upon them.[47]

The inability of water-supply organizations to satisfy the needs of growing urban regions also drew the government into direct action. Some old companies continued to function, and as late as 1857 a new one, the Jamaica Pond Aqueduct Corporation, received a charter to supply Roxbury, West Roxbury, and Brookline. But legislators and voters recognized with growing frequency that only an agency not interested in profit could supply this commodity, universally needed and related to the health and safety of the whole community.[48] Boston established the municipal Cochituate Water System, a precedent followed by Lowell and Charlestown, while special water districts arose, as in Pittsfield, to serve the needs of several towns. Here, the unlikelihood of profits discouraged private enterprise and left tasks undone which only the government seemed capable of coping with.[49]

Elsewhere, fierce recriminatory competition among rival capitalists, obdurate in the sight of gain, cast doubts upon the propriety of individual initiative and invited state action. The expansion of Boston through reclamation of the surrounding bays rested in the hands of profit-making chartered companies in the half-century after 1800. But in the 1830's filling operations by the Charlestown Branch Railroad and the East Boston Wharf Company evoked bitter protests.[50] As a long series of surveys exposed the desirability of pushing out the shore line and yet protecting the navigable channels of the South and the Back bays, of the Charles and the Mystic rivers, excited voices offered

46. St. 1857, chs. 257, 268; "Building of the Essex Bridge," *Essex Inst. Hist. Colls.*, XXX (1893), 92; st. 1860, ch. 64.

47. See *Revised Statutes*, ch. 25, secs. 1–27; st. 1856, ch. 82; *Senate Docs., 1856*, no. 66. For the allocation of responsibility see *Braintree v. Norfolk County Commissioners* (1851), 8 Cushing 546; *Senate Docs., 1859*, no. 65, p. 6. See also st. 1859, ch. 99; Mellen Chamberlain, *Documentary History of Chelsea* (Boston, 1908), II, 165.

48. St. 1857, ch. 135; Mayor's address, *Bowen's Boston News-Letter*, Jan. 27, 1826, p. 33; H. A. Hill, *Memoir of Abbott Lawrence* (Boston, 1884), pp. 45–47.

49. See *Boston Commercial Gazette*, July 21, 1836; *Boston Daily Herald*, Oct. 15, 1836; *Boston Daily Advertiser*, Nov. 20, 28, 1844; st. 1852, ch. 210; st. 1855, ch. 435; *Senate Docs., 1860*, no. 88; st. 1861, ch. 105; Jamaica Pond Aqueduct Corporation Papers (MSS, Baker Library, Harvard University).

50. St. 1836, ch. 187, sec. 7; *Senate Docs., 1845*, no. 107; *House Docs., 1845*, no. 58.

contradictory suggestions about the best means.[51] The earliest work on the South Bay was privately done; a semipublic corporation in which Charlestown participated undertook the task for the Mystic River; but the claims and refutation of claims resting on utterly chaotic titles to the Back Bay led the Commonwealth itself to formulate plans and supervise the filling.[52]

Bridges and waterworks, the flats, and roads fell directly into the province of government when the simple passage of regulatory laws did not achieve a balance of contending interests.[53] Though the transition often seemed acceptable to all concerned, it was shadowed with doubts about where the Commonwealth would find limits to its activity. To draw a stalwart line of principle was difficult or impossible. If the agricultural college and grammar schools were public, why not universities and academies; if the sale of liquor, why not of bread? In 1851 Josiah Quincy, a member of the Athenæum, stated categorically, "Our government, from its nature, does not comprise within its cares" the support of libraries. But not long before, that society had asked financial aid of the city of Boston, and within the decade a rival municipal institution was in active operation.[54]

If it was difficult to draw the line with reference to libraries or schools, how much more so with reference to economic activities close to the purses of the citizenry? If bridges and roads were "fit for the action of government," would anyone "be so hardy as to attempt to make a distinction between . . . a bridge and a railroad?"[55] Indeed, Massachusetts retained the right to purchase all lines after twenty years, and regulation often reflected an intention to do so.[56] But if the state by design undertook such enterprises, how would it answer the sponsors of a government-

51. See *Senate Docs., 1846*, no. 64; *Boston Daily Advertiser*, Jan. 13, 1847; res. 1850, ch. 3; *Senate Docs., 1852*, no. 45.

52. For the Mystic see R. H. Dana, Jr., *Improvement of the Mystic River* (n.p., n.d.), pp. 1–7; st. 1852, ch. 105. For the Back Bay see *Senate Docs., 1852*, no. 45; st. 1852, ch. 79; *Senate Docs., 1855*, no. 115; *Senate Docs., 1859*, no. 103; *House Docs., 1860*, no. 13. See also *Boston City Documents, 1850*, no. 14.

53. See also, in this connection, the question of railroad termini on Boston Common, *Boston Daily Advertiser*, Sept. 9, 11, 14, 21, Oct. 7, 11, 1843.

54. Josiah Quincy, *History of the Boston Athenæum* (Cambridge, Mass., 1851), I, 9, 186; *General Statutes*, ch. 33.

55. [B. R. Curtis], "Debts of the States," *North Amer. Rev.*, 58 (1844), 128, 129.

56. See, e.g., the discussion of regulation of building and depot expenses, *Senate Docs., 1840*, no. 50, pp. 6ff, 9ff; *Boston Daily Advertiser*, Mar. 13, 1843; also, *Fuller v. Dame* (1836) in which Judge Lemuel Shaw ruled that a bribe to a railroad director was against public policy (18 Pickering 472, 479). For the purchase provision see *Revised Statutes*, ch. 39, sec. 84, and the correspondence of Hülsemann and J. P. Bigelow, September, October, 1839, Bigelow Papers.

owned mine who pointed out: "Not an argument can be produced in favor of constructing Canals and Rail Roads for the public good, at the public expense, which is not equally applicable to the object of developing the minerals of the country, at the expense of the government, and especially that of Coal." [57]

As yet these were questions, not threats. Businessmen were uneasy lest the alternative of free government operation nibble away the limited security from political interference. In the absence of a clear distinction between "what the People must do as a *state* & what they may safely & advantageously do in their looser capacity, as a society bound together by common national ties," any enterprise, individual or corporate, might now find some hulking public exigency, unmindful of private profits, ponderously, blindly, opening a breach for direct action by the Commonwealth.[58]

A vague consciousness of the possibility of remote consequences gave added point to doubts about the proper sphere of regulation. By 1860 uncertainty was characteristic. It was as if, imperceptibly, all the familiar metes and bounds that marked off one man's estate from another's vanished, to leave a vast and open space, familiar but with the old landmarks gone. Somewhere, everyone knew, the state could act directly, somewhere it could legislate as arbiter, and somewhere it had no place at all. But where one field ended and another began, no one knew; the master map was not yet drawn. With many issues still unformulated, consistency, even in theory, was beyond the reach of any group of citizens. In practice a society that found "a disposition in the people to manage their own affairs" also witnessed a remarkable extension of government interference with the personal lives of its members.[59]

For the time being, few people in Massachusetts considered the paradox intolerable. The transformation of the role of government in the economy had proceeded in a seamless web. The society which faced the crisis of Fort Sumter differed radically from that which met the challenge of Lexington Common. But continuity of development joined the two, with no precipitous divide to mark the break. The later was visibly the outgrowth of

57. *Boston Commercial Gazette*, Jan. 17, 21, 1839; *House Docs., 1841*, no. 66.

58. Everett to Whewell, Sept. 3, 1849, Everett Papers, XC, 143.

59. Governor Washburn's address, *Senate Docs., 1854*, no. 3, p. 10; also, *Senate Docs., 1853*, no. 5, pp. 20, 21; Rantoul, *Memoirs*, p. 354; Edward Everett, "Accumulation, Property, Capital, Credit," *Orations and Speeches on Various Occasions* (Boston, 1853–1868), II, 299ff.

the earlier. The regulatory police state had replaced the Commonwealth, but the germinal tendencies that produced the forces animating the policy-makers of 1860 had been present from the start.

The Revolution had left to Massachusetts a conception of government prominent in the direction and management of productive enterprise. The aspiration of a weak young state for economic independence had given shape to a positive program; a narrow purse and the obsession of debt had channeled activities through the grant of privilege. The modes of political action in terms of which men thought thus bore marked resemblance to the mercantilist patterns already evolved in western Europe and evolving almost contemporaneously in the less advanced societies of Prussia and Russia.

But a unique dynamic factor had from the start enriched American development. Those who held the balance of power in Massachusetts did not constitute the rigid, coherent class which managed the affairs of state in European countries. In the United States there were neither gentry nor Junkers. The new merchants, Revolution-bred, aspired to such places but lacked coherence, assurance, stability of status, and the discipline to subordinate individual to class interests. Furthermore, ultimate authority rested on a much broader base. Other groups who normally tolerated control by a minority were capable on occasion of turning competition within the mercantile community to the service of a larger purpose. Finally, participation in the insurrectionary effort that gave birth to the Commonwealth had fostered the conviction that everyone should share in the advantages of the new form of government and, almost at once, had added an emendatory gloss to the mercantilist conceptions.

Within the new faith in the old forms the instruments of state action, like privilege and incorporation, became widely accessible. Spread destroyed the exclusive character of these institutions and their link with the Commonwealth. Multiplication, with the intent of furthering the common interest, made it difficult to conceive of a common interest inextricably tied to any specific enterprise. Diffusion opened the way for a body of rights enshrined in law, standing between the government and the citizen and his property.

The battle of privilege that resulted from the fragmentation of society was therefore half won before it started. With the ties to the state already sundered, there was no need for an attack upon all political action to do away with special favors. The laissez-faire argument found no place in Massachusetts thinking; transformation came from the internal development of the institutions themselves.

Failure to develop a case against all government economic measures acquired particular significance when liberal humanitarianism placed ever heavier emphasis upon the police and reform functions of the state. There was no counterpart in America of the transatlantic tendency to transpose objections against privilege into objections against government regulation. In the United States the people who favored reform were not held back by a fear of the state; the people were the state.

The transition from the Commonwealth to the police state, from mercantilism to liberalism, was not peculiar to Massachusetts or to the United States. But the unique aspect of the American experience as represented by Massachusetts was the concatenation of three distinct forces against the background of a rapidly expanding economy. The democratic widening of opportunities that grew out of the instability of the class structure and of political alignments, the recognition of a body of vested private rights free of state interference, and the humanitarian doctrine of reform reshaped the conception of the place of the state in the productive system and demolished, in a distinctive manner, the heritage of Commonwealth ideas.

No longer able to look backward for solutions, many Massachusetts men attuned their ears to advice from across the Atlantic when the impact of another great war raised a new series of critical questions. English theorists had by then charted a consistent solution known and respected in America. Before 1860 some Bay State thinkers, like Francis Bowen, tended to accept their principles; others, like George Sumner, rejected them. In either case, the classical generalities were unimportant: for both those who accepted and those who rejected the English teachings conceived that the question of the role of their government in the economy "does not relate to the correctness of the general principle in economical science, but only to its applicability under particular circumstances." [60]

After the Civil War the British theories, reformulated and

60. Francis Bowen, "Phillips on Protection," *North Amer. Rev.*, 72 (1851), 414; Francis Bowen, *Principles of Political Economy* (Boston, 1856), pp. vi, vii; "Bigotry of Laissez-Faire," *Living Age*, 1 (1844), 338ff; Orestes Brownson, "The Policy to be Pursued," *Boston Quarterly Review*, 4 (1841), 83ff; George Sumner to Prescott, June 16, 1845, W. H. Prescott, *Correspondence, 1833–47* (Cambridge,

strengthened by Darwinian conceptions, assumed a new importance as the old issues of government-granted privilege disappeared and as further economic changes created a powerful interest against any state action. By then, four years of fighting and the aftermath of belligerent peace had profoundly altered the relation of Massachusetts to its economy. Intensified industrialization and the nationalized scale of business enterprise transformed the nature of the government's problems, while the enormous growth of federal powers introduced a new regulating factor which was to mount steadily in importance and ultimately to overshadow the state.

Neither element was new. The factory system had been long in maturing; and there were occasional appeals for the services of the United States from the earliest period, for the tariff and control of commerce, for the improvement of harbors and the maintenance of lighthouses, and for the regulation of banking.[61] But the exigencies of a military economy shifted the focus of attention. It was no longer possible to think in parochial terms; the center of gravity had moved to Washington. The consequential issues of policy would now be considered in the national arena. A significant chapter in the role of government in American economy had drawn to a close.

Mass., 1925), pp. 543, 544; Theodore Sedgwick, *Public and Private Economy* (New York, 1839), I, 89; above, p. 52.

61. See on lighthouses, st. 1783, ch. 19; st. 1784, ch. 18; st. 1786, chs. 27, 62; st. 1787, ch. 31; st. 1790, ch. 4; st. 1795, ch. 18. For banking see *Senate Docs., 1858*, no. 17, p. 17.

Appendixes | Note on the Sources | Index

Appendix A

Statistics of the Constitutional Convention of 1780

Table 1

Daily Average of Votes Cast

Date		Average
Sept.	3	251.0
	4	237.0
	4*	198.0
Nov.	5	113.0
	8	119.0
Jan.	27	102.0
Feb.	1	46.0
	2	57.0
	3	59.0
	9	57.5
	10	66.0
	11	68.0
	12	57.3
	14	52.0
	15	73.0
	16	86.0
	18	67.0
	20	80.0
	21	73.5
	22	63.0
	23	64.0
	24	56.5
	25	36.0
	28	35.0

* Afternoon session.

SOURCE: *Journal of the Convention for Framing a Constitution of Government for the State of Massachusetts Bay, September 1, 1779, to June 16, 1780* (Boston, 1832).

Table 2

Critical Votes

Subject	Date			For	Against	Majority
Judiciary, structure and powers	Nov.	5,	1779	78	35	43
	Nov.	5,	1779	62	57	5
	Feb.	12,	1780	36	22	14
	Feb.	12,	1780	32	24	8
	Feb.	12,	1780	36	22	14
	Feb.	16,	1780	62	24	38
Senate	Feb.	1,	1780	28	18	10
	Feb.	2,	1780	57	39	18
Council	Feb.	10,	1780	36	30	6
				38	32	6
Representation	Feb.	18,	1780	52	15	37
Form of submittal	Feb.	9,	1780	46	11	35
				33	25	8
Property qualifications	Feb.	24,	1780	37	27	10
Legislative pay	Feb.	19,	1780	60	20	40

SOURCE: *Journal of Convention, 1780*, pp. 42, 43, 69, 70, 94, 98, 99, 104, 116, 118, 122, 124, 136.

Appendix B

Representation in the General Court, 1780–1820

The tenuous nature of political control in Massachusetts referred to in Chapter 3 reflected in some measure a system of representation that gave each town the option of electing members of the House of Representatives or not. Since the cost rested upon the local community, the temptation was strong to forgo the privilege in the interest of a lower tax rate. There was therefore enormous variation in the size of the legislature from session to session and in the number of towns represented (Table 1, below). Generally this situation put the commercial cities, and particularly Boston, at an advantage; their membership in the House was consistently larger since the burden of support was less weighty on the seacoast (Table 2, below). In periods of crisis the inland towns could, of course, make use of their reserve of potential representation to retake control (Table 3, below). (These three tables were derived from the statistics of each session collected in *Senate Docs., 1854*, no. 56.)

Table 1

Representation in the House of Representatives, 1780–1820

Years	Number of legislative sessions	Number of towns		Number of towns represented		Number of members	
		Average	Minimum Maximum	Average	Minimum Maximum	Average	Minimum Maximum
1780–1785	11	301	294 304	161 *	125 192	172	130 301
1785–1790	15	351	346 357	181	98 220	200	108 252
1790–1795	13	369	336 390	168	117 224	179	123 245
1795–1800	11	407	394 435	176	163 199	186	171 213
1800–1805	12	441	419 455	230	200 258	260	221 286
1805–1810	11	474	470 477	309	264 363	458	346 585
1810–1815	12	549	477 577	376	323 417	636	512 739
1815–1820	10	578	583 606	261	195 345	368	226 543
1780–1820	95	431	294 606	225	98 417	302	108 739

* Figures for 1780 and 1781 are not available.

Table 2

Per Cent of Towns Represented in the House of Representatives, 1780–1820

Years	*Average per cent for Suffolk County**	*Average per cent for Massachusetts*
1780–1785	76	53
1785–1790	68	52
1790–1795	67	46
1795–1800	58	43
1800–1805	76	52
1805–1810	86	65
1810–1815	86	68
1815–1820	58	45
1780–1820	71	52

* Includes Norfolk County after its separation from Suffolk.

Table 3

Per Cent of Towns Represented in the House of Representatives, 1785–1788

Legislative year	*Session*	*Berkshire and Hampshire Counties*	*Massachusetts*
1785–1786	1	60	58
1785–1786	2	63	56
1785–1786	3	61	56
1786–1787	1	40	44
1786–1787	2	39	42
1786–1787	3	35	40
1786–1787	4	14	28
1787–1788	1	69	62
1787–1788	2	57	59
1787–1788	3	54	57

Appendix C

Letter to The President and Directors of the Banks in Boston [1]

Boston March 6, 1807.

To the President & Directors of the
Banks in Boston

Gentlemen,

We beg leave respectfully to trouble you with business of great import & Magnitude to yourselves & the public — We hope it will meet with that serious attention from you, which the nature of the subject demands. It is, gentlemen, a case of importance to our fellow-citizens — & feeling conscious of the rectitude of our intentions, we doubt not, the result of your deliberations will ultimately tend to the object of this address.

On the 20th of Feb. last, we sent to Amherst, a considerable number of bills of the Hillsborough Bank — that from that period to the present (16 days) we have obtained payment for only $13807 — though during most of this time, we had two agents there, & alternately one — that this delay of payment does not arise from any altercation with the Bank whatever — but a *fixed determination* of the Directors, not to *redeem* no more than $3000 of their bills in one day — be there ever so many at market, or presented for payment.

But the fact is, they do not pay $3000 in a day, or we should have obtained, before this, double of what we have received! — The manner of their proceeding & weighing out the specie, does not produce but little more than $2000 in a day — it is weighed out in parcels of $100 each, & takes all their Bank hours to obtain this sum. — But to make up the sum of $3000 a day, they want you, from day to day to give back to the Bank, the specie, & receive a draft on Boston for $3000 at sight!! — What, give back to the Bank the specie after you have worked hard all day to obtain it? Could any thing be more inconsistent? — Our agent is now at Amherst, & the line of conduct as marked out, the Directors say they shall not deviate from. — Our market must be filled with their bills, & yet they will not redeem only this sum in a day. Shall this Bank have the privileges & advantages of putting into circulation, say one, two, or three millions of money, & only redeem $3000 in a day? Besides, gentlemen, could they not employ some of their agents to be at the Bank every day, & weigh

1. Directed to Joseph Chapman, Esq., March 6, 1807, marked Urgent (MS, Baker Library, Harvard University, Small Collections).

out the gold the same as they do to us — thereby excluding *every one* & the public, from ever presenting a bill for payment?

The consequences, from such a procedure, will be seriously felt by all who have payments to make in Boston money — besides setting the example for other Banks to do the same. As the Banking business now is, it is a well known fact that the premium on Boston bills is much lower than it would be, in consequence of the bills of the country Banks being sent home. — Shall bills of another State fill our market, without the possibility of being redeemed, if such conduct continues? A critical observer, will find, already, that a great part of foreign bills in circulation are of Amherst Bank, & daily increase.

We should beg leave further to state although our authority may not be conclusive, (yet we have no doubt of it) which is, that Agents are placed here, with large sums of bills of said Bank, *for the sole purpose of purchasing bills of other Banks, & sending them home for payment* — expecting that other will redeem their bills *promptly & without delay*. These facts are weighty & impressive — & shall such deviations from banking, go on without some check? — We hope & pray not, & that our Banks will estimate such conduct accordingly.

We also understand, as another mode of getting & keeping their bills in perpetual circulation, is, that large sums are loaned out for FOUR PR CENT per annum — the person who hires the money, agreeing to redeem all such bills as may be sent home or pay the premium on Boston as often as they are sent home — provided the Bank will not redeem but $3000 in one day.

From these statements we hope our Banks will adopt some prompt & decisive measure — & guard against the evils which will arise from the proceedings of the Amherst Bank.

We are gentlemen, your servants

> Oliver C. Wyman
> Jon^a. Allen
> Gilbert A. Dean

Appendix D

Opinion of the Attorney General of Massachusetts, on the Life of the Corporation, 1802

The approaching expiration of the charter of the Union Bank in 1802 brought the question of the life-span of its rival, the Massachusetts Bank, to the attention of the General Court. The charter of the first bank in the state, granted in 1784, contained no hint about duration; nor had an amendment in 1792 touched on the subject. Puzzled by the legal implications, a committee of the legislature, charged with the duty of considering the matter, turned for advice to James Sullivan, Attorney General of the Commonwealth.

Sullivan was well qualified to answer. An attorney of long experience, historian, author of a legal treatise, he was no doubt as familiar as anyone in the state with the development of the law. Furthermore, he possessed both political and business experience of significance in this context. Sullivan had been chairman in 1784, of the legislative committee that drafted the charter. In 1792 his Path to Riches *had presented an elaborate argument sustaining the power of the government to terminate charters. And he was, in 1802, heavily engaged as an investor in some of the corporations then mushrooming in Massachusetts. His reply is a significant reflection of the confused state of the best opinion concerning the nature of the corporation in a period of sharp change.*[1]

Sir —

In obedience to the direction of the Committee, of which you are Chairman, I have endeavoured, in the course of the last evening, to arrange my ideas on the question arising from the subject matter of your commission.

The first question proposed for my consideration is,

Whether the Act creating the corporation called the Massachusetts Bank, makes it a perpetual corporation.

The Act is, that

> William Phillips, Isaac Smith, Jonathan Mason, Thomas Russell, John Lowell, and Stephen Higginson, so long as they continue proprietors in the said Bank, together with all those who now are, and all those who shall become proprietors to the said Bank, shall be a corporation, and body politic, under the name of etc

1. The document is in MA, Senate, 2957. See also O. and M. F. Handlin, "Origins of the American Business Corporation," *Jour. of Econ. Hist.*, 5 (1937), 80; Thomas C. Amory, *Life of James Sullivan* (Boston, 1859), I, 146, 387.

There are no express terms of duration, or limitation in the act.

There is provision that their real estate shall never exceed fifty thousand pounds value, nor their goods, chattels, and effects more than five hundred thousand pounds. There is no provision for the quantity of their stock, any restrictions as to the proportion their debts shall bear to their capital, nor any definition of their powers.

By a subsequent Act made in 1792, that bank is restrained from issuing notes to more in sum, than double the amount of their capital in gold, and silver, actually deposited.

When that Bank appeared under the first act, or charter, there were doubts, whether the creation of a corporation, as a perpetual body, without limitation, as to the quantity of credit it should assume, or any regulation in regard to the proportion its debts should bear to its stock or property, was compatible with the constitution of the Commonwealth. The clause in view was, that 'no man or corporation, or association of men, shall have any other title to obtain priviledges, distinct from those of the community, than what arises from the consideration of services rendered to the public.'

There has also been an objection, that this charter is against the constitution of the United States, by which it is provided, that no State shall issue paper money.

The Act of 1792, in some measure, obviated the first objection, by limitting the credit of the bank, and by defining its powers. But even this put it in the power of that corporation, to receive a use of twelve per cent on their real money, while private subjects are punished for taking more than six.

This is now no objection, because all the subsequent Banks have the same priviledge, and it must be right.

The provision of the first act, in 1784, is for six persons, named therein, to be a corporation so long as *they* shall continue proprietors in the same Bank. Whether this is to be construed as a trust committed to them jointly, and to cease as soon as either of them should cease to possess the qualification mentioned, may be a nice question. The trust is undefined, but the grant is, that they shall be a corporation for a Bank. If we consider this as a description of the authority delegated, we must suppose, it had those requisites incident to corporations of the same nature.

The rule seems to be well settled in the English Laws, that where a number of persons are made an agregate corporation, the death of one, does not dissolve the charter: and where there are no words of duration or limitation, the corporation shall survive to the last member.

Where a corporation is made without defined or express powers, yet it shall have the powers usually incident to the nature of such corporation —

But here is a difficulty again; there was no usage then, as to banks in this country; if there is now: and there was none in England, because there is but one Bank corporation there, and its powers depend on its charter, and not on usage.

By this Act, the M. Bank was capable of purchasing real Estate to a great value. It is a well known rule in the learning on corporations, that on the dissolution of such a body, the Lands they have purchased revert to the original owner. Co Litt 13. Lev. 237 etc.[2] I think it would be a severe construction of this act, that any one of the persons named in it might dissolve the corporation by ceasing to be a proprietor; or that it should be dissolved by the death of either. Yet it is an established rule, that, where the grant is from *mere grace and favour*, it shall have a rigid construction against the grantee.

The Act provides, further, that *they together*, with all those who are, and who shall become proprietors, shall be a corporation and body politic. There is no word expressive of a succession, other than that those six men *together* with all who shall become proprietors, shall be a corporation etc.

Whether the Act intended, by the word *together*, that these six men, or some of them at least, should be constitutionally necessary to the existence of the corporation, and that it should, on their deaths, or on the death of either, or on their all ceasing to be proprietors be dissolved is an important and critical question. The act is inartificially drawn; but I cannot conceive, that to have been the intention of the legislature — Indeed the preamble suggests ideas quite to the contrary. The idea is opposed to those in the books, which describe corporations, as *invisible* immortal etc — .

If I am to form an opinion upon this point, I should be inclined to believe, that if the legislature has power to create a perpetual, unlimitted corporation, if the M. Bank is such a one, as can be created by the legislative authority, consistently with the Constitution, it would be considered, that the words in the act imply a grant of perpetuity.

If the act was in itself unconstitutional, then it may be classed

2. The reference to Coke is to the discussion of escheat of lands held in fee simple in which a distinction is drawn between a natural body and "a body politique or incorporate." In the case of lands held by "a deane and chaptor, or . . . a major and commonalty," after "such body politique or incorporate is dissolved, the donor shall have again the land, and not the lord by escheate. And the reason . . . is, for that in the case of a body politique or incorporate the fee simple is vested in their . . . capacity created by the policy of man, and therefore the law doth annex the condition in law to every such gift and grant, that if such body politique or incorporate be dissolved, that the donor or grantor shall reenter, for that the cause of the gift or grant faileth; but no such condition is annexed to the estate in fee simple vested in any man in his naturall capacity . . ." (Coke, *Commentary upon Littleton*, I, 13 b).

The other reference is to the case of *Edmonds* v. *Brown and Tilliard* (20 Car. II), 1 Levinz 237, *English Reports*, LXXXIII, 385, and seems to have no particular relevance.

amongst those, where the sovereign power is deceived in his grant, because he has granted that, which he had no authority to grant. But this objection, so far as it regards the perpetuity of the grant, does not apply to this corporation alone; for a great number of other corporations, are expressly made perpetual.

The most important question, and that which involves in its discussion, all those submitted by the committee, is what the effects, and consequences of any act of the legislature on this subject, would be.

Should the powers ascribed to the parliment of Great Britain, be considered as in the possession of our legislature, there would be no necessity of saying anything on the subject, in regard to legal decisions, or established precedents. Blackstone, Coke, and others say, that corporations may be dissolved by the parliment, which is *omnipotent and uncontroulable.*

Towns in England, as well as here, are corporations for certain purposes; but they have no common seal. In this State, towns and parishes have been created, altered changed, and dissolved, at the pleasure of the legislature — The tenants in common of Lands may act *quasi* a corporation but, they clearly are not such; and their mode of existence is not much more remote from a corporation, with a common seal, than that of towns, and parishes are.

There were no corporations with a common seal, within Massachusetts, before the revolution. They have been, since that event, so greatly multiplied, that no one can examine, or or [sic] define, their powers, and priviledges.

The Corporations here which possess a common seal, may be classed, as those which have a foundation on real Estate: such as Bridges, turnpikes, canals and aqueducts. Those which are for the promotion of religion, morals, literature, and the arts and sciences. And those which are for the management of money and the maintainance of corporate credit. All these by the forms of their institutions may acquire, and hold real Estates.

Of these corporations, some again are made perpetual, by the use of words in their grants, such as *perpetual succession, succession,* or *forever.* Others are restrained and limitted — as to the term of their duration. There is not one which by express words is during the pleasure of the legislature. Nor any one, excepting the M. Bank, that has not, either express words of perpetuity, or limitation, as to the term of its duration of existance.

But if the legislature can dissolve those which are created with a grant of perpetual existance, they can dissolve those which are created for a term of years only, before the term expires. There have been no decisions on the point in the country, and it is therefore out of my power to determine the question. I have lived long enough to learn, that reasoning, merely on principle, is quite an uncertain business in its event. Men often adopt false, for true principles, and conceive that they are reasoning from anology where there is no natural connexion in the premises. I feel myself in duty bound to add, that although the increase of corporations may ultimately involve the community in difficulty, yet the public opinion is, and so far as I understand it, always has been, (that is for eighteen years past) that the legislature cannot, at pleasure dissolve corporations, possessing the priviledges indicated by the emblem of a common seal. Whether there has been an existing distinction in this opinion, between banks, and other corporations I do not know; it is a pity that so great a variety of corporations have been formed before general rules for their government had been agreed on.

As to the principles of the common Law of England, it may be made a question how far, they have been adopted and practised upon here. Our constitution provides that all those Laws which had been adopted, and practised upon before the revolution, shall be continued as law here untill they shall be altered by the legislature; but as there were no corporations here, like those to which the english authorities principally apply, those principles could not have been adopted. Indeed as to banks, there are none in particular because the bank of England is not governed by usage, but by its charter.

If the Legislature suppose themselves in possession of the power ascribed to the english parliment in regard to corporations, an act may be passed repealing the laws of 1784 & 1792, made for creating and reforming the corporation of the M. Bank, or in other words may pass an act for its dissolution. Or there may be a new charter granted on condition that the old one may be surrendered.

There is an important consideration, which relates to all the banks; as they can all hold real Estate. On their dissolution by an expiration, or otherwise, their real Estate reverts to the original owner. This more essentially affects those, which can take mortgages. Even a renewall of a charter is a creation of a new bank.

If the general Court shall believe the act creating the M. Bank, to be void because it was unconstitutional, or because the grantor was deceived in its grant, or that the charter has expired on the cessation of one or more of the original nominal grantees ceasing to be proprietors, an order may be passed to the solicitor, or attorney general, or to both, to bring a *scire facias*, or *quo warranto* against it. or if the legislature, under a sense of parlimentary omnipotence, shall repeal the laws in regard to that bank, and yet the stockholders should continue to exercise corporate functions, the same process, or one on the statute against private associations for banking, will settle the contest in the Judiciary department of the government.

On this point, the only question would be, whether the legislature has authority to dissolve corporations for the purpose of banking at their pleasure, and yet have not the same power over other corporations holding a common seal. Or whether the legislative power extends to a dissolution of every species of corporation indiscriminately, so far as to subvert them at pleasure. These questions would be of such magnitude, and involve in them the fate of so much property, and so many priviledges, that the whole state would stand oppressed with anxiety untill they should be decided.

Mankind do not ordinarily consider the consequences of adopting certain principles, untill they are carried to such an extreme as may expose their natures. Was the scheme of banks a novelty now, the government, under its present experience, would act with caution — Notwithstanding the objections to a legislative controul over corporations, the acts to restrain their issuing bills less than five dollars, and all restrictive additional acts must be founded in that idea alone.

On the question, whether the act of 1784, was constitutional, there may be a great deal said to shew that it was so, and that it remains to be yet unconstitutional, unless the act of 1792 has aided the defect. If the corporation has accepted the last act as a part of their charter, then that bank is nearly on a standing with the others. I observe that in the memorial of the corporation to the committee, the existance of the corporation, is emphatically placed on the first, and no notice taken of the second act.

Upon the point, whether the sovereign power was deceived in its grant, if the grant was originally consonat to the principles of the constitution, or was made so by a subsequent act, then the rules of Law in England, if they have been made a part of our Laws, are very plain and decided.

I define them thus: where the soverign power is deceived into making grants which it had no right to make. As in Cokes institute 13, the principle is laid down, and which rule is the voice of common reason, the grant is void.[3]

Where the grant is incompatible with the public safety, it must also be void: for a power, is certainly deceived, when it grants that, the exercise of which, would destroy the public authority which makes the grant. This principle is well explained in Cokes 5th report.[4]

Where the sovereign power has been deceived by false suggestions of the grantee; as in the case of Alton Woods, 6th Cokes reports 43 to 46;[5] where all the principles are described on this point, and the result is, what every one will realize, that where the sovereign power, more especially in grants of *mere grace and favour,* and which are of doubtful construction and therefore shall be construed most strongly against the grantee, is deceived, the grant is voidable — Where the

3. See above, note 2.
4. This citation is vague, and no case in the fifth report seems to have a specific bearing. See *English Reports,* LXXVII.
5. This citation is inaccurate. *The Case of Alton Woods* (37 Elizabeth), 1 Coke Reports 26 b, *English Reports,* LXXVI, 64ff, deals with the grant of a manor by the king.

King shall be deceived in his grant, by false suggestions of the grantee, the grant is voidable. This principle is hinted of, and explained in 6th report 55 etc,[6] and in the Bishop of Winchester case, as reported in Raymond 298 Comberbach 334 Levinz 350.[7]

Where the sovereign power has made an imprudent and foolish grant, but which it had a right to make; and where the mistake, and error was from itself, there the grant is not voidable. As where the King grants a certain estate, worth a larger annuity than is expressed in the deed, yet if he uses apt words to make a grant, and the estate is well described the grant is good.

This principle seems to render it certain that the sovereign power cannot avoid its grant merely because it was *imprudent or inexpedient to make it.*

I believe I have attended to all the questions your honorable committee saw fit to propose to me; but I cannot say, that I have directly answered any one of them. There is no legal decision, no precedent established in the government, on which to predicate an opinion, or to form decisive answers. This subject may eventually engage the attention, and employ the learning of all the men in the commonwealth. The feelings of interest, the dictates of prudence, the calculations of policy, and even the prevalency of parties, may give the whole contest a complexion which is at this time inconceivable to any one. The giving a decided opinion, therefore, without a precedent, or established rule to guide my mind would be of little avail; and might hereafter be considered as presumptuous and imprudent.

The great end of government, is to unite and consolidate the interests of all the subjects. A sense of security, and an assurance of protection, concentrates the public favourable opinion in support of the social compact. The creation of a great variety of corporate interests, in themselves powerful and important, must have a direct tendency to weaken the powers of government. When those are multiplied, and all the ability of the state is engaged in one or the other; and when the interests may militate with each other essentially, it is in vain to reason upon naked principles unfortified by established rules. No one can foresee what the event will be, no body can predict the consequences, while every one will lament the calamity —

I am sensible that this is going out of the line proposed to me, but I never laid aside the man for the Lawyer, or the citizen for the officer: and this suggestion is only intended, to exemplify the main drift of my argument, that forensic learning is rather useless (in my opinion) on the present occasion —

6. This citation refers to *The Duke of Chandos's Case* (4 Jac. I), 6 Coke Reports 55, *English Reports*, which held that where less passes in the grant of a manor than the king intended, the grant is good; where more, the grant is void.

7. These citations are clearly inaccurate. See *English Reports*, LXXXIII, XC, XCI, XCII.

I am happy, when it is in my power to be of use to the honorable Legislature: and consider myself honoured with the commands of your committee, with high respect to whom, I remain
Your most humble
Servant

JASullivan

Boston 5th March 1802
The Honorable
Elijah Brigham Esqr
Chairman of the Committee on
the question of the Massachusetts Bank

Appendix E

Edward Everett on the Public Debt [1]
To Lord Grenville

Boston United States of America
16th . July . 1828.

My Lord,

I have just finished reading yr lordship's essay on 'the supposed advantages of the sinking fund,' in the second Edition & with great satisfaction. You have succeeded, I think, in demonstrating the utter inutility of a sinking fund, kept up by borrowed resources, & the only wonder, that remains on the mind, in rising from the perusal of the Essay, is that truths, capable of being made so obvious, sh'd ever have been overlooked by wise statesmen.

Yr Lordship is aware, that the sinking fund, in this country, tho' evidently modelled, in its machinery, from that established in England, by the Act of 1786, differs from it in the very important fact, that its operations have been generally carried on, particularly of late years, not by borrow'd means, but by an effective surplus revenue; & that consequently the debt of the United States, w'h amounted nominally, on the first of Jan. 1817 to 118,882,865 dollars, (of w'h all but a small portion bore an interest of at least 6 p'r cent,) has been reduced to about 65,000,000 dollars; altho', in the interval several large additions have been made to it. The sinking fund, as at present organized, in the U States, consists of an annual appropriation of ten millions of dollars, of surplus revenue, to the payment of the principal & interest of the debt, with any further surplus, w'h remains in the treasury, after satisfying all the other appropriations. Sh'd nothing unforeseen occur, to increase the expenditure or diminish the income of the U States, the existing public debt will be entirely p'd in seven or eight years. It is obvious, therefore, that all the objections urged by your Lordship, to a sinking fund like that of England, do not apply to the sinking fund of the United States.

It has, however, on former occasions, occurred to me, & I have ventured even to express the opinion, on the floor of Congress, that the whole system of paying a public debt, not merely by a sinking fund raised by surplus taxation, like yours, but raised by surplus revenue, like ours, is illusory; — a sort of financial or state fiction, having no other value, than what the imagination gives it. This value, however imparted by the imagination, I am inclined to think is considerable. Unless writings like those of yr Lordship & the gen-

1. Edward Everett Papers (MHS), Letter Book, LXIII, 49ff.

eral diffusion among the community of sounder views sh'd disturb the popular faith, I am inclined to believe, that any Government in Great Britain would find it easier, to borrow money, with a debt of £900,000,000, of which £300,000,000 stood in the name of the Commissioners of the sinking fund, than with a debt of £600,000,000. This opinion, however, I express with great diffidence, as touching a matter, of w'h, as a foreigner, I cannot be a competent judge. At all events, I think there is no doubt, that the imagination clothes with great importance, the process of paying off a public debt, by actual redemption from surplus revenue, as the U States have done for several years, & are now doing. —

And yet who gains, by paying the public debt, even in this way? There can, substantially, be but two parties to the public debt. The tax-paying inhabitants of the country are the debtor party; the holders of the evidences of the debt the creditor party. W'h of these parties gains, by the payment of the debt? Not, surely, the tax-paying inhabitants, because every portion of the debt redeemed, is redeemed only by raising an equal amount of money, by taxation. Not the stockholder, because he considers it a disadvantage to be paid off, & his stock is valuable, just in proportion to the term, for w'h it is irredeemable. — The lawful rate of interest in Massachusetts is 6 p'r cent. The market rate, on good private security, carries from 5 to 6 p'r cent. For the first time, since the settlement of America, money has within a month, been loaned in Boston, on private security, at 3 per cent. — This loan was obtained for a popular object, & the lenders were partly actuated by public spirit; the loan was but of 100,000 doll's, & even this taken in numerous share. — But the U States three p'r cent stocks have ever been at a high premium.

It is then, neither, the interest of the creditor nor of the debtor, that the public debt sh'd be paid. The latter saves nothing, the former loses, by all the difference in value, between a redeemable & an irredeemable stock.

The reason of this becomes more obvious, when we consider two things. —

1^0. That a public debt represents money, w'h the Govern^t has borrowed in the public service, & *consumed* in the public service. Now what is consumed or destroyed, cannot be reproduced. It may have been wisely consumed, & for proper objects; but no fiscal operation can restore it. — It is forever gone. — You may pay the debt, but you can do so, only by consuming just so much more of the taxable wealth of the Country, in the act of payment.

2^0. That it can be no benefit to the tax-payers, to redeem a debt on any plan, appears further, than this; that *all* taxation is (if I may use an expression bordering on solacism,) *extra.* You apply that term to the taxation, by w'h money is borrowed, for a sinking fund; & justly — but I do not perceive, that the case is really different, with a surplus of ordinary revenue applied, as at present, in the U. States, to pay the public debt. — Every man sees, that to pay $5,000,000, of old debt, by creating $5,000,000 of new debt, is trifling. But is it, in reality, anything better than trifling, to releive tax-payers of $5,000,000 debt, by taxing them $5,000,000 to pay it? —

These remarks hold, with strictness only of a people stationary in numbers & wealth. Of a people declining in one or both, — as perhaps Spain — , they do not hold at all. It is the interest of the tax-payers then, to pay the debt as soon as possible; because the longer it is delayed, it falls on a smaller number, & decaying resources. — Unluckily, however, a People in this condition is precisely the People, least able to pay its debts & least likely to attempt it. — To a stationary people, what is called the payment of a public debt is a financial fiction, wholly inoperative, as far as concerns a saving to the Community.

But in the case of Countries like England & the U. States, w'h are rapidly growing in numbers & wealth, it is plain that to pay off the public debt is, in reality, to increase the burden of each individual tax-payer, who contributes his part. Our population doubles itself in about twenty three years: & our wealth of course in the same period does much more than double itself. But assume, for argument's sake, only a duplication; & in 1851 our debt, tho' it sh'd remain nominally the same, w'd plainly impose a burden only half as heavy on each tax-payer. The same is true of England, according to her term of duplication. —

This I take to be the true secret, (as far as finance is concerned,) of the power of England to support burdens, so much beyond previous anticipation. It seems to me very possible, that Mr. Hume's memorable prediction, that England c'd not bear a greater debt than £100,000,000 has not yet been falsified, by Experience. In other words, so vast & unexpected has been her growth since he wrote, principally in consequence of the great improvements in machinery, that perhaps the present debt of England, compared with her resources, is really less than a debt of $100,000,000 w'd have been, compared with her resources as conceived of by Hume.

Whilst it appears to me, therefore, that all sinking funds are delusive; & that the arguments, by w'h that of the U. State is shown to be so are corollaries of those, w'h y'r Lordship employs, to prove the futility of the English system — I w'd return to the proposition, that all sinking funds — & especially one like ours — have a value & consequently an efficacy derived from the *imagination*. The Govern't w'h is really no party to the debt, has, as agent of the debtor less trouble in managing a small debt, than a large one. — so rooted, too, in the popular mind is the supposed analogy between public debt & debt of man to man (things alike only in name,) that it is commonly easy to borrow money, in precise proportion to the smallness of the debt already existing, & the activity of the system organized for paying it.

All that I have taken the liberty to say has, like y'r Lordship's Essay, been intended in a financial view of the subject. In a political view, under a Govern't like that of the U. States, the payment of the public debt is highly important, & demanded by the character of all our institutions. No administration c'd neglect it without certain & well deserved ruin.

I owe an apology to y'r lordship for troubling you with these hasty remarks, expressly as they come from an individual personally a stranger. My respect for y'r lordship's public character & the excitement given, by the reading of y'r Essay, to ideas, w'h have been for some time floating in my mind, have led me to venture on this intrusion. I sh'd be pleased & proud to find, that my views were in any degree sanctioned by y'r concurrence. I have taken the liberty to send, with this letter, a copy of some remarks made by me, on another subject; — remarks of a very unpretending character; in the course of w'h, I had occasion to hint at the opinions expressed in this letter. —

I have the honor to be,

With high respect,
Your lordship's most faithful, humble servant,
Edward Everett

Appendix F

Artisan Grievances Against the Corporation [1]

Remonstrance of George W. Cushing & Others, Journeymen Carriage Makers, against a petition of Robert C. Kid & Others, to be incorporated as the Amherst Carriage Company, Feby 8 1838 John Rayner

To the Senate and house of Representatives of the Commonwealth of Massachusetts in generel Court asembeled

We the subscribers respectfully represent

That we regret that a petition is now pending in the Legislature to encorporate Robert C Kid and others by the name of the Amherst Carrage Company, and we beg leave to state our reasons why the prayer should not be granted.

We being journamen at the Coach chaise and harness manufactoring business, do look forward with anticipation to a time when we shall be able to conduct the buisness upon our own responsibility and receive the proffits of our labor, which we now relinquish to others, and we believe that incorporated bodies tend to crush all feable enterprise and compel us to worke out our dayes in the Service of others.

And also because that incorporations puts means into the hands of inexperienced capitalists to take from us the profits of our art which has cost us many year of labour to obtain, and which we consider ought to be our exclusive privilege to enjoy.

And furthermore because large carriage manufactorys is not necessary to suply the market and the reduction of prices benefits only the rich they being the only purchasers, while it greatly injures the poor.

Therefore as the publick can receive no benefit from an incorporation of this kinde and as the publick is liable to gross imposition from incorporations of any kinde and for the reasons above stated and for the protections of equal rights and for the encouragement of enterprise and honest industry we respectfuly and earnestly pray that the request of the said petition may not be granted

February 6th 1838.

[Fifty-one signatures follow.]

1. MS, HCL, US 12565.41 (no. 1).

Appendix G

Memoranda on the Role of Government in American Economic Development

1. *Committee on Research in Economic History, July 15, 1941*

Ideas and Economic History

The Committee is convinced that a study of economic ideas about the role of government is essential for an understanding of American economic development. But a study of ideas is only important because it lays bare the preconceptions of legislators, or the opinions of groups about legislative needs. Ideas partly reflect economic processes and partly censor them; they affect the rôle of government positively and negatively, acting either as a demand for new legislation or as restraints upon the demands of legislative minorities.

Some portion of the idea crust will therefore be transformed into legislation, and any purposeful study of ideas must be carried through into a study of legislation which is designed to have some specific effects upon economic development. These effects will often be sought by means of appropriate governmental agencies, and hence the study of ideas must go beyond ideas to legislation and beyond legislation to governmental agencies.

Lastly, the impact of legislation and governmental agencies upon economic institutions must be appraised if an accurate estimate of the place of government is to be attained. An ideal program of research in the rôle of government in economic development would, therefore, embrace a sequential study of ideas through time and a cross-sectional tracing of the effects of ideas on economic institutions by means of legislation and governmental agencies. Nor would the cross section be a one-way street; economic processes will obviously affect governmental agencies, the course of legislation, and the pattern of economic thought.

The division of jurisdiction between state and federal authority presents a further complication. Economic development is surely influenced by the two types of governmental activity, and hence an integrated program of research should provide opportunity for exploring the effects of both state and federal legislation. How this can be done will be explained below.

Methodology

The preceding section has indicated that there are six dimensions which must be considered in dealing with the rôle of government in American economic development:

Ideas
Legislation
Governmental agencies
Economic institutions
Time
Jurisdiction

If the Committee had unlimited funds that it wished to devote to a complete study of government and economic development, it is conceivable that all these dimensions could be followed. Yet even if this were financially possible, the Committee would quite surely have misgivings about the wisdom of such a program. There is no necessary unity, either in thought or legislative trends, within a period of time. One area of economic activity may require more governmental intervention, another less. Some intellectual currents will be in sharp conflict with others. Accurate historical research must make classifications in terms of comparability. Hence worthwhile research in the history of the relation of government to economic life should be a series of studies designed to reveal the various kinds of interaction between government and the enterprise system. It should not attempt to tell the entire story, for the simple reason that there may well be no "story" that is consistent and meaningful. A least this hypothesis is the safest upon which to lay our plans.

Worthwhile projects which are manageable can, however, be located within the historical dimensions already described, projects which can give a meaningful explanation of what was attempted and what was accomplished either within jurisdictional areas or with reference to particular segments of the enterprise system.

An Ideal Program

In the opinion of the subcommittee, an ideal program of research in the rôle of government in American economic life would embrace the following:

(a) *A series of cross-sectional studies about the rôle of government.*

The first of these studies would be restricted to the period 1750–1790. The primary focus would be upon the latter date (1790) but sufficient attention would be given conditions relative to the earlier one (1750) so that changes could be clearly appraised. The question to which an answer should be sought might be phrased: to what extent were the ideas and governmental activities in the economic field after the Revolution and the "critical period" mere continuations from those of the late colonial era, and to what extent were they novel, at least for this country.

This first study would attempt to discover the contemporaneous currents of economic thought; the conflicts of opinion about governmental functions; the relation of these idea-currents to legislation, to colonial and royal governmental agencies, and to institutions set up under the new regime; the appropriateness of legislative and administrative action to the economic problems of the late-colonial and early national periods. This cross-sectional study would serve as a platform on which to erect the studies described under # (b), and as a frame of reference for subsequent cross-sectional studies, say at 1830 and at 1870. An ideal program would include three or four such horizontal surveys at fixed points in time — surveys designed to reveal comparative ideological patterns and comparative degrees of governmental intervention among all the significant segments of the economy.

(b) *A series of studies designed to show the range, and scope of governmental activity in particular states.*

These studies would be longitudinal in the sense that they would be projected through time. They would be confined to one jurisdictional level except incidentally, e.g., when federal action is immediately relevant to state action. The primary purpose is to discover the scope, the techniques, and the sequences of governmental tentatives within special areas. States representative of economic regions should be selected, the ultimate number, of course, being dependent upon the fruitfulness of the studies themselves. Such state studies ought to include a New England, an east-central, a southeastern, a mid-western state, and a southwestern state. Thus, in the ideal program, studies should be made, for example, of politico-economic relations from 1790 onward in Massachusetts, Pennsylvania, South Carolina, Illinois, and Texas. The linkage between state action and colonial precedents will be drawn largely from the study just proposed under # (a) but these state inquiries would also contribute to the latter. Such state inquiries would be directed primarily at changes over time, and at the emergence of new concepts of public policy appropriate to regional economic problems. Moreover, because of our constitutional system, it was the states rather than the federal government which were responsible for the greatest range of politico-economic activity for many decades.

The time span over which these state studies should extend cannot now be definitively set. They should surely proceed down to the Civil War . . .

A Minimum Program

. . . In area (a) : A study of economic ideas and legislation for the period 1750–1790. As already indicated, the chief purpose of this inquiry is to discover the late-colonial attitudes of government toward enterprise and of enterprise toward government, and the changes that had occurred by 1790. The greater attention would be given the later date. It should reveal the pluralistic demands for

economic policies in relation to particular economic problems arising from the balance of payments, from mercantile and planter indebtedness, from the imperfections of markets. This project will
require the services of an investigator and his research assistant for
about two years.

In area (b) : Studies of the developing pattern of politico-economic
relations in Massachusetts, Pennsylvania, a southeastern state, and
a western one, from 1789 onward. Massachusetts is a logical nomination since it seems to offer the best example of New England thought
and experience. Pennsylvania has been selected not only because it
represents an agricultural-commercial-manufacturing state, but also
because important work has already been done on the governmental
activities of that state. Either South Carolina or Georgia would represent another economic region, both have also been partly surveyed,
and it seems possible that the Committee can avail itself of these find-
ings. The choice between the two would depend upon the results
of further exploration into available sources of data. Yet either would
be satisfactory and it seems unnecessary to delay decision on the
general program because of this detail of choice.

2. Herbert Heaton, *General Memorandum of State Studies in the
Role of Government in American Economic Development, July
14, 1941*

The general aim of this series of studies is to examine the range
and scope of governmental activity in a number of states up to 1860
. . . Apart from the value of these studies for their own sake, the
time element played some part in leading the committee to decide
upon them. It was felt desirable to destroy, (if that be possible,) the
popular notion that until the fourth of March, 1933, the United
States was the land of laissez faire, and the alternate notion that governments, when they have acted, have done so only in a regulatory
capacity. Historians know that both these notions are fantastically
untrue; yet the story of the role of governments in American economic enterprise has not been adequately studied and presented.

Our business, therefore, is to see how far and in what ways state
governments were interested in economic developments, and to examine the four possible aspects of such interest: —

(a) aid, in its various forms,
(b) government enterprise, where such is to be found,
(c) regulation, including prohibition,
(d) public finance, where the furthering or defraying the cost of
some economic enterprise was the aim of taxation, borrowing or
spending.

The first of these four aspects, government aid, takes on a motley
of shapes and colors, ranging from bounties to state fairs or progressive farmers, to financial support of public utilities. It crops out

in a number of questions such as, for instance, the contrast between the suspicions with which European governments approached the question of corporation law and the eagerness of American states to get companies established. In a very useful Ph.D. thesis, done at Harvard recently, the regulation of economic enterprise in Pennsylvania was carefully studied, but assistance to enterprise was scarcely touched upon. Hence, this aspect of state policy should be carefully watched and dealt with as fully as possible. It will probably be found that government aid in many states was available on demand, and it was especially generous as a measure of relief in time of depression; in fact, all our work might with advantage be done against a backdrop-curtain on which is a graph of business fluctuations during the period.

(b) Public enterprise. Professor Heath, in his study of eleven southern states, has been so impressed by the willingness of governments down there to undertake banking and other enterprises that he even talks of "state capitalism" as a prominent characteristic feature of the area and period. How far this trend goes in other states I do not know, but suspect it may be rather a question of degree than of kind. At any rate, we should try to get a measure of the extent to which state governments were willing to "go into business," or at any rate permit subordinate units of government, such as a city or county, to do so.

(c) The regulatory functions are so well known that nothing need be said about them here, except on one point. Professor Warren, (Princeton Institute for Advanced Study,) is doing a separate job on state banking policy up to 1862. To some extent this relieves the rest of us from the arduous task of studying state banking in detail; but nevertheless, we should know in general what our states are doing, and should make note of any references which might be useful to Professor Warren and send them on to him. It will however, be necessary to examine the way in which regulations were amended or abandoned in the light of experience or under the influence of pressure or protest from the regulated.

(d) Public finance. The main difficulty here is to fix boundaries. It is impossible to study the whole public finance history of each state; yet we should look at those parts of the story which are concerned with any of the three preceding topics. Money raised for paying purely governmental costs need not worry us; but funds raised and devoted to bounties, public improvements, interest on productive loans, etc., does come inside our parish. When any doubt arises on this, *or any other matter,* a note should be made on the question pending consultation with me.

Line of Attack
Governments did not do most of [the] things they were asked to

do, and countless agitations or proposals failed to win favour. Perhaps the best starting point is the statutes, for here, at any rate, we see what legislatures did decide to do, and the first stage of our work might therefore with advantage be the examination of the state's legislative records. This, however, is only the end of the beginning, or rather it is Chapter 2. From the acts themselves we need to go back to see what events, conditions, ideas, and interests led to the passage of the law; and then go forward to see how the act was put into effect, what difficulties it encountered, and what results it achieved, so far as results are capable of discovery or measurement. The prelude to legislation will take us into party politics of the state, and possibly into the higher reaches of idealists and crackpots; but too much time should not be spent here, or none will be left to see how the policies worked. Committee reports and governors' messages should throw light on the steps to the passage of laws, and other printed or manuscript reports of ministers or committees may show how the acts were operated. Judicial decisions will be useful, especially in indicating the snags which are encountered in enforcing regulatory policies.

The place of the federal government in the economic life of states is a matter which has me puzzled. In the old states, federal influence on land policy, internal improvements, and other fields, may be much smaller than it is in the west. Nevertheless it cannot be ignored and an examination of federal documents is necessary. This in itself is a huge task and there is no reason why each one of us should do it, for that would be unnecessary duplication, or rather, quadruplication, of effort. The relevant documents for each state might possibly be found by consulting the Index of Federal Documents done by Poole — I think that was his name. It may prove worthwhile before we have gone very far to get one person to do the job for all of us, and distribute the references; but for the time being each worker should look up references for his state in Poole.

Concluding Comments

Some idea concerning the further plans which are being considered by the committee may be helpful. In the first place, it is hoped that these initial state studies can be completed and manuscripts finished, at least in first draft, within a year, though that may not prove to be possible. In the second place, it is hoped that each state study can be used as a starting point for a comparison with neighboring states and the drawing of regional patterns. In the third place, the committee is now considering its second main subject, which is the role of the entrepreneur in American economic development; and the third field which may be marked out will probably be economic growth and fluctuations. The shape and extent of the entrepreneur study has not been decided yet; but it is fairly certain that it will embrace such topics as farming as an enterprise, merchandising (both foreign and domestic, retail and wholesale,) the accumulation and administration of capital, the problems of monopoly and competition, the part played by entrepreneurs in the economic development and the political life of their communities, the rise of the corporation, and the development of public attitudes toward the entrepreneur. I don't know how far this information can help in giving direction to the state studies; but at least on such points as the development of corporation law, the encouragement of corporations, and the discussion of monopoly, your digging may unearth material useful for this later task.

3. *Oscar and Mary F. Handlin Report of April 20, 1942*

Our work thus far has been largely exploratory, although at least one significant area of material has been covered. We have been attempting to clarify our problem within the broad objectives set down by the committee but are keenly aware that a premature statement may prejudice and distort them. The complex economic pattern of Massachusetts in these years, complicated reflections from the intellectual cross-currents that transformed its thought, and uncertain political alliances and alignments must all enter our picture. The place, or even the form, that these factors will ultimately take will become clearer as we get deeper into our material; as yet we hesitate to make even the most innocent assumptions about them. Already we have had to discard some of our preconceived formulations. When we entered upon the study, it seemed possible, for instance, that one of our topics would be "Regulation in the Public Interest." By now we are dubious as to whether that is a meaningful category, whether all the state activities in that realm might not better be classified as the expressions of private or group interests, or in some other fashion.

But whatever the organization or form of our study, we are by now convinced that it will have to pursue four main lines of inquiry. Within our field we distinguish the following spheres:

1. Action — the actual application, or attempts to apply the instrument of the state or of its agencies to the control of the economic system. Here we distinguish of course between laws passed and laws enforced, and between various degrees of state power and influence. The passive authority of the leather grader or hay weigher is obviously different from the active use of the state's credit by a railroad, or the delegation of the state's fiscal powers to a bank.

2. Motivation — the causes of action or lack of action, and of the forces which support or oppose it. We have thus far been chiefly concerned with relationship of political to economic lines: on the

issue of banks and currency, for instance, where do the lines of Whig-Democrat meet those of Merchant-Industrialist-Farmer? But we can see other lines of division, of lesser importance perhaps, rising out of ideological, sectional, and even personal considerations.

3. Rationale — the justification for action or lack of action. Public interest, monopoly, competition are typical of the concepts which seem to enter here insofar as they are used to support specific activities.

4. Ideas — the fundamental conceptions and basic assumptions whose interplay with other factors produces the causes and justification for action. The basis of the distinction between this level and that of Rationale is the possibility that certain concepts (e.g. Contract) have an internal development, independent to some extent of the particular function they assume at any given time.

The actual amount of work we have finished varies from category to category, partly because these were not defined in our minds until fairly recently and partly because we have thought it best at the beginning to cut the pattern of our research to fit the sources rather than the objectives. We have covered the Massachusetts Public Documents — legislative and executive — from 1826 to 1861. This gives us a substantial framework for those years though we may have to go back to that source for more details later. In the period before the public documents were issued serially, we still have much work to do. We have also begun an examination of judicial decisions and have completed some ten years (1822 ff.) of the reports of the Supreme Judicial Court (Pickering). In addition, we have examined a large number of dreary and not very profitable pamphlets in the Massachusetts local history collection of the Harvard College Library. Then we have initiated a systematic examination of biographies, memoirs, and correspondence of merchants and businessmen (Appletons, Lowells, Lawrences, etc.) and intend to work back from there through the politicians to the "thinkers" in the stricter sense. Finally we have made a beginning in the vast newspaper sources (*Boston Commercial Gazette*, 1836–40) and have surveyed some of the more important secondary works. Naturally, there still remains a tremendous amount of material yet to be covered.

4. *Oscar and Mary F. Handlin Report of August 23, 1942*

Our work in the past four months has, by and large, followed the lines indicated in our last report to the committee. In addition, we have begun to examine some of the abundant manuscript materials available for the period. We have also covered the Acts and Resolves for about half of the period before 1826, when the public document series begin, and have made a thorough study of the revision, both tentative and final, of the public statutes in 1835.

Meanwhile, we have pointed a considerable amount of research towards the not too distant time when we begin to write. We realized some time ago that our study would have to be pushed back to the adoption in 1780, of the state constitution which remained fundamental law throughout our period. The collapse of colonial government in 1774 was attended by a reversion of functions to local agencies, by a dissolution of restraints, and by a vigorous release of sectional attitudes and interests from the shackles of centralized government. This interregnum, regarded by most contemporaries as a return to the "state of nature," and the necessity of restoring a full "civil society" fostered a thorough-going discussion of the functions and purposes of government.

Our first section, which we hope to begin writing soon, will therefore be devoted to a discussion of the origin and development of ideas of government in the late 1770's and 1780's. We expect to arrive at a clear picture of what various groups — economic, political, and sectional — expected the government to be and do, and of the limitation of these interests by, and rationalization in terms of, the basic intellectual assumptions of the era.

In this discussion we expect to find that the economic functions of the government fell into a number of well defined categories of power such as the grant of monopolies, the creation of legal persons, and the extension of security to property. At present we expect that the body of our study will trace the evolution of these functions in their interplay with economic, political, and intellectual forces through the period. The organization of this section will be complicated by chronological development and by the necessity for dealing with differences in the application of these powers to various spheres. But our first section will at least furnish a valid point of departure. This renders it important not only for its own sake but also as the basis for much that will follow, and justifies the attention we expect to give to it.

5. *Oscar and Mary F. Handlin Report of March 18, 1943*

Research

It is difficult to say much beyond our previous reports under this head. In general we have pursued the same lines of investigation. We early realized the hopelessness of any attempt to cover *all* the sources completely. It would take years of solid research to go through all the economic materials in the state archives alone. Our chief design was first to sample various types of material and then to rely on judicious selection for adequate coverage.

The first six months (January–June, 1942) were spent in covering certain large blocks of material like the Public Documents, and in reading widely to get an over-all view of the problem. By the Fall we had a fair picture of what we were trying to do. From November to January we concentrated our work on the first section (described below), beginning to write at the same time. At present most of our attention is devoted to the period 1790–1830.

Organization

The organization of this study is fairly well crystallized by now. Logically it falls into five sections:

      I. The Sources of Political Power, 1774–1787
     II. The Commonwealth Period, 1780–1830
   III. The Period, 1830–1861
   IV. Persistent Forms
    V. Conclusion

I. This entire section stretches back beyond the opening date set for the study by the Committee; but we were driven back into it by the materials themselves. The later sections are incomprehensible without an understanding of the underlying forces emerging in these years. This was a revolutionary period, a time when the complex relationships that enter into the exercise of political and economic power were brought into sharp relief. The crisis acted as a precipitant. The great majority of government activities went on without interruption; but those which were critical and involved the control of power were segregated. In the political sphere, the collapse of the old government and its organization into new forms stripped away the conventional patterns which normally cloak the struggle of diverse groups for power. The patterns themselves no longer existed because all the customary forms were outmoded.

The dissolution of old forms was particularly thorough-going since it was accompanied by a significant social upheaval. To the extent that class divisions rested upon economic foundations, the disruption of the state's economy upset the equilibrium of the class structure. In any case, lines became remarkably fluid. The ruling class was eliminated at one stroke by emigration. "New men" appeared in old classes, and new issues, derived from the war's economy, tended to mark out new lines of class division.

In fact, one can hardly speak of etiher classes or parties in this period. Because the state no longer had fixed policies, emergencies drew it into strange fields of activity. New issues continually cropped up. Economically and socially, various groups struggled to find cohesion as the state emerged from the crisis. Politically, a confusing mixture of shifting and dissolving factions, based on personalities, sectionalism, and interest, held power from time to time. In both respects the issues of the period served as clarifying factors. From the conflict of interests emerged classes, from that of faction, parties.

The critical character of the period emphasized another aspect of the whole problem. Control of power brought with it immediate, concrete advantages, and served immediate ends. But the forms of political control were hardly less important. The elaborate theorizing which characterized the era lent an unusual importance to the forms and rationale of government. Extensively discussed and earnestly fought over, the forms ultimately emerging from the contests over current issues set the conditions for subsequent control of power. Though their adoption was due to special circumstances and interests, these forms ultimately acquired a vitality and strength which outlived their immediate ends.

Specifically, in this section we trace the influence of war and the general revolutionary crisis upon economic policy, the interests which emerged in the course of the evolution of economic policy, and the struggle by various interests for control of the state between 1774 and 1780. The year 1780 is a dividing point. The constitution of that year put control of the state in the hands of a relatively small group which in the next seven years used the economic and, ultimately, the military machinery of the state, to consolidate their power.

II. In the course of the struggles described in the first section, a clear conception of the role of the state in economic matters emerged. Briefly, and therefore crudely stated, the role of the state was that of a participant with interests of its own in economic as in other affairs. This section will trace the evolution of this concept in doctrine and legislation.

III. This period is not yet clearly defined in our minds; therefore we hesitate to give it a name. But we do know that somewhere "around 1830" the conception of State action as described in "II" broke down and was replaced by one that was quite different. Here we will attempt to define and describe the change.

IV. We have found certain forms of government activity which seem to persist apart from their immediate background. Here we intend to examine their degree of importance and the causes of their survival.

V. We hope to derive some valid conclusions concerning the role of government in Massachusetts economy, the changing ideas of what the role should be, and the reasons for and influence of these new ideas.

Writing

A first draft of section I is just about finished. The material for section II is fairly well blocked out. We plan to begin writing section II as soon as section I is completed to our satisfaction — in the immediate future.

The only "difficulty" worth mentioning to the Committee is that of length. We have, in rewriting, cut section I to somewhat under one hundred typed pages. But on the same scale the work as a whole will run to some two hundred pages [sic]. It would be helpful if we could know whether the Committee has any feelings about that question in view of the problems of publication.

6. *Oscar and Mary F. Handlin, Preliminary Outline, 1944*

A Study of Commonwealth: The Role of Government in the Economy of Massachusetts, 1780–1860

Part I. The Sources of Political Power in Massachusetts, 1774–1789
  1. Political Power in a Time of Crisis
  2. Revolutionary Finance
  3. Control of Commodities in Wartime
  4. Interests and Politics
  5. Constitutions and Constitution Making
  6. Consolidation of Political Power
  7. The Commonwealth Idea

Part II. The Commonwealth Period, 1780–1830
  1. The Conditions that Influenced State Action
  2. Debt and the State's Domain
  3. To Encourage Industry and Economy
  4. The Power to Regulate
  5. The State in Association
  6. The Law of Private Rights in a Commonwealth

Part III. The Liberal Humanitarian State, 1830–1860
  1. Industry and the Boston Merchant Class
  2. The Quest for a Through Route
  3. The Fight against Monopoly and the Dissolution of Commonwealth Ideas
  4. The Emergence of the Police State

Part IV. Conclusion

Part I is at present about 150 pages, Part II, 200, and Part III, 225, but revision will alter the size and proportions.

Note on the Sources

The conception behind this study, the attempt to find in the life of the people of Massachusetts a key to the role they expected government to play in their economy, stood in the way of any simple delimitation of sources. With this end in view, many diverse areas of thought and action became pertinent. Voluminous records made the quest for data simple; indeed, from the start, the more serious problem was that of selection from a wealth of riches. With no hope of complete coverage, it was necessary to rely upon judicious choice as a guide through the ranges of complex material.

Controversial Tracts

A good deal of first hand information came from contemporary observations on specific problems in controversial tracts. Provoked by immediate grievances or written in the interest of some concrete measure, these documents nevertheless contained, explicitly or implicitly, appeals to general principle that were often enlightening precisely because they were unformulated and free of dogmatism. Furthermore, the very fact that these pamphlets espoused a determinable cause made it possible to locate their bias and judge their orientation.

Through the whole period the problems of banking and the currency called forth much writing of this character. In the transitional period after the Revolution, James Sullivan's *Path to Riches* (Boston, 1792) thus examined the role of money in the productive system. In the 1830's the national crisis occasioned by the struggle over the Bank of the United States and the local one precipitated by the recharter of the Massachusetts institutions prompted Nathan Appleton, Richard Hildreth, and others to set forth their views in pamphlets. Somewhat later, hostility to the proposals to fix a specie reserve led James B. Congdon, cashier of the Merchants Bank of New Bedford, to defend the status quo in a series of vigorous publications, while the climactic panic of 1857 produced, among other things, an illuminating *Report* by the Boston Board of Trade in 1858.

The literature on internal improvements is probably even more extensive than that on banking. Various proposals for bridges in and around Boston generated a voluminous pamphlet literature, as did the controversies over railroad routes and regulation. Indeed, each of the great economic questions that agitated opinion in this period, and there were many, produced a like array of printed material: the tariff, the corporation and industry, land, and the Indian problem. The footnote references to discussions of these issues contain a sampling, though far from a complete catalogue, of this rich literature.

Nor were economic attitudes confined to publications on economic questions. It was profitable to stray into the controversial writings of such men as Lyman Beecher, and to consult tracts on the license and Sabbath laws and on pauperism. Sermons, election and commemorative, by divines like William Ellery Channing, Samuel Cooper, and S. K. Lothrop, had a contribution to make, as did secular speeches by such men as John Lowell and T. H. Perkins.

Of a somewhat more general nature were the purely political tracts, which, nevertheless touched upon a considerable number of economic subjects. Massachusetts was early familiar with reviews of political affairs, and it was not uncommon for organized movements to state their case in print. But the most informative material came in the statements of party conventions, first on the local and county level and then through the legislative caucus. Year after year each partisan group issued its own *Address* to its constituents and made vigorous appeals *To the Electors* or *To the People*, while the printing of the *Proceedings* of the conventions and reviews of the actions of the legislature supplied ammunition for arguments. In addition, personal expositions of political points of view came from such well-known figures as George Bancroft, J. G. Palfrey, and A. H. Everett, to say nothing of pamphleteers like Amaziah Bumpus, who sought safety in pseudonym.

Periodical Literature

Facility in reaching print made possible the issue of a great body of periodical literature. There were noteworthy journals in this period, but not one attained a position from which it could exclude competitors. This circumstance permitted the easy launching of new ventures which gave expression to diverse points of view.

Newspapers in particular thrived in impressive variety.[1] The old *Boston Gazette* lived through important revolutionary experiences but failed to hold its place after the peace. The limelight in the next two decades was shared by the *Independent Chronicle* and *Columbian Centinel*, whose inveterate rivalry after 1795 took the form of alliance with the Republicans and Federalists. The turn of the century saw the appearance of a flock of smaller party organs. The biweekly *Repertory* and *New-England Palladium* and the *Weekly Messenger* spoke for the Federalists, the *Boston Patriot* for

1. For details concerning ownership, changes of title, and present repositories, see, e.g., C. S. Brigham, "Bibliography of American Newspapers, 1690–1820," *American Antiquarian Society Proceedings*, Vols. XXIII–XXXVII (1913–1927); *American Newspapers, 1821–1936*, ed. Winifred Gregory (New York, 1937).

the Jeffersonians. The early publications were important as a source of news and even more important because they furnished an outlet for the work of essayists on political and economic subjects.

The War of 1812 and its settlement took the ground out from under many of these sheets and made way for a new generation of editors and newspapers. In 1816, for instance, the *Boston Commercial Gazette*, after twenty years of experiment with other formats and under other designations, appeared in its ultimate aspect. For a quarter-century thereafter it supplied a reliable guide to the concerns of business and mirrored many important shades of opinion in the state. In the 1830's appeared the *Boston Daily Herald* and the *Daily Evening Transcript*, while the *Boston Daily Advertiser* advanced steadily in importance as spokesman for the merchants. The last-named paper was particularly valuable for its reports on legislative and judicial proceedings, often fuller than the official versions.

No other city enjoyed the variety of publications that flourished in Boston. Almost everywhere else there were solid and respectable journals, but their news and often their opinions were primarily derivative, reflecting the attitudes of the metropolitan press. Worcester profited at the expense of the state capital when first the *Massachusetts Spy* and then the *American Herald* moved to the interior. Competition between the *Salem Register* and the *Salem Gazette* enlivened for many years the reading of Essex County citizens. Farther west the *Hampshire Herald* and the *Springfield Gazette* prepared the ground for Samuel Bowles and the *Republican*.

The news in the rural press came almost completely from the urban papers. The gentry dominated policy, as the correspondence of Theodore Sedgwick with Loring Andrews of the *Stockbridge Western Star* and the *Albany Centinel* showed. Such organs as the *Hampshire Gazette*, the *Haverhill Observer*, the *Franklin Herald*, the *Woburn Journal*, and the *Middlesex Journal* were of value primarily for occasional items of local interest. The same limitations applied also to the press of the District of Maine: the *Kennebeck Intelligencer*, the *Eastern Herald*, the *Castine Journal*, and the *Eastern Repository*, among others.

For the early period, the line between newspapers and magazines was difficult to draw. Such publications as the *Boston Magazine* and the *Worcester Magazine* were not far different, except in size and frequency of issue, from the weekly and semiweekly press. But as newspapers clarified their own field of interest, they made room for other organs willing to print long, serious discussions.

The establishment of the *Monthly Anthology and Boston Review* in 1804 marked the beginning of a long magazine tradition in the Hub. This journal was primarily devoted to belles-lettres but found space for occasional articles on law and economics by such writers as Isaac Parker, Joseph Story, and William Tudor. The *North*

American Review, its more famous successor, followed the same practice. An impressive array of names appeared on its roster of contributors — Loammi Baldwin, Alexander H. and Edward Everett, Jared Sparks, Nathan Hale, J. T. Austin, Charles Francis Adams, George Bancroft, Willard Phillips, and Francis Bowen — many of whom found their way into print for the first time through the pages of the *Review*.

Among the competitive journals with briefer life spans in this period were the *Literary Miscellany*, Buckingham's *New-England Magazine*, Brownson's *Boston Quarterly Review*, *The Atlantic Monthly*, the *American Monthly*, and the second *Worcester Magazine*. In addition, more specialized periodicals made their appearance as the century advanced. *The Massachusetts Agricultural Repository* began its career as the organ of the Society for Promoting Agriculture but dealt with a broad range of subject matter. *Bowen's Boston News-Letter* focused its attention on matters of municipal interest. The *American Jurist* and the *American Law Magazine* served the lawyers as *Niles' Weekly Register* and *Hunt's Merchants' Magazine* did the merchants. The latter two were not published in the state but carried frequent contributions by Massachusetts authors.

Contemplative Works

Those fugitive writings, whether published as pamphlets or in periodicals, were often more important than the more imposing contemplative works, which attempted to present a systematic analysis of the problems of politics or the economy. The great revolutionary outburst of theoretical speculation about the nature of the state that reached a peak in the writings of John Adams fell off with stability and was not again repeated. There were glimmerings of the old interest in the works of John Quincy Adams and in those of George Bancroft, but discussion, by and large, took another turn.

The new generation of thinkers was no longer concerned with the just structure of politics. They shifted, instead, to problems arising from philosophic inquiries into ethics, as did W. E. Channing, R. W. Emerson, and their followers, or to the construction of legal systems, as did Joseph Story and Rufus Choate, or, finally, to studies of the proper functioning and efficient organization of production.

The first substantial works in the last category did not appear until the third decade of the nineteenth century. Loammi Baldwin's earlier *Political Economy* (1809) displayed some acquaintance with Malthus and dealt soberly with problems of population, internal improvements, and banks. But Baldwin was well aware of the limits to his own knowledge and tempered his conclusions with earnest appeals for further study. Seven years later, J. W. Clark's Bowdoin Prize dissertation, "Of the Importance of Commerce as a Source of Private and Publick Wealth" (Harvard University Archives), showed the depth of interest in the subject, and also the shallowness of knowledge.

The economic problems of the next four decades — the tariff, money and banking, internal improvements, and the rest — provoked widespread discussion; the impact of English ideas in the same period supplied an intellectual frame of reference; and the pages of the *North American Review* furnished the facilities for apprenticeship in writing.

Under the stimulus of these circumstances appeared a school of Massachusetts economists, the leading representatives of which were Willard Phillips and Francis Bowen. Phillips' *Manual of Political Economy* had a particular importance for this study. Published in 1828, at a point when economic ideas were highly fluid, it contained reflections both of the era that was just closing and the period that was just beginning. Bowen's *Principles of Political Economy* almost thirty years later (1856) propounded a scheme that was more systematic and more formalized. Yet his work had elements of originality derived from preoccupation with the problems of the immediate environment. Phillips and Bowen both spoke for the mercantile community of Boston in a sense, just as O. A. Brownson spoke for the displaced artisans, as Amasa Walker spoke for the local industrialists, and as the younger Theodore Sedgwick spoke for the lawyer-gentry group of western Massachusetts.

Massachusetts Archives

Speculative material, whether it was controversial or contemplative, threw light on what people as individuals or in groups thought the role of government should be in the economy. But it was also necessary to seek light on the nature of those conceptions through an examination of what the government actually did and of the forces that pressed it into action. The most important body of material in this respect lay in the Massachusetts Archives (referred to throughout as MA). These materials are admirably arranged and contain all the documents of government through the whole period. The papers connected with the Revolution are bound in volumes bearing roman numerals. This file includes the records of the Provincial Congress, of the constitutional conventions, and of a great mass of important petitions. After 1780 the legislative documents are organized separately by years, bearing a chapter number in the case of bills passed and a continuous numbering by House and Senate in the case of bills not passed.

Acts and Resolves

The Acts and Resolves of the General Court have been frequently reprinted and are readily accessible. For measures prior to 1780 the praiseworthy twenty-one-volume edition published under Chapter

87 of the Resolves of 1867 was entirely satisfactory and contained as well informative historical notes. Volumes V, VI, and XVIII to XXII were particularly important for the years after 1774.

A comparable project undertaken under Chapter 104 of the Resolves of 1889 brought the acts and resolves down to the close of the eighteenth century. These volumes, however, lacked notes and cross references and contained omissions, which were supplied in E. M. Bacon's *Supplement to the Acts and Resolves* (Boston, 1896).

For the rest of the period, the situation was chaotic. Compilations of *Laws* and *Perpetual Laws* in 1801 and 1807 omitted those expired or repealed as well as private and special legislation, as did Theron Metcalf's edition of the *General Laws* (Boston, 1823–1832). The last named, however, was useful for its thorough system of cross references. To fill the gaps, the *Private and Special Acts* were published in a separate series. For the *Resolves*, which were excluded from almost all collections and, indeed, for the *Laws*, it was safest to refer to the sessional publications, which were complete for each legislative year and which are referred to in the text as *Acts and Resolves*.[2]

Massachusetts never adopted a code, but on two occasions the legislature through a commission revised the statutes passed since 1780, to eliminate obsolete and contradictory provisions: the *Revised Statutes* of 1835 (with a supplement by Theron Metcalf and L. S. Cushing in 1844) and the *General Statutes* of 1859. In both cases the commissioners' reports and the legislative amendments were also published.

The legislative debates were not published in full in these years; the only reports of this kind were in the newspapers and in occasional compilations, such as the *Reports of Controverted Elections* by L. S. Cushing, C. W. Storey, and Lewis Josselyn (Boston, 1853). The *Journals*, which contained the bare framework of the proceedings, when printed, proved of slight value. More useful were the documents collected and published for the use of the lawmakers. The *House, Senate,* and *Public Documents* contained the drafts of bills, the results of committee investigations and of public hearings, and the reports of the executive departments.

In contrast to the proceedings of the legislature, those of extraordinary state assemblies have been published in detail. *Journals* have appeared of the business of each Provincial Congress and of the constitutional conventions of 1780, 1820, and 1853, as well as of the body that met to ratify the federal frame of government in 1788.

There was no formal system of reporting cases in the Massachusetts courts until 1804. Earlier the only information on litigation

2. The legislative year was not identical with the calendar year until 1830. An act inscribed in a given legislative year could thus have been passed either in the same or in the following calendar year.

was found in the records of lawyers, as in William Cushing, "Notes of Cases Decided in the Superior and Supreme Judicial Courts in Massachusetts from 1772–1789" (MS, Harvard Law School). After 1804 Ephraim Williams, D. A. Tyng, Octavius Pickering, L. S. Cushing, and Horace Gray, Jr., in turn supervised the publication of the decisions of the state supreme court. In addition, the rulings of inferior tribunals were gleaned from newspapers and from manuscript records, such as those kept in Berkshire County (1790–1799) by Azariah Egleston (MS, Harvard Law School) and in Dukes County (1790–1833) by James and George Athearn (MSS, Houghton Library, Harvard University). Finally, Francis Hilliard (1837) and Theophilus Parsons (1836) prepared digests of the law as handed down in the Massachusetts courts, and the textbooks of James Sullivan (1801), of Nathan Dane (1824), of J. K. Angell and Samuel Ames (1832), and of Samuel Batchelder (1868) contained useful summaries.

The governor's office was less important in the formulation of policies, though occasional chief executives exercised personal influence. From time to time, formal letters, messages, and proclamations bore witness to their activity, but more striking evidence appeared in less formal, personal material.

Town Records

Since many functions of government devolved from the state to the local level, it was frequently necessary to shift the focus of attention away from the records of the central government and to examine those of the towns. The Boston materials were most familiar, but there was also much that was usable in the records of such places as Fitchburg, Braintree, Plymouth, Watertown, and Weston, as well as in unofficial publications like John Bacon's *Town Officer's Guide* (Haverhill, 1825).

Town Histories

Not every locality in Massachusetts attained the dignity of seeing its archives go into print. And there were gaps even for those which did; taxpayers who evinced enough interest to provide for the colonial and revolutionary papers grew cold when it came to the prosaic nineteenth century. But these deficiencies of coverage were amply compensated for by numerous scholars in every part of the state who made up with devotion for what they lacked in skill and who compiled honest and useful, if unimaginative, town histories.[3] Liberal quotations from the records raised many of these works to the status of firsthand sources.

3. Jeremiah Colburn's *Bibliography of the Local History of Massachusetts* (Boston, 1871) and Charles A. Flagg's *Guide to Massachusetts Local History* (Salem, 1907) give adequate coverage for nineteenth-century works.

The Massachusetts Historical Society had expressed eagerness over the accumulations of local materials from its very foundation, and the first series of its *Collections* (beginning in 1792) included a large number of communications on the subject. But attention seems to have subsided until well after the end of the War of 1812, when the general awakening in national consciousness gradually revived interest in this field as in other fields of historical study.

Although the Historical Society lost its early solicitude for local history, others took over the task. The Bay State towns, rich with colonial and revolutionary incident, were particularly attractive to those in search of a patriotic tradition. The half-century after 1820 saw a rapid output of publications. J. E. A. Smith, *History of Pittsfield, (Berkshire County,)* . . . *from* . . . *1734 to* . . . *1800* (Boston, 1869), with a second volume to 1876 (Springfield, 1876), is representative of the best of these works. The *Worcester Magazine* and similar journals provided an outlet for the less ambitious essays. Anniversaries and other celebrations were occasions on which enterprising orators could commemorate their native places. Sometimes, indeed, these lectures grew into full-fledged tomes. Finally there were some, like W. H. Sumner, who knew how to make Clio serve the purposes of real-estate speculation and other practical ends. These authors were almost all amateurs. They were clergymen, and lawyers, and politicians. But by and large they wrote for the love of their subject, labored hard in the sources, and left much of value in their books.

Town history continued to attract attention after 1870, and the succession of centennial celebrations after 1876 produced a crop of new publications. This later generation of local historians was more professional in its attitude and had greater regard for formal scholarly methods. But, unfortunately, it was also more concerned with genealogy. In addition, its products were sometimes less useful because they tended to skirt the day-to-day level of common occurrences in order to concentrate on the great events. This period also saw the establishment at Danvers and elsewhere of worthy historical societies issuing publication series. More recently, some communities have received quite another kind of treatment, generally emphasizing economic and social factors. Vera Shlakman, M. T. Parker, Oscar Handlin, and B. W. Labaree have dealt with Chicopee (1935), Lowell (1940), Boston (1959), and Newburyport (1962).

The history of the churches in many places threw some light on the history of the town; often, of course, the two were indistinguishable. Here, too, the habit of the commemorative discourse had useful consequences. In an analogous category belonged the accounts of some of the secular local institutions — mechanic associations, marine societies, schools, libraries, and charities.

The works on counties and other regions larger than the town were decidedly inferior. At best, as in the case of Josiah G. Holland's *Western Massachusetts* (Springfield, 1855) and Frederick Freeman's *History of Cape Cod* (Boston, 1869), they brought together chronicles, uneven in quality, of separate towns. At worst, they were massive and chaotic agglomerations of antiquarian, genealogical, and personal odds and ends assembled for the crudest commercial motives. On the other hand, Richard D. Birdsall, *Berkshire County* (New Haven, 1959) was an interesting cultural history, and the publications of some of the county societies, the Essex, the Worcester, and the Berkshire, were quite praiseworthy.

Personal Papers

In the records of government were the surface indications of its operations. To illuminate the workings of the inner machinery, however, it was often necessary to inquire into the lives of the people who made the government run. Fortunately, the men of this period were conscious of history and of their possible place in it. They kept excellent records that extended to their most private and most intimate affairs; they threw practically nothing away; and the resultant accumulation of their personal papers in and out of print contains a rich lode of information on many aspects of life in the Commonwealth.

The Adams family had a collection for almost every member of importance. These papers are now being systematically published by the Harvard University Press in an edition sponsored by the Massachusetts Historical Society. In the interim, older if less meticulous editions are available. The *Works* of the second president were piously edited by his grandson (Boston, 1850–1856), supplemented by four volumes of *Familiar Letters* to and from Mrs. Adams (New York, 1876). These supplied an excellent introduction to the wide range of affairs in which John Adams was concerned. John Quincy Adams was represented by multivolumed editions of both *Memoirs* (Philadelphia, 1874–1877) and *Writings* (New York, 1913–1917), and Charles Francis Adams by an autobiography (Boston, 1916).

The revolutionary statesmen were as well off in their mementos preserved for posterity. E. C. Burnett assembled an interesting selection of *Letters of Members of the Continental Congress* (Washington, 1921–1936), including a good many by Massachusetts men. There were also collections of *Writings* for Samuel Adams (New York, 1904–1908) and of *Memoirs* for William Heath (New York, 1901). There were, in addition, numerous biographies of the main participants in the revolutionary events in Massachusetts.

The personal data for the first four decades after the establishment of the state government were also ample. Alexander Hamilton's *Industrial and Commercial Correspondence* (Chicago, 1928) included communications from many New Englanders. Some of the writings of governors Gerry and Strong were published. T. C. Amory's *Life of James Sullivan* (Boston, 1859) contained copious selections from his private correspondence. Timothy Pickering's Papers (MHS) and the voluminous *Life and Correspondence of Rufus King* by C. R. King (New York, 1894–1900) contained letters from men prominent in all phases of the Commonwealth's life. By and large, this material was heavily weighted with the materials of men affiliated with Federalism.

On the period before the Civil War, the Papers of Edward Everett (MHS), governor, congressman, and elder statesman, proved of great value. Daniel Webster's *Works* (Boston, 1853) gave the public utterances of the Marshfield giant. J. P. Bigelow's Papers (Houghton Library, Harvard University) were informative for his career as mayor of Boston and as secretary of state. For the 1840's and 1850's, the great mass of Charles Sumner's Papers (Houghton Library and Harvard University Archives) were extremely useful. The *Memoirs* of Robert Rantoul, Jr. (Boston, 1854) and the correspondence of George Bancroft (MSS, MHS) and of Marcus Morton (MSS, MHS) revealed some of the forces at work in the Democratic party.

There were, of course, no precise limits to politics, and political information often appeared in the personal materials of many men who disclaimed the politician's vocation. The papers of businessmen often had much to tell: in the earlier period, some of the documents in Kenneth W. Porter's *Jacksons and the Lees* (Cambridge, Mass., 1937), the papers of Benoit Merlino de St. Pry (MSS, Houghton Library, Harvard University), the Bourn Manuscripts (Houghton Library), the Davis Papers (MSS, MHS), the Willard Phillips Papers (MSS, MHS), the Letters of Boston Merchants (MSS, Baker Library, Harvard University), the Lee-Cabot Papers (MSS, MHS), and the "Bowdoin and Temple Papers," *Massachusetts Historical Society Collections*, Sixth Series, Vol. IX, Seventh Series, Vol. VI; in the later period, the Ginery Twichell Papers (MSS, Baker Library) and the files of such corporations as the Jamaica Pond Aqueduct (MSS, Baker Library), the Amoskeag Canal (MSS, Boston Public Library), the Western, the Nashua & Lowell, and the Newburyport Extension railroads (MSS, Baker Library). There were pertinent data in the *Selections from the Diaries of William Appleton* (Boston, 1922) and the *Recollections* of Samuel Breck (Philadelphia, 1877). Nor was it wise to neglect the gentry outside Boston. The Theodore Sedgwick Papers (MSS, MHS), for instance, provided invaluable information for three generations in the history of western Massachusetts.

Lawyers hardly formed a distinct group in this period. Many were politicians or had business interests. But some of the more influential figures retained a degree of detachment. W. W. Story's *Life and Let-*

ters of Joseph Story (Boston, 1851) thus dealt with a jurist who did not serve on the Massachusetts bench but whose opinions had great influence in the state.

The memoirs of ministers and writers had a relevance independent both of the extent to which these people were directly involved in politics and of the influence they may have exerted upon public opinion. Often these men were acute, and sometimes the only, recorders of what went on about them. The *Smith and Deane Journals* edited by William Willis (Portland, 1849), for instance, were valuable sources of information for the local history of Portland, and William Bentley's *Diary* (Salem, 1905–1914) contained a pithy commentary upon three decades of Salem's history. The recollections, correspondence, and journals of such authors as George Ticknor (Boston, 1880), William Ellery Channing (Boston, 1848), William H. Prescott (Cambridge, Mass., 1925), and T. L. Nichols (New York, 1937) gave frequent assistance.

Secondary Works

Except perhaps for the town histories, all the sources mentioned thus far were primary. But we were not confined to these. We were fortunate to be able to labor in a field deeply tilled by many devoted scholars before us. Secondary works often proved sound guides, and if we sometimes arrived at different results, we were nevertheless grateful to those who first broke the soil.

Since the publication of our first edition, a number of useful volumes have been added to the already rich store of biographies of Massachusetts figures. These include Martin Duberman on Charles Francis Adams (Boston, 1961), E. C. Kirkland on Charles Francis Adams, Jr. (Cambridge, Mass., 1965), C. P. Smith on John Adams (New York, 1962), S. F. Bemis on John Quincy Adams (New York, 1949–1956), Martin Duberman on James Russell Lowell (Boston, 1966), F. O. Gatell on John G. Palfrey (Cambridge, Mass., 1963), Leonard W. Levy on Lemuel Shaw (Cambridge, Mass., 1957), David H. Donald on Charles Sumner (New York, 1960), John Cary on Joseph Warren (Urbana, 1961), and Richard N. Current on Daniel Webster (Boston, 1955).

The general histories had little to say for the purposes of this study; their attention was focused almost exclusively on doings in Washington. For New England, the old-fashioned volumes of W. B. Weeden (Boston, 1891), which reached into our period, were still valuable, while the later ones of J. T. Adams (Boston, 1926) were useful for the eighteenth century if handled with caution. The level of writing in the *Commonwealth History of Massachusetts*, edited by A. B. Hart (New York, 1927–1930), was high although not everywhere sustained. The older publications on Massachusetts by Alden Bradford (Boston, 1825–1829), J. S. Barry (Boston, 1857), and G. L. Austin (Boston, 1876) also repaid reading, the first two particularly since they were written by persons prominent in the administration of the state. For Maine in the period when it was part of Massachusetts there were satisfactory contemporary accounts by James Sullivan (Boston, 1795), Moses Greenleaf (Portland, 1829), and W. D. Williamson (Hallowell, 1832).

The organization of government in the Commonwealth was the subject of a number of comprehensive treatments. S. E. Morison's excellent brief history of the constitution (Boston, 1917) was supplemented by our introduction to the collection of documents on the Constitution of 1780 (Cambridge, Mass., 1966). There were more specific considerations of individual branches of government by Robert R. Bishop on the Senate (Boston, 1882), by W. T. Davis on the judiciary, and by John F. Sly on the town (Cambridge, Mass., 1930). There were adequate treatments of the state's currency by J. B. Felt (Boston, 1839) and of its financial structure by C. H. J. Douglas (New York, 1892) and C. J. Bullock (New York, 1907).

The great bulk of monographic studies covered narrower time spans. For the colonial background we found useful Roy H. Akagi on the town proprietors (Philadelphia, 1924) and George Haskins on legal origins (New York, 1960). Valuable contributions by Bernard Bailyn and others in recent years have added to the immense literature on the Revolution, much of it with a bearing upon Massachusetts. The best general survey of the internal history of the Revolution however remains Allan Nevins, *American States during and after the Revolution* (New York, 1927). E. C. Burnett's *Continental Congress* (New York, 1941), though exhaustive, was diffuse and generally unenlightening. Robert A. East handled the problems of *Business Enterprise* (New York, 1938) satisfactorily although we cannot agree, on the basis of the Massachusetts experience, with his conception of the perpetuation of the prerevolutionary merchant class. The works of Robert E. Brown touched off a considerable controversy, the details of which are not, however, particularly relevant to our subject.

Discussions of the decade after 1780 have usually centered either in Shays' Rebellion or in the ratification of the federal Constitution. For the latter, Samuel B. Harding, *Contest over the Ratification of the Federal Constitution in . . . Massachusetts* (New York, 1896) was still useful, and there was additional material in Forrest MacDonald, *We the People* (Chapel Hill, 1958). E. P. Douglass, *Rebels and Democrats* (Chapel Hill, 1955), L. N. Newcomer, *Embattled Farmers* (New York, 1953), and R. J. Taylor, *Western Massachusetts in the Revolution* (Providence, 1953) contained material on the uprisings of 1786. But the clearest picture of what happened was found in Minot's contemporary report, although it was by no means neutral in its sympathies (Worcester, 1788). The chapters on Massachusetts in J. R. Pole, *Political Representation in England and the Origins of the American Republic* (London, 1966) dealt with the development of politics down to 1787, in terms of the issue of representation.

The political history of the three decades 1790–1820 is familiar. The standard monographs of A. E. Morse (Princeton, 1909) and William A. Robinson (New Haven, 1916) were reliable but have now been supplemented by J. E. Charles, *The Origins of the American Party System* (Williamsburg, 1956) and Paul Goodman, *The Democratic-Republicans of Massachusetts* (Cambridge, Mass., 1964). There was some material on Massachusetts in David H. Fischer, *The Revolution of American Conservatism* (New York, 1965), an account of the Federalists in the Jeffersonian period. C. A. Beard's *Economic Origins of Jeffersonian Democracy* (New York, 1915) contained an essay on John Adams which showed flashes of insight but which, we think, proved our point rather than his.

Developments in Massachusetts in the forty years before the Civil War were covered in William G. Bean, "Party Transformation in Massachusetts . . . 1848–1860" (unpub. diss. Harvard University, 1922, University Archives) and A. B. Darling, *Political Changes in Massachusetts, 1824–1848* (New Haven, 1925), works solid in detail but shaky in the general attempt to establish an interpretation in terms of sectional conflict. The brief chapter on Massachusetts in Richard P. McCormick, *The Second American Party System* (Chapel Hill, 1966) added little to them. A. M. Schlesinger, Jr.'s, *Age of Jackson* (Boston, 1945) contained a scintillating analysis of the political ideas of the artisans but was weaker for those of other groups, and we cannot agree to the identification of reform with the Democratic party. Also useful on the issues of the Jacksonian period were T. P. Govan, *Nicholas Biddle* (Chicago, 1959) and Bray Hammond, *Banking and Politics in America* (Princeton, 1957). The literature on reform is voluminous.

Economic History

The volumes published under the auspices of the Committee on Research in Economic History, of which this was the first, provided helpful comparisons. These include: Louis Hartz, *Economic Policy and Democratic Thought: Pennsylvania, 1776–1860* (Cambridge, Mass., 1948); Milton Heath, *Constructive Liberalism* (Cambridge, Mass., 1954); and J. N. Primm, *Economic Policy in . . . Missouri, 1821–1860* (Cambridge, Mass., 1954).

For the Massachusetts economy, the weakest field of coverage was agriculture: P. W. Bidwell's accounts were not altogether satisfactory, and Elizabeth Ramsey's book was sketchy. The situation for commerce was happier. S. E. Morison's excellent *Maritime History of Massachusetts, 1783–1860* (Boston, 1921) dealt with the whole subject.

Since the first edition of this work, a number of impressive volumes have added substantially to our knowledge of the development of transportation. Stephen Salsbury, *The State, the Investor, and the Railroad* (Cambridge, Mass., 1967), is a careful account of the Boston & Albany Railroad; and Edward C. Kirkland, *Men, Cities and Transportation* (Cambridge, Mass., 1948) is a lively analysis of all New England. Carter Goodrich, *Government Promotion of American Canals and Railroads* (New York, 1960) and his *Canals and American Economic Development* (New York, 1961) contain material on other states, helpful for comparison, while Albert Fishlow, *American Railroads and the Transformation of the Ante-Bellum Economy* (Cambridge, Mass., 1965) is an economic analysis.

Histories of industry have not ventured far in discussing the role of politics except in the case of the tariff. The general accounts, like that by A. S. Bolles (Norwich, 1889), tended to concentrate on techniques and the organization of production. The most valuable studies of individual branches of manufacturing were A. H. Cole's *American Wool Manufacture* (Cambridge, Mass., 1926) and C. F. Ware's *Early New England Cotton Manufacture* (Boston, 1931).

With a few notable exceptions, most of the business histories were either antiquarian or apologetic. Among the exceptions were N. S. B. Gras on the Massachusetts First National Bank (Cambridge, Mass., 1937), J. T. Holdsworth on the first Bank of the United States (Washington, 1910) and W. B. Smith on the second (Cambridge, Mass., 1953), and D. R. Whitney on the Suffolk Bank (Cambridge, Mass., 1878). J. Van Fenstermaker, "The Statistics of American Commercial Banking, 1782–1818," *Journal of Economic History*, XXV (1965), 400ff, was an important analysis.

For our purposes, the most serious gap in coverage existed in the broad field where economic and legal forms overlap. The American lottery, for example, was more often treated rather as a curiosity than as a significant institution, and there were only superficial accounts of such integral features of the economy as auctions or pilotage.

The most important politico-legal form was the corporation. Our "Origins of the American Business Corporation," *Journal of Economic History*, 5 (1945), 1ff, discussed some of the general problems of historiography. The studies of W. E. Rappard (Paris, 1908) and E. M. Dodd, Jr. (Cambridge, Mass., 1954) contained useful summaries but did not go beyond the legislation. The most comprehensive history of the institution in the United States was by J. S. Davis (Cambridge, Mass., 1917), but the presentation was not systematic and there were blind spots in interpretation. Shaw Livermore in 1939 attempted to reinterpret the whole question by demonstrating that there was no difference between incorporated and unincorporated business associations. In the process he disregarded the types of evidence presented in Chapters 4 and 5 above, and he fell into serious contradictions, pointed to in our "Origins of the American Business Corporation."

Twenty years ago, in acknowledging our debt to a number of monographs on specific subjects, we complained of the paucity of useful studies in American legal history. Few contributions in the intervening decades have helped fill the gap. The history of law in the United States remains largely a field still to be exploited.

Index

Abolition, 202
Academies: farmers and, 188; private, 231, 232, 240
Act of amnesty, 47
Act of 1779, 23
Adams, Charles F., 282
Adams, John: on banking, 99, 117; and corporations, 133; father of, 186; ideas on government, xiii, 24, 25, 28–31, 47, 282; and manufacturing, 123; politics of, 55; and the Revolution, 3, 6
Adams, John Quincy, 55, 117, 282
Adams, Samuel, 154
Adams family, 186
Administration, public, 229
Advertisements, 25
Agawam River, 69
Agency: law of, 204; liquor, 234, 235, 236
Agricultural college, 240
Agriculture: aid to, 37–38, 48, 52, 53, 78, 80, 81, 87, 98; education in, 232, 240; relations to industry, 123–124, 182; after the Revolution, 57, 59, 60, 186, 187; during the Revolution, 12, 13, 35; societies for, 130, 210, 232; survey of, 210. *See also* Farmers
Albany: railroad to, 172, 178, 211; trade with, 59, 187

Ale, 206
Alewives, xi, 72, 73
Alford & Egremont Turnpike, 152
Alger v. *Thacher*, 226
Allen, Jonathan, 253
Allen, Thomas, 16, 18, 126
Almshouses, 230
Amendments, constitutional: for cities, 236; demand for, 43, 44, 46; expectation of, 32; proposed, 26, 27, 54
American Academy of Arts and Sciences, 97
American system, 182
Ames, Fisher, 154
Ames, Samuel, 147
Amesbury Nail Company, 124
Amherst, 5
Amherst, N.H., 252, 253
Amherst Carriage Company, 266
Andover & Medford Turnpike Corporation v. *Gould*, 142
Andover & Medford Turnpike Corporation v. *Hay*, 142
Andrews, Loring, 281
Androscoggin River, 106
Angell, S. K., 147
Annapolis convention, 46
Anti-Masonic party, 202
Appleton, Nathan, 163, 166, 198, 279